P9-EEG-361

Labor's Home Front

Labor's Home Front

The American Federation of Labor During World War II

Andrew E. Kersten

CONSULTING EDITOR: Harvey J. Kaye

NEW YORK UNIVERSITY PRESS
New York and London

NEW YORK UNIVERSITY PRESS
New York and London
www.nyupress.org

Library of Congress Cataloging-in-Publication Data
Kersten, Andrew Edmund, 1969–
Labor's home front : the American Federation of Labor during World War II / Andrew E. Kersten.
p. cm.
Includes bibliographical references and index.
ISBN-13: 978-0-8147-4786-5 (cloth : alk. paper)
ISBN-10: 0-8147-4786-8 (cloth : alk. paper)
1. AFL-CIO—History—20th century. 2. CIO—History—20th century. 3. Labor policy—United States—20th century. 4. World War, 1939–1945—United States. I. Title.
HD8072.K38 2006
331.880973'09044—dc22 2006009946

New York University Press books are printed on acid-free paper, and their binding materials are chosen for strength and durability.

Manufactured in the United States of America
10 9 8 7 6 5 4 3 2 1

Contents

Preface: Labor's Grave Hour vii

1 The Politics of "Equality of Sacrifice": The AFL and Wartime Labor Relations 1

2 Putting the Shackles on Labor: The AFL and the Fight Against the Open Shop 41

3 Building Ships for Democracy: The AFL, the Boilermakers, and Wartime Racial Justice in Portland and Providence 68

4 "Under the Stress of Necessity": Women and the AFL 100

5 Union Against Union: The AFL and CIO Rivalry 139

6 Death in the Factories: Worker Safety and the AFL 166

7 Planning America's Future: The AFL and Postwar Planning 189

Epilogue: Labor's Moment 223

Notes 227

A Note on Sources 263

Index 269

About the Author 274

Preface
Labor's Grave Hour

Nearly nine months after the vicious, surprise attack on the military installations near Pearl Harbor, on September 5, 1942, President Franklin D. Roosevelt delivered his tenth Labor Day statement. Although the American victory at Midway Island in June 1942 had given the nation cause to be optimistic, the war was not progressing quickly, and the liberation of Europe and the defeat of Japan were years away. President Roosevelt and his wartime cabinet knew that winning the war would require enormous sacrifices and Herculean efforts. FDR never missed a chance to remind Americans of these essential truths about the Second World War. He also never missed a chance to emphasize the stakes of war. "There has never been a Labor Day as significant as this one," he began his Labor Day statement. Alluding to the conflagration that was engulfing the planet, he noted that in a great many countries, free labor had ceased to exist. "A blackout of freedom has darkened Europe from the tip of Norway to the shores of the Aegean and sturdy working men who once walked erect in the sun now stumble and cower beneath the lash of the slavemasters." Perhaps more unsettling than the eradication of "the rights of free labor and free men in the conquered lands" was the undeniable reality that free labor was "threatened and besieged everywhere." "This is indeed labor's grave hour," FDR observed. But, he pointed out, "happily our good right arm is strong and growing stronger." "In our own country . . . the people who live by the sweat of their brows have risen mightily to the challenge of the struggle." Roosevelt then expressed his "appreciation to the working people of the United States for the energy and devotion with which they have met the demands of the present crisis." Finally, applauding them as much as challenging them, he concluded that American workers "know too democracy has made labor's advances possible. They know just what stake they have in America, just what they are fighting for." They "are pledged to the war effort" and were willing to make "sacrifices of wage increases, crop price increases, profit increases, bodily comforts." "All this," the president opined hopefully, "is little enough for free men to sacrifice in a world where freedom is imperiled."[1]

This book is about the wartime sacrifices, the accomplishments, the triumphs, and the failures of American workers who during the Second World War rose to meet the challenge of "labor's grave hour." In particular, it is an investigation into the wartime history of the American Federation of Labor (AFL). I came to this topic while researching my first book, a history of FDR's Fair Employment Practice Committee (FEPC). In *Race, Jobs, and the War,* I drew from the works of such scholars as Nelson Lichtenstein, August Meier, Elliott Rudwick, Ruth Milkman, Joe W. Trotter, Jr., and Robert H. Zieger. These historians' examinations of the working class and of the Congress of Industrial Organizations (CIO) and its affiliates not only inspired me but also made my job easier. Since the FEPC worked with labor organizations, particularly CIO unions, I was able to look up much of what I needed to know in monographs rather than assemble the information solely from primary documents. Curiously, when I turned my attention to the FEPC's relationship with the American Federation of Labor, I found that recent labor historians had been nearly silent on the subject. I soon discovered that in fact almost no one had examined the AFL's wartime experiences. I also learned that I was not the first to notice this historiographical lacuna. In a review of Irving Bernstein's *Turbulent Years: A History of the American Worker, 1933–1941* (1970), the historian Roger Daniels pointed out a "major weakness of a very strong book": Bernstein failed to deal with the AFL, although he noted in passing, on pages 773 and 774, that "by 1941 the AFL had gained a decisive and permanent victory" over the Congress of Industrial Organizations. Despite the fact that Philip Taft's two-volume AFL history does cover the war years, until now there has been no AFL counterpart to Nelson Lichtenstein's *Labor's War at Home: The CIO in World War II,* which focuses almost exclusively on the CIO. In part, this book is an attempt to bring my interests in labor history to bear on the AFL during the Second World War and thus to fill the historiographical void.[2]

The practitioners of the new labor history have not completely ignored the AFL, but most treatments carry the Federation's story only through the First World War.[3] There have been important exceptions, such as Christopher L. Tomlin's important 1979 article about the AFL in the 1930s and Dorothy Sue Cobble's provocative 1997 essay about reviving the AFL organizing strategy.[4] But few others have been tempted to examine the AFL outside its early heyday. In this, they are much like the "old" labor historians of the Wisconsin School. Typically, when historians look at labor during the Age of FDR, the CIO quickly takes center stage and the AFL all but disappears. This is unfortunate for several reasons. First, there are the membership numbers. As one can see from Table 1.1, the American Federation of Labor was always larger than the CIO. By the end of the Second World War, the AFL was roughly twice the size of its main rival. Moreover, while the CIO had added more than 1.5 million workers during the war, the Federation had increased its membership by more than 2.5 million. Clearly, if one wants to discuss wartime union workers, one must examine the federation to which nearly 60 percent of all unionists belonged. Second, an analysis of the AFL in the 1940s can yield new insights into issues that are central to recent historical inquiry, such as the importance of race and gender and the transformations on the shop floor. Finally, a look at the Federation at war points to a dramatic change in the labor organization. The basic argument here is that, although the AFL's reputation for conservative, "pure and simple" unionism is well deserved, during the war the AFL became much more active in American politics and society. Thus, as the AFL's power grew, so did its commitment to political activism.

The standard treatment of the AFL at war remains Philip Taft's *The A. F. of L. from the Death of Gompers to the Merger.* As one of the last disciples of the Wisconsin School of Labor History, Taft brought the notion of "job consciousness" to the Federation's war years.[5] The main issue for the AFL, according to Taft, was wages. The union's leadership fought constantly with the National War Labor Board (NWLB), which largely set the structure of worker compensation during the war. In particular, AFL president William Green and the Executive Council tried to relax the Little Steel Formula whereby the NWLB had limited wage increases to 15 percent above the hour wage rates that had prevailed in January 1941. Nevertheless, despite the criticism of the Board, Taft concluded that the "Federation commented favorably . . . upon the volume and quality of work the [NWLB] performed during its tenure." In sum, Taft maintains that the AFL continued its commitment to "pure and simple" union politics, which focused largely on lobbying and on bread-and-butter issues.[6]

In the five decades since Taft published this analysis, scholars have not revisited the subject of the AFL at war in the 1940s. Why? One answer could be that since the 1960s, labor historians have made it a priority to examine the role of radical and liberal politics in the American labor movement. Since, with the exception of a few stalwart socialists like A. Philip Randolph, most left-leaning unionists joined the Congress of Industrial Organizations, these more recent labor historians naturally followed their subjects and their political interests into the CIO. Additionally, scholars critical of the Wisconsin School, which largely focused on the AFL and the union's institutional politics and policies, sought to break with that tradition by looking not only at the CIO but also at nonunion workers and, more important, working-class culture. Indeed, the study of these latter issues has been the hallmark and the most important contributions of the new labor history. Moreover, perhaps the AFL gets scant attention because, unlike the those of the CIO or the Industrial Workers of the World, the Federation's membership drives were rather undramatic. There were few stunning climactic organizing struggles like the 1937 Battle of the Overpass, which lend themselves to great writing.[7]

Finally, one reason why the AFL is ignored relates to the research difficulties inherent in the topic. The American Federation of Labor was an organization whose parts seemed larger than their sum. The Federation was made up of thousands of chartered unions, local affiliates, and Internationals. Although there was a central leadership, its influence was often limited. Furthermore, the story of the AFL is not merely the summary of the pronouncements, lobbying, and activities of the Federation's hierarchy. By focusing on just the administrative leaders—as Philip Taft did—one risks forgetting about the average AFL union worker. Hence, to understand the AFL at war, one has to turn to the unions and the workers themselves. But which workers and what unions? How does one write a history of thousands of union organizations? The answer is, of course, that one does not. Rather, I have taken my cue from the historian David Brody, who many years ago talked about "circling back to old Selig Perlman" and the old labor history with an eye on new concerns and new historical ideas.[8] For this study, I organized the AFL's wartime experience into seven major themes.

The essential questions that *Labor's Home Front* answers are these: how did the AFL respond to the Second World War, and how did the war shape the Federation? In some ways, the AFL changed very little. In terms of race, gender, shop-floor politics, and the struggle against employers and against the CIO, the Federation remained virtually unaltered. However, wartime conditions fundamentally recast the AFL's political outlook. During the war, the AFL developed an extremely close working relationship with Franklin D. Roosevelt's administration. By the war's end, the Federation's leaders and many rank-and-file workers had become liberals. They helped to develop FDR's vision for a postwar America. Although it appears as though the weight of the Federation's conservative beliefs and their adherents held more sway in determining how much the organization changed during the war, one should not underestimate this shift toward New Deal thinking. In many respects, the AFL abandoned its two cherished principals—volunteerism and pure and simple unionism—by the war's end. This book chronicles that transformation.

Most of *Labor's Home Front* centers on the challenges of the Second World War and the AFL's generally conservative response to them. The book, however, begins with an example of how the Federation changed. Chapter 1 lays out the core wartime struggles, namely the bread-and-butter issues and "equality of sacrifice." Although the Federation, as well as the CIO, did not win that struggle, it transformed organized labor's relationship with the federal government. The AFL became a proponent of federal intervention in the economy and in labor relations, whereas it had once opposed this. The next several chapters emphasize continuity as well as change. As chapter 2 demonstrates, the Federation was dedicated to defending this new relationship from employer attacks and the decades-old open-shop movement. Significantly, working with New Dealers did not mean that the AFL adopted all aspects of liberalism. Specifically, when confronted with federal demands for racial equality or gender equity, the AFL maintained its prewar ideology. In general, despite their multiple public platitudes about equal rights, the Federation's unions remained a bulwark of white male hegemony. These are the themes of chapters 3 and 4. Chapter 5 provides another case study of the AFL's unbending nature. Simply put, early in the war, President Roosevelt desperately sought to resolve the mortal conflict between the AFL and the CIO. But, much to FDR's chagrin, both labor federations refused to bury the hatchet during the war. There were limits to what the American Federation of Labor was willing to do for the sake of the war. And then there were extraordinarily important issues that it virtually ignored, such as shop-floor safety. As chapter 6 shows, the AFL remained as interested in factory safety during the war as it had been before the war. Suffice it to say that the Federation believed that it was the employers' job to maintain an injury-free work environment.

Do these conservative reactions to wartime exigencies mean more than the AFL's fundamental wartime transformation? There is no easy answer. Certainly, the challengers and movements that the AFL rebuffed and rejected saw the Federation's intransigence as evidence of the old bromide about *plus ça change, plus c'est la même chose*. But, as chapter 7 illustrates, the AFL had changed its outlook greatly. President Roosevelt's postwar vision for establishing the Four Freedoms, for creating a Second Bill of Rights, and for fixing the crisis of poverty in America appealed to the members of the Federation. They gave FDR their utmost support for his political plan to expand the New Deal and offered their own interpretation of that vision. In other words, the AFL came up with its own Beveridge Plan. The fact that the federal government put this vision into practice only for veterans should not diminish the scope of this wartime change in the AFL's philosophy. Ideologically, the Federation was fundamentally different in 1945 from what it had been in 1941. Although the difference is hard to quantify, there is no doubt that the AFL had become part of the New Deal's liberal coalition.

This book took nine years to research and write. Along the way I benefited greatly from the kindly prodding of my former graduate school mentor, Roger Daniels. In fact, he was the first to encourage me to pursue this topic and has aided me in numerous ways. I deeply appreciate Roger's interest and support of my work, both then and now. Closer to home, I would like to acknowledge the tremendous help of my colleague, Harvey Kaye, who has probably heard more about the AFL than any left-leaning, decidedly pro-CIO academic might want. Harvey has been gracious and generous. He read large chunks of the manuscript, helped me to improve my writing and my thoughts, and, most important, introduced me to Debbie Gershenowitz, my editor at New York University Press. Thank you, Harvey. Debbie has been an incredible editor. She and I began talking about this book five years ago. She patiently waited for me to develop it, research it, and write it. And, she offered valuable insights into the organization of the book. It has been my pleasure to work with her and her colleague Despina Papazoglou Gimbel. I would also like to acknowledge many people who have answered my innumerous questions, read parts of the manuscript, and offered me advice, support, comments, and encouragement: Mike Barry, Eileen Boris, Don Caswell, Dorothy Sue Cobble, Clete Daniel, Joshua Freeman, Michael Kazin, Fred Kersten, Paul Moreno, Kim Nielsen, Peter Rachleff, David Witwer, and Bob Zieger. I also must acknowledge the help of several libraries, librarians, and people who gave me money to finish the research. This book would not have been written without the assistance of the staffs at the Franklin D. Roosevelt Presidential Library, the George Meany Memorial Archives and Library, the National Archives (Building I and Building II in Washington, D.C., and the Rocky Mountain Regional branch), and Cofrin Library at the University of Wisconsin-Green Bay. Specifically, I would like to thank three UW-Green Bay librarians. Deb Anderson, our brilliant archivist at UW-Green Bay, worked tirelessly to get me the collections I needed to complete the research on this book. I also need to mention the wonderful assistance of Mary Naumann, the head of the UW-Green Bay Interlibrary Loan, and Anne Kasuboski, who helped me find several important government documents. Bob Reynolds, of the George Meany Memorial Archives and Library, and Tab Lewis, of the National Archives, also offered invaluable guidance. Similarly, I would like to acknowledge the help and encouragement of Mark Renovitch, of the Franklin D. Roosevelt Library; Lee Grady, of the Wisconsin Historical Society; and Donald Caswell, of the International Brotherhood of Boilermakers. This book was made possible by grants from the Franklin D. Roosevelt Institute and the UW-Green Bay Research Council. Finally, the Greenwood Publishing Group has graciously allowed me to utilize material from my book chapter "Joseph A. Padway and the Open Shop Movement During World War II," published in Andrew E. Kersten and Kriste Lindenmeyer, eds., *Politics and Progress: The American State Since 1865* (Westport, CT: Praeger, 2001). The book is dedicated to my wife, Vickie, and my daughters, Bethany and Emily. Guys, the book is done. Let's go for a bike ride!

Green Bay
May 2006

1

The Politics of "Equality of Sacrifice"

The AFL and Wartime Labor Relations

This story begins with a bang and winds up with a wallop. The bang, which shocked American ears in the dawn of December 7, 1941, was the explosion of the first Japanese bomb at Pearl Harbor. The wallop, which will ultimately destroy the enemy, was the instantaneous response of American labor to the bugles of war.

—William Green, 1942[1]

The price for civilization must be paid in hard work and sorrow and blood.

—President Franklin D. Roosevelt, 1942[2]

Sacrifice defined the American generation—now dubbed the "greatest generation"—that endured the twin scourges of the Great Depression and the Second World War.[3] Examine the wartime story of Pauline Szymanski, a hardworking member of the International Ladies' Garment Workers Union (ILGWU), affiliated with the American Federation of Labor (AFL). A mother of seven, she was by her employer's estimation "one of the best sewing operators" he had ever seen. Her dedication to her work and to her family was legendary around the plant. Every morning she rose at five o'clock and made sure that her youngest son, Harold, was ready for school. Then she would get herself ready for eight hours on the sewing machines. Off at three o'clock, she was home in time to greet Harold at the door. Despite the hectic days and nights, Pauline was happy to have her full-time job at the mill. Like so many of her Detroit neighbors, she vividly remembered the personal and economic sacrifices that had been necessary during the Great Depression, when jobs and money were scarce. But she and her husband had made it through, and the new war had brought steady work. The war had also brought tragedy, more sacrifices. While Pauline worked, washed, cooked, and cared, she thought constantly about her six sons in the military. In her spare moments, she wrote to them and waited with bated breath for their replies. It was not long after the war began that she received the mail that no mother wants. Edward died first, in Africa, in 1942. Raymond was killed next. Unlike Edward, Raymond suffered, lingering briefly. The agony did, however, give him the chance to tell his captain his dying wish: he desired someone to kiss his mother for him one last time. Pauline's union, the ILGWU, made certain that Raymond's wish was granted. In 1943, union officials, along with the Red Cross, arranged for her to travel to Washington, D.C., to meet President Franklin D. Roosevelt. She was one of fifty-seven Gold Star mothers who saw FDR that day in March 1944. "I've never been away from Detroit before," Pauline told an AFL reporter upon her return. "I was so—so green about traveling. But the Red Cross looked after me. . . . It was comforting to talk to [the president]." She did not remember what FDR had said to her. She only remembered "that moment when he kissed me—just a touch of the lips on my cheek. I can't ever forget that." As the reporter editorialized in the Federation's monthly magazine, the *American Federationist:*

> Mrs. Szymanski's name may be hard to spell and even harder to pronounce. But she is the kind of American we of the labor movement can well be proud of. She is doing her job. She is doing the best to win the war regardless of sacrifices. She is not letting anyone down. May she be spared further suffering!

But, of course, to win the war, AFL unionists like Pauline had to sacrifice much more to defeat the Axis armies.[4]

American workers, and in our case unionists who belonged to the American Federation of Labor, were more than willing to do nearly anything it took to win the war. Significantly, that did *not* mean that they stopped their rekindled quest to bring equity and equality to American life. Moreover, it did *not* mean that the AFL's members relinquished their cherished beliefs, traditions, or policies without good cause or without a fight. On the contrary, if anything, the resumption of war in Europe in the late 1930s focused labor's attention and energies on the Federation's organizational drives and political missions that the New Deal had helped to unleash. Thus, there were limits to the amount and kinds of wartime sacrifices AFL workers were willing to make. They were willing to commit their labor and their lives, but not if their sacrifices lined the pockets of big capitalists, emboldened reactionary politicians, aided the upstart Congress of Industrial Organizations (CIO), or forced them begrudgingly to recast their ideology. From the first hints of war in Europe in the 1930s and throughout the entire war period, there existed a politics of sacrifice that often put labor's demand for democracy, equality, and fairness in direct conflict with the programs for defense preparedness and, later, war production. The negotiated solutions to these political battles—which involved labor and its readiness, or, as some maintained, its reluctance, to make the required sacrifices—shaped much of the history of the home front during the Second World War.

These fights also set the parameters of the American Federation of Labor's response to the war. Initially cool to the defense preparedness program, the Federation reversed its political stance as the war with the Axis became inevitable. By the time of Japan's attack on Pearl Harbor, the AFL was staunchly pro-defense. By working with FDR's wartime administration, the AFL began to transform its core ideas, especially volunteerism and "pure and simple" unionism. No longer did AFL leaders eschew government intervention in labor relations or in workers' lives. The Second World War became a watershed when the AFL finally realized that economic security and stability would come only with an alliance with the federal government. As we will see in later chapters, the Federation eventually bought into President Franklin D. Roosevelt's wide-ranging vision of a future America where the Four Freedoms were not an aspiration but a reality. This change was tempered by continuity elsewhere in the Federation. The AFL refused to use its power to redefine the economic and political positions of African American and women workers. It also failed to cease its internecine battle with the Congress of Industrial Organizations. In addition, the AFL continued to be vigilant in its efforts to stop employers from destroying the advances made through New Deal labor relations. Nevertheless, despite the continuity, the AFL had changed fundamentally by the war's end. It was committed to a Rooseveltian vision of security and citizenship that sought to transform the lives of all Americans. This break from the past happened quickly and represented a stark departure from the prewar AFL worldview.

A Glimpse of the AFL on the Eve of the Second World War

Initially, as dark and dreadful war clouds gathered in Europe, the AFL, especially its leadership, refused to make any major sacrifices for the sake of the impending crisis. In general, the AFL's position reflected the nation's isolationist mood. Simply put, the Federation challenged any policy or action that brought the United States closer to war. That said, AFL leaders strongly opposed fascism in Europe. They sternly rebuked Adolph Hitler's and Benito Mussolini's warmongering and antidemocratic public statements and actions. In fact, the Federation was among the earliest and staunchest critics of Hitler and the Nazi Party. As early as 1933, the AFL's Executive Council expressed its "profound regret and indignation" at the violent suppression of the German labor movement, as well as the vicious attacks upon German Jews. "We abhor racial persecution and we protest vigorously against the persecution of the Jewish people of Germany," the Council proclaimed shortly after Hitler took power.[5] In a vain attempt to aid German trade unions, the AFL subsequently passed, at its 1933 annual convention, a resolution that sympathized with the downtrodden German unionists, called for the reestablishment of an independent German labor movement, and instituted a voluntary boycott of German imports. Throughout the 1930s, the AFL echoed these sentiments at its conventions. In 1935, the Federation voted to extend a boycott of German goods and services, urged American Olympians to forgo the 1936 Berlin games, and authorized funds to be sent to Hitler's and Mussolini's victims.

Yet, even when war finally broke out, in September 1939, the AFL clung to isolationism. Soon after Hitler unchained his armies, AFL president William Green released an official Federation pamphlet titled *No European Entanglements,* in which the AFL's president detailed the labor organization's isolationist stance. Green reminded his readers (who theoretically included President Roosevelt, who received a personal copy of the pamphlet) that it was unlawful to "enlist with the belligerents, taking any part in activity to aid or abet" them. That was the letter of the law, and Green voiced some concern that the May 1939

William Green (1870–1952), courtesy of the Franklin D. Roosevelt President Library, image NPx66-323-38.

revisions to American neutrality laws, which created the so-called cash-and-carry provisions, failed to live up to the spirit of George Washington's famous diplomatic dictum. As Green stated bluntly:

> Labor firmly believes that we should have no part in this European War. We have no part in its causes, and can have no responsible part in its adjustments. We want policies best calculated to keep us free of European entanglements.[6]

Green did condemn Hitler's invasion of Poland: "We denounce it. We abhor it." Moreover, he believed that the German people, particularly the working class, did not favor the war. "Their bodies and their lives will be sacrificed on the field of battle. They will be called upon to kill other workers whose interests are common. . . . And what for?" Green's misguided notion that average Germans were unwilling to make any sacrifices for their Führer greatly underestimated the situation. Regardless, he and the Federation were not prepared to sacrifice their beliefs and mobilize for war. This put the Federation at odds with President Franklin D. Roosevelt, who was beginning to put the United States on a war footing with the creation, in 1939, of the War Resources Board, whose name rankled many isolationists across the country.[7] Green maintained that American working people did not desire an agency to ready the nation for battle. Rather, he called on the president to use any means in his power for "mediation efforts" and to make "use of all moral interference at our command in the interest of peace."[8] During the "phony war" period, between October 1939 and March 1940, when it seemed that the German cannons had rested, the AFL stuck to its ideological guns and renewed its call for FDR to pursue a foreign policy based upon "strict neutrality and peace" while at the same time reaffirming its condemnation of Germany and the Soviet Union for their imperialist actions.[9]

Despite the AFL's strong public support for isolationism, when the Nazis moved again, in the spring of 1940, President Green and the Federation quickly changed their position on the European conflict. On April 9, 1940, Hitler ordered his armies to invade Norway and Denmark. Success encouraged the Germans to broaden the war still further, using their blitzkrieg on France, Luxembourg, the Netherlands, and Belgium on May 10, 1940. Less than a week later, President Roosevelt requested that Congress appropriate more money for defense. The Federation's leadership watched these events carefully, and the Executive Council passed a confidential memorandum committing the AFL to Roosevelt's defense efforts in the event that the United States became a belligerent. The resolution also stated that the Federation expected equal representation on civilian wartime agencies.[10] Moreover the AFL expected that the Federation's representatives "be consulted in connection with all questions affecting civilians and civilian activities during a period of national emergency."[11] Publicly outspoken support for the defense preparations came shortly thereafter. The final straw was the fall of France four weeks later. William Green jumped to action. He again called the Executive Council together, and it issued this statement to the press:

> In the present emergency caused by the necessity for a rapid development of the nation's national defense, the American Federation of Labor again pledges its active and cooperative support with industry and with every appropriate governmental agency having to do with the production and construction of material for national defense, or any other national requirement to that end.[12]

Following that public announcement, several influential members of the AFL wrote to President Roosevelt to indicate their "willingness to cooperate in every possible way to do everything in our power to further the National Defense Program." And yet, the AFL's director of organization, Frank P. Fenton; its International representative, Robert J. Watt; and Harvey W. Brown, the International president of the International Association of Machinists, wanted to make clear that their full support had a price. In polite language, and echoing the sentiments of that confidential Executive Council memorandum, the three wrote that they recommended that, "in order to coordinate [defense activities] in a more realistic manner," FDR "appoint a coordinating committee with equal representation of employers and representatives of labor."[13]

The AFL leadership wanted to make certain that in the defense emergency, all stakeholders shared the burdens of making policy decisions. No unionist wanted a return to the situation of the First World War, during which employers and their government allies, no matter how progressive, basically ran the show. In theory, equal representation of labor (meaning in this instance the AFL) and business would guarantee that the Roosevelt administration would not call on workers to give more to the defense effort than their employers. Here, then, was the essence of "the equality of sacrifice," a phrase popularized by the leaders of the Congress of Industrial Organizations. Both houses of labor demanded that the work of the war must be shared and that no one group unduly profit from the circumstances. Fears that businessmen were already gaining an upper hand prompted public protest from both the CIO and the AFL. As the Federation president noted in a speech in the spring of 1940, "already selfish business interests are calling for the repeal of the Walsh-Healey Act [which obliged the federal government to respect prevailing minimum wages in manufacturing and service contracts] and demanding that the Wage and Hour Act be scrapped." Green declared firmly that "the American Federation of Labor will oppose such moves." "If the day ever comes when all of us must tighten our belts and pitch in to defend our country, there will be no slackers in the American Federation of Labor," he promised. But he also warned that such sacrifices for defense preparedness must be accompanied by guarantees that "workers' gains [over the previous decade would] not vanish."[14]

These concerns grew as the United States inched toward involvement in the conflicts in Europe and Asia. One year into the defense mobilization, it was clear that, instead of sacrificing, employers were profiting greatly from the defense emergency. In the first quarter of 1941, 295 leading manufacturing companies earned profits of 12.5 percent. In airplane factories alone, profits were up by about 33 percent compared to 1940 profit levels. Put another way, airplane manufacturers were making a profit of $544 per worker. In summary, as the Federation editorialized in its magazine, "Industry has been protected from loss due to plant expansion; profit averages earned before defense are exempted from excess-profits taxes; profits of leading companies are tremendous, and throughout industry profits are running well above average." Employers did not seem to be suffering that much. "How's business?" the AFL mused in the summer of 1941. "Business, brother, is *just fine.*"[15]

Long before Japan's attack on Pearl Harbor, President Roosevelt tried to ensure that the burdens of war fell as equally as they could. In May 1940, he scuttled the War Resources Board and established a new, less aggressive, and less militaristic-sounding agency, the National Defense Advisory Commission (NDAC). To lead the NDAC, he chose one leader from industry and one from labor. Perhaps not surprisingly, FDR tapped the head of General Motors, William S. Knudsen, to represent the employer side of the defense mobilization. Roosevelt's choice for the labor representative, however, stunned the American Federation of Labor. The president chose Sidney Hillman, head of the Amalgamated Clothing Workers of America and one of the original founders of the CIO.

The selection of Hillman illustrates in dramatic fashion the transformed nature of the labor movement by 1940 and how far the AFL had fallen in the realm of American politics. From roughly 1890 through 1935, the American Federation of Labor had been the bulwark of the American labor movement. The fact that Roosevelt had picked someone from the Congress of Industrial Organizations to head up his defense preparedness agency speaks to how quick and complete the Federation's decline was. In only five years, the labor movement had witnessed the rise of a new generation of leaders who seemed to outshine and outperform the older, more conservative AFL leaders. This, of course, was a total reversal of fortune. At one time, the movers and shakers within the AFL had seemed to provide all the answers to workers' problems.

The AFL Before the Second World War

The American Federation of Labor had its origins in the heady years of the Gilded Age, and its founding was the direct result of a vicious interunion battle. The key protagonist (or, in the Knights of Labor's view, antagonist) was Samuel Gompers. Born in London's East Side in 1850, Gompers learned his trade, cigar making, from his father. Immigrating to America in 1863, Sam quickly joined the labor movement and rose in its ranks. In 1875, he was elected president of Local 144 of the Cigarmakers' International Union (CIU). Gompers worked tirelessly to improve the working conditions for cigar makers. These independent tradesmen lived hard lives. Seemingly everyone from the wholesalers to the tax officers who charged the cigar makers for selling on their own stock took advantage of them. To turn a profit, cigar makers often enlisted the entire family, old and young alike, to make cigars. They generally lived in overcrowded tenement apartments and barely made ends meet. Gompers and his allies, particularly his fellow cigar makers Adolph Strasser and Karl Laurrell, sought to change the system through unionization.

At first, Gompers's union struggled. Local 144's first treasurer embezzled all of the workers' funds. Gompers saw to it that he was arrested, tried, and convicted for betraying the cigar makers' trust in him. Perhaps worse than an empty coffer was the Knights of Labor, which had launched a challenge to the CIU. Formed in 1869 by a group of garment workers, the Knights based its efforts on various principles of equality. Workers of any skill, of any sex, and, eventually, of any race were welcome in the organization. The Knights fought hard for an eight-hour day, an end to child labor, and equal pay for equal work and addressed equity issues such as the need for a graduated tax system. From the late 1870s through the late 1880s, the Knights of Labor was a working-class juggernaut with a membership of more than seven hundred thousand. The Knights had built its organization with its clarion call for equality and fairness and by co-opting other unions.

By the early 1880s, the Knights of Labor was looking to expand. In 1882, the organization weighed in on a divisive controversy within Gompers's Local 144. Socialists in the union wanted the CIU to support their proposals for developing an independent political party. Gompers, along with Strasser, disapproved, while continuing to support prolabor politicians within the traditional parties. Eventually, the Socialists broke away and formed a rival union directly affiliated with the Knights of Labor, Local Assembly 2814. To protect their craft, Gompers and Local 144 developed a blue label for their cigars. Local Assembly 2814 countered with a white label. Although Local 144 won the battle of the cigar bands, the dispute left Gompers with a bitter distrust for the Knights of Labor and its ideology. It also propelled Gompers toward developing an umbrella organization dedicated to the protection of trade unions.[16]

A year before the Knights of Labor initiated its cigar-worker drive in New York City, nearly sixty trade unions had met in Pittsburgh to discuss ways of organizing a federation of trade unions. At this November 1881 meeting, Gompers, Samuel Leffingwell, of the International Typographical Union, and John Jarrett, of the Amalgamated Association of Iron and Steel Workers, helped to establish the Federation of Organized Trade and Labor Unions (FOTLU). Although the Knights of Labor had sent representatives to the meeting, the FOTLU was not its kind of group. The Federation's leadership opposed a dynamic social reform agenda and refused to align itself formally with political parties. In 1886, at the height of his conflict with the Knights of Labor, Gompers was elected president of the FOTLU. Yet, he failed to build a viable trade union movement. The FOTLU was a moribund organization and did not excite craft workers. Instead of quitting, however, Gompers decided to restart the movement for a national association of trade unions.[17]

To revive the Federation and to devise some way of resisting the encroachment of the Knights of Labor on trade unions, Gompers sent out a call for a meeting in Philadelphia on May 17, 1886. This meeting, which took place just weeks after the Haymarket Square Massacre, led to the drafting of a peace treaty between the FOTLU and the Knights. It called for an end to the Knights' attempts to raid trade unions, to organize outside jurisdictional lines, to disband existing trade unions, and to interfere with existing trade union strikes or labor disputes. Although hopeful that some accord could be reached, the Knights of Labor's Grand Master Workman, Terence V. Powderly, rejected the offer. Several FOTLU leaders then called for another meeting in Columbus, Ohio, on December 8, 1886.

It was at Columbus that Gompers, Strasser, and others made the call for a new federation to foster and assist the development of trade unions and to "secure national legislation in the interest of the working people, and influence public opinion by peaceful and legal methods in favor of organized labor."[18] The newly established American Federation of Labor shared some similarities with the now defunct Federation of Organized Trade and Labor Unions. Both were umbrella organizations, and both sought similar labor reforms, such as the eight-hour day, an end to child labor, and restrictions on immigration. And, indeed, both federations had similar leadership. But Gompers, who was unanimously elected AFL president in 1886, built a much tighter organization. More than its predecessor, the new Federation was modeled closely on the British "new union" model, which emphasized high dues, worker benefits, centralization over state and local union bodies, and collective bargaining over "indiscriminate" work stoppages.[19]

The AFL began inauspiciously enough. The Federation's first office was an eight-by-ten-foot room with a small window and a brick floor. It was hot in the summer and cold in the winter. The office furniture was makeshift, consisting of salvaged old kitchen furniture. That was the good stuff. Gompers's desk chair was an old wood box. The office staff was Gompers's second boy, Henry, who worked when he was not in school. What drove the Federation were Gompers's dynamism, his charisma, and his ideology, which by default became the ideology of the AFL. The AFL stood for three main principles: (1) volunteerism, (2) "pure and simple" unionism, and (3) exclusivity. All three made the Federation one of the most conservative factions in the American labor movement. It also helped the Federation become successful.

Arguably the central tenet of the AFL was the belief in volunteerism to build a movement of trade unionists. Vladimir Lenin once called the notion a "rope of sand." But Gompers saw it as a "chain of iron."[20] As his personal secretary and biographer (and autobiographer), Florence C. Thorne wrote, he "put his faith and trust in voluntary principles and never wavered in that course."[21] In the AFL context, volunteerism was a way for the Federation to connect with one of the essential aspects of American life: the freedom to join a group of like-minded individuals. As de Tocqueville had noted earlier in the nineteenth century, Americans were gregarious social joiners. According to Gompers, it was that human freedom that allowed each worker to "choose union membership as his method of securing things that had to be achieved jointly with other workers."[22] Volunteerism also meant that the AFL's president and its Executive Council could not dictate to the unions that made up the Federation. Rather, it was the standard line that "decisions and policies of the union were the result of discussion and agreement and that the union relied upon educational methods for progress." As Gompers himself put it:

> There is no power vested in the officers of the Federation. They can act in an advisory capacity; they can suggest; they can recommend. But they can not command one man in all America to do anything. Under no circumstances can they say, "You must do so and so," or, "You must desist from going so and so." And this is true in the governmental affairs of the local organizations anywhere on the continent of America, industrially and politically.[23]

Finally, volunteerism translated into an aversion to governmental action in labor's sphere. Unionists wanted to meet, negotiate, and sometimes fight with employers on their own. The fear of government action, interference, or compulsion was partly based upon the repeated use of federal troops to crush strikes. Keeping the federal as well as state and local governments at bay was another way to ensure free and voluntary action, as opposed to governmental obligation. Politicians and especially government bureaucrats could not be trusted. "If the workers surrender control over working relations to legislative and administrative agents," Gompers wrote, "they put their industrial liberty at the disposal of state agents."[24] As a foundational philosophy, volunteerism encouraged membership from a broad spectrum of workers. It made the AFL seem less threatening as an organization and perhaps appealed to Americans' antiauthoritarian nature. At the same time, as we will see when discussing race and gender, volunteerism slowed the Federation's snail-paced movement toward equality for women and African Americans. Rarely, for instance, did the AFL's leadership take any action to reign in the racist and antidemocratic attitudes and policies of its member unions.

The second of the AFL's great principles was "pure and simple" trade unionism. In general and ideally, AFL unionists did not represent any particular politics or particular political party. They merely sought economic gains. In this way, the Federation's leaders, especially Gompers, who initially had ties to Socialism and to Socialist leaders like Eugene Debs, sought to avoid ideological battles with radicals and moved quickly to keep them out of the trade union movement. "Pure and simple" unionism also translated into a certain kind of outlook. The AFL leadership was not interested in grand social schemes. Rather, it emphasized and struggled toward immediate, short-term economic results. Socialists, and, later, Communists, too, decried the Federation's dedication to antiradicalism and antipartisanship. To revolutionaries like Daniel DeLeon, founder of the Socialist Labor Party, Gompers was a "labor fakir" and the illegitimate head of the Federation.[25] At various times, radicals sought to remove Gompers from his post as president. They succeeded once, in 1895, when Socialists within the Federation helped to elect John McBride as the head of the AFL. McBride's tenure lasted only one term. Gompers constantly fought with radicals within and outside the Federation. Increasingly, he saw them as a threat to the AFL. In 1905, when several radical unions, including the Western Federation of Miners, launched the Industrial Workers of the World (IWW), the AFL leadership wasted no time, quickly denouncing and opposing them. The heads of the IWW responded in kind, calling the AFL "the American Separation of Labor," and worked to capture the hearts, minds, and dues of American workers.[26] Gompers never shied away from a fight against what he called the "barnacles of labor."[27] He berated the Wobblies, Socialists, and, later, Communists in the press and even in person, as in his famous public debate, in 1914, with Morris Hillquit, a leading American socialist. To Gompers, the radicals did not offer the trade unionist any hope. Rather, they were "destructive" to the labor movement, "fanatical" and "unscrupulous."[28]

"Pure and simple" unionism did not neuter the AFL, making it apolitical. Taking their cue from Gompers's dictum to "defeat labor's enemies and to reward its friends," AFL unionists voted for local, state, and federal politicians who supported their agenda. But their nearsighted political plans, with some notable exceptions (such as the 1924 Presidential election), tended to be nonpartisan and tended center on immediate economic circumstances.[29] The AFL's political outlook made the Federation popular with employers who preferred to work with the AFL's business agents rather than those of the IWW or the Trade Union Unity League, the AFL's left-wing rivals. Within the labor movement, the cozy relationship that developed between the AFL and many employers was the source of much criticism. It was often said that the Federation organized employers before it organized workers. In some cases, this was true. Again, Gompers cared little, and he even became a founding member of the National Civic Federation, an organization of employers and unionists dedicated to achieving industrial peace through negotiation rather than labor activism.

The final founding belief of the AFL was exclusivity. In their basic essence, trade unions were organizations of workers "with the same problems, the same purposes and the same needs." A trade unionist's union card provided the key to his needs as a worker: apprentice training, employment placement, contracts, and representation in disputes between employers and between unions. This concept stood in stark contrast to the platforms of the Knights of Labor, the Industrial Workers of the World, and the Socialist Party, all of which wanted workers to combine into large organizations to establish a social and political power base from which to challenge employers and various governments in the United States. Although the AFL's predecessor, the Federation of Trade and *Labor* Unions (emphasis added), had tipped its hat to such organizations of semiskilled and unskilled workers, the AFL was adamant that only craftsmen could join. The idea was at the heart of its commitment both to volunteerism and to "pure and simple" business unionism. Gompers and the rest of the AFL believed that only workingmen who had common backgrounds would form a successful union. Why would, for instance, carpenters join a miner's union? What would they have to gain? Furthermore, such a combination might weaken the carpenters or force them to do things that they opposed. What if the miners decided to let African Americans or women into the union? Such affronts to white manhood could prove intolerable and destroy the union from within. Thus, of their own choosing but with some notable exceptions, such as the United Mine Workers and several federal unions, the chartered unions of the AFL were divided by craft and clung almost religiously to policies that excluded people of color and women. Exclusivity also engendered an extremely conservative outlook that resisted any change that could open further the union admission gates. For example, the Federation was at the forefront of the movement to restrict immigration into the United States. In particular, President Gompers lent his political weight to the movement for the exclusion of Chinese workers and cautioned others not to "militate against our policy of protecting our people from the evil effect of the Chinese invasion."[30] The AFL's most sympathetic historian, Philip Taft, noted that, "while there were undoubtedly racial aspects to the agitation against the Chinese the basic objection of labor leaders was to the competition of Chinese workers in the labor market."[31] Of course, organizing Chinese workers was simply out of the question for the AFL. The same went for organizing women, especially married women. If the husband joined the AFL union and worked hard to advance his "pure and simple" economic interests, then, as Gompers once wrote:

> I entertain no doubt but that from the constant better opportunity resultant from the larger earning power of the husband the wife will, apart from performing her natural household duties, perform that work which is most pleasurable for her, contributing to the beautifying of her home and surroundings.[32]

Thus, keeping women as well as African Americans and some immigrants in their place and under the control of white American men was a byproduct of the AFL philosophy. Gompers once said that trade unions were "born of the necessity of the workers to protect and defend themselves from encroachment, injustice and wrong."[33] Men voluntarily formed them to improve their immediate economic conditions, pure and simple. And they preserved their organization and their gains through negotiations with employers, by backing prolabor politicians, and by excluding anyone, male or female, native or immigrant, black or even white, who seemed to threaten the trade unionists' position economically, socially, or sexually.

By the Second World War, all three major parts of the AFL's philosophy had come under fire. In fact, the Federation's façade had been cracking and crumbling for some time. On the eve of the First World War, however, the AFL had seemed poised to become the singular labor organization in the United States. The Federation's lobbyists, along with its president, had secured what they considered to be the workers' Magna Carta, the Clayton Act. Passed in 1914, the law declared that "the labor of a human being is not a commodity or article of commerce." In addition to this call for respecting the dignity of work, the legislation was also designed to shield labor unions from antitrust lawsuits and similar antilabor legal devices that had hindered the AFL and other organizations since the Gilded Age. The future also looked promising because, by the early twentieth century, the Federation had seemingly found a way to reduce the amount of jurisdictional disputes among its member unions. The Federationwide agreement, called the Scranton Declaration, encouraged unions to seek broad alliances among kindred crafts. The AFL also was moving forward in its plans to organize unskilled workers with federal labor unions, the use of the category of "helpers" within existing trade unions, and the creation of international unions whose membership consisted primarily of the semiskilled and unskilled. Finally, during the First World War, the Federation gained respectability as well as new access to the federal government by not only throwing its weight behind President Woodrow Wilson but also participating on various government boards. Samuel Gompers himself embodied the AFL's temporary rapprochement with the federal government; he served on Wilson's National Defense Advisory Commission and made frequent public appearances to support the war.

The AFL's wartime loyalty and activities did not translate into a postwar boom for the organization. Rather, the "normalcy" of the 1920s meant a resurgence of attacks upon the labor movement. Although the employer-driven open-shop movement began well before war in Europe, it gained steam in the 1920s and found fertile ground among business and political leaders. Organized labor's gains of the war period were precipitously lost by the mid-1920s. In the case of the AFL, it suffered not only from the open-shop movement but also from competition from rival unions such as the IWW. Additionally, the Federation lost ground because its Magna Carta, the Clayton Act, proved to be a phony document. After the war, the government used all sorts of "legal" remedies to forestall and stall union actions. Finally, the AFL experienced a stern blow on December 13, 1924. On that Friday the thirteenth, Samuel Gompers died. In his place, William Green was selected to lead the AFL.

Who was William Green? No one except for Ohio miners knew who he was. Moreover, he seemed like the last person who should have been tapped to succeed Gompers. There were other, more logical choices: John L. Lewis, the impetuous head of the United Mine Workers; the charismatic Tom Rickert, of the United Garment Workers; the stately Mathew Woll, of the International Photo-Engravers Union; the ultraconservative John Frey, of the Metal Trades Department; and Gompers's first lieutenant, James Duncan, of the Granite Cutters International Association. Behind the scenes, these leaders fought for the top spot, without success. Eventually, the Federation Executive Council settled on Green, Lewis's seemingly rather mild-mannered protégé. Clearly, Green was the compromise candidate, and one thing was for sure: William Green was not Samuel Gompers.

Born on March 3, 1870, to parents who had recently emigrated from England, William was the son of a coal miner. At a young age, he joined his father in the mines of eastern Ohio. Hard work and sacrifice shaped his life. "Even as a child," Green later recalled, "I realized the horrors of mine accidents and saw the sorrow and deprivation which loss of bread winners brought to families and sensed the ever-present fear of impending tragedy that dwells in miners' homes."[34] Two institutions gave the Greens hope, succor, and courage to continue: the United Mine Workers and the Baptist Church. And the union and the church had an enormous influence upon the AFL's wartime leader. As Green's biographer Craig Phelan has written, "religion was so much a part of his life that it was impossible for him to separate his union principles from his religious beliefs."[35] In Green's view, his job as AFL president was to serve the will of the Federation, its membership, and its Executive Council. He also saw himself as a peacemaker in the conflicts between employers and workers and between rival unions. His outlook was generally conservative and conciliatory. And amid the doldrums of the 1920s, President Green had an awful time keeping the AFL together. His initiatives, such as the higher-income plan (otherwise known as the "social wage") and the union label campaign, were unsuccessful. Green spearheaded two major organizations drives, one in the automobile industry and one in the South. The AFL made few inroads in Detroit, and Green's timid precursor of Operation Dixie was a complete failure as his appeasing rhetoric and actions only encouraged southern textile owners to ignore the Federation.[36] By the 1930s, under Green's tenure, the AFL had hit rock bottom. According to Lewis L. Lowrin, a Brookings Institution labor economist, the Federation was "on its deathbed" in 1933.[37] One could point to external factors such as the Great Depression and the open-shop movement to explain the AFL's demise. The insurgency that eventually resulted in the creation of Congress of Industrial Organizations also provides a historical explanation to the Federation's apparent downfall in the early 1930s. However, some historians who have studied the labor history of the era have not been so oblique. According to Craig Phelan, President Green deserves much of the blame. He was a "constant failure," a "weak, unimaginative, ineffectual peacemaker," and, by the eve of the Second World War, "fast becoming a nonentity" in American politics and economics.[38] No wonder that when President Roosevelt went to pick his labor representative, he chose Hillman, an up-and-coming unionist of considerable clout, influence, and acumen. Green and the AFL seemed out of the game.

The AFL and the Defense Preparedness Program

The AFL might have been down on the eve of the Second World War, but it was far from out. In fact, everyone from politicians to labor leaders (and later historians) may have been too quick to pronounce the Federation's death. They might also have misjudged William Green. In terms of charisma and leadership skills, Green was hardly the dynamic force that Gompers was. However, Green did begin the process of modernizing the AFL, moving the Federation away from both volunteerism and "pure and simple" politics. Unlike Gompers, Green believed that the federal, state, and local governments had a vital role in assisting the labor movement. As a two-term state senator in Ohio in the early 1910s, Green had spearheaded efforts to pass the Ohio Compensatory Workmen's Compensation Act, the state's nine-hour-work-day-for-women statute, and a law that improved miners' rates of compensation. Additionally, he campaigned vigorously for a state minimum-wage bill, as well as a state health-insurance plan, but neither was enacted before he left office. As president of the AFL, Green backed similar federal legislation in support of a minimum wage, maximum hours, and federally supported collective bargaining. As Green explained in his 1939 book, *Labor and Democracy* (whose text was actually written by the AFL's Florence Thorne and Boris Shishkin and approved by Green)[39], his experiences as an Ohio coal miner had convinced him that workers could advance much further "by using our heads than by using our fists."[40]

Green was also much more receptive to industrial organizing than Gompers ever was. In "AFL Unions in the 1930s: Their Performance in Historical Perspective," the labor historian Christopher L. Tomlins challenged "traditional historiography [that] exaggerates the extent to which competition between AFL and CIO was responsible for causing changes of strategy and structure in the AFL's affiliates."[41] There is no doubt that the rivalry with the CIO sparked change in the AFL. But President Green was already moving toward industrial unionism before

TABLE 1.1
Membership of Labor Unions in the United States Compared, 1933–1945
(in thousands)

Year	*All Organized Workers in the U.S.*	*AFL affiliates*	*CIO affiliates*
1933	2,973.0	2,317.5	—
1934	3,608.6	3,303.0	—
1935	3,753.3	3,218.4	—
1936	4,107.1	3,516.4	1,204.6 (est.)
1937	5,780.1	3,179.7	1,991.2
1938	6,080.5	3,547.4	1,957.7
1939	6,555.5	3,878.0	1,837.7
1940	7,282.0	4,343.0	2,154.1
1941	8,698.0	5,178.8	2,653.9
1942	10,199.7	6,078.7	2,492.7
1943	11,811.7	6,779.2	3,303.4
1944	12,628.0	6,876.5	3,937.1
1945	12,562.1	6,890.4	3,927.9

SOURCE: Christopher L. Tomlins, "AFL Unions in the 1930s: Their Performance in Historical Perspective," *Journal of American History* 65 (March 1979): 1023.

the schism with the Congress of Industrial Organizations. Moreover, the AFL grew during the 1930s at a faster rate than the CIO. Although Green's AFL did not meet all the changes of industrial unionism, the Federation did in fact transform itself. By 1939, out of 102 national unions, there were only 12 pure craft unions left. Moreover, under President Green, the AFL made great strides in the manufacturing, construction, transportation, communications, and service industries. In 1940, the AFL was more than twice the size of the CIO. (See table 1.1.) Despite this record of success, the CIO captured the hearts of some American politicians. Again, nothing demonstrated this better than Hillman's appointment to the NDAC. Like later labor historians, FDR operated on the mistaken assumption that the Congress of Industrial Organizations "was more significant . . . because its unions organized the center firms which set the general price and wage levels of the major manufacturing industries."[42]

Roosevelt's selection of Hillman, of course, angered the AFL's leadership. Moreover, it added strain to a relationship that was already under pressure. FDR and Green did not see eye to eye on several issues. Since Roosevelt's first inaugural, Green had publicly challenged the New Deal several times. For instance, he objected to the creation of the Civilian Conservation Corps, which he viewed as a step toward a military solution to the problem of joblessness.[43] Then there was the uproar over Roosevelt's choice for secretary of labor. Green and the AFL Executive Council had expected FDR to choose Teamster president Daniel J. Tobin. They were bewildered when the President had instead tapped the progressive social worker Frances Perkins for the post.[44] Finally, as we will see in a later chapter, the AFL eventually grew to resent the National Labor Relations Board (NLRB), Roosevelt's primary labor relations agency. The AFL came to see the NLRB as a very imperfect instrument to create fair collective-bargaining rights.

Despite these hard feelings generated in the 1930s, the AFL leadership did not allow the Hillman snub to damage further the relationship between President Roosevelt and President Green and the AFL. Rather, Green began to court and cooperate with the administration, as he had not done before. And he was successful in shaping the development of wartime production and labor policies. Put another way, after the initial shock of the Hillman appointment wore off, Green was able to negotiate the terms of the Federation's support for FDR's emergency and, later, wartime labor policies. In the final analysis, the AFL agreed to wartime sacrifices, but not without significant concessions from the Roosevelt administration. The AFL's goal was to ensure equality of sacrifice.

Hillman took the first steps toward meeting the AFL's reservations about the defense effort. By September 1940, NDAC co-chair Sidney Hillman had selected his team to shape labor policy. Significantly, his top assistant was an AFL unionist, Joseph D. Keenan, secretary of the Chicago Federation of Labor. The NDAC Advisory Committee on Labor Policy consisted of an equal number of members from the AFL and the CIO. For the Federation, there was Harry C. Bates, of the Bricklayers; Harvey W. Brown, of the Machinists; John P. Coyne, of the Building Trades Department; George Q. Lynch, of the Pattern Makers; Charles J. MacGowen, of the Boilermakers; George Masterton, of the Plumbers and Steamfitters; and D. W. Tracey, of the Brotherhood of Electrical Workers. For the CIO, there was Van A. Bittner, of the Steel Workers Organizing Committee; S. H. Dalrymple, of the United Rubber Workers; Clinton Golden, also of the Steel Workers Organizing Committee; Allen S. Haywood, of the Utility Workers Organizing Committee; Emil Rieve, of the Textile Workers; and R. J. Thomas, of the United Automobile Workers.[45] There were no sinecures here. It was a serious group, a veritable Who's Who of the American labor movement. Moreover, the composition of the committee made it nearly impossible for the AFL's concerns to go unheard. Several months after the appointments were in place and after the NDAC had morphed into the Office of Production Management (OPM), Hillman took a second decisive step to get the AFL behind the defense effort. And, in so doing, Hillman solved one of the outstanding problems with defense mobilization, namely the construction of new military facilities and defense housing.

The Roosevelt administration's emphasis on building and, in some cases, rebuilding military infrastructure quickly outstripped workers' and employers' patience. As was the case in other areas of the economy, such as the automobile industry, employers and workers preferred to labor for the consumer markets rather than on federal projects. Tension developed quickly. By 1940, federal construction goals and timetables created urgent problems. The government, private contractors, and workers were scrambling for scarce building materials. The inflationary pressures caused by this and by the rapidly shrinking labor pool produced serious conflicts between workers and employers and between contractors and the federal government. These fights resulted in strikes and construction delays. The AFL, which housed most construction workers, tried, at the 1939 Building and Construction Trades Department convention, to resolve the jurisdictional disputes, but without much luck. Moreover, unionists rebuffed jawboning efforts to cajole the construction trade unions and private contractors into adopting the NDAC's building and material priorities, as well as the request to forgo work stoppages, particularly when they involved interunion fighting with the CIO. At the November 1940 meeting of the AFL's Building and Construction Trades Department, the AFL's secretary-treasurer, George Meany, acknowledged that the defense emergency was the "most critical period, not only in the history of our country, but . . . for the trade union movement [as well]." And yet, in discussing the government's pressure to give up their fights on the job, he stated that "I feel that, desirable as labor peace is, the American Federation of Labor is not prepared to sacrifice the ideals and the principles upon which this organization was founded in order to attain peace. Peace is desirable, but not at the price that would allow us to adopt the philosophy that we know in the final analysis would be destructive."[46] Thus, as war approached in Europe, AFL construction workers were not ready to sacrifice their aims for the government's. As the OPM's point man on labor issues, Hillman was responsible for figuring out how to get them to make those sacrifices for the good of the defense effort.[47]

On July 22, 1941, the OPM's Hillman and John Coyne, who was still at the top of the AFL Building and Construction Trades Department, signed an incredible and exclusive industry stabilization agreement that affected 1.5 million Federation unionists.[48] The "epochal pact," as the AFL leaders called it, was essentially a closed-shop agreement between the Building and Construction Trades Department and the U.S. government for the construction of all defense-related buildings. In other words, only AFL unionists were to work on any structure constructed for the defense emergency (and, later, for the war). Additionally, the government promised to honor prevailing wages, pay overtime, create uniform shifts, and create a review board within the OPM to mediate disputes. Finally, the AFL was able to eliminate an annoying practice that had evolved during the New Deal. In the Hillman-Coyne accord, the federal government agreed to stop immediately and to prohibit the future use of nonunion workers on Work Projects Administration defense-related construction.

In order to get this unbelievable deal, the AFL had to make two major sacrifices. First, the Federation's construction workers had to agree to obey the federal government's plan for job and material allocation. The choice of jobs and of building materials was fundamental rights to building unionists, and the curtailment of this prerogative fed the workers' discontent.[49] But, once the agreement was signed, the OPM, with Coyne representing the AFL building trades, issued this statement:

> Organized labor in the Building and Construction industry has pledged its unstinted cooperation in every phase of the defense program. Building and construction workers recognize that speedy and effective prosecution of defense is of foremost importance—they are united in their belief that defense comes first and that their interest and even their jobs come second.
>
> The construction industry has been subjected to more drastic restrictions under the limitations placed on the allocation of materials to private building, than any other major industry. The committee agrees fully with the objectives of the order of Supplies, Priorities and Allocations Board and of the other regulations that prior consideration should be given to the availability of steel and metals to the direct defense needs of

the nation. It is the purpose of the committee to examine thoroughly every phase of the materials supply situation and to determine methods and procedures whereby greater flexibility can be attained in assuring continued construction essential to the welfare of the people and the maximum employment stability of the workers in the industry.[50]

The second sacrifice was equally substantial, if not more so: the right to strike. Although, at this moment, the tradeoff was not called a "no-strike pledge," in essence, that was the quid pro quo.[51] The construction agreement read: "The Building and Construction Trades Department of the American Federation of Labor agrees that there shall be no stoppage of work on account of jurisdictional disputes, or for any other cause. All grievances and disputes shall be settled by conciliation and arbitration." When ink hit the paper for this one, Sam Gompers probably turned over in his grave. To Gompers, striking, or the potential to strike, was the greatest tool a unionist had to advance his causes. "Unless they occasionally strike, or have the power to strike," Gompers wrote in 1899, "the [economic] improvements will all go to the employer and all the injuries to the employees."[52]

Whether or not Gompers's ghost was frowning, this OPM-AFL construction stabilization agreement was a boon from heaven. For nearly a decade, the construction industry had been a "sick industry." What exactly had caused the illness was in dispute. Antiunion businessmen and bankers claimed that unions were the pathogens. In a 1939 article for *Collier's*, conservative journalist John T. Flynn argued that the AFL's construction unions hampered economic growth because of their adherence to high-cost and retrograde building methods, as well as their deep-seated corruption and racketeering.[53] Indeed, many construction unions were corrupt and flagrantly discriminatory against women and minority workers. One example will stand for many. In 1942, Martin Christiansen, a thirty-year master carpenter, tried to get a job on the massive federal construction project at the Brooklyn Naval Yard. He was turned away because, according to Christiansen, he was not an "able bootlicker." In a letter to AFL president William Green, he decried the nepotism and corruption in the building trades in New York City. Christiansen claimed that he had tried to follow his grievance through the proper local channels. But, the local building trades business agent, Charles Hanson, was completely uninterested. Hanson allegedly told Christiansen that favoritism was "human nature" and that "you can't expect anything else." To this, Christiansen responded, "thieving and lying is also human nature, and so is murder, but we cannot justify these things for that reason." So, "God Damn bitter about things as they are," Christiansen sent his complaint to the federal Fair Employment Practice Committee, FDR's wartime antidiscrimination agency. But because he was not a minority worker, the complaint was dismissed. Unemployed and at the end of his rope, Christiansen appealed to President Green, who sent a letter to William L. Hutcheson, president of the United Brotherhood of Carpenters and Joiners. Nothing was ever done.[54]

Although there was no denying the corruption charges of John Flynn or even of the antiunion muckraking journalist Westbrook Pegler, a closer examination of the construction industry points to a different cause for the economic illness. The Great Depression had a devastating effect upon the construction industry. As W. C. Bell, chairmen of the Seattle-based Western Homes Foundation, stated, in 1939, "the building industry . . . was hit earlier and harder than any other by the depression."[55] The AFL Building and Construction Trades Department president John P. Coyne agreed: "In the past ten years building trades men have had to bear the brunt of the economic crisis and to grapple with many tough problems of recovery and readjustment."[56] The lack of available capital was one problem. Another was the high unemployment and low wages among construction workers. The worst year for construction jobs was 1935, when at no time was the unemployment rate in the sector less than 45 percent. Moreover, at the start of the New Deal, wages for most construction workers had dropped by an average of 15 percent.[57] (See tables 1.2 and 1.3.) Housing starts increased in the late 1930s; in the first five months of 1939, loans totaling $33 million were made in Los Angeles, breaking a thirteen-year drought in the city's construction business.[58] But that development appeared Lilliputian compared to the war-spurred building boom. The money that was spent in L.A. in that record year was nearly the same amount that the federal government spent on *one* Marine base in San Diego, where AFL construction workers built a training station, a hospital, an air station, an armory, and defense housing. Similarly, near the small communities of Umatilla County, along the Columbia River, the federal government spent $8 million for an ordnance depot.[59] In the fifteen months of the defense emergency, July 1940 to September 1941, the federal government spent almost $10 billion on construction.[60] In 1942 alone, the Roosevelt administration expended $13 billion. Although the expendi-

TABLE 1.2
AFL Building Trades Unemployment Aggregates and Percentages, 1935

Month	*Percentage Unemployed*
January	60%
February	61%
March	59%
April	57%
May	54%
June	51%
July	51%
August	49%
September	46%
October	47%
November	46%
December	48%

SOURCE: "AFL Building Trades Unemployment Aggregates and Percentages, 1935," American Federation of Labor Papers, Series 4, Box 26.

TABLE 1.3
Average Wage Rates for Selected Building Trades, 1929–1939

	Average Rate Per Hour		
Trade	*1929*	*1933*	*1939*
Bricklayer	$1.53	$1.27*	$1.50
Carpenter	1.19	1.04†	1.23
Electrician	1.28	1.19*	1.36
Hoist Engineer	1.54	1.31	1.50
Painter	1.18	1.00	1.14
Plasterer	1.53	1.28	1.51
Plumber	1.34	1.15	1.37
Stone Mason	1.49	1.16*	1.47

* 1934; † 1932
SOURCE: John Coyne, "Building Trades and Defense," *American Federationist* 47 (November 1940): 32.

tures dropped significantly in 1943 (to $8.3 billion) and in 1944 (to $4.6 billion), these were fat years for AFL construction workers, the only ones who could work on federally funded projects.[61]

Because of Hillman's actions regarding construction contracts, the AFL was now on board the defense emergency bandwagon. At the same time, however, Hillman created new divisions within the Congress of Industrial Organizations and between the AFL and CIO. John L. Lewis was outraged at Hillman and never forgave him for forsaking the CIO's

United Construction Workers, which incidentally was led by Lewis's brother. Union politics aside, Hillman had done the right thing. Denny Lewis's post was a sinecure, and the UCW was never more than a "paper" or "nuisance" union set up to give the AFL construction unions grief.[62] Moreover, Hillman's hands were tied. The AFL had the bulk of the construction workers. If the NDAC and, later, the OPM wanted union peace and if they wanted defense construction to move forward, the NDAC had little choice other than to give the AFL what it wanted.

Still, there is no doubt that Hillman was giving preferential treatment to the AFL. In September 1941, the NDAC, acting upon Hillman's advice, rejected a low bid from the Currier Lumber Company (which had a CIO union) and awarded a contract to build defense housing near Detroit to a different company, the Esslingler & Misch Company, which had a union shop agreement with the AFL Building Trades.[63] John L. Lewis was now even angrier, but for the moment his wrath was the least of Hillman's worries. Shortly after the AFL construction pact was announced, Denny Lewis filed a complaint with Assistant U.S. Attorney General Thurman Arnold, who pledged a thorough investigation. The official minutes of the NDAC and the OPM offer no clue about whether such promises from FDR's trust-busting and occasionally anti-union assistant attorney general scared anyone. In any case, Arnold failed to follow through. Undeterred, Denny filed a complaint with Senator Harry S. Truman's (D-Missouri) special committee, which was probing fraud and inefficiencies in the defense program. Although the Truman Committee gave the complaint—which contained fifteen allegations, including a charge of unfairness in the Currier Lumber case—a full hearing, no action was taken to reverse the contract or to upend the construction stabilization agreement.[64] No one close to FDR, the OPM, or the defense effort wanted to upset the defense building plans or return the nation to the chaotic, strike-ridden situation that had dominated the months before the "epochal pact." Thus, Hillman and the AFL had won that round, but the labor situation on the home front of the Second World War was far from settled.

The Outbreak of War and the Fight for "Equality of Sacrifice"

As it became clear to the AFL's leadership that Hillman was not a CIO hardliner, was a willing negotiator, and, most important, could deliver

William Green and George Meany presenting President Franklin D. Roosevelt with the AFL's new defense poster, May 1941, courtesy of the George Meany Memorial Archives, image 392.

on his promises, Green and his colleagues began to shift the Federation's considerable political weight toward the defense effort. In May 1941, President Green commissioned the Washington, D.C., artist George Lohr to create fifty thousand color posters to express the AFL's backing of FDR's defense policies. On May 26, 1941, Green, along with George Meany, personally gave President Roosevelt his copy of the "A. F. of L. 100% for Defense/Buy Defense Bonds" poster. The president loved it and promised the Federation officials that he would send it to his library in Hyde Park, New York, which he indeed did. At the meeting with the president, Green also announced that the AFL planned to purchase $50,000 worth of national defense bonds and that it would send out invitations to its local labor organizations to similarly "invest in American democracy."[65] During the summer of 1941, the Federation formed its own AFL National Defense Committee, largely made up of Federation officials already serving on Hillman's labor policy board. Over the next several months, the AFL National Defense Committee issued several pamphlets to the Federation's membership on a range of controversial issues, including defense contracts, material and job priorities, price control, and "the responsibility of central labor unions." In this last one, the AFL leadership made it clear that in "the most stupendous production job in the history of the world [that] lies ahead . . . personal and financial sacrifices" would have to be made. The AFL leadership demanded that local labor groups help managers retool their workshops, retrain workers, and resolve grievances through mediation, not through "interruption of production."[66]

The AFL's new proadministration, prodefense position was cemented on December 7, 1941. Within a week of the ferocious attack at Pearl Harbor, the AFL Executive Council met and adopted an organization-wide "no-strike" policy for the duration and called for a new "War Labor Board for the purpose of dealing with disputes, differences and grievances which may arise between employers and employees through mediation, conciliation and arbitration."[67] Although now in the parlance, the no-strike pledge had in reality been in effect for the AFL since the creation of the NDAC in the summer of 1940. On June 20, 1940, the Federation's Metal Trades Department had agreed that, in return for its the shipbuilding stabilization agreement with the federal government, "there shall be no stoppage of work . . . neither strikes no lockouts."[68]

Like the AFL, the CIO also supported the defense program, and after the United States formally entered the global conflict, it quickly announced its no-strike pledge. Also exactly like the AFL, the CIO did not give its support for the war without a just price. As the UAW's R. J. Thomas and Richard Frankensteen wrote to FDR, "is the CIO to be expected to make sacrifices which may result in its own destruction to the aggrandizement of those who are lending aid and comfort to the enemies of the country?" In other words, sacrifice was not free. Despite the friction between the two labor organizations, the Congress was basically saying the same thing as the AFL. In early 1942, CIO president Philip Murray, along with the United Automobile Workers's Walter Reuther, developed the "Victory through Equality of Sacrifice" program. It was far more specific and detailed than the AFL's position. To the CIO, equality of sacrifice meant that, in return for its support for Roosevelt's war mobilization efforts and in exchange for the no-strike pledge, the CIO demanded that government control employer profits, executive salaries, and inflation. Additionally, the CIO proposed wage increases to meet the rise in prices. Finally, the Congress wanted Roosevelt to help institute a nationwide industrial management plan through which labor-employer councils would help orchestrate the conversion to war production and ensure that war production schedules were met.[69]

Even before the Japanese surprise attack, the AFL and the CIO were squabbling about which labor federation had the better plan, which had sacrificed the most, and which was the most patriotic. Early in the war, the CIO often pointed to its battle with the International Association of Machinists (IAM), an AFL affiliate, as evidence of AFL negligence. In 1942, the UAW launched a major organizational drive in the aircraft industry. In Buffalo, New York, it faced stiff competition from the IAM, which eventually trounced the UAW. The central issue was the UAW's (and the CIO's) concession to the federal government over premium pay. The IAM refused to give up time-and-a-half for Saturday work and double-time for work on Sunday. As a result, Buffalo Curtiss-Wright employees voted for the Machinists. Bitter, the UAW issued a statement after the NLRB election stating that "while the AFL has been loyal to the country it has also been loyal to its members, IT HAS NOT FELT CALLED UPON TO MAKE SACRIFICES OF WORKERS' PAY OR OF LABOR'S GAINS."[70] Although the statement was meant as an attack, the AFL might have taken it as a badge of honor. In any case, the AFL's President Green had a powerful way of demonstrating the AFL's sacrifices, patriotism, and loyalty compared to those of the CIO. As he explained in a widely distributed pamphlet, during the first ten months of the defense emergency, there had been sixty-one strikes involving forty-seven CIO unions and only nine AFL unions. Five of the worker protests involved jurisdictional battles between the two organizations. In terms of man-days lost, 91.5 percent were a result of CIO strikes, 5.3 percent were a product of AFL job actions, and 3.2 percent related to AFL and CIO fights. As Green said, "the record speaks for itself."[71]

While the AFL and the CIO engaged in this rather frivolous public debate, a more serious problem was developing in American wartime labor relations over wages and prices. During the entire defense emergency and war period, inflation was rampant, triggering bad memories of the First World War. When that conflict broke out, in 1914, inflation in the United States was minimal. Steep increases in prices hit hardest during the second year of the war, and, by 1917, both consumer and wholesale prices were more than 50 percent above their prewar levels.

Although President Woodrow Wilson used powers established within the National Defense Act of 1917 to reign in the upward spiral, federal price control efforts largely failed. By 1919, the average cost of living had doubled, and wholesale prices were on average 145 percent higher than prices during the prewar period.[72] During the year before the Pearl Harbor attack, prices were rising at a similar pace. Depending on the particular locale, average food costs in June 1941 were 8 to 13 percent higher than a year earlier. Some items were dramatically higher: eggs were up 34 percent, pork chops 30 percent, butter 25 percent, and sugar 10 percent.[73]

Higher costs of living infuriated most workers. They were indeed making more money during the war years than during the lean depression years. However, they were not receiving raises commensurate with the rise in inflation. Moreover, employers were making their profits. Workers wanted equality of sacrifice. As negotiations with employers broke down, more and more workers went on strike. Additionally, the AFL and CIO engaged in work stoppages as part of their ongoing battle for supremacy. (See table 1.4.) The situation was already bad in late 1940. That December, there were 147 strikes, costing employers 458,314 idle man-days. However, by March 1941, the number of strikes per month had doubled to 316, with 1,543,803 idle man-days.[74] Normally, the jobs of resolving these disputes would have fallen to two federal agencies: the National Labor Relations Board and the Labor Department's Conciliation Service (USCS). But both were largely nonentities during the war. As the historians of the NDAC wrote after the war, the Conciliation Service was primarily known for its weakness and inefficiencies. Labor Department officials were more than willing to hand their defense-related case load off to other agencies, particularly the National Defense Mediation Board and, later, the National War Labor Board. As USCS director John R. Steelman announced, in October 1941, "we have carefully instructed the entire staff of the Conciliation Service to give utmost attention to any potential board case and to earmark at the earliest possible moment every situation which may at any time, in the interests of the defense program, became deserving of certification to the board."[75]

The National Labor Relations Board (NLRB) also kept its war activities to a minimum. The NLRB was neither weak nor ineffectual. And, the NLRB remained the principal arbiter in representational issues. But on issues such as unfair labor practices, other wartime labor agencies

TABLE 1.4
Work Stoppages During World War II

	Work Stoppages		Man-days Idle	
Period	*Number*	*Workers Involved*	*Number*	*Percent of Available Working Time*
Total-World War II	14,731	6,744,000	36,601,000	0.11
December 8–31, 1941	84	16,000	303,000	0.06
1942	2,968	840,000	4,183,000	0.05
1943	3,752	1,981,000	13,501,000	0.15
1944	4,956	2,116,000	8,721,000	0.09
January 1–August 14, 1945	2,971	1,791,000	9,593,000	0.17

SOURCE: "Work Stoppages During the War," *Monthly Labor Review* 60 (May 1946): 723.

stepped in so that resolutions could be quickly reached. Additionally, the NLRB was happy to have a lower profile since it was under constant political attack during the war. In 1943, the reactionary Virginia Democratic Representative Howard W. Smith launched an investigation into various New Deal agencies, including the NLRB. Smith's goal was to dig up dirt, embarrass, and delegitimize Roosevelt's most controversial alphabet agencies. In this battle, Smith found some odd political bedfellows. By the 1940s, the AFL demanded several reforms to the Wagner Act to make the NLRB less friendly to the CIO and more hospitable to the Federation's craft unions.[76] Although Congress failed to pass the AFL-sponsored amendments to the the Wagner Act in 1943, it did approve the so-called Frey rider to the 1944 Appropriations Act. John Frey, the head of the AFL's Metal Trade Department, successfully lobbied Congress to limit funds to the NRLB to take action on unfair-labor-practices claims that had been filed less than three months before the signing of a collective-bargaining agreement. Frey introduced this limit in order to shield the AFL from CIO challenges to its exclusive closed-shop agreements in construction and in shipyards. It worked very well, perhaps too well. The AFL contracts were generally safe, but by 1945, employers were using the Frey rider provision to impose a kind of cooling-off period for union grievances before collective-bargaining contracts had been signed. The AFL backed off its support for the measure, and the 1945 Appropriations Act restored the NLRB funding for resolving unfair-labor-practices grievances.[77]

With the NLRB and the Conciliation Service taking a back seat, two other federal agencies dealt with labor unrest: the short-lived National Defense Mediation Board and the more permanent National War Labor

John P. Frey (1871–1957), courtesy of the George Meany Memorial Archives/Harris & Ewing, image 1858.

Board. The AFL and the CIO tried to control both in order to create their version of equality of sacrifice on the home front. Historians have been quite critical of both the NDMB and the NWLB.[78] However, with some important exceptions, these boards were able to keep the "arsenal of democracy" on its production schedules. That was no easy task. Initially, Hillman's Labor Advisory Committee of the NDAC and, later, the OPM had tried to handle the growing number of labor disputes and strikes. The Labor Advisory Committee set up a subcommittee with an equal number of AFL and CIO representatives. Quickly, however, the subcommittee members realized they were in over the heads. Therefore, on March 19, 1941, President Roosevelt stepped in and issued Executive Order 8716, which created the National Defense Mediation Board to resolve conflicts between employers and unions in the defense industries. Commencing under the leadership of University of Wisconsin president Clarence A. Dykstra, the board began with a backlog of cases.

Unlike the OPM's conciliation subcommittee, the NDMB had more CIO than AFL members. George Meany was the lone Federation representative, while Thomas Kennedy, of the United Mine Workers, and Philip Murray held the CIO's stake.[79]

Three out of every four of the 118 cases before the NDMB dealt with wage increases. The rest dealt with other kinds of issues, including proper bargaining representation. Ninety-six of the 118 cases (involving 1,191,664 union workers) were settled. In addition to quickly resolving grievances, the NDMB also earned a reputation for fairness. Nothing demonstrates this more than the fact that by December 1941, all workers engaged with the NDMB gave up their strikes and went back to work while awaiting the Board's final decision. In most cases, the Board was able to provide some sort of wage increase. Moreover, the Board set an enormously consequential precedent for all wartime unions. This precedent grew out of a fight between the United Brotherhood of Carpenters and Joiners (AFL) and the Weyerhaeuser Timber Company. Weyerhaeuser's managers were dedicated to keeping an open shop, while the Carpenters were on strike for a union shop. The NDMB heard the sticky case and offered a novel solution. Rather than establish the union shop, the AFL union and Weyerhaeuser agreed to a "maintenance of membership" contract, which allowed the union to keep its members for the life of the contract. In other words, although no one was obliged to join the union either at employment or soon after, once in the union workers had to stay there and pay dues until a new contract was ratified. Although in some ways the compromise was equally unappealing to both parties, the deal stuck for the entire war.[80]

In early 1941, the NDMB was on the verge of establishing another precedent, this one concerning wages. Both the AFL and the CIO were pressuring the NDMB to grant larger wage increases. Regardless of affiliation, all workers were struggling with inflationary prices of household goods. During the five-month period from February to June 1941, the cost of living increased by a shocking 3 percent, and wholesale prices rose 10 percent.[81] The Board, however, was under pressure to keep raises to a minimum in order to guard against more inflation. The CIO and its fallen leader, John L. Lewis, were much more adamant than the AFL about fighting for higher wages; in some ways, the AFL had already made its deals with Roosevelt's war agencies. In September and October 1941, Lewis, who was still the head of the United Mine Workers, closed the so-called captive mines, those that were owned by the steel companies. Fifty-three thousand UMW workers demanded higher wages and the union shop. The mines were essential for war production, and the strike drew angry denunciations from every corner. The AFL publicist Philip Pearl called the strike "not only a betrayal of America . . . not only a betrayal of the workers involved, but . . . a dastardly and indefensible betrayal of the best interests of all labor in America."[82] President Roosevelt warned that defense production "cannot be hampered by the selfish obstruction of a small but dangerous minority of labor leaders."[83] Everyone knew FDR was referring to Lewis. The NDMB tried in vain to resolve the dispute. On October 30, 1941, the Board voted against the UWM's plea for the union shop. Both CIO representatives on the NDMB—Murray and Kennedy, who were also members of the UMW—resigned in protest. The Board was effectively dead.

On December 7, 1941, a special mediation committee that Roosevelt set up to deal with captive mines granted a union shop for the United Mine Workers. The miners immediately and patriotically went back to work, but the other issue, a wage increase, had yet to be resolved. In January 1942, FDR created a new war labor relations board by resurrecting the old National War Labor Board of First World War fame.[84] The first order of business for the NWLB was to settle the dispute with John Lewis. In July 1942, the NWLB issued its "Little Steel" decision, raising wages by forty cents per day, sixty cents less than was asked for. Moreover, the NWLB stated that the Little Steel formula of a 15 percent wage increase would apply to all workers in war factories everywhere. Employers praised the wage cap, and workers denounced it. The small raise was an affront to the idea of equality of sacrifice.

Strikes were on the rise months before the Little Steel decision and spiked sharply afterward. The labor situation was beginning to unravel, and in April 1942, President Roosevelt attempted to settle things down. On April 27, 1942, FDR sent Congress a seven-point plan to stop the spiraling inflation and economic unrest. He encouraged Congress to establish an economic stabilization program to increase taxes, fix prices, expand rationing, stabilize wages, encourage the purchasing of war bonds, and discourage installment buying. The next day, he told Americans about his ideas during one of his famous wartime fireside chats. The chat, which was titled "A Call for Sacrifice," started as all his wartime radio messages did, with an update on the battlefronts. The news was decidedly mixed. "We have passed through," the president explained, "a phase of serious losses." Much of the Pacific, Europe, Africa, and Asia were "in the hands of the enemy." Most Americans probably already knew how badly the war was progressing for the Allies. But there was some comfort in hearing the president's straight talk. Moreover, FDR answered the question on everyone's mind. Since January 1942, the White House had been inundated with telegrams and letters asking, "What more can I do to help my country in winning this war?" The answer was blunt. "The price for civilization," he said, "must be paid in hard work and sorrow and blood." The stakes were that high. The Axis Powers threatened freedom everywhere in the world. "That is why [we] fight . . . that is why we must work and sacrifice."[85]

Although he did not specifically mention it, FDR intended that all sacrifices would be equal. For example, in terms of tax policies, no one was to unduly profit from the war. Roosevelt proposed that Congress establish tax brackets so that "no American citizen [would] have a net income, after he paid taxes, of more than $25,000 a year."[86] The president set similar goals for the rationing and price-fixing system. FDR's Executive Order 8734 had created the Office of Price Administration (OPA) on April 11, 1941. After the war began, Congress widened the OPA's jurisdiction and legal powers with the Emergency Price Control Act of January 1942. FDR was clear to OPA officials that he wanted the agency to conduct business with an eye on fairness. As the OPA official historian Harvey Mansfield stated, however, fairness did not mean equality. "Equitable distribution in some cases [meant] equal distribution among the people, in other cases not." "Equality of sacrifice," Mansfield explained, was required "for the purpose of maintaining civilian morale."[87] Thus, rationing and price controls were more than tools to control inflation. They were a means to maintain patriotism.

Publicly, the AFL strongly supported Roosevelt's equality-of-sacrifice plan. In his 1942 Labor Day message, Federation president William Green promised that all AFL workers "would accept the sacrifices" involved in FDR's anti-inflation plan "for their own ultimate good and the nation's welfare." Green continued: "Let us resolve to do everything in our power, without stint and without reservation, to win this war. And let us resolve to see to it that when victory comes an enduring peace will be established, based on the extension of freedom and democracy to all the peoples in all the lands of the earth. . . . The Army, Navy and Air Forces will not fail us. We must not fail them." He then reaffirmed the no-strike pledge, rhetorically asking, "isn't it clear that strikes for any cause now will help Hitler deprive us forever of the right to strike?" "We must refrain from work stoppages of any kind now in order to maintain our freedom." Finally, Green echoed the president and declared that "the price of victory is sacrifice."[88]

The problem was that for the AFL, wartime sacrifices were not unconditional. Everyone agreed that sacrifice was needed. But the Federation was willing to support the President just so far. In terms of price controls and rationing, the AFL was solidly behind the Office of Price Administration. It backed, for example, the OPA Consumer Division's publicity campaigns. On July 31, 1942, President Green sent out letters to all unions and AFL state and local councils, along with millions of copies of the AFL Consumer War Pledge. The form asked each unionist to take the following oath:

> TO HELP MY COUNTRY AND MY PEOPLE WIN;
> TO MAKE OUR COMMON SACRIFICE EQUAL, FAIR AND JUST—
> I join my fellow unionists in the solemn pledge that:
> 1. I will not buy above the ceiling prices.
> 2. I will not attempt to get more than my share of rationed goods.
> 3. I will buy only what I absolutely need.[89]

Scores of AFL members signed Green's pledge cards. President Roosevelt commended Green on his Consumer War Pledge, as well as for his mobilization of the American Federation of Women's Auxiliaries of Labor to work with AFL families and to help enforce the OPA's price regulations.[90]

The AFL's backing of the OPA, however, mattered little. As Mansfield wrote in his short history of the OPA, the agency was nearly universally hated and could neither "buy good will, nor even tolerance."[91] In any case, price controls and rationing were largely unsuccessful at curbing inflation. By the end of summer 1942, prices had risen another 10 percent. When victory over the Axis powers was finally declared, in September 1945, consumer prices on average were almost 30 percent over their prewar levels. Prices had actually stabilized by mid-1943. But that was little consolation for workers who were paying the higher prices. Put in simpler terms, in spring 1943, in Canton, Ohio, a one-pound pot roast cost more than twice as much as it had before the war. In January 1941, a peck of potatoes fetched twenty-five cents. In April 1943, the same peck cost eighty-nine cents, a 256 percent increase. A dozen eggs in

January 1941 cost twenty-nine cents. The price in April 1943 had risen to forty-five cents, up 56 percent.[92] What made matters worse was that not all consumers suffered to the same degree. As the editors of the AFL's wartime monthly newsletter, *Labor's Monthly Survey,* wrote, in November 1943, not all "groups [had] made equal sacrifice." From 1942 to 1943, while inflation had gone up another 10 percent, workers' wages had risen only 6 percent. Corporate profits, however, were up 13 percent. Feeling the pocketbook pinch, American workers became increasingly restless, prompting the newsletter editors to state:

> It is this basic unfairness which creates the current labor unrest. Labor feels, and rightly, that in spite of our outstanding contribution to the war effort we have been discriminated against in the matter of stabilization control. If democracy is to be preserved in this country, we must have justice for all groups in America. Else why are we fighting a war to "save democracy"?[93]

Shop-floor reactions to inflation and wage stagnation were more decisive. From late 1942 though July 1943, the number of work stoppages doubled.[94] Striking workers did not merely wanted raises. They were fighting for an equality of sacrifice.

In the summer of 1942, President Roosevelt let it be known that he was considering freezing wages as a way to deal with the inflation. This drew severe criticism from organized labor. In late July 1942, AFL president William Green wrote to President Roosevelt demanding that he act quickly to deal with inflation, wages, and the strikes. "We have reached a crisis in war administration which threatens the fundamentals of our democratic way of life," he stated. Green reminded the president that "we voluntarily agreed not to strike for the duration of the war, but to submit our disputes to conciliation or to the War Labor Board. We did this with the definite understanding that collective bargaining was to remain fully operative." "But the developments of the past week," he continued, "have convinced me that as the spokesman for the American Federation of Labor, whose membership has proven their loyalty through over sixty years of trial and in two world wars, that I must speak plainly against proposed invasion of Labor's basic rights."[95] Clearly, FDR's suggestion of a wage freeze hit the AFL in two ways. It was a violation of the prewar agreements not only to include labor in the war's administration but also to ensure that wartime sacrifices would be as equitable as possible. It was also an affront to the very foundations of the AFL's ideology, in particular to what remained of volunteerism.

Green's protest earned him a trip to the White House. On July 23, 1942, FDR called an emergency meeting of his Combined Labor War Victory Board, a quasi-public advisory group that included AFL president William Green, first vice president Daniel J. Tobin, and secretary-treasurer George Meany. The AFL leaders made clear their position that "this principle of equality of sacrifice [had been] forgotten as soon as the President's voice speaking to the nation faded from the air" in April 1942. They argued that the key to stopping inflation was not a wage freeze but more effective price controls and wage stabilization, which ideally would fix "inequalities in wage rates."[96] And they reminded Roosevelt that wage stabilization was already in play and working in two industries, construction and shipbuilding. Thus, Roosevelt did not need to take any drastic action but could implement more widely the administration's current labor policies.

Green, Tobin, and Meany left the meeting feeling that Roosevelt had heard and understood their complaints and suggestions. Yet, FDR waited almost two months to take action. On September 7, 1942, FDR gave a fireside chat on the war's progress and the rising cost of living. He began by telling the story of a navy airman, Lieutenant John James Powers, of New York City, who sunk or severely damaged four Japanese war ships, including an aircraft carrier, on a single raid. Roosevelt then asked his audience to consider whether Americans back home "were playing our part . . . in winning this war." The president's answer was clear: "we are not doing enough."[97] More sacrifice was required. FDR was still interested in equality of sacrifice. He refreshed his seven-point anti-inflation plan, which Congress had ignored. A week later, on September 15, Congress passed Roosevelt's Economic Stabilization Bill, giving the president more powers to deal with inflation, prices, and wages. On October 3, 1942, President Roosevelt issued Executive Order 9250, creating the Office of Economic Stabilization (OES). James F. Byrnes headed the OES, the most powerful domestic wartime agency, which had supervisory control over both the OPA and the NWLB. In other words, Byrnes, and his successor, Frederick M. Vinson, had the power to set both wages and prices on the home front.

Both AFL and CIO workers were unimpressed. The strike wave continued to rise through the rest of 1943. After a brief period of labor peace in early 1944, the epidemic of work stoppages resumed after the launching of the D-Day invasion and continued unabated until after the war. President Roosevelt, the OES, the NWLB, and the OPA did little to assuage union displeasure at the cost-of-living increases and the stagnation of wages. If anything, Roosevelt's actions in 1943 further angered workers. In April 1943, in response to another United Mine Workers strike, FDR issued his "Hold the Line" executive order (#9328), which mandated that the heads of the OPA, the NWLB, and the OES stop issuing price and wages increases except in cases of dire emergency. Roosevelt's hard line on inflation was softened somewhat by the creation of the President's Committee on Cost of Living, with George Meany as the AFL's representative and R. J. Thomas the CIO's. The Committee was a sop and did little. While it researched the proper way to calculate inflation rates, workers walked off their jobs. Conservatives in the U.S. Congress had had enough. In 1943, Congress passed the War Labor Disputes Act (a.k.a. the Smith-Connally Act), which mandated a thirty-day cooling-off period before strikes and allowed the president to seize a struck war factory. The bill, which was passed over FDR's veto, was aimed directly at John L. Lewis's coal strike and was intended to send a chilling message to all union workers. Although it was an attack upon organized labor, the War Labor Disputes Act was a mild piece of legislation compared to the much bandied-about idea of a labor draft.[98] The Smith-Connally Act had no involuntary service provision, nor did it have much of an effect. The number of strikes actually increased after its passage.[99]

The AFL lost the fight for equality of sacrifice. In the end, very little was done to ensure that all Americans shared equally in the pain on the home front brought on by the war. Unsurprisingly, the burden fell mostly on the working class. And those atop the economic ladder earned the greatest wartime benefits. By the war's denouement, in 1944, corporate profits before taxes had risen 329 percent over 1939 levels. Industrial workers saw their wages increase only 58 percent. Moreover, by D-Day, there was little administrative pretense to equality of sacrifice. By late 1942, FDR had given up on his plan to limit all net personal incomes to no more than $25,000 per year.[100] Roosevelt's wage stabilization and price control plans did little to help workers' earnings keep up with inflation. More often than not, the wartime economy pinched workers. And unionists responded with strikes. In 1944 and 1945, there were more than 9,700 strikes, with 46.7 million man-days idle. And yet, despite all the protest, industrial production was barely affected. To the rest of the world, the United States remained the indefatigable arsenal of democracy. Moreover, despite the battle for equality of sacrifice, the AFL remained firmedly entrenched in Roosevelt's camp. The marriage between the Federation and the New Deal had been consummated with the prewar construction agreement. Afterward, the AFL's leadership was more than willing to cooperate with the president in securing his wartime and postwar goals. In particular, the Federation committed itself to a labor-government partnership that promised to bring eternal economic security. In their purest forms, both volunteerism and "pure and simple" unionism were causalities of the Second World War. The AFL, however, was unwilling to give up the other basic parts of its ideology. As the following chapters detail, these parts, such as exclusivity, were not sacrificed. Neither was the fight with the CIO. Thus, the history of the AFL during the Second World War must include the prewar ideas and practices that the America's largest labor organization kept and those that it left behind. By 1945, the Federation was no longer the bastion of conservatism that it had been before the war. Nor was it liberalism's great exemplar. Frustratingly enough for historians, it existed somewhere in between.

2

Putting the Shackles on Labor

The AFL and the Fight Against the Open Shop

> The anti-union shop—and that is generally the "open shop"—is a shop in which the employer pursues a militant policy in opposition to organization. It is the shop of the crusading employer, bent upon maintaining industrial autocracy and upon restoring it where trade unionism has broken it down.
>
> —Samuel Gompers, 1921[1]

Japan's attack on Pearl Harbor and other American interests and assets in the Pacific Ocean marked the United States's formal entry into World War II. It also signaled a period of unusual (but perhaps expected) unity on the home front. Employers and workers temporarily gave up their fights for the sake of the war effort. Nothing illustrated this more than the six months of industrial peace that followed America's entry into the war. Strikes and lockouts virtually disappeared as the country retooled for battle. Yet, this wartime unity did not last long. Neither managers nor unionists were willing to sacrifice permanently their antagonism or their stakes in the fight to control the shop floor. Industrial conflicts were on the rise by the middle of 1942, and by the middle of the war, the old antagonisms that were the hallmark of the 1930s had fully reappeared. Employers and unionists resumed their fight for control of the shop floor. Employers again sought the elusive goal of rolling back organized labor's gains established during the New Deal. But, this time, they eschewed the strong-arm tactics exposed by Senator Robert M. La Follette, Jr. (R-Wisconsin). Rather, during the war, employers revived the open-shop movement. To a significant extent, their efforts were rewarded both during the war and after. The first major piece of postwar labor legislation, the Labor-Management Relations Act, otherwise known as the Taft-Hartley Act, was the culmination of employers' wartime work.

The Taft-Hartley Act was the hottest topic at the October 1947 American Federation of Labor (AFL) Convention, held in San Francisco. The passage of the "slave labor bill" over President Harry S. Truman's veto meant that the yearlong energetic lobbying activities by the Federation's legislative and legal teams had failed. In essence, the Taft-Hartley Act was a series of amendments to the Wagner Act. The legislation had nine main features, each intended to limit the power and influence of labor unions. The law mandated a sixty-day cooling-off period before a union could resort to a strike. It authorized the federal government to obtain court injunctions to impose an eighty-day cooling-off period for any strike in an essential industry. It outlawed the secondary boycott, a tactic that sympathetic unionists often employed to support striking workers in another union. The legislation permitted employers and unions to sue each other for breach of contract. It required union officers to file affidavits that they were not members of the Communist Party. The law required unions to file copies of their constitutions and financial statements with the Department of Labor. It forbade unions or employers to make direct or indirect campaign contributions to party campaign funds. And it ended the dues check-off system whereby employers collected union dues from workers. Most important for our purposes, the act outlawed the closed shop. The union shop was allowed to exist but only if the union represented a majority of the employees eligible to vote and if the union gave equal rights to new members.[2]

Joseph A. Padway, the American Federation of Labor's chief counsel, appeared before the 1947 convention to tell his story of frustration in opposing the Taft-Hartley bill and to chart a course for future action against the retrenchment of federal support for labor unions. Padway began his remarks by modestly noting that it had been the "most hectic and trying year" of his decade of legal service to the Federation. In addition to fighting against the forces supporting Taft-Hartley, he had also been one of the lead attorneys defending John L. Lewis, of the United Mine Workers, in a federal prosecution. The full truth was worse. Padway was completely exhausted. He had developed high blood pressure and ulcers while working overtime. As one of the nation's leading attorneys fighting what he once called "shackling labor by legislation,"

Padway intended to summarize for the convention delegates the new challenge to unions with a title-by-title attack on the new labor relations law. However, ten minutes into his presentation, he faltered and grasped the podium for support. Regaining his composure for a few minutes, Padway began his diatribe against Taft-Hartley and then suddenly stopped midsentence and fell to the platform's floor. California State Federation of Labor president John L. Shelley caught the AFL's lawyer, who begged to be allowed to return to the stage. Instead, Padway was rushed to Stanford University Hospital, where he died a short time later of a cerebral hemorrhage.[3]

In his eulogy, a few days later, AFL president William Green paid tribute to his friend and predicted that "when the pages of history of the American labor are written there will be no brighter page in the book than the story of the service rendered by this great man."[4] Yet, historians have largely forgotten Padway's accomplishments for the AFL and the labor movement generally. His major contributions came in his role as one of the principal defenders of labor rights and security and a catalyst to the Federation's political transformation during the age of Franklin D. Roosevelt. By the end of the Roosevelt years, the AFL leadership, as well as its rank and file, had become accustomed to and come to rely on state intervention on behalf of labor unions. This chapter explores the AFL's fight to maintain one of its main means of union security, the closed shop. The AFL was unwilling to sacrifice this tool for the sake of the war. The story is told, in part, through the eyes of Joseph Padway, the Federation's primary lawyer during the war years. Unlike the history of the CIO, little about the AFL's lieutenants and professional staff has been published. While President Green made pronouncements, it was the dedicated work of people like Padway who tried to make labor's desires into realities. And during the war, the stakes were quite high. Under the cover of wartime conditions and distractions, employers resumed their battle against organized labor. They argued that the closed shop hindered the war effort, an accusation tantamount to a charge of treason. Thus, while American soldiers, many of whom left union jobs to fight, were battling fascism in Europe and Japan, American employers fought to eliminate the closed shop at home. They were opposed primarily by the American Federation of Labor, which used the closed shop more frequently than the Congress of Industrial Organizations. In the end, despite the AFL's vehement legal protests, employer associations and their allies were moderately successful, particularly in southern states, where a few state legislatures passed laws prohibiting the closed shop. After the war and after Padway's death, these employer gains were solidified and dramatically expanded with the passage of the Taft-Hartley Act in 1947.[5]

A Stalwart for Labor's Rights

Born on July 25, 1891, in Leeds, England, Joseph Padway emigrated with his parents to the United States when he was fourteen. His primary schooling was in England, and when his family relocated to Milwaukee, Wisconsin, he enrolled at Marquette University, graduating from its law school in 1912. For three years, he practiced privately as a labor lawyer. Then in 1915, he became the Wisconsin State Federation of Labor's general counsel. As his connections with organized labor increased, so did his commitment to political activism. Like many AFL unionists, Padway found that his political stripes changed with the environment. In the 1920s, Padway became involved in state politics, originally as a Socialist and an ally of Robert M. La Follette. Padway helped to draft and lobby for progressive legislation, served one term as a state senator, and was appointed judge of the civil court of Milwaukee. By the late 1920s, perhaps like many progressives, disillusioned, Padway abandoned his political career in Wisconsin and returned to his private practice. During the Great Depression, however, he reentered politics and the labor movement. This time he was a Democrat and a staunch supporter of Franklin D. Roosevelt and the New Deal.[6]

In 1934, Padway rose to national prominence when the Wisconsin State Federation of Labor hired him to assist in the legal battles stemming from the infamous and violent Kohler bathroom fixture factory strike in Kohler, Wisconsin.[7] Because of his dedicated efforts, at its 1938 Miami convention, the AFL hired Padway as the organization's first full-time lawyer.[8] Joseph Padway's political views were consistently progressive. He valued and fought for a beneficial role for the state in labor relations. Until the 1930s, this political position was quite out of place in the inner circles of the AFL leadership. From the AFL's founding in 1886 to the early 1930s, its leaders were dedicated theoretically to what they called volunteerism, a main tenet of which was the avoidance of state influence in labor relations. Ranking AFL members such as John Frey, of the Metal Trades Department, were adamantly opposed to state

Joseph A. Padway (1891–1947), courtesy of the George Meany Memorial Archives/Gordon W. Powley, image 1857.

imposition of rules governing organizing and bargaining. As Frey put it, "management and labor should have an outstand-ing voice in the determination of policies and rules" that related to labor unions and contracts.[9] Additionally, "pure and simple" unionism meant, ideally, that the AFL focused on short-term objectives, relied more on economic power than on party politics, limited membership largely to skilled workers, and organized strictly along occupational lines. The goal of this conservative agenda was to create a common ground, albeit a narrow one, on which workers of varying nationalities might unite. Unions within the Federation also preferred a type of organizing and bargaining that favored working closely with employers while tending to exclude any government interference. AFL leaders occasionally "organized" an employer before his workers. The resulting agreements met the needs and desires of the AFL leadership and the businessman but not necessarily those of the rank-and-file workers. For their part, employers welcomed the AFL and its conservative "business unionism" over the more radical—if not Communist—unionism of other organizations such as the Congress of Industrial Organizations.[10] And, of course, employers generally preferred to operate outside the purview of government agencies, as well, unless there was a dispute that they could not settle themselves. Thus, Padway's views seemed to call into question much of this philosophy on union organizing.

In addition to challenging its method of organizing, Padway also seemed to push the Federation toward another change. In principle and by tradition, the AFL and its affiliates were also to be nonpartisan, whereas Padway was an outspoken progressive, Democrat, and New Dealer. But, until the 1930s, the AFL sought to avoid the partisan divides that often separated workers. In practice, AFL unionists engaged in party politics at the local and national levels where they worked with and backed prolabor candidates. In 1924, for instance, the Federation had embraced the presidential campaign of Senator Robert M. La Follette. Still, generally speaking, on the national level, the AFL tended to remain aloof. Partly because of this political malleability and partly because of its conservative, procapitalist outlook, the American Federation of Labor was quite successful. By the 1930s, 85 percent of all union workers were under its aegis. Furthermore, despite the challenge presented by the Congress of Industrial Organizations, the Federation remained the largest and most powerful union during Franklin D. Roosevelt's presidency. But, during the FDR years, the AFL began to tilt toward the politicians who favored New Deal policies.[11]

Mainly because of what the New Deal meant to unionists, the AFL changed its formal stance on state intervention, coming closer to the views of some prostate labor activists and politicians such as Padway. Although at times the Federation sought to revise the 1935 National Labor Relations (or Wagner) Act and the National Labor Relations Board, it embraced the New Deal's labor reforms. As the lawyer for the AFL, Padway was responsible for ensuring that the gains brought by the Wagner Act were not lost to attacks from organized labor's foes or from AFL rivals. In fact, Padway was central to the AFL's stance on modern labor relations. When Padway died, in 1947, the Federation and the labor movement in general lost one of their most ardent supporter of labor rights and of the federal government's influence in and support of union activity.

Padway's primary task was to lead the campaigns to defend and "improve" the Wagner Act. He shared William Green's disdain for what they perceived as the pro-CIO leaning of the National Labor Relations Board (NLRB). Close observers both then and now dismissed accusations of bias made by both the AFL and the CIO. As the NLRB historian Fred Witney wrote, the charge of prejudice against the NLRB is akin to a "charge against the voting machine because it registers more votes for one candidate than another."[12] Nevertheless, while the AFL leaders approved of the principles behind the New Deal's labor relations, they wanted reform. In the late 1930s, Padway drafted several amendments to the Wagner Act that would have recognized craft unions, prevented the NLRB from setting aside existing contracts when the workers shifted union affiliation, allowed employers to voice preference for one union over another, and empowered the U.S. Circuit Court of Appeals to review NLRB finding. Had they passed a willing Congress and been signed by an approving FDR, Padway's modifications—particularly the proposal to recognize craft unions—would have benefited the AFL in its fight against the CIO. Although Padway had public backing, according to Gallup polls, and (somewhat embarrassingly) the encouragement of antiunion business organizations such as the National Association of Manufacturers and of congressional conservatives like Representative Clare Hoffman (R-Michigan) and Senator Edward R. Burke (D-Nebraska), Wagner Act supporters such as Senate "Laborcrat" Elbert D. Thomas (D-Utah) and Teamster president Daniel Tobin were able to stop the reform movement, at least temporarily.[13]

As explained in chapter 1, during the war, the AFL dusted off its list of Wagner Act reforms and was able to wrangle a major concession from the U.S. Congress. In July 1943, Congress passed the 1944 NLRB Appropriation Act, which contained an amendment based on Padway's original proposals and introduced by AFL Metal Trades Department president John Frey. The Frey or "Craft" Amendment significantly limited the power of the NLRB to take action against unfair labor practices. The Board was forbidden to spend any funds to prevent unfair labor practices that grew out of collective bargaining agreements unless the charge of unfair practices was filed before the agreement was three months old. At issue was a fight between the AFL and the CIO at the

Kaiser Shipyards in Portland, Oregon. In January 1941, Kaiser had received a contract from the federal government to build a new shipyard and begin to build ships for the navy and the merchant marine. Even before the shipyard opened, Kaiser signed a closed-shop agreement with AFL-affiliated unions such as the International Brotherhood of Boilermakers. Only eighty-six employees had been hired at the time, and only sixty-six of them belonged to the AFL. Kaiser officials later admitted that they knew that these five dozen workers would constitute less than 1 percent of the yard's eventual workforce. When the Kaiser Portland shipyard was completed, thousands of workers found jobs building ships. However, because of the closed-shop agreement, they had to join the AFL. Since most of the workers belonged to the CIO's affiliated union, the Industrial Union of Marine and Shipbuilding Workers, they were soon discharged for failing to honor the closed-shop agreement. Immediately the CIO filed a petition with the NLRB on behalf of its union to have a new election to determine the proper bargaining agent.

The CIO had a good chance of winning a favorable decision from the NLRB. Clearly, this was another case where the AFL had organized the employer before it organized the workers. Sensing that it might lose the shipyard, the AFL turned to the U.S. Congress for relief. And the plan worked. The Frey Amendment meant that the Kaiser Shipyard was safe. Since the CIO had not filed its papers before the three-month period ended, its complaint was dismissed. The AFL closed shop was secure for the war period.[14]

Although Padway was not directly involved with the passage of the Frey Amendment, he clearly had an important role to play in its development. It was an example of Padway's role as the AFL's general legal troubleshooter. In addition to influencing legislation, he led the charge against legal actions aimed at the Federation. Padway frequently clashed with the head of the Justice Department's Antitrust Division, Thurman Arnold, who brought several antitrust lawsuits against AFL unions.[15] As the defense preparedness program began, in 1940, Padway represented the AFL at government conferences in order to develop uniform hiring policies and labor standards. He also spent considerable time voicing the AFL's position against the antistrike bills such as the Smith-Connally law. Moreover, in 1940, he won one of the most important Supreme Court cases of the twentieth century, *Thornhill v. State of Alabama.*

In 1939, Brian Thornhill was arrested for violating a 1923 Alabama law that forbade picketing. Thornhill and several other unionists were on strike at the Brown Wood Preserving Company and picketed the factory every day. As even witnesses for the prosecution testified, the strike was peaceful. Clarence Simpson, one of only four employees who was not a member of the AFL, told the court that Thornhill had approached him "in a peaceful manner, and did not put fear in me, and did not appear to be mad."[16] Thornhill's quiet words said must have made an impact, as Simpson joined the striking workers. Later, to force an end to the strike, Thornhill was arrested.

Thornhill was initially convicted and fined, but under Padway's direction his case quickly wound its way to the U.S. Supreme Court. In their decision, the justices agreed with the AFL's lawyer and in so doing established what Padway and others labeled the "Thornhill doctrine."[17] The Supreme Court ruled that a worker's right to picket (specifically, AFL unionist Brian Thornhill's) was constitutionally protected. "The freedom of speech and of the press, which are secured by the First Amendment against abridgment by the United States," Justice Frank Murphy, the former governor of Michigan, who had supported the GM sitdown strikers, wrote, "are among the fundamental personal rights and liberties which are secured to all persons by the Fourteenth Amendment against abridgment by a state."[18] During the Second World War, Padway continued to defend worker and union rights as he engaged in a fierce battle with the open-shop movement in many states. Importantly, he utilized the legal strategy that he developed in the *Thornhill* case. As we will see, in his struggle against the wartime open-shop movement, he argued that denying the closed shop was against the First and Fourteenth Amendments.

The Roots of the Open Shop Movement During World War II

Padway's various legal assignments for the AFL reflected the changes brought by the New Deal. The Roosevelt administration, more than any of its predecessors, recognized organized labor as an essential political constituency. The cornerstone of New Deal labor policy was the Wagner Act, which outlawed company representation plans, sanctioned independent unions, and recognized collective bargaining.[19] It dramatically reshaped the shop floor, as well as the political scene. Whereas, before the New Deal, unions had to contend with employers, their spies, and federal troops, beginning with the Roosevelt administration the federal government ostensibly supported unions. "The president wants you to join the union," organizers told prospective recruits who responded in droves during the 1930s. During the Roosevelt years, organized labor added more than ten million workers to its ranks. In particular, despite the defection of more than a million workers to the CIO in 1936, Federation membership increased by two million workers by 1940. Labor was thankful for Roosevelt's support and in turn backed New Deal Democrats.[20]

As the AFL grew in size and political stature, it needed a full-time lawyer to look after its legal interests, because almost immediately after the Wagner Act's passage, employers and their business associations launched legal attacks against union activism, recognition, and collective bargaining. Challenges were first brought through federal courts, but in 1937 the U.S. Supreme Court affirmed the constitutionality of the act with its ruling in *NLRB v. Jones & Laughlin Steel Company.* Afterward, the battlefield shifted to the states. The Wagner Act originally contained several weaknesses. One critically important one was that the act did not legalize specific union practices (such as the all-union or closed shop, where union membership predicates continued employment) in instances where state governments had outlawed them. Initially, many states had supported the intent of the Wagner Act by passing their own "baby" Wagner Acts. But, in the late 1930s, under pressure from chambers of commerce, manufacturing associations, and other businesses interests, many states revised their labor codes. The model example was Wisconsin. In 1937, the Wisconsin state legislature had enacted a bill (which Padway drafted) that provided guarantees similar to those included in the Wagner Act. Two years later, the legislature passed the "Employment Peace Bill," which reversed many of those provisions by severely limiting the rights to strike and picket and reopened the way for court injunctions in labor disputes. Additionally, the law required a supermajority three-fourths vote of the employees involved to create a closed shop.[21]

Padway vehemently opposed the changes to the Wisconsin law. As *Time* magazine reported, "no man likes to have his ox gored, least of all A.F. of L. Counsel Joseph Padway." In February 1939, Padway testified before the state legislature in Madison, but to no avail. Wisconsin, one reporter explained, was "in step with the rightward trend of U.S. politics." [22] Although defeated in his home state, in the 1940s, Padway redoubled his efforts for union rights, which were under constant attack. Wisconsin was not the only state with a "reactionary legislature" (as Padway termed it);[23] in fact, several states went well beyond the Dairy State in curtailing the power of labor unions. In 1938, Oregon's legislature enacted a labor law that legally limited all employment disputes to issues of wages and working conditions. It outlawed sympathy strikes and secondary boycotts. It virtually ended the closed shop, union political fundraising, and job actions. To challenge these laws and thus the rightward swing of state legislatures, Padway and the AFL challenged the Wisconsin law at the U.S. Supreme Court. In a surprising 1942 ruling that reversed its Thornhill precedent, the Justices upheld Wisconsin's reactionary state labor law, thus giving a green light to other states so inclined to limit organized labor's activities such as picketing and strikes.[24] As table 2.1 illustrates, similar laws against organized labor were considered and enacted in many states, from Alabama to Arkansas, from Massachusetts to Minnesota, and from South Carolina to South Dakota.[25]

The fierceness of the legal and legislative assaults upon the Wagner Act, which Padway and the AFL sought to repel, was a reaction to labor's dramatic gains in the 1930s and early 1940s. Moreover, to the angry chagrin of employers, the promise of the Wagner Act to strengthen unions was further realized while the United Sates fought World War II.[26] Again unionists could thank FDR for maintaining his commitment to organized labor. President Roosevelt expected labor to make sacrifices, but such concessions were to be the products of a deliberative process. In 1941, Roosevelt called his first defense labor-management conference at the White House to discuss defense production. Two major policy developments came directly from that meeting: (1) labor's blanket no-strike pledge for the duration of the war, and (2) the creation of the National Defense Mediation Board (NDMB). Both policies were ways of avoiding strikes and maintaining, as far as possible, uninterrupted wartime production. No one imagined that the no-strike pledge would work in all cases; if a dispute between a union and an employer seemed intractable and the United States Conciliation Service failed to reach a settlement, then the case would go to the NDMB for a fair adjustment. Strikes might still happen, but the emphasis of the federal government was on what it termed "responsible" action and procedure. Despite the obvious limitations of this policy whereby managers attempted to assert their "rights" and unions could only "grieve,"

TABLE 2.1

Examples of State Controls Over Labor Unions, 1944

State	*Financial Statement*	*Union Membership*	*Picketing*	*Assembly*	*Strikes*	*Licensing*	*Penalties for Violation*
Alabama	Filed annually	Free to join or not join	No force or threat may be used to prevent any one from working	No assembly at or near a place of labor dispute forcibly to prevent work	By secret majority vote reported within 24 hours	N/A	Misdemeanor to participate in or urge an outlaw strike
Arkansas	N/A	N/A	No force or threat may be used to prevent any one from working	No assembly at or near a place of labor dispute forcibly to prevent work	N/A	N/A	Felony, 1–2 years in state prison
Colorado	Industrial commissioner makes annual examination	Free to join or not join	No mass or secondary picketing. Industrial commission can limit manner and quality of picketing	N/A	By majority vote on 20 days notice (30 in agricultural work)	N/A	$50–100 fine
Florida	Filed annually; open to members	Free to join or not join	No secondary picketing	N/A	By secret majority vote; no force or violence; no jurisdictional strikes	Agents must be citizens of good character and approved by governor	Criminal

Idaho	Filed annually	Forbidden on farm premises. No secondary boycotting	No agent may enter premises without owner's consent	N/A	N/A	N/A	$300 fine, 90 days
Kansas	Filed annually	No violent picketing or secondary boycott	N/A	By majority vote; no sitdown or jurisdictional strikes	Agents must be citizens	Revocation of agent's license	
Minnesota	Union must report to members	N/A	No interference with marketing of farm products	N/A	By majority vote; no jurisdictional strikes	N/A	Labor referee can disqualify union
South Dakota	Filed annually	N/A	Forbidden on farm premises; no secondary boycotting	No agent may enter premises without owner's consent	N/A	N/A	$300 fine, 90 days
Texas	Filed annually; open to members	Public hearing before expulsion	N/A	N/A	N/A	Agents must be citizens without criminal record	Union, $1000; individual $300, 60 days
Wisconsin	N/A	N/A	No violence; majority vote required, limited to workers, no secondary boycott	N/A	By majority vote	N/A	Union $1000, individual $500, 60 days

under the NDMB and its successor, the National War Labor Board, unions made phenomenal advances. At the war's peak in 1944, almost fourteen million workers, or 45 percent of all workers in private industry, were employed under union agreements.[27] Some industries continued to be much more widely organized than others. Of all manufacturing wage earners, 60 percent belonged to a union. In such industries as aluminum fabrication, automobiles, shipbuilding, and basic steel, more than 90 percent of workers worked under union agreements. Almost 100 percent of all longshoremen, coal miners, and railroad workers labored under the terms of union contracts. Another significant change was related to union status. From 1941 to 1945, there were increases in the proportion of manufacturing workers covered by agreements that required maintenance of membership during the term of the contract by employees who were or chose to become members and a decrease in the proportion of workers under agreements that made no membership requirements. There were sizable gains in the numbers of workers covered by all-union or closed-shop (where only union members were hired), preferential-shop (where employers gave preferential treatment to union members), and union-shop (where to remain employed workers had to join the union) agreements. In January 1944, for instance, closed-shop contracts covered nearly 20 percent of all union workers, and union-shop agreements covered another 20 percent, for a total of almost seven million workers. Many AFL unionists must have agreed with Padway and the AFL's leadership, which regarded the Wagner Act as "the Magna Carta of labor." During the tumultuous war years, the act and federal agencies that upheld labor rights brought opportunities for greater job security and better working conditions for American wage earners.[28]

At the same time, employers and their political allies responded to union advances by rejuvenating the open-shop or right-to-work movement.[29] The concerted activity by American employers to destroy forms of union security, if not the unions themselves, dates back to the early 1800s, when the first trade unions appeared in the United States. Well before the era of collective bargaining, union leaders sought union or closed-shop agreements. The rationale was simple: workers who benefited from union contracts ought to contribute their fair share to support the organization. The closed shop also safeguarded against union rivalries and the hiring of nonunion workers. Challenged by union power, employers countered with the open shop. Although the phrase "open shop" is temporally sensitive, prewar and wartime advocates subscribed to a theory that the open shop meant that an employer did not discriminate against a worker because that person was or was not a union member. Unionists and their allies were not fooled but rather insulted by the phony democratic connotation of the words "open shop" and "right to work." In practice, the open shop did not uphold the principles of employment at will or the liberty of contract. Rather, the open shop simply meant that employers did not recognize unions and often used the courts to seek injunctions against union activity. More militant forms of the movement relied on violence to eradicate union activities.[30] As AFL president Sam Gompers stated, in 1903, the open shop was nothing more than a nonunion shop that itself was closed to union workers. Moreover, union leaders maintained that there was no right to work in America; rather, a worker had a vague right to apply for a job, with hiring decisions resting generally with the employer.[31]

At the national level, the open-shop push was stifled somewhat by the Wagner Act and the subsequent *Jones & Laughlin* decision. Moreover, federal investigations into employer antiunion activity encouraged some employers to make their campaigns less visible. The most comprehensive examination of open-shop tactics was conducted by the Senate's La Follette Committee from 1936 through 1939. The measures that capital undertook to defeat organized labor were eye-opening. In the early 1930s, American industry reportedly spent yearly $80 million to support forty thousand labor spies who not only informed on organizers and unionists but also sought to disrupt their work. During the automobile workers' sitdown strikes of 1936, in Flint, Michigan, General Motors reportedly spent $900,000 in three weeks on Pinkerton detectives. In addition to their network of spies, company managers hired hordes of thugs who, as one sheriff testified before the La Follette Committee, declared "open season on organizers." Some of the worst labor-related violence happened in Harlan County, Kentucky, where a series of unsolved murders of union organizers and sympathizers prompted local residents to sardonically joke that a shooting death in Harlan was "death by natural causes." The La Follette Committee also revealed that the open-shop movement had been quite successful. In Los Angeles, California, for instance, several employer associations, including the Merchant and Manufacturing Association, the Chamber of Commerce, the Association of Farmers, the Southern California Industries, Inc., and two all-women groups, the Neutral Thousands and the Women of the

Pacific, had virtually eliminated the influence of unions in the city. Using a war chest of several hundred thousand dollars, these organizations waged a tireless public-relations campaign. By controlling the airwaves and the major newspapers, open-shop organizers effectively created an antiunion environment. The results were tangible. For example, wages in Los Angeles were lower than in other areas; in 1939, a Los Angeles milk truck driver made eighty dollars a month, whereas a driver doing similar work in San Francisco made seventy dollars more.[32]

Padway himself had witnessed antiunion attitudes and the violent methods that some employers used oppose unions. In 1934, he was hired by the Federal Local Union 18545 (AFL) in Kohler, Wisconsin, as its chief counsel. Local 18545 was engaged in a pitched battle with Walter J. Kohler, Sr., who not only founded the plumbing-supply and bathroom-fixture company but also was a former conservative Republican governor. Kohler's workers resented many things, including the speed-up of machinery and wage cuts. However, the main grievance was Kohler's flat refusal to negotiate with Local 18545. Rather than deal with the AFL union, Kohler chose instead to form a company union, the Kohler Workers Association, which competed unfairly for employee support. When Local 18545 went on strike for recognition and bargaining rights, Kohler deputized more than a thousand antiunion men from surrounding communities, armed them, and brought them into the conflict. On the evening of July 27, 1934, company thugs attacked picketing strikers, many of whom were accompanied by their wives and children. Several were injured, and two men workers were shot to death. This episode had a powerful effect on Padway, who was Local 18545's legal adviser. Afterward, he became only more dedicated to defending the Wagner Act and to the elimination of antiunion activities by employers.[33]

Because of the negative publicity connected with the La Follette hearings, as well as incidents like the Kohler strike, the open-shop movement and its champions, such as Walter Drew, of the National Erectors Association, virtually disappeared from the national scene from the late 1930s until the middle of the Second World War.[34] The reappearance of antiunion and anticlosed-shop activities coincided with the surge in wartime strikes. Immediately following the attack on Pearl Harbor, there were few strikes. Nineteen forty-two witnessed only 2,970 work stoppages involving 840,000 workers. The next year, the number of strikes increased by 730, and the number of strikers more than doubled.

Antiunion politicians, who never lost their animosity toward the Wagner Act, now had a chance to act.[35] In the midst of the rise in strikes and with public support for such job actions dwindling, in 1943, Congress passed, over President Roosevelt's veto, the War Labor Disputes (a.k.a. Smith-Connally) Act, which compelled unions to delay strikes for thirty days, required all strikes to have the approval of union members, and authorized the president to seize any struck war plant. Some congressmen sought other ways to curtail union power during the war. For instance in 1943, Representative Howard K. Smith (D-Virginia) and Carl Vinson (D-Georgia) introduced a bill to "freeze" closed-shop contracts in defense industries, thus stopping further union advances. Although a similar action had been taken during World War I, the Smith-Vinson bill never became law. Rather, the open-shop movement's successes occurred not at the national but at the state level during World War II.[36]

The Wartime Open-Shop Movement

In some respects, the wartime open-shop movement that Padway and the AFL fought resembled that of the 1930s. The vast public-relations campaign that the La Follette Committee had exposed continued, albeit on a smaller scale. Again, the marketing of the open shop had two parts. First, employers rallied their peers and organizations. Second, the leaders of the open-shop drive sought to influence the press. An excellent example of the former can be seen in the work of William Frew Long, of the Associated Industries of Cleveland. Established in 1920 (like many such employers' groups), this association served a purpose similar to that of the Southern California Industries, Inc.[37] The Cleveland group was dedicated to crushing the closed shop and ending all union security arrangements, including union and preferential shops. As its general manager, Long led the public charge against Cleveland's unions. On January 29, 1941, he delivered an address at the Association's twenty-first annual meeting. Long charged that the closed shop was a "threat to national defense." He likened the closed shop to "local industrial slavery" that made the nation's high moral principles unattainable; unionism, he asserted, promoted immorality and thus debauched "our social life." According to Long, any organization that compelled membership went against the liberties established by the Constitution.

With the support of only "various pink and red societies," unions sought to create the closed shop so that they could, Long claimed, engage in lawless activities like racketeering. During peacetime, he continued, such union activity was dangerous enough, but in wartime it was tantamount to treason. Without concrete examples or numbers, Long estimated that unions slowed defense production by 20 percent. Long asked his audience to use the same label on unionists as they would on "American soldiers and gunners [who were] intentionally to direct their fire 20 degrees off their targets. . . . 'Traitors,' we would call them." In conclusion, Long called on his business colleagues to join him in support of the "freedom of employment," that is, the open shop.[38]

Long's remarks were reprinted and widely distributed. Perhaps more effective than the rants of antiunion, anticlosed-shop businessmen like Long's were the newspaper articles written by conservative journalists who argued for the open shop. Although not quite of the stature of the antiunion, anti-New Deal journalist Westbrook Pegler, the journalist Ray Parr, of Oklahoma, was influential.[39] In the spring of 1942, Parr spent two weeks visiting several war plants in eastern Oklahoma. While on assignment, he infiltrated unions to gather information on what he termed "labor racketeers."[40] His observations were later serialized in the *Daily Oklahoman* and published as a widely distributed pamphlet entitled *America Is Also Fighting for Freedom to Work*. All the factories that Parr encountered were closed shops. Thus, to get work, he had to join the union. He first signed up with Local 318 of the International Hod Carriers, Building and Common Laborers Union of America (AFL). The initiation fee was $16.65, which meant to Parr that he had to work thirty-three hours at fifty cents in order to break even. As his friend and fellow union member "George" put it, "this union business is a big graft."[41] Moreover, according to Parr, there was not much one could do to change the situation, since the federal government went along with the unions. "Through no fault of its own," he reported, "the United States Employment Service [USES] has been placed in the unhappy position of stooge for the unions because of the closed shop nature of the tremendous war projects." Hence dealing with the USES was "just another boondoggle."[42] Finally, Parr estimated the overall effect of closed-shop contracts. Aside from the hardships placed on workers, many of whom were unemployed, these union agreements, Parr asserted, "slowed construction progress in minor instances." Although his conclusions were more restrained than Long's had been, Parr asked his readers whether workers were "fighting for the preservation of American liberty or merely to make the world safe for labor racketeers?"[43]

Parr's articles had a political effect in Oklahoma. Readers of the *Daily Oklahoman* wrote their congressional representatives and demanded an end to the closed shop in defense production.[44] But a more significant impact happened outside the state. As Parr noted in the preface to his pamphlet, the "fire [that he started in Oklahoma] spread to California, to Massachusetts, to Florida, to Oregon, to Rhode Island." Two organizations led the open-shop charge in the states during the war. Building on its previous anticlosed-shop activities before the war, the National Association of Manufacturers helped to introduce legislation and funded a publicity campaign through its propaganda arm, the National Industrial Information Committee. Additionally, the Christian Americans, a proto-fascist group formed in Texas in 1936 by the big-business lobbyist Vance Muse and his wife, Val Sherman, was at the center of the wartime open-shop movement. With funds from the du Ponts, the Armours, Sam Insull, John J. Raskob, Alfred P. Sloan, and others, Muse and Sherman organized a grassroots movement with Senator Wilbert "Pappy" O'Daniel (D-Texas), S. Valentine Ulrey, and the fundamentalist minister Gerald Winrod as its spokesmen. All had far-right credentials, as was revealed in John Roy Carlson's book, *Under Cover: My Four Years in the Nazi Underworld of America*.[45] Ulrey was the leading advocate for the twelve-hour day and the six-day work week, and Muse had connections with several fascists, including Gerald L. K. Smith. Winrod's reputation among the American far right was almost equivalent to Smith's. A publisher of several anti-Catholic and anti-Jewish newspapers and magazines, Winrod translated the Nazi ideology into English and disseminated it widely. In fact, he was close to many Nazis both in the United States and in Germany. As Carlson explained, Winrod helped to create a "Nazified 'Christianity'" in the United States. The primary mission of the Christian Americans was to reverse New Deal labor policy. Although it sought to repeal the Wagner Act and to outlaw striking and picketing, much of the group's activities focused on the enactment of so-called right-to-work or open-shop amendments to state constitutions.[46]

The plan to use constitutional amendments was ingenious. As mentioned earlier, the Wagner Act did not supercede state law where states had specifically enacted legislation that limited unions. Proponents of these amendments believed them immune not only to the federal courts

This rare cartoon about the Christian Americans appeared in the *Boilermakers Journal* (April 1945): page 95, courtesy of the International Brotherhood of Boilermakers.

but to state ones, as well, as Padway noted in an article in the *American Federationist.* During the war, the Christian Americans and their political allies pushed for open-shop amendments in eleven southern and western states, including Alabama, Arkansas, California, Florida, Georgia, Kansas, North Carolina, South Carolina, South Dakota, Tennessee, and Texas. Although the AFL and its local affiliates fought these referenda politically, Padway joined the fight only after the amendments were adopted.[47]

Several state electorates were set to vote on these amendments on the same day they were to vote for the next president of the United States —November 7, 1944. The key battle states for the right-to-work referenda were California, Arkansas, and Florida. In California, Paul Shoup, the seventy-year-old president of the vigorously antiunion Merchants and Manufacturers Association of Los Angeles, had initiated the open-shop proposition. Proposition 12 had been placed on the ballot after 180,449 supporting signatures were obtained. Not surprisingly, 160,000 signees were from Los Angeles County, the heart of antiunionism in California before World War II. At first, it seemed that Shoup's plan would succeed. He had the backing of the Christian Americans, the Women of the Pacific, and the Los Angeles Chamber of Commerce. The state CIO unions were silent and did not oppose the measure. In fact, nationally, the CIO did not actively defend against the open shop. The historian Gilbert J. Gall has suggested that Lee Pressman and his CIO legal team were engaged in another and different court fight to broaden and redefine labor's rights. Still, for practical reasons, the CIO might have chosen to remain on the sidelines. Smashing the closed shop might have freed thousands of AFL members to join the CIO in places like the Kaiser shipyards in Portland. Additionally, breaking a closed-shop contract might have allowed the CIO to raid an AFL union or might have led to new job opportunities for CIO members.[48]

Despite the lack of a unified labor front, the proposition ran into a few critical obstacles. First, the California Federation of Labor, along with the American Federation of Labor, outspent Shoup two to one, getting the message out that the bill not only would jeopardize the average unionist's economic position but would also destroy the business relationships that AFL unions had built with California employers. Although they might have opposed the close shop, many employers did not oppose unions per se or collective bargaining. Most California chambers of commerce agreed. Moreover, the last thing employers wanted was to nullify their AFL agreements, possibly setting the stage for the CIO organizing drive. As a 1941 American Council on Public Affairs study concluded, "As a result of antipathy toward the CIO because of Communist influence in its unions, a large number of companies long opposed to the closed shop have accepted it under A. F. L. contracts." Second, the state's Republican leadership refused to support Proposition 12 because they feared that workers who voted against the amendment would also vote against the GOP presidential candidate, Thomas Dewey. Thus, the amendment went down to defeat.[49]

Although the Christian Americans lost in California, Muse's plan had achieved results. In October 1944, after a political campaign that cost the Christian Americans and their local partner, the Arkansas Free Enterprise Association, almost $50,000,[50] Arkansas voters narrowly adopted Amendment 34 to the state's constitution. It read:

> No person shall be denied employment because of membership in or affiliation with or resignation from a labor union, or because of refusal to join or affiliate with a labor union; nor shall any corporation or individual or association of any kind enter into any contract, written or oral, to exclude from employment members of a labor union or persons who refuse to join a labor union, or because of resignation from a labor union; nor shall any person against his will be compelled to pay dues to any labor organization as a prerequisite to or condition of employment.[51]

The open-shop amendment sparked fear in the hearts of the leaders of the American Federation of Labor and the Arkansas Federation of Labor, which had spent more than $20,000 on newspaper advertising opposing the proposed constitutional change. Rank-and-file unionists were also upset. In December 1944, Wesley High, the business agent for the Bakery and Confectionery Workers, International Union of America, Local 422 (Little Rock), was "doing his bit for Uncle Sam" in the Sea Bees when he learned of Amendment 34. In a letter home, High exasperatedly wrote:

> We service men are out here fighting and dying so we will be free American Citizens, and so we can bargain collectively for hours and wages, and now since so many of us are away from home the big business men have worked their little labor laws in by playing up the people that it was to keep the service men and women, and they went as far as passing of Act 35 [*sic*]. But the papers refuse to print some letters that we wrote against Act 35 [*sic*]. So you see we guys from Arkansas would be just about as well off under the yoke of Hitler.[52]

Despite the money spent on the Arkansas right-to-work fight and the possible rollback of union gains in the state, the decisive legal battle was in Florida, which had also added an open-shop constitutional amendment.[53] The history of the Sunshine State's attack on the closed shop was unique among its peers. Florida's attorney general, J. Tom Watson, hated unions and the closed shop. During his 1941 election campaign, candidate Watson had kept his views hidden. But, once in office, he announced his antiunion opinions during a jaw-dropping speech before the AFL's state convention.[54] Shortly after, he initiated *quo warranto* proceedings against major labor unions that had closed-shop contracts, claiming that they were exercising authority that they had not been legally granted. The legal maneuver was designed to bring unions to court in order to void their contracts. By 1943, Watson had brought suits against the state's largest unions, including the United Association of Plumbers and Steamfitters and the International Brotherhood of Boilermakers, as well as companies such as Tampa Shipbuilding, which had agreed to the closed shop. Although he was no race liberal, had Watson's challenge been successful, it might have had the ironic outcome of opening the employment doors for black workers, which the IBB had excluded from the Tampa yards. The initial signs were promising. Watson won the first legal round. A Tampa judge ruled that the closed-shop contract in a war industry was against public policy. Upon learning of the ruling, the AFL's Joseph Padway filed an appeal. Before the Florida Supreme Court, the AFL's lawyer argued persuasively, and, on November 10, 1943, the state's high court ruled that, since there was no law prohibiting the closed shop, managers were free to hire only union workers if they so chose. Padway viewed the victory as "one of the most momentous decisions in labor history."[55]

The Florida court's ruling was not exceptional and was in line with rulings from other state courts (such as that of the Massachusetts Supreme Court in 1944) that had ruled in favor of the closed shop. Rather than accept this defeat as final, Watson responded to the Florida Supreme Court's ruling by proposing an open-shop amendment to the state constitution. The Florida provision was similar in wording to the other right-to-work initiatives put forth by the Christian Americans and sought to make the closed shop illegal. After its passage in November 1944, Watson assumed the enforcement of the measure.[56] Again, Watson instituted *quo warranto* proceedings against companies and unions that had entered into closed-shop contracts. His first targets were the Tampa Central Trades and Labor Assembly and three local employers. Initially, the Assembly resisted assistance from Padway and the AFL's legal team and hired its own attorneys. When Padway discovered that these lawyers had charged the Assembly $25,000 for their services, he was outraged. Padway had offered to challenge the Florida amendment for free. Eventually, he convinced the AFL affiliate to let him join the lawsuit and take the lead. Padway decided to proceed as he had in the

Thornhill case, using the federal courts with the hope that the amendment's restrictions on the ability of unions to organize would be found to be in violation of the U.S. Constitution's First Amendment and that the amendment would in addition be found to be in violation of the Fourteenth Amendment's guarantee of equal treatment and due process under the law. Additionally, Padway maintained that the amendment ran counter to the Contract Clause of Article I, forbidding states to impose laws that impair the obligation of contracts. With a positive ruling, he would have had legal leverage to overturn other state laws. Padway was confident that the open-shop laws had no future. At the 1944 AFL convention, he told the Federationists that they "might as well here and now tell the State of Florida and the State of Arkansas" that the right-to-work amendments would never work. "It cannot and will not be done!" he exclaimed.[57]

In 1945, Padway and his team brought the case before a federal district court in Florida. There Padway argued about the incongruities between the state amendment and the U.S. Constitution. Moreover, Padway contended that the Florida amendment was inconsistent with the Wagner Act, which gave employees the right to bargain collectively for the closed shop. Finally, he pointed out that enforcement of the right-to-work amendment would have damaging economic impacts. First, the state's unions, particularly AFL unions, would lose, on average, $3,000 a year in dues. Second, the amendment would throw into chaos the five hundred closed-shop contracts operating in Florida, affecting about 100,000 employees. Perhaps as expected, the district court sympathized with the state attorney general and those who supported the amendment; it dismissed the case and denied the request for a temporary restraining order.[58]

Padway immediately brought an appeal to the U.S. Supreme Court, where he repeated his arguments, hoping to find a friendlier audience.[59] It was a reasonable thought. The New Deal Court had earlier viewed his *Thornhill* defense approvingly. On February 8, 1946, the Court heard the case. Although generally favorable, the Supreme Court handed down a mixed ruling on March 25, 1946.[60] Writing for the majority, Justice William O. Douglas agreed with Padway that outlawing closed-shop agreements would disrupt the "harmonious relations between unions and employers." However, the majority of Justices were less convinced by Padway's constitutional arguments. Virtually ignoring the

First Amendment issues that Padway raised, Justice Douglas focused on the Wagner Act and wrote that the Florida amendment could be construed to eliminate any conflict with that act. Moreover, he maintained that one could see how the law might avoid a conflict with the Fourteenth Amendment. But, in the end, the Justices who supported Douglas felt that the state amendment first needed an authoritative ruling from a state court. "A decision today on the constitutionality of this Florida law would be based on a preliminary guess concerning its meaning, not on an authoritative construction of it." Thus, the Supreme Court reversed the judgment of the federal district court and remanded the cause to the state courts for "an orderly and expeditious adjudication of the state law questions."[61]

Justices Harlan Fiske Stone and Frank Murphy dissented. Stone wanted the case dismissed outright until the state courts could decide on the issue of the closed-shop amendment. Although he was sympathetic to unions, Stone wrote a dissent that was legalistic in tone. Murphy's was decidedly not. Padway's argument convinced him that Florida's amendment posed a "grave threat to collective bargaining." Moreover, he thought that quite possibly the amendment violated the U.S. Constitution on the grounds that Padway had outlined. Finally, Murphy thought that his colleagues should have made a clearer ruling, since the "efficacy" of relying on a state court decision was "less real than apparent."[62]

Although in a sense Padway and the AFL had won the case, the Supreme Court's decision was not a conclusive victory, since there was no ruling on the constitutionality of laws prohibiting the closed shop. Thus, the door was still open to conservative forces bent on destroying forms of union security. During the war, the closed shop was in fact safe. From January 1942 to December 1945 (when it was disbanded), the National War Labor Board steadfastly and consistently refused to void closed-shop agreements between unions and wartime employers. Whether or not a state had an open-shop amendment or had passed a law outlawing any form of union security, including maintenance of membership, the NWLB held to its basic principle as explained in its *Termination Report* (1947):

> Board policy with respect to union or closed shop conformed to President Roosevelt's statement . . . in 1941 that the Government would not

> order a closed shop. The Board did not direct a union or closed shop in any case where such a provision had not previously existed in a collective agreement.

Thus, in states such Florida and Arkansas, which banned the closed shop during the war, and in other states, including Alabama, Colorado, and Wisconsin, where union security arrangements were under similar attack, the NWLB ignored state labor law and granted the closed shop.[63]

However, in the end, the timidity of the U.S. Supreme Court on the closed-shop issue proved unfortunate for both the AFL and the CIO. The year after the war ended and the NWLB disappeared, Congress passed New Jersey Republican Clifford P. Case's Labor Disputes Mediation Bill (H.R. 4908), a sweeping and retrograde revision of the 1935 Wagner Act. Although President Truman vetoed the measure, similar legislation proposed by Senator Robert A. Taft (R-Ohio) and Representative Fred A. Hartley (R-New Jersey) was successful. The 1947 Taft-Hartley Act explicitly outlawed the closed shop and made many other changes to American labor relations. Thus, in the larger sense, Padway's fight against the Christian Americans and the wartime open-shop movement had not succeeded in stemming the tide of opposition to organized labor.[64]

Conclusion

Only a few months after the passage of the Taft-Hartley Act, the AFL convened its sixty-sixth convention, in San Francisco. President William Green had asked Joseph Padway to focus on the act during his address. Although Padway himself barely made it past his opening joke before he collapsed, the entire speech was printed in the report on the convention proceedings. It reveals Padway's thoughts on several key issues. First, he believed that the forces behind the Taft-Hartley Act, such as the right-wing Liberty League lawyers and congressional conservatives, were motivated by a desire "to make this Nation an open shop industrial nation."[65] Second, Padway thought that the act was not only unworkable but also unconstitutional. By stripping the National Labor Relations Board of its review section and by increasing the number of required union elections, the act, he predicted, would never properly function. In any case, he maintained that basic parts of the law were unconstitutional, and he predicted that the Supreme Court would agree with him.[66]

Finally, Padway's speech revealed exactly what he thought the Taft-Hartley Act meant to the labor movement. To him, it was a crowbar that would upset what he and the AFL had "had reason to believe . . . [was] a permanent foundation stone" of American labor relations. In other words, by modifying the Wagner Act and New Deal labor policy to give the advantage to employers, the act tilted the power of the state in opposition to organized labor. It threatened to undo the work that Padway and so many others had fought hard to accomplish. One can only imagine that, had he lived longer, he would have again tried to use the courts to motivate the federal and state governments to secure and expand the rights of workers and convince his colleagues to completely abandon volunteerism. Padway's former colleagues were certainly less outspoken about opposing the new labor-relations law. In a remark that could have easily come from the AFL's president, William Green, the CIO's president, Philip Murray, said, after the passage of Taft-Hartley, "What the hell—pendulums swing . . . and we have our cycles in life, and we [have] got to make the best of it, using the tools at hand."[67] These tools that had been used by both the CIO and the AFL to build strong unions had been damaged during the war. Under the cover of wartime emergency, antiunion forces had succeeded in stripping the big labor federations of their ability to fend off employer attacks. The results have been clear. Since the 1950s, unions have experienced a steady decline in influence and membership due to restrictive laws and policies as well as to larger structural changes in the economy. Moreover, governmental support for unions has been much more ambiguous since labor's heyday during World War II, and organized labor has had a difficult time meeting the challenges of the late twenieth century.[68]

3

Building Ships for Democracy

The AFL, the Boilermakers, and Wartime Racial Justice in Portland and Providence

We live in that house; we didn't build that house; and we were not the architects of it.

—Leland Tanner, Lawyer for Boilermaker Lodge 72, speaking in reference to the Boilermakers' policy of racial exclusion and separation, 1943[1]

By his own admission, Thomas Doram was a family man and a zealous patriot. Three weeks after the United States declared war against the Axis powers, in late December 1941, the twenty-nine-year-old Doram sought a new job that would achieve his goals of establishing financial security for his growing family and helping win the war. On December 29, he found employment at the California Shipyards (Calship) as a janitor. The pay was decent, and Doram must have seen the possibility for advancement. Well-paying, skilled wartime work was becoming readily available, as war contractors in the Los Angeles area had just been promised more than $11 billion in federal contracts. Calship was one of the "Big Three" local shipbuilding companies that, along with Consolidated Steel's Shipbuilding Division and Western Pipe and Steel Company, employed roughly ninety thousand workers during the war. Three months later, Doram joined Local 92 of the International Brotherhood of Boilermakers, Iron Ship Builders, and Helpers of America, was given his union book and insurance policy, and became a helper. Despite the exigencies of the wartime situation, this was quite unusual. The Boilermakers did not allow African Americans directly into their union. But he had passed his initiation ceremony, because he could pass for white. Within another three weeks, Doram was promoted to burner on production. Keeping his racial identity a secret, in January 1943, he applied for another promotion and became an instructor training white burners. Shortly thereafter, his troubles began.[2]

Youlen Dixon, Doram's leadman, suspected that his burner instructor was in fact African American. Initially, Dixon planned to make Doram quit his job by calling him "nigger" and by threatening him with bodily harm. When that did not work, Dixon tried to get Doram fired by making frequent adverse work reports to the foreman. Doram pleaded with the foreman not to fire him, pointing out his excellent work record and the fact that he was well liked by coworkers. The foreman dealt with the situation by putting Doram on the nightshift, believing that the other workers would "think that [he] was Mexican and [thus wouldn't] pay much attention."[3] But this was not good enough for Dixon, who, in Doram's words, was committed to upholding "undemocratic and unpatriotic white union powers."[4] On June 29, 1943, soon after Doram started his shift, Dixon and his friend Paul Morris cornered him in the bowels of an unfinished ship. Dixon fired the first punch and missed. Doram's return landed and knocked Dixon to the floor. Dixon then grabbed for a knife while Morris jumped on Doram's back. Stronger than his assailants, Doram quickly shook himself free, causing Dixon and Morris to run off. The fight thus abruptly stopped. Doram had got the better of Dixon, who had a broken jaw. Yet, despite the fact that the attack was vicious, unprovoked, and potentially murderous, Local 92 leaders and rank-and-file sided with Dixon and Morris, and Doram was fired and booted out of the union.[5]

A week later, Doram had secured a new wartime job, at Bethlehem Steel Company, in San Pedro. On July 6, 1943, he went to pick up his paycheck and was arrested by San Pedro police officers, who jailed him on the charge of assaulting Dixon and Morris. Doram called Thomas Griffith, a lawyer associated with the Los Angeles branch of the National Association for the Advancement of Colored People (NAACP). Strangely, instead of taking him pro bono, Griffith charged him fifty dollars as a private-practice client. Doram's legal representative was incompetent and showed up only for the trial. Unsurprisingly, Doram lost the case and was given thirty days, even though that day his wife was at White Memorial Hospital in labor with their second child. From jail, Doram sent an urgent letter to President Roosevelt's Committee on Fair Employment Practice (FEPC). Established by executive order in June 1941, the FEPC was created to hear complaints of employment discrimination and seek redress. The committee quickly dispatched a staff worker to record Doram's story. Even though when the federal worker arrived, Doram had been released from jail (thanks to the efforts of Doram's new lawyer, Walter Gordon) and had found another new job, at Consolidated Steel Company, he was still justifiably bitter. After relating his sad tale, Doram told the FEPC official that he "continued to labor and pray that the heavens would not always be silent; that the force of right and justice would in the end prevail."[6] Doram's "unusual" case (as one committee member termed it) was added to the dozens of complaints about the Boilermakers that the FEPC had collected since the war had begun.[7] For five wartorn years, the president's committee, in concert with civil rights organizations and some unionists, tried in vain to change the Boilermaker's stance on race. In the end, however, the IBB clung to its biased traditions of exclusivity, unwilling to sacrifice them despite the wartime emergency.

The history of the FEPC's attempts to end discrimination in the International Brotherhood of Boilermakers has been recounted several times.[8] This chapter adds to this tale in a couple ways. First, it examines the fight over fair employment from the perspective of the Boilermakers, rather than that of the federal government or civil rights groups, although both are essential to this history. Second, the chapter brings a nuanced view of the Boilermakers by analyzing two very different locals, one in Portland, Oregon (Lodge 72), which supported racial discrimination, and the other in Providence, Rhode Island (Local 308), which opposed it. It is absolutely clear that employment discrimination against African Americans was a well-ingrained union practice. In fact, one can go so far as to say that there were definite racial limits to the wartime patriotism of most white IBB members. The Boilermakers fulfilled a central role in the war for democracy, but in general they never relinquished their undemocratic policies or altered their prejudices, even when absolutely necessary in wartime conditions. And, as Doram's story illustrates, some rank-and-file members were willing to fight (and murder?) to uphold racial discrimination. Nevertheless, the Providence local did indeed break ranks and accept blacks as equal members. Although their actions literally became a footnote to the standard version of the Boilermakers' wartime story, it nevertheless shows the possibilities and failures of racial justice during World War II. Those opportunities for changing the racial status quo were based not only on geography and the social fluidity of wartime but also upon the personalities involved. In particular, Portland's Thomas Ray, Lodge 72's business agent, and Providence's Americo Petrini, president of Local 308, had a tremendous influence upon the racial politics of their respective unions. The history of the IBB at war is a tale of people, as well as of economic and social structures.

The Boilermakers' record on race also points to the AFL's own struggles over the issue during World War II and at other times. From its inception, the Federation failed to make racial equality—let alone gender equality—a core principle. Despite its lip service to democracy and egalitarianism, the AFL, with some notable exceptions, was a bastion of racial conservatism and discrimination. Although World War II provided the conditions for change, the Federation and its member unions, including the IBB, rebuffed most efforts to relax racial bias in employment.

The IBB in Depression and War

Doubtless, ten years before the outbreak of World War II, the members of the International Brotherhood of Boilermakers could have scarcely imagined the economic boon that awaited. During the Great Depression, the Boilermakers' fortunes had fallen hard, along with those of the shipbuilders. In 1920, the major yards built 3,475,872 deadweight tons of new shipping. The year before Franklin D. Roosevelt was elected president, yearly output had dropped to 355,771 tons, and in 1935 only 49,054 tons of new shipping was launched, the lowest amount since 1820.[9] In that same depression year, only 64,000 wage earners were employed in shipyards.[10] This changed dramatically in 1937 when President Roosevelt and the U.S. Maritime Commission (the federal government's shipping regulatory agency) initiated a new shipbuilding program. The plan was justified by the simple fact that there had been virtually no new shipbuilding in the United States since World War I. Not only was the U.S. Navy aged, but the merchant marine was outmoded and decrepit. Under this peacetime building program, old ships were to be replaced by modern, fast vessels and high-speed tankers. The immediate goal was to build fifty ships a year for ten years. But the long-term hope was to revitalize a sick industry.[11]

The outbreak of war in Europe in 1939 dramatically accelerated the Maritime Commission's shipbuilding program. Even before war had been declared, the commission had doubled its 1937 production schedule and made contracts for one hundred ships a year. By 1940, the program had doubled its goal to two hundred ships per year. Bottlenecks rapidly appeared. The American Federation of Labor's Metal Trades Department (of which the Boilermakers were a key constituent) acted quickly to remove the labor roadblocks by calling a general conference. Meeting for two days in early January 1941, the Metal Trades Department and its member unions issued a declaration and a program for the defense emergency. The conference document, which was so comprehensive and reasonable that it became the basis for other industries, suggested that the nation be divided into production zones with regional stabilization boards so that employers and unions could set employment rules. It also pledged unions not to strike, and employers agreed to forgo lockouts. The tradeoff was employer acceptance of unions, collective bargaining, and the closed shop. The agreement hammered out by the Metal Trades Department was adopted virtually in toto by the shipmakers and the federal government. The Office of Production Management and the U.S. Maritime Commission broke the country into four zones (Pacific Coast, Great Lakes, Gulf Coast, and Atlantic Seaboard) and then agreed to the Metal Trades Department's general outline for hours of labor, wage rates, premiums, and grievance machinery. The basic hourly wage was $1.12. Time-and-a-half pay was given for work that exceeded eight hours in a day or forty hours in a week or for Saturday labor. Double time was given for Sundays and holidays. Finally, shift work was permitted, with a forty-cent premium for second and third shifts. Shortly thereafter, master agreements were reached in each of the zones. The agreements held during the entire wartime period with some modifications. In January 1942, President Roosevelt called for around-the-clock, seven-day-a-week operation on the Pacific Coast. The Boilermakers and all other Metal Trades Department unions agreed to the increase and dropped the double-time pay for Sunday work. Despite the hardships and pressures of this breakneck production, the contract for the Pacific Coast was quite a victory for the Boilermakers.[12]

With the labor obstacles surmounted, at least on paper, defense shipbuilding began in earnest in mid-1941. There were still some other hurdles. The lack of shipways and plant capacity to make geared-turbine engines slowed production. The Maritime Commission responded by designing a ship for mass assembly. Although it lacked the most modern technology, the Liberty ship, which was based on old-style steam engines, was sturdy, reliable, and inexpensive. With a relatively contented workforce and improvised ship designs, new records were set. In 1941, a million deadweight tones of shipping were built. That number increased twelve times in 1942. At the war's height, more than twenty million tons were launched. Seen another way, in early 1943, the United States was producing nearly 126 ships a month. The chairman of the U.S. Maritime Commission, Admiral Emory S. Land, and John Frey, the cantankerous head of the AFL's Metal Trades Department, both credited the Boilermakers for the accomplishment. Commenting on the important role that the Boilermakers were playing in the war, Land affirmed his belief that "nearly every great war in history [has] been won primarily in the shipyards of the victorious nation."[13]

Helping the arsenal of democracy win the war was only one aspect of the Boilermakers' experience during World War II. The war's enormous increase in shipbuilding reversed the Boilermakers' decline. The manpower shortages in the yards were acute. Large production quotas meant that thousands of workers had to be hired quickly. Just three months before the Japanese raid on Pearl Harbor, the U.S. Labor Department estimated that to meet their contracts, shipyard employers would have to hire an additional 300,000 workers by November 1942. This educated guess was quite accurate. By mid-1943, there were almost 700,000 men and women working in America's shipyards. Yet, more workers were needed. Although, during the first four months of 1943, 263,000 new workers were hired, shipyard operators were still short 70,000 of the number that they considered necessary to meet their quotas.[14] Despite the human-resources headaches that this kind of employment situation caused management, this was an unprecedented boom and boon for the Boilermakers.

Just how World War II affected the Boilermakers can be seen in the experiences of Mt. Hood Lodge 72. This IBB local was based in Portland, Oregon, which had been reshaped by wartime economic conditions. As one reporter aptly noted, the "City of Roses" had truly become the "City of Ships."[15] Six major shipyards were at full capacity constructing new ships and repairing others. To meet the demand for workers at Willamette Iron and Steel, Commercial Iron Works, Albina Engine Works, and the three Kaiser yards—Oregon, Swan Island, and Vancouver—thousands migrated to the Portland area. Many even left East Coast shipyards to seek jobs at Kaiser, which was known for its innovative fringe benefits and expansive, well-equipped facilities.[16] By far Kaiser was the largest area employer, with more than eighty thousand workers. Willamette's work force was about a fifth of that, and Commercial's was about a tenth. At the war's peak, Albina had hired about four thousand workers. Because of the insatiable de-mand for labor, from 1940 to 1943, the city's population nearly doubled. Sixty-five percent of all shipyard workers belonged to Lodge 72. The reasons for this were obvious. Since receiving its charter, in 1891, the Portland Boilermakers had maintained a closed-shop agreement with the shipbuilders. In essence, the union controlled the employment of workers. Such a contract was tremendously useful. During the Great Depression, the union rebuffed employers' attempts to cut wages and weaken work standards. On the eve of American participation in World War II, Lodge 72, along with all unions affiliated with the American Federation of Labor's Metal Trades Department, entered into a master agreement with the Pacific Coast shipbuilders. Again because of the strength of the closed-shop environment, this contract was a major victory for these Boilermakers. Employers agreed to the closed shop for the entire Pacific Coast for the entire "national emergency." It also outlined working conditions that were quite favorable. A five-day, forty-hour week was granted, as were overtime and vacation-pay provisions. It also gave the union some control over trade jurisdiction. For instance, the contract specified that foremen and leadmen would be selected "as far as practicable from the trades they are supervising." They also had control over training facilities.[17] The West Coast Boilermakers were rightfully pleased with the results of their contract. Two years later, Lodge 72 boasted the highest pay scale in the nation, established equal pay for equal work for women, and created its own training schools. But the Lodge members were most proud of their building accomplishments. From the start of the defense emergency, the Portland Boilermakers had laid 300 keels and launched 266 vessels, including 203 Liberty ships.[18]

In Providence, Rhode Island, the Boilermakers also profited from the war. Yet, the situation was vastly different. Whereas war was a dramatic boon for Portland, similar fortunes did not rain down on Providence. The U.S. Maritime Commission's plan to expand shipbuilding did include money to fund a new facility near Providence. But, unlike what happened at Kaiser in Portland, the initial effort to boost shipbuilding in Providence was a disaster. The contract to build the Providence yards and ships went to Rheem Shipbuilding Company, which, in March

1942, broke ground at Field's Point, an area close to rail, highway, and other local infrastructure. Additionally, it was thought that the shipyard was ideally positioned to tap the labor supply. At it turned out, Field's Point could not have been a worse choice. The area was a diked-in, muddy tideland that required more than two million cubic yards of fill to make the facility's 144 acres functional. An additional two million cubic yards of mud was so unstable that it had to be dredged. Three months after the site had been prepared, the first buildings went up. The yard's centerpiece was the gigantic 255-by-643-foot Plate Shop, which was destroyed by fire on New Year's Eve, 1942. By the time the government canceled Rheem's contract, Rheem was $12 million over budget. Its shipyard was literally a mud hole that had produced only one ship at the cost of 3.1 million manhours, nearly four times the usual amount.[19]

To replace Rheem, the federal government selected the Kaiser Company, which teamed up with the Walsh Company (thus forming the Walsh-Kaiser Company) to finish the construction. Walsh was in charge of completing construction, and Kaiser was under contract to build the vessels, namely twenty-one twin-screw frigates. Soon after Walsh-Kaiser received the $9.3 million it had requested for the job, construction resumed, and the first keel was laid. By June 1943, there were two thousand construction and fourteen thousand shipyard workers employed. And, by July 1943, construction on what many considered one of the finest facilities in the nation was complete. Walsh had replaced the mud with asphalt, had constructed fireproof buildings, and had installed modern electrical wiring.[20]

Even though the yard had been created in dramatic fashion, Walsh-Kaiser suffered from poor labor relations. In testimony before the U.S. Congress, War Manpower Commission officials attributed low productivity and morale problems to excessive turnover, lack of worker training, shortage of tools and materials, and poor supervision. Additionally, Walsh-Kaiser treated women much differently from men, creating more tensions. Managers hesitated to give women equal pay for equal work —as the union demanded—claiming that women could not keep up with men and that men would protest wage equality. Walsh-Kaiser also blamed the IBB Local 308, which had been formed in September 1942, for not working harder to raise morale.[21] But there were limits on what the new (and, as we will see, embattled) union could do. Nonetheless, despite the labor-relations problems, Walsh-Kaiser was productive, albeit not like the yards in Portland. But, incredibly, in just eighteen months, it built ten Liberty ships, twenty-one frigates, and thirty-two combat cargo ships. By the war's end, there were twenty thousand workers at the yards, most of whom belonged the IBB Local 308, which, like its counterpart in Portland, had a closed-shop agreement.[22]

Although, in some ways, the Boilermakers' World War II story is one of largely unmitigated success, IBB locals encountered some severe problems. One was industrial safety. The around-the-clock operations quickly had an effect on workers' "mental alertness," as U.S. Maritime Commission's vice chairman Howard L. Vickery termed it. Overwork led not only to injury but also to absenteeism, the bane of wartime production. From November 1942 to January 1943, more than seven million man-hours were lost in the shipyards due to unexcused absences.[23] Not all the downtime was attributable to fatigue. Strikes and slow-downs were all too frequent. The primary issue was the failure of managers to respect craft lines. To employers such as Kaiser, the goal was the building of ships as quickly as possible. If that meant placing able but perhaps not union-certified bodies on jobs, so be it. The Boilermakers responded with job actions. Eventually, the fights over hiring and other issues, such as jurisdictional boundaries, became so severe that the head of the War Production Board's labor division, Joseph D. Keenan (who before the war had been an official with AFL's International Brotherhood of Electrical Workers) worked out a statement with the Metal Trades Department. The resolution reaffirmed the department's opposition to work stoppages arising from jurisdictional "differences" and advised all locals that all disputes would be adjusted by the International union officials.[24] This rift between employers and the Boilermakers, as well as between locals and the International, affected the way that the Boilermakers' leaders dealt with concerns such as fair employment, the most divisive wartime issue for the Boilermakers. The federal government looked to the International to solve all union problems, thus eschewing local unions and local solutions. Although it may have appeared logical to some in the federal government, reliance upon the International stalled the wartime efforts to end job bias against African Americans.

AFL, IBB, and Race

At root, the issue of race and unions concerned admissions policy. In American trade unionism, the right of a worker to join a union has traditionally been governed by the international association, as in the case of the International Brotherhood of Boilermakers. These organizations' constitutions generally laid out membership guidelines, while local by-laws often supplemented them. Most admission rules related to job skills, gender, creed, nationality, political beliefs, and race. Out of the 185 international unions that existed on the home front of World War II, nine explicitly made race a criterion for membership, limiting those eligible for membership to "white" workers. A few unions, such as the Railway Mail Association, were more specific, stating that only those of the "Caucasian race or native American Indians" could join, while the Firemen's constitution defined "white" as excluding "Mexicans, Indians, or those of Spanish-Mexican extraction."[25] Five of nine that set racial requirments for membership (Airline Dispatchers, Railroad Telegraphers, Railway and Steamship Clerks, Railway Mail Association, and Switchmen) were affiliated with the AFL, and four (Locomotive Engineers, Locomotive Firemen and Enginemen, Railroad Trainmen, and Railway Conductors) were independent. Five more AFL unions (Boilermakers, Blacksmiths, Maintenance of Way Employees, Railway Carmen, and Sheet Metal Workers) openly excluded African American workers by admitting them into segregated, auxiliary unions. In some cases, notably among longshoremen, separate locals allowed some opportunities for black workers.[26] However, in most cases, segregated locals created distinct disadvantages for African Americans. Those auxiliaries had no voice in local or national union affairs, were represented solely by the white officers of the main local, had no grievance procedure, and frequently provided fewer benefits than were afforded to white members. As the black economist Robert C. Weaver once put it, black workers in these setups had second-class union status but paid first-class dues.[27]

More wartime international unions (124 of them) either took no position on race or expressly protected the right of African Americans to join the union (47 of them). These numbers, however, are a bit deceiving. For the first few years after its formation, the American Federation of Labor and its affiliates sought to uphold liberal policies on racial equality. Unions that wished to join the Federation were made to pledge "never to discriminate against a fellow worker on account of color, creed, or nationality." In 1890, the AFL refused to admit the International Association of Machinists until it dropped its constitutional clause denying membership to African Americans. But, five years later, the AFL had abandoned its open policy.[28] Although it still gave lip service to equality in employment, the Federation accepted the Machinists in 1895 even though they transferred their ban on black membership from their constitution to their induction ritual. In 1896, the Boilermakers were accepted into the AFL without having removed their constitutional ban on black workers.[29] Moreover, locals had considerable power to exclude workers not specified by union constitutions. In the absence of an International's demand that a local accept black members, locals often established their own policies on race. Five major AFL affiliates (the Flint Glass Workers, the Brotherhood of Electrical Workers, the Plumbers and Steamfitters, the Asbestos Workers, and the Granite Cutters) denied admittance to blacks with the tacit consent of the locals.[30]

From the beginning, attempts to eliminate discrimination within the AFL and the Internationals were rebuffed. When questions were raised, the AFL's leaders merely "reiterated, re-endorsed, and reaffirmed" the fact that the AFL had no (explicit) color bar and proclaimed their desire that workers organize and unite under its banner without regard to race, color, creed, or national origin.[31] After 1900, the AFL formally recognized the policy of placing blacks into segregated locals or into affiliated and directly chartered federal unions when they were refused admission into national or international unions that had racial proscriptions. African American unionists began their formal protests to change the AFL in 1920, when several federal locals introduced resolutions to condemn some Internationals, including the Boilermakers, for discriminating against blacks. The resolutions committee made a mock investigation and reported that in fact the Boilermakers had "no law in their constitutions prohibiting the admission of colored workers."[32] Although it was true that the Boilermakers' constitution did not bar blacks from joining the union, the membership induction ritual did, which the members of the resolutions committee surely knew. During the resurgence of trade unionism in the 1930s, the fight to end discrimination gained a new leader. In 1934, A. Philip Randolph, president of the Brotherhood of Sleeping Car Porters (AFL), succeeded in having the AFL establish a committee to investigate the "conditions of colored workers." Although the report could not have solved the problems of job bias in the AFL, it might, if it were taken seriously, have provided a framework for significant reform. As it was, the report was issued at the 1935 AFL convention at 10:00 P.M. on the eleventh and final day of the contentious convention, which had been divided by the craft-industrial union controversy. Randolph continued to propose convention resolutions in support of fair employment. At the 1941 convention, AFL president William Green, vice president Matthew Woll, and Metal Trades Department president John P. Frey supplied a formal answer. They said that the AFL did not discriminate, that discrimination as it existed could not be altered as "human nature cannot be altered," and that African Americans ought to be "grateful" for what the Federation had done for them. In the wartime fight to change the racial policies of unions like the Boilermakers, the AFL's leaders were of nearly no assistance.[33]

Clearly, when African Americans encountered job discrimination, they could not rely on the AFL for help. In the case of black shipyard workers, they could not look to the Boilermakers' International leadership for assistance, either. Since its formation and entry into the AFL, the Boilermakers had pledged themselves to excluding workers of color. The economist Herbert Northrup has suggested two reasons for this. First, "to admit Negroes to their ranks on an equal footing would be, in the minds of many white members, tantamount to admitting that the colored man is a social equal." Second, excluding blacks, "craft unionists have discovered, is a convenient and effective method . . . [of obtaining] a larger share of the available work for themselves and/or to command a higher wage."[34] It is difficult to assert which of the two was more important. Although economic advantage was clearly key, the Boilermakers seemed just as concerned about the social position of blacks. Proof can be read in the *Boilermakers Journal,* which ran a column (until 1943) called "Uncle Twink Sez."[35] Written in a pseudo-black dialect, each article began "All I know is whut de white folks say." Usually, the article's message concerned the benefits of unionism or some current event such as defense preparedness. In every case, Uncle Twink Simpson gave homespun advice. Although not overtly racist, the articles did depict African Americans as something less than the educated white Boilermaker who might be reading the magazine.[36]

Whatever the case, the Boilermakers' relationship with black workers was not static. Shortly after the U.S. Maritime Commission announced its new shipbuilding plans, the Boilermakers met at their 1937 convention. There the union members voted to remove "white" from the ritual and passed new by-laws to allow for the chartering of segregated auxiliary locals for black workers. They did so for three reasons. First, they understood that, as shipyard production increased, more African Americans would be hired. In some yards, such as Virginia's Newport News

Company, hourly rates for blacks were half those of white shipyard workers. To maintain some control over wages and job opportunities, white boilermakers saw the logic of biracial (not interracial) organizing. As one delegate explained at the convention, "I have been taught all my life to keep the Negro down. To keep the Negro out of our organization is arming him with a weapon that he can use for the purpose of bringing down the wages, conditions, and hours in the Southern shipyards."[37] Second, to counteract the activities of the Congress of Industrial Organizations (namely the Industrial Union of Marine and Shipbuilding Workers of America), which theoretically accepted African Americans on equal terms, the Boilermakers thought it best to offer some type of membership status to blacks. Third, they sought to control the competition from newly unionized black shipyard workers without granting them full admission into the union. In these workers' minds, to do so would elevate African Americans' social status. As another 1937 delegate stated, everyone "knows that the Negro is either beneath or above the white man. He never will be his social equal."[38]

The all-black auxiliary locals that were created after the 1937 convention were woefully unfair. The Jim Crow unions did not have political rights within either the local or the International. They were under the jurisdiction of the closest white local and were not seated at national conventions. Auxiliary locals had no business agent or grievance committee, and these locals could not deal with employers directly. Limits were set on advancement from helper to mechanic, and blacks were not allowed to be apprentices. There were race-specific penalties for such misconduct as public intoxication. Auxiliary members were forbidden from transferring to other locals and could join the locals only if they were between the ages of sixteen and sixty, even though whites could be admitted into the Boilermakers at the age of seventy. In what might be termed the "fringe benefits of whiteness," union insurance policies granted to black members offered half the benefits offered to whites. Death benefits were $500 for blacks and $1,000 for whites. Unlike whites, African Americans could not carry an extra $2,000 for their wives and an extra $2,000 for each child. If blinded, a black boilermaker would receive $250, while a white would get $500. Dismembered arms garnered $400 for blacks and $800 for whites. As Northrup explained the situation to federal officials, "the only matter in which there is entire equality, without discrimination, is with reference to dues. *The dues are equal.*"[39]

The Boilermakers upheld these rules on race with a fanaticism seen perhaps only in the railroad industry.[40] In other words, even in terms of violence, the Doram case was not so unusual. In 1938, the Metal Trades Department, along with the Boilermakers, negotiated a closed-shop contract with the Tampa (Florida) Shipbuilding and Engineering Corporation. The Tampa shipbuilder had employed hundreds of skilled and unskilled African Americans. In fact, 50 percent of its 1,200 workers were black. Instead of organizing an auxiliary local, the Boilermakers forced the dismissal of five hundred black workers and the demotion of all but two of the remainder to unskilled jobs. One African American hoisting engineer with twenty years' experience was assigned the job of picking up paper in the yard. When the African American shipyard workers protested, the local Ku Klux Klan demonstrated in front of their houses. Similar but perhaps less threatening situations existed in Mobile, Alabama, at the Gulf Shipbuilding Corporation, and at the Delta Shipbuilding Corporation, in New Orleans. In each case, the Boilermakers used all their leverage to create economic advantages for whites and disadvantages for African Americans.[41]

Portland Lodge 72 and the Issue of Race

Unlike in southern shipyard cities, in prewar Portland, there was little concern for the city's African American citizens, who numbered 1,934, or less than 1 percent of the total population. As Edwin C. Berry, of the Portland Urban League, explained in a postwar race-relations survey, "this small group was law-abiding, self-sustaining, and unobtrusive. Nobody molested them. There was no race problem in the sense that there was danger of violence or that the Negro group represented a threat to the white residents in any way." This did not mean that Portland was either integrated or a welcoming place. As Berry put it, Portland was a "northern city with a southern exposure; northern geographically but southern in many traditions, attitudes, and approaches to things interracial in character." In fact, Portland had been a main center for the Ku Klux Klan in the 1920s. Its reputation for antiblack (as well as anti-Jewish and anti-Catholic) rhetoric and activities grew during the 1930s and 1940s. In his magisterial *Inside U.S.A.* (1947), John Gunther wrote, "I heard more and more bitter anti-Negro talk [in Portland] than in any other northern city." The Federal Bureau of

Investigation considered the city a center for Nazi sympathizers. African Americans were not only vilified but also had few employment opportunities. Because of union and employer prejudice and discrimination, only low-skill jobs, mostly in domestic service and the railroads, were available in good times. During the Great Depression, blacks took advantage of the Work Progress Administration and direct relief as whites took all the jobs that they had formerly held. And yet, there were few prewar protests. In his survey, Berry concluded that "it would be nearly accurate to say that Negroes accommodated themselves to the position in this community."[42]

World War II upset this social equilibrium. From the beginning of the defense emergency in 1940 to the war's height in 1944, more than 160,000 migrants moved to the Portland area. About 10 percent were black. The city's old residents, both black and white, resented the newcomers, whom, as Berry reported, they considered uneducated "scum." Although some of the black migrants were highly trained school teachers, social workers, stenographers, and laborers, most were common workers, primarily from the South. After arriving in Portland, blacks found their reception chilling. Most did not find housing in the city. The Portland Realty Board had a code of "ethics" that stated that "a realtor should never be instrumental in introducing into a neighborhood a character of property or occupancy, members of any race, or any individual whose presence will clearly be detrimental to property values in that neighborhood." Since the Board considered black residents detrimental, they had to live in Vanport and Vancouver and commute to their jobs in Portland. As a by-product of this residential segregation, blacks in the Portland area were also disenfranchised, because municipal code forbade anyone from voting who did not live within the city limits. Clearly, whites in and about Portland were trying hard to maintain a subservient place for African Americans, not just in housing and politics but in education, as well. During the war, one Portland Parent Teachers Association recommended the creation of a nonvoting auxiliary for black parents. Although this did not happen, it indicated the extent to which what Berry labeled "boilermakers' thinking" had permeated the city.[43]

Eventually, after a few years of struggle, 96 percent of the black migrants secured jobs in shipbuilding, an industry dominated by the Boilermakers. In Portland, the IBB Lodge 72 had 65 percent jurisdiction in the massive shipyards. This accomplishment rested largely on the efforts of its energetic business agent, Tom Ray. When he joined Lodge 72, in 1923, it was small and nearly insignificant. Founded in 1891, the local's membership had never reached two hundred, even during World War I, when the federal government briefly gave organizing and bargaining rights to unions. But, after Ray became the local's secretary in 1928 and, subsequently, its business agent, the union began to grow, particularly after the birth of the Congress of Industrial Organizations, in 1936. Oregon employers were generally antiunion, but they preferred AFL unions, which (as John Gunther wrote in *Inside U.S.A.*) they considered "pretty red" compared to those of the CIO, which they considered "positively insurrectionary." As was the AFL's style, Ray organized the employers as much as he organized the shipyard workers. The hallmark of Ray's tenure as the titular head of Lodge 72 was fifteen years of industrial peace in which no one could remember strikes, lockouts, or walkouts.[44]

Ray's copasetic relationship with the large shipyard employers changed drastically during the war. Like all shipbuilders, the Kaiser Company, which managed the largest yards in Oregon, had a desperate need for workers to meet their production schedules. To secure new workers, Edgar F. Kaiser, vice president and general manager of the company that his father, Henry J. Kaiser, had founded, decided to recruit employees from New York City. Unlike many of his peers, Kaiser sought to lure both black and white workers. In fact, Kaiser had been out in front, pushing city and union leaders to accept and accommodate African American workers and migrants. As soon as President Franklin D. Roosevelt issued his famous June 1941 Executive Order 8802, which banned discrimination in the defense industries and created the Fair Employment Practice Committee to fight job discrimination, Kaiser had his director of industrial relations, J. O. Murray, meet with local union leaders, as well as heads of the national unions, like John Frey, telling them at length that the company intended to comply with the government's directive. Even before it recruited African Americans from New York, Kaiser had hired many Portland blacks. For those who had moved to take advantage of the job opportunities at Kaiser, the company had built (almost overnight) a city in which blacks and whites shared apartments, schools, playgrounds, and stores. Kaiser's company nursery was integrated, as well.[45] In early fall 1942, Edgar Kaiser met with Portland's mayor, a few city officials, and "select group of colored people," including Dr. D. N. Unthank, of the Portland NAACP, to discuss recruiting additional African American workers. From that meeting, city officials, Kaiser, and black leaders agreed that Charles Ivey, a Union Station employee, would act as the liaison between the growing black community and Kaiser. Having established the necessary links between the Kaiser Company and the black community, Kaiser set about attracting black workers from the East Coast.[46]

Such a plan required careful negotiations. First, Kaiser needed the permission of Anna M. Rosenberg, New York regional director of the War Manpower Commission (WMC), who had complete control over the labor situation, particularly the recruiting and assigning of workers through the U.S. Employment Service (USES). Second, Kaiser needed the permission of Tom Ray. Since the Boilermakers had a closed-shop agreement with the shipbuilder, any new workers would have to join the union first. Dealing with the unions about the employment of African Americans had already become a major problem. After Kaiser had hired thirteen black welders, more than 130 white welders had gone on strike in protest. Kaiser expected similar headaches from the Boilermakers. Indeed, as it turned out, working with the federal government proved much easier than dealing with the Boilermakers.[47]

In late September 1942, Edgar Kaiser traveled to New York to meet with Rosenberg and to obtain an agreement to recruit shipyard workers and send them to Portland. She agreed and instructed the USES offices to allow those seeking war work to be employed at Kaiser's Portland yards. Soon after, an initial train of job seekers that included thirty black workers left for Portland. Almost immediately, the plan hit a snag. The leaders of Boilermakers Lodge 72 refused to allow these African American recruits to take any yard jobs except as common laborers and painters' helpers. Black workers first took their complaint to the Portland police department, which referred them to the Oregon state bureau on labor relations, which passed the complaint on to the head of the Oregon USES, L. C. Stoll. When Stoll did not take immediate action, Charles Johnson, a San Francisco civil rights activist and one of the WMC's minority group representatives, traveled to Portland to hear the complaints.[48]

Upon receiving Johnson's report of the Portland situation, Rosenberg promptly instructed the USES to halt all recruiting effort for Kaiser. Equally as fast, sharp criticism was leveled against Lodge 72's officers. Charles Collins, secretary of the Negro Labor Victory Committee of New York, an organization of black trade unionists in the AFL, CIO, and independent unions, issued a statement that condemned Tom Ray as a "dictator" and a "home-grown fascist."[49] The AFL's leadership also made a statement. In a typically weak but nonetheless surprising action against racial discrimination, an anonymous Federation official close to William Green told a reporter for the New York liberal *PM* that "anyone who today prevents a man from making his maximum contribution to the war effort is little better than a saboteur."[50]

On October 6, 1942, Anna Rosenberg convened a meeting with Edgar Kaiser and Tom Ray. Before the meeting, Ray had met with a *PM* journalist, Arnold Beichman. He told Beichman that he had received "heat" from "all over the country, from Mrs. Rosenberg, from my own international president, from the AFL convention in Toronto." He intimated that, no matter what, the union was "not taking them [African American workers] in." Then, in a message for black workers, he said "you are laborers or nothing. So take it or leave it." He then clarified previous statements given to the Oregon *Journal,* which had recently run an article titled "Menace to Women Seen in New York 'Undesirables.' " Ray explained that he had been misquoted and provided this rejoinder:

> Hell, I'm no dynamiter looking to make trouble for other guys. I've been around a long time, working in Chicago, New York and helping to build the Panama Canal. New Yorkers are like anybody else. There are just as many good people there as anywhere else. But I'm opposed to having the colored working side by side with white women down in the holds of a ship.

Although Ray said he would not "budge" on this issue, he did, at least rhetorically. After the meeting with Rosenberg, Ray promised "better jobs" for African Americans, and the recruit trains resumed.[51]

On October 9, 1942, nearly five hundred Kaiser recruits boarded a train bound for Portland. Edgar Kaiser gave them a cheery sendoff. "You are coming out to Portland to do a job," he said, "It won't all be a bed or roses, and milk and honey, but you and we will get along, and you'll be glad you came."[52] Reportedly on the long trip, white and black recruits passed the time "with the greatest cordiality, singing, and playing cards together."[53] However, when the seventeen-car Kaiser Special arrived, little had changed, despite a mass meeting of white boilermakers at which both John Frey and Edgar Kaiser pleaded for racial tolerance. The state USES still refused to refer blacks to skilled shipyard jobs. As Stoll explained, his office was "not familiar with the New York agreement" and told African Americans waiting for Kaiser jobs that they would have to wait "for Mr. Ray, who is reported en route from the east." In the meantime, the black migrants were denied the jobs that they had been promised in New York City.[54]

This tail-wags-the-dog attitude meant that for all intents and purposes local federal officials continued to defer to Ray and the Boilermakers to settle the racial manpower issues of the area. Ray's seeming acquiescence to federal officials in New York City had earned him some good press in Portland. On October 9, 1942, the *Oregonian* published an editorial that praised Ray for publicly relenting. The anonymous editorialist criticized Ray for being a "labor despot" and suggested that he in fact deserved the reprimand that the "New Dealers" brought down upon him. At the same time, the writer stated that it was up to the War Manpower Commission to allay Ray's fear of "undesirable" African American workers in the yards. The article called for job quotas that would limit the number of black workers to their approximate proportion in the Portland population.[55] Although no quota system was ever instituted, Ray apparently had the local support to limit the kinds of jobs African American could get. By the time that Ray returned to Portland, he had already made provisions to create a racially segregated auxiliary of Lodge 72, a plan which had the full support of Wyatt Williams, a member of the Portland NAACP board of directors and a former chapter president. Williams, in fact, was instrumental in setting up the auxiliary, an act that eventually would lead to his expulsion from the NAACP, in October 1943.[56]

Once the auxiliary was created, union officials told African American workers, both those native to the Portland area and those who had been recruited, that if they joined the segregated local they could work in the yards at jobs other than common laborer. Immediately, black workers protested the Jim Crow setup by sending complaints to President Franklin D. Roosevelt's Fair Employment Practice Committee (FEPC). In June 1941, FDR had set up the FEPC in response to A. Philip Randolph's planned march on Washington. To prevent the march, Roosevelt had issued Executive Order 8802 and charged the FEPC with redressing instances of employment discrimination. The committee had received complaints regarding Lodge 72 as early as September 1941. Instead of taking the issue to Ray, the FEPC's executive secretary, Lawrence Cramer, had written to AFL president William Green, asking that blacks be admitted into the Boilermakers on equal terms. If that was not possible, Cramer requested that they be given clearance anyway so that they could be employed in essential war industries. Green replied promptly, stating that he would investigate the situation, but, not surprisingly, no action followed.[57] A year later, the March on Washington Movement (MOWM), Randolph's civil rights organization, petitioned the FEPC to act quickly. The telegram stated:

> The refusal of the AFL to admit . . . qualified Negroes into membership in the Kaiser shipyards in [Portland] is worth several crack divisions to our enemies, for the Japs and Hitler will broadcast to the colored world that all that they could expect if the democracies are victorious is Jim Crowism and a denial of equality of opportunity.
>
> Negroes are even at this moment dying on the battlefields in the Owen Stanley Mountains of New Guinea, on the high seas, and in Egypt, so democracy may live, and Tom Ray and the AFL in [Portland] and America can have the right to exist.[58]

When the MOWM complaint reached the FEPC, it was in the midst of an administrative reorganization and was unable to respond. In fact, the committee did not investigate the Portland situation for nine months. The spur that finally prompted FEPC action was a series of formal complaints from the Portland NAACP and the newly formed Shipyard Negro Organization for Victory (SNOV). In July 1943, under the terms of the closed-shop agreement with Lodge 72, Kaiser fired more than three hundred African American shipyard workers because they had refused to join the segregated auxiliary. After receiving the complaints (forwarded by the NAACP and SNOV), the FEPC sent its investigator, Daniel B. Donovan, and an independent observer, James H. Wolfe, who was the Utah Supreme Court's chief justice, on a survey trip to Portland. The Donovan-Wolfe report, as the FEPC called it, was not encouraging. In their "photostatic view of the situation," the two concluded that the problem resided in the minds of white unionists who were not "accustomed to seeing Negroes in new positions or situations." Because of the recalcitrant nature of Lodge 72's officials, they suggested quick and strong action against the union.[59] This was exactly what the FEPC attempted to do.

To fight the Boilermakers' discriminatory policies and practices, the

FEPC resorted to its most trusted method, public hearing. As a government agency created by executive order, the committee did not have the power to fine, subpoena, or jail violators. Instead, through its public hearings, the FEPC sought to persuade violators of the president's order to adopt more democratic employment practices. On November 15, 1943, the FEPC convened a hearing in Portland to consider complaints from black workers concerning the Kaiser Company and several IBB locals, in particular Lodge 72.[60] Following a lengthy statement about the history of the Boilermakers and their stance on black workers, the committee called on several African Americans to testify. Sidney Wolf reported that he had been a victim of discrimination. He had been among those who traveled to Portland on the Kaiser express train in October 1942. Kaiser's men in New York City had promised him, as well as white and other black recruits, good jobs at high wages. Initially, Wolf explained, he was to have an entry-level shipyard position at ninety-five cents per hour. When he arrived in Portland, he received a job at eighty-eight cents per hour. Later, he was promoted to a sheet metal job at $1.20 per hour but was fired in July 1943 because Lodge 72 refused to take him as a member. After several other African American witnesses had told their stories, the FEPC called Lodge 72 officials to defend the charges.[61]

Although Tom Ray was present, he did not speak on the record. In fact, the IBB already had removed Ray from office for unrelated financial blunders.[62] Leland Tanner, Lodge 72's lawyer, presented the union's three-pronged defense. First, Tanner asserted that Lodge 72 was not culpable. Speaking for his clients, Tanner "disclaim[ed] responsibility for the unfortunate situation in which we find ourselves." It was not Ray's fault but rather the fault of International officials, particularly IBB president Joseph A. Franklin, who had established the auxiliary system. As Tanner explained, "we live in that house; we didn't build that house; and we were not the architects of it." Second, Tanner contended that the white people of Oregon were not tolerant and recounted a story about his oldest daughter, who several years before had witnessed a white robed Klansman threatening to "kill the Catholics, the Jews, and the Negroes." By telling this anecdote, Tanner sought to show that he had egalitarian sympathies, while alerting the FEPC officials to the possibility that the Portland community might actually approve of the Lodge's auxiliary system. Third, Tanner summed up his arguments by stating that Lodge 72 had to have an all-black auxiliary because "the history of Negroes in unions had been a very short lived one." In other words, only white Boilermakers knew enough about collective bargaining to take independent action.[63]

While the FEPC was writing its decision in the Portland hearing, the Boilermakers's International vice president (and heir apparent to replace the aged President Franklin) Charles J. MacGowan weighed in with his opinion on the matter. At the 1943 AFL convention, he answered the criticisms of the FEPC and of A. Philip Randolph, who had delivered a diatribe against racial discrimination in the IBB. Speaking in what he termed the language of "trade unionism" and not in "the refined cultural language of Washington drawing rooms" or "in [a] polished Harvard" accent (a clear reference to Randolph), MacGowan summarized his arguments against interracial unionism. He maintained that biracial unionism was a political compromise between Boilermakers in the South who objected to any system that allowed African Americans to be members and those elsewhere who wanted all Boilermakers, regardless of race, to belong to the union. Moreover, he stated that the system was quite successful except on the West Coast, where "so-called Negro leaders" had stirred up trouble and appealed to the FEPC. MacGowan flatly denied any discrimination. "Look at the record," he implored. By September 11, 1943, there were 1,592 black shipyard workers in Portland, 42 percent of whom received mechanic's pay. Hence the problem was not job bias but what he called the "professional Negro" who objected to the "pure and simple advancement of the economic welfare of all people—regardless of color."[64]

The FEPC did not agree with MacGowan, Tanner, or Ray and ruled, in December 1943, that the IBB and its local lodges had indeed engaged in job discrimination. The Committee issued a cease-and-desist order telling the Boilermakers to end its unfair employment practices by eliminating the auxiliary system.[65] Charles W. Robinson, another lawyer for Lodge 72, responded to the FEPC's position this way:

> Let me make it clear to you the structure of the Union, the local Union, and the relationship between the International and the local. It is contractual. They protect and provide us with a constitution, and they give us a constitution which is contractual, by which we protect and provide for our membership. As I pointed out to you and point out to you now, change that Constitution by the International. Give us an opportunity and we will change our procedure. But you can't tie our hands and say

> "make so and so" with our hands tied. We can build no further than our blueprint. Let me make that plain to you now, ladies and gentlemen. Because we are restricted.[66]

In other words, it was wrong for the FEPC to expect a local union to change International policy. But Lodge 72's officials were not being truthful. In fact, they, along with other Boilermaker locals, had changed their membership rules without action from the International. Early in the war, many IBB lodges refused to admit or clear white women for work in shipyards. When Local 6 (San Francisco) turned white women workers away, these women organized and complained. Eventually, Local 6's business agent, Ed Rainbow, reversed the policy and put white women on the job, saying publicly that he would "rather get hit by a baseball bat than to become embroiled with a pack of women who wanted to work." Unlike Rainbow, Lodge 72's Tom Ray did not try to uphold the gender line in employment. The first white women in the United States to work in the wartime shipyards were employed in Portland and became members of the IBB. Ray even boasted that he had secured equal pay for equal work.[67] The FEPC may have been unaware of these instances, but, regardless, it took Robinson's words seriously and began to focus on Charles MacGowan and efforts to change the International's policy toward African American workers.

Born in Argyleshire, Scotland, MacGowan was considered a "hefty Scotsman" who had struggled to build up the Boilermakers for decades. The FEPC's chairman, Malcolm Ross, viewed MacGowan as an ally in the fight for fair employment and as "an honest-minded Scot [who] was touchy about the charges of unfairness from Negro members." In January 1944, MacGowan was set to succeed Franklin as IBB president. Ross understood that he could not approach the topic of black equality before the election. Privately, MacGowan had promised the FEPC that if he were to become president, "a solution would be reached if he could swing it." He also invited Ross to speak before the 1944 IBB convention. As Ross recalled in his memoir, "so it happened that a bureaucrat, minced up into little pieces, was served during a several-hour ceremony to the International officers and heads of lodges as an hors d'oeuvre to whet appetites for the main racial dish at the convention itself."[68] Although Ross's appearance did not go well, the convention altered its policies concerning African Americans. What seemingly changed the minds of IBB officials was a letter from President Franklin D. Roosevelt, which was read at the convention. He thanked the Boilermakers for the "wonderful job" they had done so far to aid the war effort. Appealing to the unionists' belief in "American traditions of freedom and fair play," he asked them to continue their efforts and that "every worker capable of serving his country be permitted to serve regardless of creed, race or national origin."[69] Shortly after MacGowan's election, the IBB voted to give auxiliary lodges the power to elect their own convention delegates, to join the Metal Trades Council, and to use of the business agent of the white local. The IBB also (in theory) opened all job classifications to African Americans, allowed black members to transfer their membership to other auxiliaries, and equalized the insurance system.[70]

Although the FEPC recognized that the IBB had indeed moved forward, it did not accept the changes as full compliance with its posthearing directives. In particular, the committee objected to the maintenance of the auxiliary system, believing that it would perpetuate discrimination. The following year, at their national convention, the Boilermakers again took up the issue and sought to solve their differences with the FEPC by dissolving the auxiliary system altogether. The IBB, however, remained committed to biracial unionism, and, in place of auxiliaries, the Boilermakers established segregated subordinate lodges for African American members. The FEPC saw this essentially as old wine in new bottles. Yet, the committee also feared that the new system might also lead to problems with collective bargaining and to a racial job-quota system. The FEPC had already gone on record as opposing employment quotas and fundamentally thought that the new system was illegal in light of New Deal labor relations law and policy. It thus ordered the IBB to integrate its organization. Despite the sympathy that Ross had nurtured with MacGowan, the union leader was unwilling to do this, complaining that the FEPC "seems to think that by the mere waving of its magic wand, it can socially amalgamate the white and Negro workers in this great union." In the final IBB response to the FEPC, the union's leadership argued that historical and legal precedent was on their side. They cited the U.S. Supreme Court's 1849 *Roberts v. City of Boston* ruling and the more influential 1896 *Plessy v. Ferguson* decision—both of which upheld racial segregation—and argued that these rulings had made their actions perfectly legal and constitutional. In fact, MacGowan and the white IBB leaders viewed the FEPC's efforts to create "social" (as opposed to economic) equality as "harassment" and "discrimination" against the union.[71] With both sides firmly entrenched, a stalemate resulted, and the FEPC was unable to resolve the Lodge 72 cases by the time the committee was disbanded in 1946.

Providence Local 308 and the Issue of Race

As mentioned earlier, the conditions in Providence were nearly the opposite of those found in Portland. Whereas Kaiser and its Boilermakers had a decades-long history, modern shipbuilding in Providence was had recent and rocky development. Providence was a much more tolerant place to live than Portland. The city's WPA guide noted that it had become an agglomeration of contrasting and often antagonistic regions and influences. European traditions were strong. In the Federal Hill area, there was, the WPA guide recorded, "an Old World atmosphere, especially at night [when] shrill cries, excited crowds, mingled odors and colors, to which occasionally arises the whine of a grind organ, render[ed] this gustatory paradise an exciting experience for those who enjoy the more vivid aspects of human activity." Although the various ethnic groups may have been antagonistic in Europe or at some time in the past, in Providence in the 1930s and 1940s, they lived in perhaps unsurpassed harmony.[72]

Rhode Island had a history of open-mindedness since the seventeenth century. Yet, under its New Dealer governor Theodore Francis Green, the state's Democrats forged an established a new liberal political force that consisted of the working class, the poor, and recent immigrants. This new alliance assumed power held previously not only by the Republican Party but also by the "glacially aristocratic families" (as the rapporteur John Gunther put it) who had controlled the state since the Civil War. A combination of Irish, Italians, French-Canadians, Yankees, and, later, African Americans gave the Democrats a firm root in politics. As a result, Rhode Island's little New Deal enacted several laws to improve the lives of workers and to secure the position of organized labor.[73]

While economically liberal, New Dealers in Rhode Island were not social liberals. In particular, most politicians, as well as white citizens, took a conservative view of race relations and thus steered clear of issues such as the racial integration of social institutions. During the war, attempts to create social integration were opposed, sometimes with quick police action. For example, in October 1943, police canceled a dance at which Count Basie was scheduled to perform out of fear of racial violence; white southern sailors stationed at Narragansett Bay objected to the event because they resented "Negro men dancing with white women." Rather than defend the black and white fans of Count Basie, the police chose instead to uphold the color line in entertainment.[74] African American organizations like the Providence NAACP (established in 1914), which was dedicated to pointing out the lowly social and economic position of blacks, were largely unsuccessful and were viewed as outside agitation. Supported by the conservative black newspaper the Providence *Chronicle,* moderate civil rights groups that concentrated primarily on economic issues were much more productive, given the political climate. An example is the Providence Urban League (PUL), whose sole focus was jobs, education, and training. Formed shortly after the U.S. Maritime Commission's announcement that it would build the shipyard at Field's Point, the PUL immediately instituted a vocational training program. The league's white president, Bradford H. Kenyon, manager of the Providence Base Works, a subsidiary of General Electric, and its black executive secretary, James N. Williams, created extensive business networks within the city. Thus, when the shipyard opened, it was not surprising that hundreds of black boilermakers were hired. Eventually, they numbered five hundred, which was 6 percent of the eight thousand boilermakers working at Walsh-Kaiser.[75]

In this nexus of Rhode Island's social and political traditions as well as New Deal liberalism, the Boilermakers Local 308 was founded at Walsh-Kaiser in September 1942. Unlike all other Boilermakers locals, this one was interracial by design.[76] In appearance, the union typified Rhode Island's New Deal coalition. Its president was an Italian-American, Americo "Joe" Petrini, its vice president, Caesar Archambault, was French-Canadian American, and its business agent was an Irish-American, John Maguire. The union itself was composed of Italian-Americans, French-Canadian Americans, African Americans, and Yankee workers. The union's politics were out of step with the International but were in line with Rhode Island's New Dealers. Although union officials might not have been in-terested in social integration, they were committed to interracial unionism. The main reason for this stance was the tireless activities of the PUL's John Williams, who worked with Walsh-Kaiser, Local 308, and the U.S. Employment Service to bring well-trained black boilermakers to the shipyards. Additionally and importantly, Americo Petrini supported interracial unionism while abhorring biracial unionism. From September 1942 until July 1943, Local 308 operated without making any distinction between the races in terms of membership and status. In the IBB, let alone the AFL, this was truly exceptional.[77]

Despite its statements about local autonomy and supporting fair employment, the International's leadership was in fact firmly opposed to Local 308's setup. In early summer 1943, it began a campaign to segregate Local 308, thus bringing it in line with national policy. In July 1943, the Providence Urban League began to field complaints that there were attempts within the union to establish a "Jim Crow union and to form all Negro laboring crews" at Walsh-Kaiser. At the same time, the International started to send new membership application forms. Before July, all forms had been white. By September, Local 308's business agent, John Maguire, had begun to give white cards to everyone except African Americans, who were given pink card to fill out. In September 1943, the International contacted Petrini and told him to segregate his local. With the support of the PUL and the local NAACP, Petrini held a union meeting and put biracial unionism to a vote. The overwhelming majority of Boilermakers members voted against changing Local 308. At the time this resolution passed, only a handful of AFL unions, such as Local 308 and the New York City's local of the Railway Mail Association, had gone against their International's wishes on race. Despite the Boilermakers' vote, the issue was not settled.[78]

In October 1943, Paul Hovey, a representative of the International, visited Providence to directly pressure Petrini into bifurcating Local 308. Petrini responded by meeting with the PUL's Williams, and together they planned ways of resisting the International. To show support for Local 308, Williams wrote a letter to IBB president Joseph Franklin, asking him for special dispensation to allow the local to continue its membership policies. He made clear that this was not an attempt to rid the nation of the auxiliary system but something that this particular union wanted to do. There was no reply to this or to a second similar letter. Rather, the International intensified its activities against the local.[79]

In December 1943, Local 308 had an election. Caesar Archambault and John Maguire, who had bolted from the Petrini faction and sought reelection on the other slate, opposed Petrini, who ran for a second term. The basic issue behind the election was race. Petrini pledged to maintain interracial unionism, and Archambault and Maguire promised to segregate Local 308. John A. Geremia, an IBB shipyard steward at

Walsh-Kaiser, and two International representatives, Paul Hovey and William J. Buckley, conducted the election. Before the election, Williams and Providence NAACP president John F. Lopez sent an "appeal to colored shipyard workers" at Walsh-Kaiser, encouraging them to vote.[80] On December 14, Lopez and Williams sat outside the union hall to support the black Boilermakers. As hundreds of African American and thousands of white unionists arrived, Hovey and Buckley announced that no black workers would be allowed to vote. Tensions mounted quickly. To avoid conflict, Petrini again suggested that Local 308 should put racial equality to a vote. With their black brothers waiting outside the hall, once again, the white unionists overrode the International's policy on race. After that, the election seemed to go in a orderly fashion. However, at the end, Buckley rounded up all the ballots from the black members, put them in an envelope, and set them aside. As it turned out, the ballots given African Americans had been labeled with a "C" and were disqualified. Buckley again ruled that blacks were members not of Local 308 but of its auxiliary and thus had no right to exercise suffrage. By Buckley's count, 2,700 votes had been cast, and Archambault had won by 120 votes. Of course, this result did not include the five hundred black ballots, which almost certainly would have gone for Petrini.[81]

Immediately following the election, Williams and Lopez met to discuss their course of action. They quickly ruled out working through the FEPC. The historical record does not provide a clear explanation for this. One can speculate that the lack of progress in the FEPC discrimination cases against the Boilermakers was one reason. Additionally, the FEPC's strategy relied upon convincing the International to change its policies, a process in which Local 308's leaders had no confidence. Another reason might have been the possibilities of another strategy developed by the NAACP to combat racial discrimination by unions. In November 1943, Joseph James, a civil rights activist and shipyard worker, sued the IBB and his employer, Marinship, of San Francisco, California, arguing that the union's discriminatory practices, which were supported by the company, were against public policy (namely President Franklin Roosevelt's fair employment executive orders). James and his lawyers, who were led by the NAACP's Thurgood Marshall, called for a temporary restraining order against the union, designed to allow black workers to return to their jobs regardless of union status, and for a permanent injunction to prevent future discrimination. On December 15,

1943, Lopez contacted Marshall about the situation in Providence, and he agreed to take the case. Williams was ecstatic. "What could be better! . . . We'll hold everything until Marshall arrives." he wrote the NAACP's Roy Wilkins.[82]

A few days later, Marshall visited Providence and conferred with Williams, Lopez, Petrini, Joseph LaCount, a local lawyer who worked with the Providence NAACP, and the FEPC's Malcolm Ross, who had come to show support and provide materials on the Portland cases. It was decided to proceed in the same fashion as the James suit. The first step was to gather the complainants. Four African American shipyard workers stepped forward: Gerald R. Hill, Allan Bonay, Carleton H. Blunt, and George Schmoke. Then Marshall moved quickly to get a temporary restraining order, which was granted by Judge Charles A. Walsh on December 17, 1943. The order prevented the IBB from destroying or manipulating the ballots used in the election. Finally, Marshall began the process of obtaining a permanent injunction against the International that would prohibit it from creating an auxiliary in Providence. The first phase was to seek a temporary injunction against the International; then Marshall planned to seek a permanent injunction. The case, which was named *Gerald R. Hill v. International Brotherhood of Boilermakers et al.*, was based on the idea that the auxiliary system was unconstitutional, illegal by state law, and against public policy as outlined by FDR's fair employment doctrine. In his brief, Marshall and his legal team constructed similar arguments to those of the FEPC. In fact, both relied heavily on the research of Herbert R. Northrup, who had published several articles on the exact nature of racial discrimination in the IBB. Although Buckley and the International retained counsel, they did not put up a vigorous defense. Buckley and his lawyer, Aram A. Arabian, merely responded to the complainants by stating that the union "neither admit[ed] nor den[ied] the allegations."[83]

Judge Alexander L. Churchill presided over the second trial, which was scheduled to begin on January 3, 1944. Just prior to the proceedings, the union met again in a last-ditch effort to avoid the trial. At the union hall, the Providence Boilermakers discussed the situation and voted on a motion presented by John J. Norton, a black Boilermaker. Norton wanted the union to pass a resolution telling the International to allow all votes cast to be counted. The motion was successful, and the union members presented it to Buckley, who remained unimpressed by the local's solidarity.[84] During the trial, Buckley continued to be recalcitrant. In fact, little had changed since the previous trial. Both sides repeated their arguments. Marshall did present more facts in the case as the trial went on for four weeks. He demonstrated clearly that there had not been an auxiliary at Local 308's founding. Several African Americans had joined the union after filling out white membership cards, had shared in the same benefits as whites, and had even voted in previous elections. The trouble started after Local 308 attempted to send a black delegate to the 1943 convention, an action that Buckley had personally quashed from his office at the IBB headquarters in Kansas City.[85]

On January 13, 1944, Judge Churchill handed down his decision and, in the words of Thurgood Marshall, "struck a blow for equality in trade unionism." Citing the U.S. Constitution and Rhode Island's civil rights law, he granted the temporary restraining order, stating:

> That the purpose and effect of the so-called "auxiliary" was to segregate Negroes and persons of no other race and color, in a position less favorable in substantial matters than the position enjoyed by other members of Local 308. . . . It is clear beyond doubt that such acts at this election of December 14, 1943, in respect to ballots offered Negro voters, under instructions of the officials of the International constitute a discrimination based on race and color, and the question is, is this discrimination legal? . . . I rule that the conduct at the election of December 14, 1943, and that the by-laws and constitution of the so-called "auxiliary," in so far as they discriminate between members of the colored race, Negroes, and persons of all other races, as compared with the by-laws and constitution of the Brotherhood, are illegal and void.

Marshall, Providence's black Boilermakers, and the rest of Local 308 members who wanted an interracial union could not have been more pleased. On January 18, 1944, Marshall wrote his friend Ira B. Lewis, of the Pittsburgh *Courier,* that Churchill's ruling was a "landmark" and that this case would "go far to break down discrimination against Negroes in certain other labor unions, as well as the Boilermakers."[86]

Hopes, however, were slowly dashed in the case's final phase. On May 15, 1944, Judge Patrick P. Curran heard opening statements in the permanent-injunction trial. Defense maneuvering lengthened this case. In late June 1944, both sides rested. For reasons that are not clear, Judge Curran never issued a final ruling. In a sense, he did not have to decide. By the time the case appeared in his courtroom, two things had taken place. First, the James case in California had been decided in favor of the complainant. In its ruling, the California Supreme Court unanimously found the auxiliary system to be discriminatory and unequal and ordered the IBB to end the its biracial setup. Afterwards, the Boilermakers abolished the auxiliary system and by 1948 had established racially integrated locals. What Judge Curran's ruling would have added to this process is uncertain. Second, and perhaps more important, by early 1944, Walsh-Kaiser was already planning to lay off workers. In July 1945, the Maritime Commission announced that the shipyard would close within three months. Local 308 hung on for a few more months but completely dissolved in October 1946. Thus, although Curran could have issued his ruling, the point would have been moot, and the case was discontinued on February 3, 1956.[87]

Conclusion

The wartime stories of Lodge 72 and Local 308 highlight not only the Boilermakers' experiences with racial justice but also the opportunities and challenges that the war created. It is readily apparent that in general World War II helped the union in several ways. It dramatically increased shipbuilding, which in turn allowed the IBB to grow in size. In 1940, the Boilermakers numbered roughly 60,000; by the war's end, the union had added 300,000 members. But this growth came with a number of difficult problems, such as the relationship between the burgeoning locals and the International and the introduction of black Boilermakers. Simply put, the IBB was unwilling to sacrifice its racial mores, traditions of exclusivity, and practices for the sake of the war. The Boilermakers' solution was to institute biracial unionism through its auxiliary system. Black workers overwhelming opposed this setup and in one instance, the case of Providence Local 308, were able to defeat it with the help of some white Boilermakers. Yet, because of the personalities and the ebb and flow of the economy, the history of Local 308 constitutes an aberration in the larger wartime experiences of the IBB and the AFL. Both clung to their racist traditions tooth and nail, and some Federation unionists were willing, as in the case of Thomas Doram, to kill to protect them. However, the Local 308 story highlights the beginning of the long-term transformation within the Boilermakers, the AFL, and the labor movement generally. The *Hill* lawsuit, like its California counterpart, was the first sign of change that has progressed slowly. The race discrimination lawsuits against the IBB in the 1960s and 1970s illustrated clearly the distance the union needed to go, and yet advances such as the 1970 agreement that allowed African American workers to transfer without losing seniority were made. In the end, the inescapable truth of the labor movement, certainly apparent during World War II, was that both civil rights and economic rights were (and are) firmly interwoven. The war created opportunities for the IBB and the AFL to recognize this and to move progressively toward that goal. The fact that they did not adopt the ideas and sentiments expressed by Local 308 is something that the labor movement has literally been paying for since 1945.[88]

4

"Under the Stress of Necessity"

Women and the AFL

At the end of our first year of war, we find ourselves literally in the midst of a sweeping industrial revolution.

—Frances Perkins, Secretary of Labor, 1943[1]

In a number of [ship]yards, the prejudice against women on the part of both management and labor, though still lingering in some sections, is rapidly disappearing under the stress of necessity.

—Mary Robinson, U.S. Women's Bureau, 1943[2]

Rosie the Riveter is the most recognizable and most powerful icon of the home front during the Second World War. Even more than her male counterpart, the wartime woman worker has become the symbol for American working-class muscle that helped to propel the Allies to victory. But who was Rosie? Did she belong to a union? And if so, was it an AFL or a CIO union? Although pondering these gaps in Rosie's story is akin to wondering why the Mona Lisa smiles, it is significant that historians still have not written enough about women's working and union experiences during World War II. More than thirty years ago, the eminent U.S. women's historian Alice Kessler-Harris asked a simple but profound question: where are the organized women workers?[3] Labor historians from John R. Commons on had given the matter very short shrift. Since the 1970s, dozens of historians have answered Kessler-Harris's call for historical investigation.[4] And yet, there remains more work to be done, even in the crowded literature on the Second World War. Because of the availability of historical records and most labor historians' preference for studying the Congress of Industrial Organizations and its member unions, little has been written about the millions of women who worked for, supported, and joined the American Federation of Labor in the early 1940s. This chapter seeks to begin to fill that void while contending that, like that with African Americans, the AFL wartime relationship with America's female workforce was one of expediency. Only begrudgingly and, as a U.S. Women's Bureau official put it, "under the stress of necessity" did the AFL and its unions accept women, and then only for the duration of the Second World War. This happened despite the concerted efforts and hard work of women within the AFL and their allies outside it.

Women Workers in the Context of Two World Wars

The outbreak of armed conflict in Europe and Asia only served to quicken trends in the American labor force, particularly in the case of women. As table 4.1 shows, since the Civil War, women's participation rates in the paid work economy had been increasing steadily. The 1870 Census, the first to analyze the labor force in terms of gender, indicated that nearly one out of every six American workers was female. And this ratio was the low mark of the period 1870–1940. At the turn of the twentieth century, one in five workers was a woman. One year before Japan attacked Pearl Harbor, nearly 25 percent of the labor force was female. In terms of the labor movement, too, women were making

TABLE 4.1
Women in the Labor Force, 1870–1940

	Gainfully Occupied Women in the Labor Force: Employed, Seeking Work, Public Work Projects		
Year	*Number*	*Percentage in the Labor Force*	*Percentage of All Women of Working Age*
1870	1,836,288	14.7	13.1
1880	2,647,157	15.2	14.7
1890	4,005,532	17.2	17.4
1900	5,319,397	18.3	18.8
1910	7,444,787	19.9	21.5
1920	8,636,512	20.4	21.4
1930a	10,752,116	22.0	22.0
1930b	10,679,048	22.0	24.3
1940	12,845,259	24.3	25.4

NOTE: Figures for years before 1940 are for persons 10 years old and over. Figures for 1940 are for persons 14 years old and over. Numbers for 1930a include women 10 years old and over; those for 1930b include women 14 years old and over.
SOURCE: Mary Robinson, *Woman Workers in Two Wars* (Washington, DC: GPO, 1944), 1.

TABLE 4.2
Union Membership of Women Workers, 1910–1944

Year	*Estimated Number of Women in Unions*	*Percentage of All Union Members*
1910	76,750	3.6
1920	397,000	7.9
1930	260,000	7.7
1940	800,000	9.4
1944	3,000,000	21.8

SOURCE: Gladys Dickason, "Women in Labor Unions," *Annals of the American Academy of Political and Social Science* 251 (May 1947): 71.

advances. As table 4.2 demonstrates, the percentage of women in labor unions had been increasing, albeit slowly, since the turn of the twentieth century. In 1910, women made up 3.6 percent of all unionists. In 1940, they were almost 10 percent. In 1944, they accounted for more than one-fifth of all union workers. The Second World War accelerated—and did not create—these decades-long trends.[5]

Of course, saying that women were an essential part of the American work force does not mean that there were not impediments to their participation. Only 15 percent of married women worked in 1940. They also tended to earn less than single women. In the prewar period, discrimination against married women was omnipresent. Borrowing concepts from another historical context, there was both de jure and de facto bias against women workers. An example of the former was the infamous Section 213 of the 1932 Economy Act. The law's general goal was to streamline the federal bureaucracy in a time of rapidly deteriorating economic conditions. Section 213 required that in cases of civil servant layoffs, married persons who had spouses who also worked for the federal government would be let go first. The gender-neutral language confused no one. It was assumed that married women would be released, not their husbands. The 1932 Economy Act's Section 213 typified a much broader cultural, not just legal, consensus about the role of women. Simply put, it was expected that women would be married and confine their labors to the household. The widespread currency of such notions about women's work and working women can be seen in a 1936 Gallup poll. Eighty-two percent of all respondents, who were both men and women, felt that wives should not work outside the home. Significantly, 75 percent of all women thought so. Immediately before the

Pearl Harbor attack, several state legislatures tried to pass laws prohibiting married women from wage work.[6]

The coming of the war against the Axis powers dramatically altered the role that American women, regardless of marital status, played in the labor force, while at the same time reinforcing the decades-long pattern of increasing roles for women in the economy. Married women benefited the most from the new wartime job opportunities. From 1940 through March 1944, more than three million married women entered the labor force. About 1.7 million single women joined the workforce over the same period. Furthermore, married women workers outnumbered single women workers by 300,000. (See table 4.3.) Although it was common for Americans to talk about married women working for "pin money," a U.S. Women's Bureau survey in 1944 and 1945 indicated clearly that increasingly women's wartime wages were becoming a family necessity. Eighty percent of the thirteen thousand women polled were living at home with their families, and 90 percent made weekly contributions to the household budget. Of the remaining women workers, one in six still provided some of her wages to support dependents. Although these numbers startled some, as with other aspects of women's employment, wartime conditions had only accelerated the pace of prewar changes. This was true for both married and single women.[7]

Seemingly these changes happened overnight. Well into 1942, employers and male union officials remained skeptical of the benefits of the widespread use of women workers. Immediately following the Pearl Harbor attack, a Federal Security Agency report revealed the depth of resistance to hiring women. Of the 675,675 anticipated job openings in war-related factories, only 32 percent were open to women. In other words, 68 percent of all war jobs were for men only. Another federal

TABLE 4.3
Women Employed in the Civilian Labor Force, March 1944

	Number of Women Employed	*Percentage of Total*
Single	7,030,000	42.7
Married	7,310,000	44.4
Widowed or Divorced	2,140,000	13.0
Total	16,480,000	100.0

SOURCE: Mary Elizabeth Pidgeon, *Changes in Women's Employment During the War* (Washington, DC: GPO, 1944), 18.

study, conducted in January 1942, confirmed these findings. The War Manpower Commission (WMC) surveyed thirteen thousand war factories and discovered that only 30 percent of the available jobs were open to women. Although the WMC urged employers to hire women, other parts of the federal government did not bravely abandon traditional gender patterns. Well into the Second World War, the War Department continued to discourage the use of women workers "until all available male labor . . . has first been employed."[8] Yet, by the time that the War Department had issued this statement, in August 1942, the point was moot. By late summer 1942, basic industrial training as well as job opportunities for women began to appear in increasing numbers. At the war's height, in 1944, women accounted for half of the civilian workforce. The change was rapid and dramatic. In 1940, the number of women working outside the home was about twelve million. In 1945, there were almost nineteen million wage-earning women. The percentage of women in the labor force increased from 28 to 37 percent. By the war's end, women constituted 36 percent of the civilian workforce, and 25 percent of all married women held jobs outside the home. Many of these women (both married and unmarried) joined labor unions. Fewer than 500,000 women belonged to labor unions in the 1930s. By 1950, the American labor movement counted three million women in its ranks. Although it is not known exactly how many women joined the AFL, CIO, and independent unions, there are some rough measures available. If one considers that, for the war years, there were two AFL unionists for every one CIO worker, one can estimate that a similar ratio might have held for just women. By this reasoning, one can guess that there were about two million women workers in the AFL by the war's peak, in late 1944. Two million more women belonged to AFL union auxiliaries. In sum, the war had a rapid and transformative effect on working women in terms of job opportunities and union membership.[9]

President Franklin D. Roosevelt's administration actively and successfully facilitated this conversion in the workforce. FDR's wartime alphabet agencies, like the Office of Production Management, the U.S. Employment Service, and the War Manpower Commission, recruited and placed women workers. And Roosevelt's propaganda machinery sold the idea that women belonged in the factories. The most persuasive image of women during the war and long afterward was that of Rosie the Riveter, that all-important fictional character whose usefulness in motivating women workers to join the ranks of factory workers and in

TABLE 4.4
Estimates of Civilian Woman Labor Force, June 1940–July 1943

	June 1940	*June 1941*	*June 1942*	*June 1943*	*July 1943*
Civilian woman labor force					
Number in millions	13.9	13.9	15.0	17.3	17.7
Percentage of total labor force	24.7	24.7	26.7	31.7	31.9
Employment					
Total					
Number in millions	11.2	11.9	13.9	16.7	17.1
Percentage of total employment	23.5	23.7	26.1	31.3	31.5
Nonagricultural					
Number in millions	9.7	10.4	11.8	14.4	14.8
Percentage of total nonagricultural	26.5	26.5	28.2	34.7	35.1
Agricultural					
Number in millions	1.5	1.5	2.1	2.3	2.3
Percentage of total agricultural	13.6	13.8	18.3	19.3	19.0
Unemployment					
Number in millions	2.7	2.0	1.1	0.6	0.6
Percentage of total	31.4	33.3	39.3	50.0	50.0

SOURCE: Mary Robinson, *Woman Workers in Two Wars* (Washington, DC: GPO, 1944), 2.

urging men to accept her cannot be measured. Nonetheless, this wartime icon still stands for working women's tremendous efforts on the home front, as well as the general support that their male colleagues eventually gave. But women were more than just riveters. Only two years after the attack on Pearl Harbor, women were being extensively used as drill press operators, electric arc welders, electricians, painters, inspectors, draftsmen, shipfitter's helpers, and truck drivers. Furthermore, women's work in wartime agriculture and within the wartime government itself has nearly gone unnoticed by historians. Although there were no comparative Fanny the Farm Hand or Betty the Wartime Bureaucrat in American wartime propaganda, they were absolutely essential to the war effort (see table 4.4).

Women's importance to American wars was nothing new. Since the days of Molly Pitcher, women have had active roles in every military conflict. And yet, the twentieth century's world wars constituted watershed events in American women's history. Perhaps more than in any previous conflagration, during the First World War, American women assumed new economic roles, breaking into jobs that were considered exclusively men's. Significantly, women entered the iron and steel, lumber, transportation, electrical, automotive, optical, and ammunition industries. Moreover, as the draft began drawing more and more men to the front lines in Europe, women entered into work completely unheard of, such as aircraft manufacturing, railway transportation, and the service trades. For example, shortly after the second draft call in 1917, more than six thousand women found employment in the burgeoning aircraft plants. Before the war, American airplane manufacturers had employed only one woman on the shop floor![10] At first, women's entrance into factories was rather chaotic. Without proper training and without any federal government oversight, there were serious problems and abuses. In New York and Pennsylvania, army uniform contractors made women work under sweatshop conditions nearly around the clock. In one navy shipyard, women worked ten hours per shift but were paid for only eight. Even the Government Printing Office exploited the new women workers. Officials there made women work twelve-hour days.[11] Nevertheless, by all accounts, women workers performed extraordinarily well at their new roles, even without the proper training. Generally, they received just enough on-the-job instruction to keep their machines running. Although, in the return to "normalcy" after the war, women's wartime accomplishments were generally downplayed, immediately after the war, women workers' high level of job proficiency was praised. One example must stand for many. In 1920, the assistant secretary of war, Goldthwaite Dorr, wrote:

> For the successful carrying out of our program for the production of vast quantities of explosives and propellants, as well as shell loading, the women of America must be given credit on account of the highly important part they took in this phase of helping to win the war. Fully 50 percent of the number of employees in our explosive plants were women, who braved the dangers connected but with this line of work, to which they had been, of course, entirely unaccustomed, but whose perils were not unknown to them.[12]

Regardless of their performance, male workers, in particular those affiliated with AFL unions, had to be cajoled at best and forced in some cases into allowing women on the job. Only weeks after the United States declared war on the Central powers, President Woodrow Wilson sent requests to all major national and international labor organizations in the United States, asking them to adopt resolutions affirming the use of women workers. Union leaders were skeptical at first. They feared, as President John F. Hart, of the Amalgamated Meat Cutters and Butcher

Workmen (AFL) did, that women would enter by the thousands, do the work, do it "equally as well as men ever performed," and do it at a far lower wage.[13] After the war, Hart predicted and others agreed, veterans would permanently lose their jobs to this new, cheaper labor. Yet, out of patriotic duty, American unionists did pass resolutions promising no objection to women workers, but many added statements insisting that women be organized into existing unions, that they receive equal pay for equal work, and that it be understood that their employment would be only "for the duration of the emergency."[14] The American Federation of Labor led the way by adopting the well-publicized Resolution No. 92 at its thirty-eighth annual convention in 1918. The measure read:

> Whereas, The American Federation of Labor stands for equal pay for equal work, believing that these women should receive the same wages as those received by the men whose places they have taken in order to help the prosecution of this war and the elimination of the Hun; and
>
> Whereas, We believe that the best interests of the labor movement demand that a strenuous and continuous effort be made to organize these women into trade union bodies of their respective crafts, be it
>
> Resolved, That we call upon the officers and organizers of the affiliated international and national unions to make very effort to bring these women into the organizations of their respective crafts to which the men, whose places they have taken, are members.[15]

But, as was nearly always the case with the AFL and its affiliates on gender and racial issues, pronouncements were one thing and practice was another. Many local unions ignored the resolutions of their national and international officers and resisted the introduction of women to the shop floor. Some locals that did accept women also passed a "necessity clause" that limited women's membership to the duration of the war. The AFL national leaders were no better. Federation president Sam Gompers hedged considerably on his commitment to women workers. In 1917, he published an article in the *American Federationist* titled, "Don't Sacrifice Womanhood," in which he called for a cautionary approach to the introduction of women into war factories. Not only did he worry about the potentially negative impact on wages and working conditions, but in a subsequent article he also expressed concern that somehow women were being placed into positions for which they were ill fitted. Given these cultural considerations, as well as the workplace gains that the AFL had made over the decades, Gompers warned against the systematic and wholesale introduction of women.[16]

There were many local unionists who clearly agreed with Gompers. In August 1918, the U.S. Employment Service announced that there was a shortage of railway conductors in several major cities. The Cleveland Street Railway Company was already feeling the pinch and resolved to fill vacancies by hiring 190 women, whom they trained to fill the jobs left by men who had gone to war or had taken other wartime job opportunities. The leaders of Local 268 of the American Amalgamated Association of Street and Railway Employees, the CSR's main union and an AFL affiliate, immediately cried foul. Although the Amalgamated Association's national officials passed a resolution agreeing to President Wilson's call to allow the employment of women workers, it also went on record as opposing "unalterably" the hiring of women as motormen and conductors. Thus, when the CSR offered such jobs to those 190 women, Local 268's president threatened a strike and called for a federal investigation. The U.S. Department of Labor quickly dispatched two officials, who conferred with the railway and with Local 268. Surprisingly, in their report, they sided with the union and recommended that all the women be dismissed. Ignoring the Labor Department and the union, CSR's president, John J. Stanley, kept the women on the streetcars. The union then called a strike. President Wilson's War Labor Board was sent to arbitrate the case. In late November 1918, the board upheld the company's right to hire the women but also ruled that, since the war emergency was over, there no longer was a "necessity" to employ women conductors. The women and their lawyer, Frank P. Walsh, filed an appeal. In March 1919, the War Labor Board reversed its decision. With the war over, the ruling was a dead letter, however. Furthermore, President Stanley responded that he would now ignore the board's directive. The company could not afford another strike.[17] The Association had won. Experiences like this showed AFL unions that they could successfully resist gender changes on the shop floor, an important lesson and precedent for the World War II period.

The AFL and Women Workers Before World War II

The recalcitrance of a few unions not withstanding, the AFL's cautious wartime position on women workers did not surprise close observers.

Since its inception, the Federation had refused to embrace women workers, preferring to keep them at arm's length. In 1881, when the Federation of Organized Trades and Labor Unions met for the first time, no women were present. This was at odds with the history of the labor movement. Women were the vanguard in industrial unions in the 1820s in New England textile mills. They were the bedrock of the shoemakers unions in the 1850s and 1860s. And, of course, they were instrumental to the success of the Knights of Labor, which had nearly fifty thousand female members by the 1880s.[18] In contrast to these organizations, the AFL developed a reputation for theoretically favoring the organization of women workers while not actually doing it. At its second convention, in 1882, the Federation formally "extended to all unions of women equal opportunity to participate in future conventions with unions of men."[19] This call netted one female delegate the following year, Charlotte Smith, president of the Women's National Industrial League. Two year later, the Federation refreshed its call for women to join. Unsurprisingly, few did; empty platitudes rarely generate results.

The issue of women workers, however, was not going away. In 1890, Ida M. Van Etten, of the New York Working Women's Society, appeared at the AFL's annual convention, in Detroit, Michigan, to explain to the delegates the horrific working conditions under which too many women labored. She constructed her address perfectly to get the full attention of the AFL. Her argument was simple and reflective of the age:

> [Women's] utter lack of organization, combined with natural timidity and helplessness, has left them entirely at the mercy of their employers in the matter of wages and hours. Their cheaper labor is a continual menace to wages, and their entrance in any considerable numbers into a trade or calling is invariably followed by a lowering in its rate of wages.[20]

Van Etten confirmed what the men of the AFL had always feared. Women in the labor market were cheapening their trades and their worth. From its inception, the AFL had conflated the strength of the labor movement with manliness. The Federation's view of masculinity was the cornerstone of its political philosophy. At the heart of the AFL was the belief in volunteerism: men willingly entered into a contract with an employer, and employees also entered into an association on their own volition to improve working conditions and wages. Utilizing their abilities, muscle, and resolve, they fought for the union, which in turn helped to provide for workingmen's families.[21] In this view, women had little to no permanent role in the labor force. That was the monopoly of manhood. Van Etten bluntly illustrated that AFL manhood was being challenged. "In their ignorance of the interdependent interests of wage-workers," she stated coolly, "they have become the competitors of their own husbands, fathers and brothers, and unconsciously the ally of the manufacturers in lowering the conditions of their class."[22] Then came the numbers. Sixty-six percent of the employees in New York State factories were women and children. What was worse, it was now cheaper to make clothes in New York City than it was to sew them in Canada and South America. Van Etten exhorted the Federation to organize the women and pleaded with them not to put them in separate unions, as they often did African American men. "Do not expect them to become mere addenda to men's organizations, or they will be failures," she said. "Neither men nor women will long feel an interest in an organization that is not under their direct management."[23] Finally, she gave the assembly eloquent but strong words to ponder:

> When the martyrology of the proletariat shall be written, among its unknown and unnumbered saints shall be the thousands, aye, tens of thousands of women and little children—little children who have offered up their innocent young lives in the mines, in the factories, in the store, and the warehouses of our great commercial centers. But, if we are to believe the words of an eminent labor reformer, that "the death of every man hastens the end of the system under which they are sacrificed," they will not have died in vain, and we may well have blessed their lives and their deaths.[24]

Moved by Van Etten's bold words, the American Federation of Labor made its first broad statement on women workers. The convention resolved again to call on women to join the AFL. Additionally, it urged state factory inspectors to appoint women as inspectors, and it authorized organizing campaigns to bring more women into the ranks of labor. The last part of the statement was particularly meaningful. Not since the Knights of Labor had any national labor organization dedicated itself to unionizing women. In 1891, the AFL hired a female organizer, Mary E. Kenney. After a year's work in New York City, Gompers fired her. By 1892, the AFL had returned to its regular pattern. At the

1892 and subsequent conventions, the problems facing women workers were highlighted and promises of reform were made, but no action followed.[25] As one student of the labor movement put it, in 1921:

> [T]he desire to make a favorable impression in the eyes of public opinion has nearly always resulted in official pronouncements of policy that have appeared highly favorable to the organization of women. Yet the fear of arousing irreconcilable elements as well as the reluctance to dissipate its energies in unfamiliar organizing activity has usually prevented the Federation from taking very positive steps to bring the mass of women workers into unions.[26]

In the absence of AFL organizing, working women and their allies pursued another strategy to improve their lot. Beginning in the late nineteenth century, reformers sought protective legislation as a means to raise the working standards for women. The key moment came in 1908 when the U.S. Supreme Court ruled, in *Muller v. Oregon,* that a state law setting a maximum of ten hours of work per day for factory women and laundresses was constitutional. This ruling amended an earlier decision, *Lochner v. New York* (1905), in which the Justices had struck down a ten-hour limit for bakery workers. Apparently, in the *Muller* case, the Supreme Court was swayed by the future Justice Louis D. Brandeis, who, with the assistance of Florence Kelley and Josephine Goldmark, of the National Consumers' League, had demonstrated the ill effects of long hours. Not only did excessive work outside the home damage women's health, but it hurt the family, as well. Echoing the gendered ideology of the AFL, the Supreme Court, as well as the lawyers who supported the ten-hour limit, stressed that women's proper place was in the home. Long hours on the factory floor were, in Justice David J. Brewer's majority opinion, dangerous, given a woman's "physical structure" and "her maternal functions."[27] By upholding the Oregon law, the Supreme Court was in essence stating that, unlike men, women did not have liberty of contract in all cases. This made women akin to child wards of the state. They were certainly not like men, who, through their voluntary associations (which ideally had affiliated with the AFL) entered into contracts and set their own working conditions.[28]

By World War II, virtually all states, the District of Columbia, and every major territory, including Puerto Rico, had laws that limited women's wage workday to eight to ten hours (per employer), set weekly limits of no more than sixty hours, frequently prohibited or limited night work, and established a minimum wage. (See table 4.5.) The AFL wholeheartedly supported these statutes as long as they dealt with women.

Unlike social reformers and feminists who spearheaded reform campaigns for protective legislation, AFL leaders saw the laws, as one historian has written, "as a way of shoring up the family by discouraging employers from hiring women in the first place while ensuring reasonable conditions for those who did enter the labor force."[29] During the Progressive Era, AFL officials still rejected the idea that protective laws for women might be extended to all workers. Not until the middle of the 1930s did the Federation finally concede that state influence in industrial relations was a social good for men as well as women.

While adding their voices to the call to protect women workers, the AFL also supported one of the main women's reform groups, the Women's Trade Union League (WTUL). Established in 1903 by women who attended the AFL convention in Boston, the WTUL was the American version of the original league founded in England in 1890. The American League's mission was to "help secure conditions necessary for healthful and efficient work and to obtain a just return for such work" and to "assist in the organization of women workers into trade unions."[30] Gompers gave the leaders of the WTUL, particularly Mary Kenney O'Sullivan, time at the podium during several AFL conventions. Of course, it was expected that the League would organize women into AFL affiliates. Despite this common mission, the relationship between the WTUL and the AFL was often strained. In 1924, a few months before he died, President Gompers sent his personal secretary and confidant, Florence Thorne, to meet with the League's president, Mary Anderson, to see whether the WTUL "could be persuaded to go out of business." The AFL's leaders wanted a less independent organization dedicated to the unionization of women. They envisioned a women's bureau inside the Federation, not outside it. The League's leaders seriously considered the offer, but the Federation failed to develop its own women's bureau.[31]

Despite the political infighting, the establishment of the WTUL marks an important moment in the history of the women's movement, as well as that of the AFL. For the first time, feminists were drawn to the Federation and worked cooperatively with the AFL to improve the conditions of working women. The women of the WTUL, as well as those of the AFL, developed their own special kind of feminism, what the historian Dorothy Sue Cobble has aptly called labor feminism. Labor feminists,

TABLE 4.5

ypes of Labor Laws for Women, by States and Selected Territories, March 31, 1942

	Daily Hour Limit				Weekly Hour Limit			Night Work			
te/Territory	8	9	10	Other	48	54	Other	Prohibited	Limited	Prohibited or Regulated Jobs	Minimum Wage
abama										*	
izona	*				*					*	*
kansas		*				*				*	*
alifornia	*				*			*		*	*
olorado	*				*					*	*
onnecticut	*	*			*		52, 58	*		*	*
elaware			*				55	*	*		
orida											
eorgia			*				60				
aho		*									
inois	*				*					*	*
diana								*		*	
wa											
ansas	*	*			*	*	49.5	*	*		*
entucky			*				60				*
ouisiana	*	*			*	*	60			*	*
aine		*				*					*
aryland			*				60		*	*	
assachusetts		*			*			*		*	*
ichigan		*				*				*	
innesota						*				*	*
ississippi			*				60				
issouri		*				*				*	
ontana	*				*						
ebraska		*				*		*			
evada	*				*						*
ew Hampshire			*	10.5	*	*			*		*
ew Jersey			*			*		*		*	*
ew Mexico	*	*			*	*	56				
ew York	*				*			*		*	*
orth Carolina		*	*	11	*		55				
orth Dakota		*		8.5	*	*	58	*			*
hio	*				*		45	*		*	*
klahoma		*				*				*	*
regon	*	*	*		*		44, 60			*	*
ennsylvania	*		*		*		44	*		*	*
hode Island		*			*					*	*
outh Carolina	*			12			40, 60	*			
outh Dakota			*			*					*
ennessee				10.5			57				
exas		*		11		*					
tah	*			7.5	*		45			*	*
ermont		*					50			*	
irginia		*			*					*	
ashington	*				*		60	*		*	*
est Virginia											
isconsin		*	*	9.5			50, 60	*		*	*
yoming	*				*					*	
laska	*						60				*
ashington, DC					*						*
awaii					*						*
hilippines								*			
uerto Rico	*				*						*

OURCE: *Conference on the Employment of Women,* AFL Papers, series 8A, box 44, folder "Conference on e Employment of Women" in Cobble's words, "articulated a particular variant of feminism that put the needs of working-class women at its core and . . . championed the labor movement as the principle vehicle through which the lives of the majority of women could be bettered." They were the "intellectual daughters and granddaughters of Progressive Era 'social feminists' like Florence Kelley, Rose Schneiderman, and Jane Addams." What these women shared was a belief that women's disadvantages had multiple sources and could be remedied only by a broad range of actions and social reforms. Labor and social feminists also shared a strong disdain for "equal rights" feminists. Women such as Alice Paul, of the National Women's Party, thought that the best way to eliminate women's secondary status was the passage of an Equal Rights Amendment to the U.S. Constitution (or, as many in the AFL referred to it, the "so-called" Equal Rights Amendment.)[32] Labor feminists both within and outside the AFL feared that the ERA would cause a deterioration of women's wages and working conditions, thus undoing their legislative and organizing work. In their view, the ERA would not bring equality, and such an idea was a "tyranny of words."[33] Rather, they sought what they termed "full industrial citizenship," which meant improvements in the lives of working women through legislation and through the labor movement.[34]

The story of one labor feminist, Agnes Nestor, illustrates well not only the kind of women who joined the AFL at the turn of the twentieth century but also the kinds of opportunities and limitations that they faced within the Federation. Born in 1887, in Grand Rapids, Michigan, Nestor was the daughter of an immigrant Irish father and a mother who was born of Irish parents in a cabin in New York's Mohawk Valley. When she was ten, Agnes and her family moved to Chicago, as the family's fortunes had soured in Michigan. Everyone had to get a job, including little Agnes, who found employment at the Eisendrath Glove Factory. Work in the city's needle trades was hard and long. The shortest day of work was on Saturday, when workers labored for only nine hours. Breaks were few and far between, and accidents were frequent. Eventually, during a particularly bad economic period, Nestor was laid off. She found what she thought was a better job working at a five-and-dime, which was hiring seasonal help for the Christmas rush. Initially, she thought that the job was an improvement, since it was not factory work. Agnes was soon disappointed. While the store looked nice in the front, behind the scenes in the stockroom, it was a chaotic mess. Moreover, the backroom was not heated and was overrun with rats that ate

Agnes Nestor (1887–1948), courtesy of the George Meany Memorial Archives, image 631.

everything, including the employees' lunches. Nestor once tried to outsmart the rodents by hiding her lunch in the arm of her winter coat. The rats ate the coat, too.

Such experiences on the job convinced Nestor that there must be a better way. Work radicalized her and caused her to organize her coworkers and to fight for better wages and conditions. Her efforts to form a union began when she was hired back at Eisendrath's factory in 1898. Quickly she organized the workers in her department and went out on strike. Soon she found a powerful ally, John Fitzpatrick and the Chicago Federation of Labor. The factory's managers and their newspaper friends had no intention of letting the "girls" win. As soon as the strike broke out, Nestor and her coworkers formed a picket line outside the factory. When a strikebreaker tried to go through the line, one of the striking workers grabbed her arm and holding tightly threatened "the kid glove maker. . . . 'Before I let go of you, I will duck you in that water trough.'" Of course, Nestor added in her autobiography, "it was only an idle threat." But the next day the *Chicago Tribune* ran a front-page story under the headline "Strikers Dunk Girl in Water Trough."[35]

This chicanery only toughened Nestor. She replied in kind with her own article, "A Day's Work Making Gloves," which was published and reprinted in the *Chicago Daily Socialist,* the *Union Labor Advocate,* the *Women's Trade Union League of Chicago,* and the *Brotherhood of Railroad Trainmen's Magazine.* The hard-hitting expose was written in a plain, calm style and ended with this observation:

> Employers frequently complain about the big expense of "breaking in so much help." If they spent some of this money to make the factory conditions better it would not be necessary to break in so many workers. I believe it would pay them in the end.[36]

Nestor and her friends won the strike and joined the International Glove Workers' Union (AFL).

A few years after the strike, in 1904, Nestor met Mary McDowell, and her life changed again. McDowell was the president of the Women's Trade Union League, as well as the head of the University of Chicago Settlement House. One night, she and several members of the local Glove Workers Union went to Hull House and met McDowell, Jane Addams, and Ellen Gates Starr. She was particularly taken with McDowell. She shared Nestor's ethnicity, and Nestor was entranced by McDowell's "warm, friendly manner."[37] Through McDowell and Nestor's new connections in the Women's Trade Union League, which she joined, she began to meet other leaders of the labor movement. In 1907, she joined Mary Kenny O'Sullivan and Mary McDowell as the three WTUL delegates to the AFL convention in Norfolk, Virginia. There she met Sam Gompers. Always a quick judge of character, Gompers immediately liked Nestor and even had her preside over part of the meeting. Thus began a fifty-year career working with the AFL.

Unlike other AFL leaders, Nestor had no formal position within the Federation other than that of head of her own union. But, like people such as John Frey, Boris Shishkin, and Joseph Padway, Nestor had myriad temporary assignments. Her work with the AFL represented very well the Federation's and the WTUL's outlook on women. Nestor was to help organize women into the AFL while fighting for protective legislation. She helped several unions organize, and in her autobiography she claimed that she "gave Sidney Hillman his first lesson in collective bargaining."[38] She also participated in the general strikes in Gloversville and Johnstown. Her most significant work came as the driving force behind the movement in Illinois to establish an eight-hour day for women workers. The law that was passed in 1937 was the culmination of nearly three decades of struggle. In this fight, she battled not only conservative men but also radical women. Even at the end of her career, in the 1950s, she continued to consider equal-rights feminists who had proposed the ERA a "threat to all our labor laws for women," and she took great pride in the fact that she had defeated them in Illinois.[39]

Nestor also served as the AFL's representative in various positions. Her AFL work, however, demonstrated to her the limits of women's roles and influence in the Federation. At Sam Gompers's instigation, she took various temporary government posts. In 1914, she served on President Woodrow Wilson's National Commission on Vocational Education. Then, during World War I, she joined President Wilson's National Defense Advisory Commission's Committee on Women in Industry. Anna Howard Shaw, a suffragist and an equal-rights advocate, headed the committee.[40] Initially, Shaw and Nestor did not get along. Nestor, a labor feminist, was "a little prejudiced against her," and Shaw resented the appointment of people she called "antisuffragists" to her committee. Eventually both came to respect the other, while at the same time recognizing the circumscribed role they had. As they realized when their suggestions and even their presence were ignored, "this was still a man's world."[41] This was true of the federal government, and it was true of the AFL. In the Federation, women were to do women's work: help organize women, fight for protective legislation, and serve where needed. But they were not to upset the order. They were to understand and accept that at times, as Nestor wrote, they were going to be a kind of "fifth wheel" to the American labor movement.[42] In fact, women were not just a fifth wheel; they were also the spare wheel on America's home front. Such was the case during both World War I and World War II.

The AFL and Women Workers During World War II

Rosie the Riveter put a name to the millions of women who in essence functioned as a reserve industrial army during World War II. But there is a good chance that Rosie did not represent the typical AFL woman unionist. Perhaps, Beulah, whose last name we don't know but who was a real Okie shipyard worker and a member of the Plumbers and Steamfitters Union (AFL), is the better example.[43] For the duration, Beulah worked at the Moore Dry Dock Company in Oakland, California, building ships for the U.S. Navy and the merchant marine. In early 1942, Moore Dry Dock had received gigantic contracts to build these vessels. Immediately, the call went out for shipyard workers. Initially, managers at Moore Dry Dock had a difficult time hiring new workers. It was not that they were not available. Since the 1930s, California had had a large, mobile, and underemployed workforce, many of whom had come in from Oklahoma and Arkansas.[44] As war-related production geared up, they were ready and able to take these new jobs. However, the shipyard unions slowed things down. In particular, American Federation of Labor unions like the Plumbers and Steamfitters, which had organized many West Coast yards, stifled employers' attempts to hire workers, particularly women and African Americans, before they had met union membership standards. As was the case with the International Brotherhood of Boilermakers and the issue of race, the antiwomen traditions of many AFL unions tied managers' hands. Before the war, both union and employer discrimination against women had had a profound affect in the shipbuilding business. The 1939 Census of Manufacturers had shown that only thirty-six women in the entire nation worked in shipyards. In June 1942, women accounted for only .4 percent of the total number of workers in commercial yards. A year later, when women like Beulah had found work at Moore Dry Dock, they constituted 7 percent of all shipyard workers.[45] What had changed were the positions that AFL unions had taken on women workers. Bowing to pressure from the AFL's national leadership and the leadership of the various affiliated unions, locals dropped their bars to women workers.[46]

Unlike Woodrow Wilson, President Franklin Roosevelt did not have to make a formal request to the AFL to get its unions to drop their barriers to women workers. And still, the unions hesitated in practice. Six months into World War II, the AFL Executive Council had to lean heavily on its affiliated unions to change the situation. To their credit, nearly all unions relented. In this instance, pressure from the Executive Council worked. And, in 1944, the AFL dusted off its resolutions from the late nineteenth century and at its annual convention again formally called for the organizing of women workers to add to the AFL "their membership and active participation in the bona fide trade unions of

Women working in the "arsenal of democracy" during the Second World War, courtesy of the George Meany Memorial Archives/U.S. Navy, image 955.

their respective crafts," which the resolution stated was "essential to their well being, and to the general welfare of the nation."[47]

Despite the AFL's insistence that all unions accept wartime women workers, like Sam Gompers before him, William Green did not fully support women workers. In an unsigned July 1941 article in the *American Federationist,* which was most likely written by Green or his secretary, Florence Thorne, the author asserts that women workers should enter the workforce slowly, in a step-by-step process. First, they ought to "fill the needs for additional workers in occupations traditionally held by women," such as sales, clerical, and stenographic jobs. Then, women should take those jobs in war industries that require "dexterity, care and speed with a minimum of strength and craftsmanship." Finally, only when the war has drained men off of the shop floor should women then take "more strenuous and more exacting industrial" jobs.[48] Even six months into the Second World War, President Green continued to support women workers only when "home responsibilities will permit." He made clear that they were not regular workers but, rather, America's chief "labor reserve."[49]

Nonetheless, by the end of 1942, virtually all AFL unions had opened their doors to women, at least part way. Leading the way were the International Association of Machinists, the Teamsters, the Carpenters, the Foundry Workers, and the Shipbuilders. The Plumbers and Steamfitters, Beulah's union, also begrudgingly accepted women, but only at the direct request of the national leadership. Even then, women were treated as second-class members. As one observer wrote, "the intruders were often given a second-class membership, which in the Plumbers and Steamfitters Union was compensated by abrogation of half the usual initiation fee, but which in all the craft unions of the shipyard tacitly implied that the emergency, union affiliation, and women's jobs would terminate together."[50] An International Brotherhood of Electrical Workers (AFL) official called for the passage of a law requiring women who had "taken over a man's job to be laid off after the war."[51] The Teamsters shared this sentiment and passed a resolution that allowed women drivers but also stated that a "local can withdraw their membership whenever, in its judgment, the emergency ceases."[52] The last AFL union to allow women as members was the Boilermakers. Importantly, however, the IBB allowed only white women to join.[53] As demonstrated in chapter 3, the Boilermakers never relaxed their prohibitions on race. There were no black women shipbuilders on AFL docks. Furthermore, although the Boilermakers' international leaders had opened the doors to some women, some individual locals, such as IBB Locals 104 and 568 in Puget Sound, refused to abide by the wartime policy changes.[54]

In general, male shipyard workers—perhaps like most male AFL workers across the nation—may have accepted women, but they never liked having to do so. Discrimination and hostility against women shipyard workers grew out of a combination of old fears and new ones. In *Wartime Shipyard: A Study in Social Disunity,* Katherine Archibald, a sociologist who spent the war working and recording life and labor at Moore Dry Dock Company, provided the clearest picture of wartime working conditions for women. In general, many male shipbuilders felt that it was simply improper and uncomfortable for women to labor on the docks. As Archibald summed up the sentiment, like blacks and migrant Okies, women were not a part of the regular workforce. They were—and this may have been particularly true for women—only "a reserve" to be tolerated for a short period.[55] Moreover, prior to the war, ship construction had been a tremendously uncouth masculine world. As women appeared, men felt obligated, as Archibald put it, to remove their "galleries of nudes and pornography" from workplace walls and to clean up their language and even their faces.[56] But, beneath this façade of politeness, "a half-concealed resentment still persisted, not against women as women, but against them as rivals of men in a man's world."[57] As with black workers, white men in the AFL frequently viewed women as cheap labor, job stealers, and potential strikebreakers.[58] The fear of women, then, represented the old anxiety that if women appeared on the job, men would soon lose their jobs to this new, cheaper source of labor. As Archibald succinctly put it:

> In an economy where jobs are at a premium and the specter of unemployment never quite vanishes and where at best the price of a skill is subject to decline with every increase in the supply of qualified workers, the entrance of any new group [i.e., women] into the field of competition is usually resisted.[59]

This sense of rivalry was also based upon other recently changed social features of the West Coast. In particular, these hard-hatted California men were angry at the introduction of migrant workers from Oklahoma. More than 95,000 migrants had come during the Great Depression of the 1930s.[60] And more than 300,000 native Oklahomans left their state during World War II, many for the West Coast.[61] Native Californians seemed to revel in their hatred of Okies. They were the butt of nearly every joke and were seen as embodying every derogatory stereotype. As Archibald stated in her study, "Okie stupidity was second only to sex as a subject for scrawls on bulkheads and toilet-shack walls." For example, Archibald was told that in many of the men's rooms, someone had scribbled "Okie drinking fountain" above the urinals.[62] According to Archibald, in the minds of many shipyard men, Okie and women in general shared a common characteristic: "Okies, like women, were assumed to know little or nothing of the techniques of industry and to be scarcely capable of learning more."[63] For those unfortunate enough to be both an Okie and a woman, life in the shipyards could be rather rough. Such was the case of Beulah, an Okie who spent considerable time with Katherine Archibald.

An impoverished cotton farmer, Beulah came to Oakland seeking profitable war work. Archibald noted that she exceeded Okie legend in several ways. Her voice "through years of hog and children calling" had an "almost incredible power and stridency." It fit her manner, which was "all outward-going noise and bluster, and uncultivated good will." She could probably have matched shipyard men for crudeness. As Archibald put it, when Beulah blew her nose, she "employed the unassisted equipment of nature."[64] Because of their idiosyncrasies and because of the basic disapproval of other workers, Okies like Beulah were subjected to derision and discrimination. But, in at least one area, Beulah broke away from the Okie stereotype. She was "most emphatically not lazy" and was known around Moore Dry Dock as an excellent worker. She was also a good member of the AFL, sharing many of the ideological commitments of her male counterparts. In particular, Beulah either adopted or brought with her the Federation's outlook on racial issues. She did not want African Americans to join the union or to be employed at Moore. "Oh, sure," she told Archibald, "I've known a couple of niggers who were all right enough. I don't mind any of them if they keep their place."[65]

Although women like Beulah who worked in places where the AFL had closed-shop agreements had little choice about joining the union, they found at least one aspect of their union experience quite attractive: equal pay for equal work. The American Federation of Labor had long supported equal pay for both men and women. The commitment came not from any sense of gender equality; rather, male AFL members did not want similarly trained and experienced women undercutting their wages and taking their jobs. The earliest pronouncement of this policy came in 1898, when J. H. Sullivan, of the Brotherhood of Painters and Decorators of America, introduced this rambling resolution at the AFL annual convention:

> In view of the awful conditions under which woman is compelled to toil, this, the 18th Annual Convention of the American Federation of Labor strongly urges the more general formation of wage-working women, to the end that they may scientifically and permanently abolish the terrible evils accompanying their weakened, because unorganized state, and we emphatically reiterate the trade union demand that women receive equal compensation for equal service performed.[66]

In 1901, President Gompers echoed Sullivan's motion in his annual report, and, over the next four decades, the Federation repeated its support for reformers and labor feminists who worked toward equal pay for equal work.

Although state and federal labor and wage laws were moving in this direction, the Second World War pushed the issue to the forefront. With nearly six million more women in the labor force, the AFL and its allies, such as the Women's Trade Union League, began to forcefully demand equal pay for equal work. Although the Roosevelt administration had been sympathetic to equal pay, by late 1942, it had become a wartime priority. During the war, it was not just a question of cheap labor, as it had been in previous decades. Rather, it was also a question of maintaining federally set wage rates and of stopping inflation. If women were paid either too much or too little for war work, it could upset the tenuous system of price and wage controls. To avoid this problem, during the Second World War, the federal government, as it had during the First World War, mandated equal pay for equal work rules on war-related jobs.[67]

To set the equal-pay standards, the National War Labor Board (NWLB) issued its General Order No. 16, on November 24, 1942. As it was finally perfected in 1944, the Order read:

> Adjustments which equalize the wage or salary rates paid to females with the rates paid to males for comparable quality and quantity of work on the same or similar operations, and adjustments in accordance with this policy which recognize or are based on differences in quality or quantity of work performed, may be made without approval of the National War Labor Board, provide that:
>
> 1. Such adjustments shall be subject to the Board's ultimate power of review, but any modifications or reversal thereof will not be retroactive;
> 2. Such adjustments shall not furnish a basis either to increase price ceilings of the commodity or service or to resist otherwise justified reductions in such price ceilings.[68]

Almost immediately, NWLB officials went out to enforce the rule. From late November 1942 to January 3, 1944, the NWLB handled 2,250 cases related to equal pay for women, resulting in wage increases for nearly sixty thousand women workers. Unions also had a very important role to play in establishing equal pay for equal work. As the historian Ruth Milkman demonstrated, CIO unions, particularly the United

TABLE 4.6
Schedule of Wage Rates, 24 Months, Contract Period Effective September 6, 1943, for Reynolds Metal Co., Inc., Plants in Glendale, NY, New York City, Harrison, NJ, and St. Louis, MO
(in cents)

Months	*0*	*1*	*3*	*6*	*9*	*12*	*15*	*18*	*21*	*24*
Group 1	62	64	66	70	74	78	82	86	90	93
1A	62	64	66	70	73	76	79	82	85	88
2A	62	64	66	69	72	75	77	79	81	85
2	62	64	66	69	71	73	75	77	79	80.75
3	62	64	66	68	70	71	72	73	73	73
3AA	62	64	66	68	69	70	71	71	71	71
4	62	64	66	67.5	67.5	67.5	67.5	67.5	67.5	67.5
5	62	64	66	66	66	66	66	66	66	66
Male Min	62	64	66	66	66	66	66	66	66	66
Female Min	57	57	57	57	57	57	57	57	57	57

SOURCE: NWLB Case 111-3706-HO, Reynolds Metals Co., Inc., National War Labor Board Records, RG-202, box 476, National Archives and Records Administration (Silver Spring, MD).

Electrical Workers and the United Automobile Workers, strongly supported this principle.[69] During the war, AFL unions did, as well. A U.S. Women's Bureau survey, in 1944, of Midwestern war plants showed that 80 percent of all AFL and CIO collective-bargaining contracts contained equal-pay provisions. Among the most adamant unions on this issue was the International Association of Machinists (AFL), which refused to allow managers to create male and female job classifications. The combined power of the federal government working in concert with both national labor organizations led to clear gains toward equal pay for equal work.[70]

Despite this success, there were limits to union activities for women and to NWLB Order No. 16. It did not apply if the jobs that women did were similar to those of men but differed somehow in quantity or quality. Additionally, the NWLB did not allow wage adjustments for women if "for jobs which have been historically been performed by women only." Thus, women's work was still women's work. What this meant practically can be seen in table 4.6. It illustrates that women's and men's minimum wages differed significantly if they worked different jobs. In the major metal plants owned by Reynolds Metal Company, women workers started at fifty-seven cents an hour, while men (and only because they were men) started at sixty-two cents an hour. According to the NWLB, there was no problem with that kind of wage discrimination: it was a work tradition, and it reflected the differences in men's and women's work.[71] Thus, while women's wages did increase during the war years, the gap between men's and women's wages remained about the same. In 1939, the National Industrial Conference Board (NICB) calculated men's average weekly wages at $28.09. Women's average weekly wages were at $16.18. In other words, women earned about 58 percent of what men earned. In 1944, the NICB conducted another wage survey and found that women's weekly wages had increased by 90 percent, to $30.78. But men's wages had risen 94 percent, to $54.36. Thus, women's wages were still only 57 percent of men's.[72]

Although the issue of wage equity remained unresolved, labor feminists in the AFL such as Agnes Nestor strongly believed that the Federation was on the right track. Moreover, they wanted to use the equal-pay issue as a springboard for further reform. In 1943, Nestor, who was now in her late fifties, headed up the Federation's own Women in Industry Committee, which included the indomitable Rose Schneiderman and a relatively unknown unionist, Sallie D. Clinebell. In an early 1944 typescript report prepared for Florence Thorne, the Federation's director of research, Nestor set forth a plan for women workers. Of course, equal pay for equal work was central. "Equal pay on the job," she wrote, "is not a new issue but it is one that has come sharply to the fore during the past months. This standard is just as necessary to men as to protect women." Nestor believed that "the most effective way to insure equal pay on the job is to include this provision in union agreements." But other standards were necessary, too. Additionally, women needed "legal and industrial protection against industrial hazards," the "restoration of state protective legislation suspended or lowered for the war," and "state wage and hours laws fixing minimum standards for all on the job."[73] Thus, Nestor and other labor feminists saw the equal-pay issue as an important political touchstone as they worked for other protective legislation and collective bargaining agreements for women.

The AWFAL During the War

Feminist labor organizations welcomed such a plan for action. The Women's Trade Union League had been fighting against the rollback of protective labor laws for women since the 1920s. The U.S. Women's Bureau had a similar mission and also sought to maintain standards during the 1940s. Even before the war, the Bureau had pushed for the defense industries to uphold its eleven-point program—which included guidelines on job classification, safety, sanitation, wages, and hours—to ensure high labor standards for women workers.[74] The Women's Bureau's suggestions were all but ignored by the wartime agencies and defense employers. In 1942, Mary Anderson, formerly of the WTUL and then head of the U.S. Women's Bureau, tried to put the best possible spin on the futile struggle to uphold protective legislation for women workers. She told War Production Board officials worried about production bottlenecks that "there is little or no evidence that State labor laws for women are hampering war production." In fact, federal officials had rejected no requests for exceptions from limitations on hour or night work. In other words, two main pillars of protective legislation for women did not apply in practice during the war.[75]

In the wartime fight to maintain or reinstate labor standards for women, another relatively new women's organization, the American Federation of Women's Auxiliaries of Labor (AFWAL) aided the U.S. Women's Bureau and the WTUL. In 1935, Ira M. Ornburn, head of the AFL's Union Label and Trade Department, had singlehandedly established the AFWAL at the AFL's annual convention as a way to increase the power and effectiveness of his department. At first, the formation of this federation went largely unnoticed. The 1935 Atlantic City AFL annual convention faced other pressing issues, to say the least. Nonetheless, Ornburn called for the "banding together of the most energetic and diligent women in the families of the American Federation of Labor and the Railway Labor Unions" to serve as "an aggressive army for, among other policies, the spreading of knowledge of, and good will for, Union Labor, Union-made, and made-in-American products and Union-conducted services."[76] The resolution passed, and AFWAL was born, with the goal of using the economic and consumer power of the AFL's auxiliary women as a working-class weapon in the battles for collective bargaining and collective consumer action. Slowly, news of the AFWAL was revealed to the public, and the Auxiliary Federation began to make some noise. After a three-year period of near-dormancy, in 1938, AFWAL held its first convention in Cincinnati, Ohio, at the upscale Netherlands Hotel. The meeting served two purposes. First, it was a way to get the attention of national politicians. By inviting President Roosevelt, the AFWAL leaders were able to read to the delegates FDR's good wishes and his support for the use of consumer power "to support fair labor standards."[77] Second, the Federation ratified its constitution.

In its preamble, AFWAL gave itself a much wider mission than just organizing union and women's consumer power:

> The purposes of the American Federation of Women's Auxiliaries of Labor are to disseminate the principles of labor unionism throughout America; *to exert women's influence in the local, state and national legislative fields;* to include in the courses of primary and secondary schools the true facts about labor unions; and to use their collective buying power to promote the sale of Union-made goods and the patronage of union services, we, therefore, declare ourselves in favor of the formation of a thorough federation embracing all women's auxiliaries to recognized labor union organizations in America.[78]

The new organization quickly set about recruiting the two million auxiliary women—mostly the mothers, wives, spouses, and daughters of union men—already affiliated with the AFL's member unions.[79] For example, the AFWAL leaders worked with the Ladies Auxiliary of the Brotherhood of Sleeping Car Porters. Agnes Nestor and other labor feminists of the Chicago WTUL had helped organize the BSCP's Ladies Auxiliary in 1938. During the war, AFWAL reached out to this auxiliary and others like it, although they were careful not to upset the AFL's racially segregated structure. Many of the auxiliaries lined up behind the AFWAL's social, economic, and political agenda.[80] To increase membership, AFWAL officials also sought to start up new, directly affiliated locals. In some cases, this meant that the AFWAL organizers sought to poach existing WTUL locals. In this, the AFWAL was finally doing what Gompers wanted in 1924. The AFL was taking over the WTUL.

A case in point was the Tri-City Women's Trade Union League. Labor feminists in Rock Island and Moline, Illinois, and in Davenport, Iowa, had formed the group in 1941 as a way to support local organizing and strikes and to encourage the use of the union label and union service button. The Tri-City WTUL had been quite active, particularly in pushing for the union label. It sent out women to find out who supported union work and generated monthly lists of "fair" and "unfair" businesses.[81] The Tri-City local also became active in regional strikes. For this work, they had received some expert training. In January 1942, Agnes Nestor, acting as the president of the Chicago Women's Trade Union League, visited the group and led a discussion "on how the League can help in assisting workers during strike situations."[82] Just a month after Nestor visited, these WTUL women had an extraordinary meeting. At their February 6, 1942, gathering, a Mrs. Bagenstraus, the state organizer for AFWAL, joined the group, and she asked them to affiliate with the AFWAL. Bagenstraus told the women that the "Women's Trade Union League would progress more rapidly if they would affiliate with the American Federation of Women's Auxiliaries." At the end of her presentation, she explained the benefits of AFWAL membership, most likely presented her listeners with the brochure *What Is the AFWAL?,* and then "asked the members present to immediately offer their affiliations."[83] The Tri-City WTUL did not immediately affiliate. Instead, it had a serious debate. There was a livelier-than-usual meeting, with discussions about how the group could be "more patriotic" in meetings and how it could support "defense activities." The focus of the group was shifting, and now the question before it was whether it should move its local organization from the WTUL to the AFWAL. The answer was yes. In March 1942, the Tri-City WTUL women not only affiliated with AFWAL but also changed their union's name to the Tri-City AFWAL.[84] It is not known whether the WTUL or labor feminists like Agnes Nestor disapproved of this change, but neither the organization nor the women who supported it could have been terribly pleased.

Still, AFWAL organizing met little resistance. Certainly, there were some male unionists who gave a cautious look. As Ira Ornburn remarked, in 1941, "some of my associates were a little skeptical at the outset for fear that the auxiliaries might interfere with the inner workings of the unions." But, Ornburn explained, such fears quickly dissipated as male unionists realized that "this has definitely not been the case."[85] From the beginning through the middle of the Second World War, the AFWAL and its affiliates had a very intimate relationship with the Union Label and Trade Department and focused almost entirely on women's consumption habits. The leaders of AFWAL—namely organization president Mrs. Herman H. Lowe (who never revealed her given name publicly) and AFWAL secretary-treasurer Ira M. Ornburn—knew that women made nearly eight out of every ten household purchases. Encouraging them to look for the union label or the union service button could indeed have an enormous impact on organized labor's fortunes.[86]

Although the AFWAL never deviated from its consumer focus, by late 1942, it also struck out on its own to push a labor feminist legislative agenda at both the national and the local level. In this work, the

Auxiliary Federation had become a full-fledged rival of the WTUL. The critical juncture was AFWAL's 1942 convention. To outsiders, this meeting did not appear too special. In his letter to the convention, President Roosevelt wrote:

> In helping to carry on the life of our people and doing your daily duty of keeping the home fires burning and promoting the family welfare, you are helping to make the essential sacrifices—conserving resources, sharing commodities and helping in the protection of civilians against the menaces of air raids, malnutrition and epidemics.[87]

But, at the meeting, the labor feminists assembled broke out of their traditional gender roles so aptly defined by FDR. In an address to the delegates, Federation secretary-treasurer Ornburn proclaimed AFWAL a part of "all social movements" in the United States by its fight to raise living standards, to enact protective labor legislation, and to change American consumers' habits.[88] The union label campaign was still at the center of AFWAL's work, but at the 1942 convention, AFWAL began to branch out in other, more political areas. AFWAL president Lowe accepted a position within the Office of Price Administration. Moreover, by the middle of the war, the organization had taken political positions on a range of issues. For example, in addition to resolutions about the union labor, nutrition, and wartime patriotism, the delegates at the 1942 convention also passed resolutions opposing the poll tax in southern states and supporting government-sponsored price control (i.e., the Office of Price Administration).[89] Similarly, during the war, the AFWAL monthly bulletin had a regular legislative section in which members were urged to support the repeal of the poll tax, as well as the passage of bill creating a permanent federal fair employment practice commission. Similarly, AFWAL members were admonished to do all they could to defeat the anti-strike Smith-Connally bill. The AFWAL leaders also told women to get out and vote. In October 1944, the bulletin had this to say about the approaching presidential election:

> America is faced with an election by minority vote. Eligible voters are TOO busy to be concerned. IS THIS YOUR ATTITUDE? If so, think the matter over. Then WAKE UP to the fact that this is YOUR COUNTRY, YOUR home and the place the youth of the land is fighting and dying for. CAN YOU DO LESS THAN BE WILLING TO VOTE FOR IT?[90]

Political activities like this also took place at the local level. In May 1943, the Women's Auxiliary to the Tri-City Federation of Trade Unions discussed and apparently gave some support to a proposed equal-pay bill, which had been introduced in the Illinois state legislature.[91] The support of women's organizations like AFWAL and its affiliates made a difference. Before World War II, only Michigan and Montana had equal-pay laws. By 1950, Illinois, Massachusetts, New York, Washington, and five other states had similar laws.[92] By the war's end, the AFWAL had eclipsed the WTUL, which disbanded in 1950. The AFL finally had its women's bureau, or at least a kind of one.

The Limits of Wartime Change

The wartime experiences of AFWAL and labor feminists generally show that wartime conditions did provide opportunities for reform. The individual AFL woman worker also must have seen this potential for change. Although there is no way of knowing for sure, one might suppose that Beulah, the Moore Dry Dock shipyard worker, probably wanted to keep her job after the war. For women like her, who had spent most of their adult lives laboring at various, largely unremunerative jobs, the future seemed bright. At least, it did in late 1944. In fact, the entire war appeared to be heading toward an end, and there was some talk about soldiers being home for the holidays. For many women, thoughts about the postwar world included desires to keep those new, high-paying positions in the factories, in the fields, and in government service. The concern, shared by both men and women, was that layoffs would be commonplace in the reconversion process and good jobs scarce.

But initially, that did not happen. In April 1944, War Manpower Commission officials conducted a survey of five St. Louis factories engaged in production of war materials. That spring, nearly ten thousand women had been laid off as federal war planners began to sense an end to the global conflict. Federal officials recorded two interesting trends. First, although the release of ten thousand women workers was a startlingly abrupt and disturbing occurrence, women workers maintained their overall position in these factories. As table 4.7 shows, women constituted 42.4 percent of all workers in the five companies before the lay-

TABLE 4.7
Percentage of Women Employed in Five St. Louis Firms

	Before Cutbacks, November 1943	*After Layoffs, March 1944*
Company A	11.4	11.3
Company B	40.3	40.3
Company C	48.8	50.8
Company D	44.3	56.9
Company E	36.2	48.7
Five Companies	42.4	42.3

SOURCE: AFL file memo, 6 April 1944, AFL Papers, series 8A, box 32.

offs and 42.3 percent after them. The second trend that WMC investigators noted was that half of all the laid off women workers found other employment in the St. Louis area. Two thousand of them were hired in essential wartime jobs; 3,500 found work in nonessential plants. Four thousand women failed to find work. Half of those returned to the home, while the rest sought work in St. Louis and elsewhere. These numbers indicated what historians later came to see as the norm: most wartime women workers wanted to and in many cases did remain in the labor market during the transition from war to peace.[93]

For their part, at least in late 1944, many employers were indicating that they wanted to keep their newly employed female workforce. There were some who did so out of cold calculation. One shipyard production adviser commented that maintaining women on the docks after the war would serve "mainly as an incentive for greater efficiency and accomplishment from males. A limited number of women, properly employed, could possibly serve to good advantage in establishing the required tempo of production."[94] Not all managers were so devious. Many must have agreed with Under Secretary of War Robert P. Patterson, who echoed his World War I predecessor:

> In the arsenals, in the ports of embarkation, in the motor centers, in all the War Department installations, [women's] skills are invaluable and their devotion to duty is proven. They are testing guns, making ammunition, fixing motors, sewing uniforms, inspecting ordnance, driving trucks, doing many of the thousand and one jobs that are necessary to keep the machinery of war moving.
>
> I salute them for their faithfulness, their cheerful courage, and their patriotism.[95]

Survey after survey showed that American employers found their new women workers valuable, efficient, and essential. When asked whether they had plans to retain these workers, they responded affirmatively. In a 1944 U.S. Women's Bureau Survey, government investigators noted that "a prominent shipbuilder" (most likely Kaiser) had repeatedly stated publicly that it planned to employ at least 50 percent of its wartime female workforce. Officials at a major automotive company (probably Ford) stated that although it probably would not maintain its current percentage of women workers (i.e., 40 percent), it intended to make women 20 to 30 percent of all its workers. U.S. Chamber of Commerce president Eric Johnston perhaps best expressed this sentiment when, speaking for his constituents, he publicly promised that "women will be able to keep almost every gain they have made in industry—in numbers employed, in better types of jobs, in higher wages."[96]

Close observers knew that such platitudes would become empty and meaningless unless serious plans were made and put into action. The idea was to avoid the terrible mistakes from the post–World War I period, when the federal government failed to plan for reconversion. In 1919, the sudden shift from war to peace had come without warning. As government contracts were summarily canceled, thousands of women and men were thrown out of work. Compounding the problem was the War Department's thoughtless demobilization, which resulted in the creation of an army of unemployed veterans. "Better planning," U.S. Women's Bureau officials hoped in 1944, would improve on the experiences that "were seen in 1918."[97]

As we examine in great detail in chapter 7, American labor leaders invested a lot of time and energy in postwar planning, as did the federal government. In terms of women workers, by the end of the war, there were three major plans concerning the transition to peace. The AFL had one, as did the CIO. The U.S. Women's Bureau also put forth a blueprint. Agnes Nestor led the team working on the AFL report. She must have had a feeling of déjà vu, as she had done similar work toward the end of the first global war. This time, however, she was just working with the Federation. William Green had created the AFL's Post-War Planning Committee in December 1942. The Committee's chair was Matthew Woll. Green named Nestor to the Committee to represent the interests of the AFL's women workers. As she had during the First World War, Nestor discovered quickly that her concerns were secondary. Once again, it seemed that labor feminists had been invited to the party but were not allowed to dance. Nestor, Rose Schneiderman, and Sallie D. Clinebell (her colleagues on the women workers subcommittee) were largely isolated from the main group and had no impact on its final decisions concerning the AFL's ideas about a postwar United States. Nestor's comments after World War I still rang true: it was still a "man's world," and women in the labor movement were still treated like a "fifth wheel."[98] Nestor and her subcommittee colleagues nonetheless dutifully did their research and analysis. Their thoughts, however, were not included in the AFL's official and final postwar planning report. Rather, they were published separately in 1944 under the underachieving title *Women Workers* and as an article in the *American Federationist* under Nestor's name and more appropriately titled "Working Women After Victory." This pamphlet, which had a very small circulation, contained the postwar platform for the Federation's labor feminists.[99]

In *Women Workers,* Nestor summarized the dramatic wartime gains of women workers. "One of the striking developments during the war," she wrote, "has been the number of women employed in occupations which had previously been considered suitable only for men."[100] During World War I, there had been similar developments, but not on the scale seen during World War II. The growth numbers were truly staggering. Since 1939, there had been a nearly a 600 percent increase in the number of women workers in the automobile industry, an 800 percent increase in the heavy-machine industries, and a 2700 percent increase in the transportation equipment industry. Nestor then laid out the essential question: "what will happen to these women workers and how many will want to need to stay in the labor force?"[101] In answering that question, she quoted AFL statistics that mirrored the unpublished WMC survey of St. Louis. Eighty percent of all women workers, Nestor stated, wanted and needed to stay in the labor market after the war. She argued that employers would need them. Because of death, disablement, and demobilization, there would be a shortage of male workers. Because of the war, the United States now had a highly trained and able female work force willing to pick up the slack.

But there needed to be some safeguards. Adhering to her labor feminist philosophy, Nestor called for legislative protections for women, for equal pay for equal work, and for the widespread unionization of women workers. As she put it, "through trade union agreements and through legislation obtained through trade union activity, their physical, social and economic well-being must be fully protected." The AFL supported this position fully and had actually approved this exact language at its 1944 convention in New Orleans.[102] Finally, Nestor's committee also demanded the adoption of eight basic standards for women workers in the postwar period, described in the pamphlet:

1. Equal opportunity with men for training and retraining.
2. Equal opportunity for placement in work they seek through United States Employment Service and union placement service.
3. No discrimination in rates of pay on the job, or in starting rates.
4. Legal and industrial protection against work hazards and extension of legal maximum limitation of hours for women to not more than eight hours a day or six days a week in states where women are not protected by such laws.
5. Restoration of state protective legislation suspended or lowered during the war.
6. Enactment of State Wage and Hour laws to extend to intrastate workers the provisions of the Fair Labor Standards Act now applied to only workers in interstate industries.
7. Increase the minimum hourly rates; first, to not less than 65 cents, then up to 75 cents.
8. Reduction of the age eligibility of women to sixty years for retirement benefits under social insurance, with specific inclusion of the dependents of women.[103]

After the AFL Post-War Planning Committee and the Executive Council accepted it, Nestor's report was reprinted as a pamphlet. The last page of the document listed all the members of the committee, placing Matthew Woll's and David Dubinsky's names before Nestor's. Schneiderman's and Clinebell's names did not appear on the document at all. This could mean that the entire and official postwar committee took ownership of the document. Most likely, it served as a reminder that, as Nestor put it, women still lived in a "man's world." The fact that the final AFL Post-War Planning Committee report did not include a section on women workers suggests the latter.

The CIO and the U.S. Women's Bureau offered postwar visions similar to that of the AFL. Ironically, given the level of commitment to women workers, it is somewhat surprising that the CIO never produced a specific postwar plan, as the Federation had. However, in various statements toward the end of the Second World War, the Congress made its position quite clear. The leaders of the CIO backed most of the ideas of labor feminists, although no one put the arguments in that frame. Rather, like the AFL, the CIO "believe[d] in equal pay for equal work, no matter by whom performed." It also supported the movement to end "all discrimination against the employment of women."[104] Equal opportunity in training and employment were also at the top of the CIO's agenda. Finally, the Congress formally opposed the Equal Rights Amendment and chided "organized labor for . . . [not acting] vigorously enough in exposing the dangers of this proposal and its threat to protective legislation."[105]

The U.S. Women's Bureau unveiled its postwar plan at a government, labor, and women's groups conference in Washington, D.C., on December 5, 1944. Thirty-one labor and women's organizations attended to hear and debate the Bureau's plan. Two principles were the foundation of the Women's Bureau's recommendations. First, Frieda Miller, the newly appointed director of the Women's Bureau, called for more careful analysis of the impending employment transitions for all American workers. Second, with that information, Miller called on the establishment of reasonable policies to guide the reconversion of the economy and to prevent unnecessary layoffs of women, as well as job discrimination. Miller went on to outline a list of postwar guidelines that looks extraordinarily similar to the AFL's list: the unfettered use of public employment services, equal access to job training, the establishment of national equal-pay-for-equal-work standards, and the restoration of state and federal protective labor laws.[106]

Conclusion

If there was one lesson that women workers and labor feminists drew from their experience in the First World War, it was that plans and policies were one thing; action was another. Any woman organizer or WTUL member would have known this after decades of working with the AFL. But, because of all the rapid and vast transformations during the Second World War, many thought that a moment for change had arrived. In the end, they were correct, but changing the gender structure of work in the United States required a much slower and longer campaign than these reformers could have guessed. At root, the problem lay in the assumption at the root of the reconversion plans of the AFL, the CIO, and the U.S. Women's Bureau. Although largely unstated, all three clearly hinged on the involvement of the federal government to create equal educational and employment opportunities, to establish and maintain protective legislation for women workers, and to secure and enforce antidiscrimination laws and policies. But, although there were sympathetic individuals within the government, such as Eleanor Roosevelt, Frieda Miller, Anna Rosenberg, and Mary Anderson, the vast number of men in power positions did not share the labor feminist agenda. In fact, they opposed it. One can readily see that this was the case in the congressional deliberations on the 1945 Full Employment Bill, which was the cornerstone of the postwar liberal agenda to ensure employment for all Americans. The first draft of the bill stated that "all Americans able to work and seeking work have the right to useful, remunerative, regular, and full-time employment , and it is the policy of the United States to assure the existence at all times of sufficient employment opportunities to enable all Americans who have finished their schooling and *who do not have full-time housekeeping responsibilities freely to exercise this right* [emphasis added]." Utah's Democratic senator Abe Murdock raised an objection to this language, stating that his colleagues should not exclude housewives from "any opportunity that is open to any other American." Senator James E. Murray (D-Montana), who had co-sponsored the bill, disagreed, arguing that he did not want the bill to move women out of the homes and into the factories. Murdock insisted that Congress should not "make an exception of any class," but to no avail, even though labor feminists in the U.S. Women's Bureau and within both labor federations argued that women workers as consumers were an essential element to any plan for a full-employment economy.[107] As a group of labor feminists within the War Manpower Commission had written at the war's height:

> The Government and industry must not assume that all women can be treated as the reserve group during war only, nor should those who wish to stay in the labor market be accused of taking men's jobs. The right of the individual women to work must be recognized and provided for, just as the right of the individual man to work.[108]

Clearly, those who created and enforced the laws of the federal government thought differently.

In addition to the conservatives whose sentiments could be heard in the halls of Congress, the leadership of both the AFL and the CIO did not push hard for women's issues. This was especially true of the American Federation of Labor. It is not clear whether President Green ever saw women workers, beyond their roles as mothers, as supporters of the labor movement and as a reserve industrial army. Despite the changes in the American Federation of Women's Auxiliaries of Labor, to Green, women were still primarily housewives, not feminists with any particular prolabor agenda. In 1944, William Green sent a letter to all women auxiliaries of labor and the AFWAL, asking their support for continued wartime economic controls. He couched his plea in gendered words that reveal how he viewed auxiliary women:

> It is time for American housewives to speak up and make sure that powers and procedures in the hands of government agencies are not used exclusively to protect the producer and dealer and that they are used to safeguard the interests of the housewife and of all consumers.
>
> Housewives will get no protection unless they speak up and until they act. It is up to the union housewives to make sure that they act effectively through their organizations and as individuals. Congress will not turn a deaf ear if thousands of housewives all over the country make their plight and their problem known. We ask your auxiliary to launch a campaign which we feel sure will produce results. Every housewife should be asked to write down her experience and describe her needs and difficulties in buying necessary apparel for her family and her children. She should also suggest remedies. We suggest that this time housewives use a new approach to get action. We ask that they put this information in letters addressed, not to Congressmen, but to wives of Congressmen. We also ask that each housewife keeps a copy or a record of what she has written and turns that copy to her auxiliary so that reports could be prepared by each auxiliary.[109]

Women within the AFL might have mounted some resistance to the AFL's leadership view of them, but they had yet to permeate the power structure. At the national level, there were few high-ranking Federation women. Even Agnes Nestor and Florence Thorne were not taken very seriously. Moreover, at the local level, women unionists were routinely excluded from leadership positions. In its 1945 survey of midwestern unionism, the U.S. Women's Bureau concluded that, although 50 percent of the unions surveyed had women in official positions, "the majority of women members did not actively participate in the union program." Part of the problem, of course, was male "prejudice and antagonism toward women."[110] Some women themselves did not feel that their wartime union jobs were permanent positions and therefore did not see the need to participate in union business. Whatever the case, women unionists were not yet a political force to be reckoned with. Of course, this was not merely the case within the AFL. Generally speaking, the needs and desires of wartime women workers were ignored in the euphoria of the postwar period, when they were expected and in some cases forced to return to their prewar positions. After all, women had been accepted on the shop floors only "under the stress of necessity." The AFL had been willing to sacrifice its gender mores and traditions, but these exclusive rules were suspended for the duration only. It was not long afterward, however, that women's disillusionment with the immediate postwar conditions in the United States launched another movement of feminists, many of whom sought to finish the work begun by the labor feminists, including those inside the AFL during the Second War World.[111]

5

Union Against Union
The AFL and CIO Rivalry

Primarily as a result of the AFL-CIO cleavage, Manhattan cutter and Montgomery lint-head, Boston shoe-worker and Blue Mountain lumberjack alike run the risk that their new lifeline of social and economic rights will become a rope of sand; that their modern Magna Charta, the Wagner Act, will be amended into nullity; that their political potency will be castrated into a prurient eunuchdom; that their ability to strike, to boycott, to picket, will continue to be curtailed as in Oregon, Wisconsin, Pennsylvania, and many other states; that the internal affairs of unions will be more and more regulated by a national government responding to the pressure of a public opinion rendered increasingly hostile by the repercussions of the AFL-CIO feud.

—Herbert Harris, *Labor's Civil War,* 1940[1]

It may be the most famous punch in American history. At the 1935 American Federation of Labor convention in Atlantic City, New Jersey, John L. Lewis again led his supporters in an attempt to force the AFL to commit to organizing the unorganized on the basis of industry. In other words, he wanted the Federation to grant industrial union charters when workers in mass-production industries such as steel or rubber wanted them. At the 1935 convention, the heated debates over this method of organizing finally boiled over into a fist fight between two larger-than-life unionists, Lewis, president of the United Mine Workers, and William "Big Bill" Hutcheson, head of the Carpenters' Union. After several rhetorical and political defeats for industrial unionism, Lewis introduced yet another resolution, one that would give rubber workers the right to an industrywide organization. That was the final straw for Big Bill, who stridently objected that the issue had been settled. Lewis countered by raising a point of order. Hutcheson heckled back that "this thing of raising points of order all the time on minor delegates is rather small potatoes."[2] Unable to contain his animosity toward Hutcheson and the Federation any longer, Lewis strode over to Big Bill and smashed him squarely in the face, symbolically and abruptly dividing the House of Labor into two groups—those who favored Lewis's vision of industrial unionism and those who did not. Thus, the Committee for Industrial Organization (later the Congress for Industrial Organizations) sprung from a public display of union machismo. But this was much more than a contest between two union chiefs. To the leaders and members of both organizations, it was a life-or-death struggle for the hearts, minds, and dues of American workers.

This chapter examines the origins of the split between the AFL and the CIO and their rivalry during the Second World War. Historians have all but ignored this period in the twenty-year struggle between the AFL and the CIO. Rather, scholars have focused on the 1930s, and for good reason. From 1935 through 1939, despite pleas from influential politicians and labor leaders, the two organizations waged fierce battles in the factories, forests, harbors, and mines. There were some notable exceptions, such as the unique labor harmony that prevailed in Kenosha, Wisconsin. And yet, as we will see, most conflicts resembled the vicious AFL-versus-CIO bout in Oregon. The question during the war was this: were the two organizations willing to sacrifice their rivalry for the sake of the war effort? In the end, both the AFL and the CIO were unable to put patriotism above union partisanship. In other words, as the case of copper mining shows, the AFL and the CIO's near-death embrace continued, unaffected by the war.

A House Divided

American labor's most divisive internecine conflict was rooted in the upheavals that followed the Haymarket Square Massacre in 1886. Soon after the incident, in Chicago, the Knights of Labor began to decline precipitously. Into the void stepped the members of the Federation of Organized Trade and Labor Unions (established in 1881), which called for a meeting in Columbus, Ohio. There, labor representatives refashioned a new trade union movement and created the American Federation of Labor. Even more than its predecessor, this Federation was fashioned according to the British "new union" model, which emphasized benefit systems, high dues, centralized control over local unions, and collective bargaining. The AFL also set itself apart from the Knights of Labor by organizing mainly skilled workers, generally on occupational lines.[3]

Still, the AFL was begrudgingly—but not blindly—committed to craft unionism. In 1901, the Federation adopted the so-called Scranton Declaration, which encouraged the amalgamation of kindred trades into larger entities. The hope was to reduce the number of unions (and union competition) within any one industry. So, for example, the Federation's Executive Council encouraged the Metal Mechanics Union to join the International Association of Machinists and the Wood Workers' International Union to become part of the United Brotherhood of Carpenters. Although these amalgamated unions were not industrial unions per se, they were a major step in that direction. The AFL reaffirmed the Scranton Declaration in 1912, when it was being challenged by the Industrial Workers of the World.[4] Then, in the 1920s, the AFL reorganized itself to foster unions within mass-production industries. In 1927, a jurisdictional dispute within the AFL's Metal Trades Department over workers in the automobile industry developed into a full-blown conflict that threatened craft harmony. Several unions, all within the Metal Trades, claimed dominion over the automobile industry. John Frey, head of the Metal Trades, sought a compromise to stave off a membership-raiding union war. After several meetings, representatives from the Carpenters', Firemen and Oilers', and Sheet Metal Workers' Unions walked away from the conference table. All seemed lost, but at the last moment a solution was found. Autoworkers were allowed to form their own plantwide unions directly chartered by the Federation without any specific ties to an international union. Additional federal unions, as these bodies were called, were subsequently created to avoid similar craft union fights, and these were moderately successful in organizing industrial workers. In other words, in many cases, they worked. However, the old problem died hard. Union bickering was not eliminated even among the federal unions. In what might have been the most outrageous case, five different federal unions in Cincinnati, Ohio, quarreled for three months over the allegiance of one worker! As was typical, Federation leaders procrastinated in settling the dispute. Some became so disgusted with the AFL that they returned their union cards.[5]

The issue of industrial workers and the best way to organize them became all the more pressing after the election of President Franklin D. Roosevelt. The National Industrial Recovery Act, a centerpiece of the first one hundred days, contained the famous section 7(a), which encouraged workers to join unions and to bargain collectively. Thousands moved to form unions, and thousands more rushed to join. As an organization, the AFL was caught off guard, unable to handle the masses who wanted to sign up. Although about 500,000 workers joined the AFL in 1933 and roughly 400,000 signed on in 1934, the Federation could have added even more members.[6] But the organization's leadership wanted people to slow down so that crafts could claim their jurisdictions and workers could take skills tests. Of course, the AFL approached even more cautiously the recruiting of women and minorities. Some of the more radical recruiters and recruits did not want to wait while the Federation sorted its new members and while enthusiasm waned. Many feared that further delays could prove costly, and they did.[7]

At the 1934 AFL convention, in San Francisco, a cadre of AFL officials, including John L. Lewis of the United Mine Workers, Charles P. Howard of the International Typographical Union, and David Dubinsky of the International Ladies Garment Workers Union, pressed the AFL's Executive Council to be more aggressive in organizing industrial workers and to grant those new unions industrial charters. Their call was strongly opposed by John P. Frey, head of the Metal Trades Department and self-appointed defender (and historian) of craft unionism.[8] As the rift among AFL members grew, Frey and his supporters arranged a temporary compromise. Instead of having a convention vote on industrial unionism, Frey agreed to head up an investigatory committee to examine all aspects of the issue. The report was due at the 1935 convention at Atlantic City.

Frey's report probably surprised no one. He came out squarely against industrial unionism as Lewis had proposed it. At the convention, he told the delegates that a movement was "now being made by others to compel us to abandon the form of organization which we have had from the beginning, and which has proven satisfactory to us."[9] Frey upheld the declaration of the San Francisco convention, which had stated that to "fully protect the jurisdictional rights of all trade unions organized upon craft lines and afford them every opportunity for development," no change in organizing mass production industries should take place.[10]

Lewis, Howard, and Dubinsky provided the convention with their own minority report, arguing "the time had arrived when common sense demands the organization policies of the American Federation of Labor must be molded to meet present day needs." "In the great mass production industries," the report continued, "industrial organization is the only solution."[11] The presentation of the reports led to several heated shouting matches between Lewis and Frey and between Lewis and AFL vice president Matthew Woll. Then William Green put the issue to a vote. He asked the delegates to support either the majority or the minority report. Frey's report was accepted by a vote of 18,024 to 10,933. Lewis then tried several rear-guard actions, proposing an expansion of the jurisdiction of the Mine, Mill, and Smelter Workers to cover all western mines. That was rejected by a vote of 18,464 to 10,897. Lewis's next motion was his last. He helped the Rubber Workers Union propose that it be allowed to form an industrywide organization. That sparked the tussle between Lewis and Hutcheson, which was emblematic not only of the break between the AFL and the newly formed CIO but also of the relationship between the two organizations during World War II.

Shortly after the raucous AFL convention, Lewis called for a meeting of national and international unions that were sympathetic to the cause of industrial unionism. At the headquarters of the United Mine Workers, in Washington, D.C., the Committee for Industrial Organization was formed, with Lewis as chairman, Charles Howard as secretary, and John Brophy of the United Mine Workers as the CIO executive director. The other leaders were Sidney Hillman, of the Amalgamated Clothing Workers of America; David Dubinsky, of the International Ladies' Garment Workers' Union; Thomas F. McMahon, of the United Textile Workers; Harvey C. Fremming, of the Oil Field, Gas, and Refinery Workers of America; Max Zaritsky, of the Cap and Millinery Department, United Hatters, Cap and Millinery Workers' International Union; and Thomas H. Brown, of the International Union of Mine, Mill, and Smelter Workers. The CIO's original purpose was to promote industrial unions "under the banner and in affiliation with the American Federation of Labor."[12] The CIO also dedicated itself to modernizing the AFL while avoiding injury to the established federal labor unions, those catch-all unions that behaved like industrial unions. Although word of the CIO's birth spread quickly to the AFL's headquarters, John Lewis punctuated the bold move by resigning from his post as Federation vice president. Lewis's message to William Green, the AFL's president, was just two lines long. A few weeks later, Lewis wrote to Green again suggesting that the dispute could be settled with new AFL leadership and called on the AFL's president to step down and thus to "return to [his] father's house."[13] Green fired back a stern reply. He told Lewis that he would "carry out the policies adopted at annual conventions of the American Federation of Labor." In other words, the convention had voted against Lewis's plan for industrial unionism, and Green was going to uphold the wishes of the delegates. Green also told Lewis "in the spirit of good sportsmanship [to take] it on the chin" and to acquiesce to the decision. Green wrote that he had done just this on plenty of occasions. Thus he declined Lewis's offer, concluding that "I am in my father's house as part of the family of organized labor." "It is my firm purpose," he wrote, "to remain there sharing with all its members their feelings of disappointment when they fail to achieve and of happiness when victories are won."[14]

Behind the formality of the exchange, Green was seething with anger. It is somewhat ironic that William Green, Lewis's protégé in the United Mine Workers, took such a hard line against his former mentor; Green attacked the backers of industrial unions with an almost pathological animosity. But, after years as the AFL's president, Green had found the resolve and the courage to oppose Lewis, arguably the most powerful unionist in America.[15] Fundamentally, Green also believed in majority rule. Thus, regardless of the personalities involved, the issue of industrial organizing had been settled at the 1935 convention by a majority vote of the delegates. Therefore, further discussion or action was moot. Democracy had worked. Green viewed the CIO with great suspicion as an antidemocratic rival, which would foment conflict and destroy labor unity. CIO leaders of course denied that they intended to raid current or future members of the AFL.[16] It made little difference.

Whatever the differences in perception, Green quickly went on the offensive, trying to disrupt the CIO's organizational drives planned for 1936. His actions were unprecedented in the fifty-year history of the AFL. At several times, there had existed dual unions within the AFL. For instance, the National Building Trades Council and the Structural Buildings Trades Alliance, both affiliated with the AFL, competed against each other, and the AFL's Executive Council never took action or sanctioned either. But, convinced of the righteousness of his position, Green would not turn the other cheek.[17] His intent was to suspend and then expel all

CIO unions and members. Like a dog with a bone, Green refused to relinquish his quest to punish those unions that had joined the Committee.

In late 1936, despite several reassuring pledges that the CIO was committed to the AFL and was not a dual organization, Green prepared to kick it out of the Federation. There was, however, a serious legal hurdle to surmount. Did the AFL Executive Council have the power to do this? Green's lawyer, Charlton Ogburn, studied the question and the AFL constitution and concluded that it did.[18] Even sympathetic historians of the AFL, such as Philip Taft, believe that Ogburn was wrong and that he, Green, and the AFL Executive Council suffered from something that "can only be explained as a paralysis of intelligence."[19]

Why were the AFL's leaders so dead set on destroying the CIO? Certainly, given the fact that similar types of situations had existed in the Federation's past, one might have expected a more conciliatory stance. But Green and the Executive Council were not at all sympathetic. Aside from a "paralysis of intelligence," could there have been something else involved? Green and the members of the Executive Council never quite publicly explained the reasons behind their actions against the CIO. In fact, in the several AFL publications, such as the *American Federationist,* the AFL leadership made no mention of the CIO or the rift within organized labor. Nevertheless, one might surmise that it had something to do with the AFL's battles with the Western Federation of Miners (WFM) and the Industrial Workers of the World (IWW). When the WFM organized in 1893, it initially avoided all association with what it dubbed the "American Separation of Labor."[20] As the WFM made rapid gains in the western nonferrous mine fields, relations with the AFL soured considerably. At the twenty-fifth AFL convention, in 1905, Samuel Gompers spoke of the ingratitude of the WFM, which had used AFL funds to fight court battles in Colorado. Of course, the AFL leaders were horrified by WFM's critical role in the creation of the IWW in Chicago in 1905. At that famous gathering, several WFM leaders spoke of the need for an "industrial congress" because of the failures of the AFL. William "Big Bill" Haywood pronounced: "It has been said that this convention was to form an organization rival to the AFL. This is a mistake. We are here for the purpose of forming a labor organization."[21] Gompers and the AFL (with the assistance of conservative employers and the federal government) fought back the IWW's challenge. For its part, the AFL tried to convince workers that it did support industrial unionism, albeit along craft lines.[22] In any case, when Green encountered the CIO, he might have seen it as Gompers saw the WFM and the IWW. In this light, the CIO was not just a rival labor organization that threatened to divide the American labor movement. It was a syndicate trying to destroy the AFL. To Green, it was a fight for survival.

Given Green's hostility and the history of the AFL and other labor organizations, it is interesting to note that not all of the AFL's officials saw the situation the same way. In particular, not everyone supported the movement to suspend and expel the CIO unions. At an Executive Council meeting, in July 1936, the Teamsters' Daniel Tobin pointed out that the Council had refused to suspend charters when AFL unions attacked the Teamsters. AFL vice president George Harrison also disagreed with Green. He noted that in the past, Sam Gompers had opposed suspension of unions that had disobeyed the will of the Federation. The case in point was the Carpenters and Joiners, who in 1915 had refused to comply with a ruling that awarded the machinists' union jurisdiction over millwrights. Although an adjustment committee had recommended that the Carpenters and Joiners be suspended, Gompers rose from his seat in protest, saying that while the Carpenters' actions had caused "pain and anguish . . . and [had] done grave and great injustice to other organizations," the actions did not warrant such a penalty.[23] But even the invocation of Gompers's ghost did not alter Green's determination. At the end of the July meeting, charges were formulated, and a trial date was set: August 3, 1936.[24]

The August 3 meeting began with a hearing of a peace proposal from Henry Ohl, of the Wisconsin Federation of Labor. The leaders of WFL called on the Executive Council to end the conflict and to join the CIO in an organizational drive in mass-production industries. The issue of jurisdictions and union structure, Ohl argued before the AFL's high command, could be decided at a later date. The council members mocked and belittled Ohl and moved to suspend the ten CIO unions.[25] That day's actions set in motion two decades of union-against-union fights.[26]

While John Lewis and his CIO compatriots were promising that there would not be any union raiding, in fact this was going on. One of the most vicious conflicts occurred in Portland, Oregon. In 1936, twenty thousand lumber, sawmill, veneer, and furniture workers left the AFL's United Brotherhood of Carpenters and Joiners (UBCJ) and formed a rival International Woodworkers' Union (IWU), which received its CIO charter in 1937. "Big Bill" Hutcheson immediately retaliated against the IWU. One contemporary described Hutcheson as a "hard-boiled, porcine, three-hundred-pound, bellowing czar." It was commonly said of him that "God made the forests and gave them to Bill."[27] The politically conservative, irascible head of the Carpenters was not going to give an inch, and he ordered his men not to handle so-called CIO wood. He also negotiated an informal agreement with the Teamsters so that CIO wood would not get hauled. Then the goon squads appeared, carrying pickets and protesting against any Oregon mill that bought wood lumbered by CIO workers. By December 1937, the Carpenters' boycott had forced eight sawmills to shut down. In monetary terms, the local lumber industry lost more than $9 million. Local employers pleaded with AFL and CIO officials to end the bickering, but without result. Rather, IWU and UBCJ members began literally fighting in the streets. On December 8, 1937, Portland's AFL Central Labor Council issued a statement condemning the CIO and threatening to boycott any mill that cooperated with the IWU. Finally, as Christmas approached and the Portland economy began to collapse from the lack of holiday sales, the increase in the number of families on relief, and the burden of widespread unemployment, the IWU caved. Woodworkers quit the CIO and returned to the AFL. Hutcheson had won, but organized labor in Oregon was about to lose.[28]

In November 1938, the citizens of Oregon, fed up with the battle between the AFL and the CIO and the collateral damage that accompanied it, voted 197,000 to 146,500 to restrict severely the rights of labor unions in the state. Sponsored by various large business organizations (collectively known as the Associated Farmers), Proposition 316-X outlawed picketing and striking unless a majority of all the employees agreed to such job actions. So, for example, if a union that represented a plant with 500 employees, 249 of whom belonged to a single craft union, wanted to go on strike, it could not do so legally because they it not have a majority of the plant's workers even if union members voted unanimously to strike. Moreover, the law completely banned jurisdictional strikes, strikes over union recognition, and all boycotts. Not only did the Oregon law shackle labor unions, but it also became a model for similar antiunion legislation in other states, such as Wisconsin.[29]

Although the fight in Oregon represented the typical relationship between the AFL and CIO both before the war and (as we will see) during it, there were some exceptions. One occurred in Kenosha, Wisconsin, where an unusual peace had been reached and maintained between the two organizations. During the Roosevelt years, Kenosha was a union town. Ninety-five percent of all industrial workers (many of whom worked at the large Nash-Kelvinator plant) there belonged to either an AFL or a CIO union. Seventy percent of the town's government employees were union members, as were 50 percent of its service workers. In 1936, as the national leaderships of the CIO and AFL were preparing to do battle, Kenosha's local labor leaders sat down and made a deal. Those unions in Kenosha whose international organization had joined the CIO would by default become CIO unions. However, it was agreed that no other unions would move to the CIO. Dyed-in-the-wool partisans on both sides of course objected, but they were outvoted. As a result, there were no jurisdictional fights, and there was no union raiding. This was true at Nash, where the UAW-CIO was the dominant union; at Kenosha Full Fashioned Mills, where workers belonged to the CIO's Textile Workers Unions; and at the Simmons Company, where the workers belonged to an AFL federal union.[30]

Exactly why Kenosha workers got along so well is something of a mystery. The popular labor writer Herbert Harris suggested that regional sensibility had something to do with it. As he wrote somewhat sarcastically in 1940, "lacking the sophistication of their peers on the national scene, they are still 'simple' enough to believe that the systole and diastole of unionism is unity, standing together for a common cause."[31] Whatever the truth about midwestern simplicity, there may be more to it. Wisconsin's state labor leaders, such as Henry Ohl, promoted peace and unity, which no doubt had an effect at the local level. Additionally, since the turn of the twentieth century, Kenosha's residents had been strongly prounion. Every September, Labor Day celebrations were attended by ten thousand people (that is, the entire town). Sponsored by the Trade and Labor Council, the day-long party began at Market Street and flowed to Anderson Park, where there was more drinking, games, and camaraderie. The solidarity displayed there was mirrored in the unity when the town's workers went on strike. For example, in May 1901, machinists from the five big employers (A. D. Meiselbach, Simmons, Jeffries, Chicago-Rockford Hosiery, and Badger Brass) walked off their jobs. Although the striking workers accepted a deal for less than they wanted, their action encouraged others to strike. During this wave of protests, from 1902 to 1917, Kenosha workers were successful in reducing hours and raising wages. In this kind of community where, as one historian has written, "organized labor . . . stood behind the efforts of workers who fought for higher wages," the divisions that plagued the national organizations seemed to have little local effect. During the Second World War, Kenosha's workers continued to put their working-class solidarity above any seemingly outside issues that threatened their harmonious town.[32]

The Peace That Never Came: AFL, CIO, and FDR

In some ways, the central question for those watching the AFL and CIO during World War II was this: was the relationship between the two organizations going to be like the peace in Kenosha or like the fight in Portland? Most decidedly, the answer was that the AFL and CIO continued their civil war, despite the attempts of many to patch together a peace. One has to look no further than the North American Aviation strike of June 1941 in Inglewood, California. North American was an essential war plant. Workers there made the famous P-51 Mustang interceptor, a vital key to the Allies' war plans. In the spring and summer of 1941, labor relations at the factory deteriorated significantly. The Communist leadership of the local United Automobile Workers (CIO) fought to win over the plant. The International Association of Machinists (AFL) opposed them. Although the UAW won the NLRB election and thus collective bargaining rights, the IAM waged an unrelenting campaign of harassment to discredit the UAW and to win the allegiance of the airplane workers. The IAM saw its best chance in June 1941, when the local UAW went on strike. Despite criticism and calls to go back to work from CIO leaders, AFL leaders, and President Roosevelt, the strikers persisted. FDR finally sent federal troops to break the strike. The end of the strike satisfied no one. The radical leadership felt scorned; the workers felt betrayed; and the IAM was left out in the cold as the UAW remained in control of the factory.[33]

Despite his strong-arm tactics during the North American Aviation strike, President Roosevelt remained seriously concerned with the split between the AFL and the CIO. He tried in vain to get the labor federations to settle their prewar hostilities. Some historians have claimed that FDR's attempts at rapprochement were motivated by crude politics, particularly his fear that the divisions would cost the Democratic Party votes.[34] But, Roosevelt consistently wrote that it was his fear that the cracks within the House of Labor would weaken the ability of America to defend itself. Thus, as war clouds gathered in Europe, Roosevelt sought to unite the home front to strengthen the nation's defenses. Closing the breach between the AFL and CIO was a top priority. Yet, neither Dr. New Deal nor Dr. Win-the-War could heal the rift or repair the damage done to the labor movement.

From the beginning of the schism in the 1930s, President Roosevelt was interested and involved in the peace movement between the AFL and the CIO.[35] Yet, at first, he worked in the background and through intermediaries, particularly Secretary of Labor Frances Perkins. Nonetheless, it was the Federation itself that took the first initiative and offered an olive branch shortly after the CIO broke away. Lewis rebuffed the attempt immediately.[36] However, in October 1936, the AFL Executive Council called for the creation of subcommittees of the two organizations to find an acceptable formula to reunite the organizations. After a year of false starts, representatives of the Federation and the CIO exchanged proposals. The CIO wanted the AFL to publicly endorse the organization of mass-production workers only by industry, to allow the CIO to return as an independent department, and to call a conference to work out the jurisdiction details. The AFL countered with a demand for the immediate return of the unions now in the CIO, the aggressive organizing of mass-production workers along both industrial and craft lines, and the dissolution of the CIO. By late December 1937, a secret agreement had been tentatively reached. The apparent sticking point was the future of the twenty CIO unions chartered since 1936. But both sides had reasoned that jurisdictional issues like this could be ironed out after reunification. The CIO's chief negotiator, Philip Murray, took this proposed deal to his boss, John L. Lewis. Meeting Lewis in his hotel room, Murray gave him the offer. While walking over to the window, Lewis glanced it over. Then according to legend, he took the paper, tore it to bits, and scattered the pieces to the street. There would be no deal.[37]

Was it all Lewis's fault? Could there have been peace in 1937? Shortly after the news broke that the peace talks had failed, William Green publicly pointed his finger at Lewis. In a 1938 speech, Green stated that "most common-sense people see through [the CIO's] camouflage by now and are sick of it." The deal, he continued, was scuttled by "someone behind the scenes," meaning Lewis.[38] AFL vice president Matthew Woll echoed Green in an interview with a *New York Times* reporter. He angrily said that "the road had actually been cleared for an agreement when our efforts were torpedoed and the conference was brought to an end." "From all indications," Woll concluded, "it would seem that the CIO wrecked the peace negotiations at the last moment because it perceived that the restoration of peace would make it impossible for those dominating the CIO to control its own organizations and much less the American Federation of Labor."[39] However, historians generally do not place all the blame on Lewis. His biographers, as well as the AFL's main historian, Philip Taft, maintain that Lewis could not have agreed to the 1937 peace deal. Reuniting with the Federation at that moment might have destroyed his movement. The years 1936 and 1937 were high-water years for the CIO. It signed up millions of workers. Even though the AFL was willing to accept back the twelve unions it had suspended, the CIO's work most likely would have been seriously hampered by the leaders like Frey, Green, Hutcheson, and Woll, who had opposed industrial unionism all along. Moreover, there were many outstanding issues that the deal did not address. Lewis would have seemed weak at best and a traitor at worst. And yet, as time went on, it became quite clear that Lewis simply did not want the CIO to return to the AFL. He did not want peace.[40]

The peace movement remained dormant until February 1939, when President Roosevelt personally and quietly contacted William Green and John Lewis and requested that they appoint new committees and find a new accord. His letters were delivered by the secretary of labor and appealed to the labor leaders' sense of fair play and good will. He wrote that they should come together

> *first,* because it is right, *second,* because the responsible officers from both groups seem to me to be ready and capable of making a negotiated and just peace, *third,* because your membership ardently desire peace and unity for the better ordering of their responsible life in the trade unions and in their communities, and *fourth,* because the Government of the United States and the people of America believe it to be a wise and almost necessary step for the further development of the cooperation between free men in a democratic society such as ours, I am writing to ask you to appoint a committee to represent your organization and to negotiate the terms of peace between the American Federation of Labor and the Congress of Industrial Organizations.

FDR pledged "whatever assistance we in the Government can give you in this matter."[41] Both union leaders responded affirmatively, although

Green was the first to acknowledge the letter and take up the charge. "I know you are moved by the highest and most noble considerations in the appeal which you make for a settlement," Green wrote. "Please be assured of my willingness to cooperate in every possible way . . . to establish and perpetuate peace within the ranks of Labor."[42]

The public's response to this announcement was astonishing. Unionists sent thousands of telegrams to Green, Lewis, FDR, and Labor Secretary Perkins. A typical one came from the Minneapolis's Sausage Makers Union Local 615, which sent the AFL a telegram calling on Green "to put forth every effort on your part to restore peace unity and harmony in the labor movement." And the union reminded him that "[p]ersonal viewpoints sometimes may be sacrificed to gain benefits of utmost importance to great masses of working people."[43] The International Association of Machinists, Lodge No. 364 (Stockton, California) sent Green a resolution, passed at its March 20, 1939 meeting:

> WHEREAS: President Roosevelt has seen fit to recognize the present controversy between the American Federation of Labor and the Congress of Industrial Organizations as being a determining factor in the future welfare of the Nation, and
>
> WHEREAS: The President has made a personal appeal to the Officer in Chief of both Organizations to again enter into friendly negotiations for a final settlement, and
>
> WHEREAS: Such peace negotiations as the President proposes could not be carried on without prejudice while workers are being pitted against each other, therefore be it
>
> RESOLVED: That Stockton Lodge No. 364 International Association of Machinists, do hereby go on record in regular meeting of March 17, 1939, as wholeheartedly endorsing the President's program of peace and unity in the ranks of Labor, and be it further
>
> RESOLVED: That the first condition of negotiation be an unqualified declaration by both the AFL and the CIO for the immediate abandonment of all boycotts and picket lines which have been established or are being considered as a means of settling jurisdiction.[44]

To get the ball rolling, on March 7, 1939, Roosevelt himself presided over the first peace meeting. In his opening statement, FDR again called on the representatives of the AFL and the CIO to negotiate a settlement of their differences "in good faith and with honor . . . for the best interests of labor and the country generally." He told them that he personally had received resolutions from labor unions representing more than a million workers in support of the talks. He admonished them to overcome their "extreme bitterness" and to follow the example of "many cities and towns . . . where the local CIO and AFL are working together in closest harmony." Finally, he gave some advice:

> I accept the premise that both sides want peace. That means, of course, that both sides go into conference with the idea of giving as well as getting. You are all experienced negotiators. You have been doing that all your lives. From that standpoint, this job ought to be easy for you.[45]

FDR's intervention had raised hopes. Secretary Perkins, who also attended the first peace meeting, told the press that the "outlook for peace is 'good.'"[46] But it was not going to be easy. The peace committees met several times in late March and early April, without much result. Then suddenly, once again, a settlement was within reach. The AFL negotiating team, headed by Harry Bates, of the Bricklayers Union, had made a major concession; the AFL agreed in principle to allow the CIO unions back into the AFL with their new memberships. For example, the United Mine Workers could return with its acquisitions since 1935, such as the coke and chemical workers. Both Green and Lewis scheduled a meeting for final negotiations. But, as a meeting neared, Lewis pulled the plug. On April 5, Lewis called Green on the telephone and told him that he could not meet because he had to attend a congressional hearing. No date was set for another meeting. Five days later, Secretary of Labor Frances Perkins called Matthew Woll, one of Green's lieutenants, asking what had happened and whether Lewis had completely ended the peace process. Woll told her that "the conversation with Lewis was entirely on a friendly basis, that Lewis did not manifest or evidence any militancy, that he did not indicate either in words used or his manner of approach that he intended our conferences should be postponed for all time."[47] But, as the weeks past, Lewis's true intentions became clear. Peace again had been scuttled. On June 16, 1939, Woll wrote to FDR to let him know that the latest round of peace talks had failed. According to the AFL, all blame rested on Lewis. In a statement for the newspapers, Woll stated that Lewis was "pursuing a rule or ruin policy" and now believed that the CIO's conflict with the AFL was to be "a fight to the finish."[48]

Neither Green nor Lewis had any significant contact for six months. By September 1939, organized labor's infighting and failure to find a peace settlement began to seriously worry President Roosevelt and his advisers. War seemed ever more likely in Europe and in Asia, and FDR thought that the union rivalry between the AFL and the CIO could hamper the defense effort. Thus, in late 1939, nearly one month after Hitler started war in Europe, the president sought to restart the movement for union peace. Shortly before the October 1939 AFL Convention, in Cincinnati, Roosevelt sent a letter in which he urged William Green to try find a way to reconcile with the CIO. This time, FDR made his appeal in the name of democracy and national security.

> Perhaps the highest service we Americans can render at this time is to demonstrate that our personal liberty, our democratic way of life, our free representative Government, make it possible for us to disagree among ourselves over many things without bitterness and find quickly the means of settlement and adjustment of controversy when it has gone far enough. A world emergency such as the present gives us new realization of the blessings and in the face of this world necessity we must adjourn our small grudges, our differences, and find the way to peace and good will within our borders in every department of life. So we become a free and fearless nation with people of all shades of opinion and walks of life, united in common purpose to maintain and to practice and to protect this American way of life. . . .
>
> If we desire peace and good will in the world we must learn to practice these in the small and large things of our own life. The continued conflict and separation in the labor movement can hardly be overlooked, in these days, when discord in any group is so harmful to world peace. The joint committee which was appointed by your body and by your separated brothers in the Congress of Industrial Organizations has, I know, done faithful and effective service to promote reunion and negotiate a practical and sound peace in the labor movement. I take this occasion to thank the members of that committee and the two organizations, which they represent, for the intelligent and persistent efforts toward peace and to congratulate them upon the substantial progress made. This must be continued until a sound negotiated basis of peace between the labor groups is reached and agreed upon. If it is hard to continue it is all the more a challenge to the members and leaders of

> these labor bodies—to their capacity to serve the workers of America—to their capacity to put aside pride and self-advantage in patriotic service for national unity in this time of trouble and distress.[49]

Green was quite receptive to the president's request. He sent FDR an appreciative telegram that stated in part: "we have opened the door of the American Federation of Labor wide and completely. We have invited those who left the American Federation of Labor to return. We have urged them to come back home and settle differences within the family of labor in a sensible honest and fair way." Then, on October 3, the Convention's first day, Green read the letter to the delegates and formally reconstituted the peace committee yet again.[50]

FDR also sent a letter to the CIO convention held in October 1939 and called for unity amidst the world crisis:

> If we desire peace and good will in the world we must learn to practice these in the small and large things of our own life. The continued conflict and separation in the labor movement can hardly be overlooked, in these days, when discord in any group is so harmful to world peace. The joint committee which was appointed by your body and by the American Federation of Labor has, I know, done faithful and effective service to promote reunion and negotiate a practical and sound peace in the labor movement. I take this occasion to thank your members on that committee and your organizations, which they represent, for the intelligent and persistent efforts toward peace and to congratulate them upon the substantial progress made. This must be continued until a sound negotiated basis of peace between the labor groups is reached and agreed upon. If it is hard to continue it is all the more a challenge to the members and leaders of these two labor bodies—to their capacity to serve the workers of America—to their capacity to put aside pride and self-advantage in patriotic service for national unity in this time of trouble and distress.[51]

Lewis's response was short and discouraging. "Our [peace] Committee does not possess any information which would lead to the belief that conferences, if resumed at this time, would be fruitful."[52] FDR had reached his limit and, with one exception, gave up on helping the AFL and the CIO reconcile.[53]

Complicating the peace process was John L. Lewis's sharp break with President Roosevelt in 1940. Unlike FDR and many AFL and CIO union leaders, Lewis was an uncompromising isolationist. As Roosevelt placed the United States on a war footing, in 1939, Lewis became increasingly antiwar and anti-Roosevelt. Making matters more personal, President Roosevelt tapped Lewis's CIO rival Sidney Hillman to be the key labor representative on the all-important National Defense Advisory Commission. Throughout the summer of 1940, Lewis tangled with Hillman over NDAC policies and actions such as the granting of exclusive construction contracts to AFL unions. By the fall of 1940, Lewis no longer supported FDR. On October 25, he gave a national radio address in which he formally endorsed the Republican nominee in the 1940 presidential election, Wendell Wilkie, asserting that the reelection of Roosevelt "would be a national evil of the first magnitude" and demanding that the labor movement support him by voting for Wilkie. Lewis added that if unionists did not repudiate Roosevelt, he would step down as the head of the CIO. To the surprise of many, Lewis kept his promise.[54]

Even though Lewis, one of the main roadblocks to the reunification of the labor movement, was temporarily out of the way, the peace movement was all but dead until December 7, 1941. Following the merciless attack on American bases and forces in the Pacific Ocean, CIO president Philip Murray and AFL president William Green began secret talks following late December meetings with top business leaders and representatives of the Roosevelt administration. As a settlement talk progressed, ex-CIO president John Lewis surprised everyone again and announced his own peace proposal in a public letter to William Green on January 17, 1942.[55] Although not fully fleshed out, Lewis's offer involved the retirements of both Green and Murray and the promotion of George Meany to the AFL presidency. The maneuver angered the negotiating teams, which immediately stopped working. President Murray quite rightly felt that this was Lewis's attempt to regain power in the CIO. No one involved honestly believed that Lewis was interested in peace. President Roosevelt had various people investigate the episode. In addition to a report from FDR's troubleshooter, Anna Rosenberg, FDR received one from Gardner Jackson, a former journalist and an undersecretary at the Department of Agriculture, who made, in his opinion, "as thorough a check as possible in the time allowed." He concluded that Lewis had acted "to cut Phil's throat."[56] Jackson also gave credence to the strange rumor that Senator Burton K. Wheeler—whom Lewis had briefly backed as alternative to FDR in 1940—had been involved in "every phase of John's maneuver and thoroughly approved of its design to wrest control from Phil's hands."[57]

It is hard to accurately measure FDR's response to this episode. On the one hand, whatever his motives, Lewis had restarted the dialog about peace, and Roosevelt clearly wanted a unified labor movement. On the other hand, Roosevelt desired neither to increase Lewis's power (in the labor movement or in American politics) nor to create a situation that would inflame union rivalries at a moment when the threat of war demanded that American factories, mines, and lumber mills operate at full capacity. On January 21, 1942, Roosevelt called Philip Murray to the White House for a private one-hour discussion. Murray shared both of the president's concerns. Rather than seek a counterproposal to Lewis's new peace plan, they agreed to work for "peace without unity."[58] The Roosevelt-Murray plan, which was approved by both the AFL and the CIO, created a six-member Combined Labor War Victory Board. The goal of FDR's wartime "labor cabinet," as he called it, was to secure peace between the organizations and cooperation on wartime issues while avoiding the issues that divided the AFL and the CIO.[59] Within days, the AFL appointed its members (Green; George Meany, Federation secretary-treasurer; and Daniel J. Tobin, Teamster Union head), as did the CIO (Murray; R. J. Thomas, head of the United Automobile Workers Union; and Julius Emspack, secretary-treasurer of the United Electrical Workers Union). The labor board met several times but did not do much. Quite likely, it was a sop. By the middle of 1943, Philip Murray might have thought so. On May 9, 1943, Murray sent FDR a telegram complaining bitterly that neither he nor the Combined Labor War Victory Board had been consulted about the plan for national service legislation formulated by a committee consisting of James Byrnes, Harry Hopkins, Bernard Baruch, and Admiral William D. Leahy. FDR penciled the following note on the file memorandum about the telegram: "Tell [Anna Rosenberg] to hold P. Murray's hand. Also, I have no Committee, just helpers."[60] Whether it was Roosevelt's intent to use the board as a means to quell the movement for labor peace, it is hard to say. One can say that the board did not create or even foster a peace between the AFL and CIO.

A Wartime Example: Rivalry at Phelps Dodge

The failure of the unions to make peace during the war meant in practical terms that the rivalry between the AFL and the CIO continued unabated. Among the more bitter wartime conflicts between the two unions was the fight at the Phelps Dodge mines in Arizona. By 1941, Phelps Dodge was one of the oldest and most powerful corporations in the United States. Anson Greene Phelps had founded the corporation in 1781. For nearly one hundred years, the company that Phelps and his partner William Dodge built dealt mainly with the cotton trade and the importing of tin. Slowly, it branched out into manufacturing, railroads, and mining. In the late nineteenth century, the company purchased several mines in Arizona. Eventually, these and other western mines became the heart of the Phelps Dodge Corporation.[61]

From the beginning, Phelps Dodge's corporate leaders had an antiunion attitude. Its factory and mining towns were company towns, which, according to the historian Robert Glass Cleland, "were known for their churches, schools, and comfortable homes." "But the level of wages," he continued, "like any other commodity was normally to be determined by the law of supply and demand." Thus, he concluded "any organized opposition to the employer's policies or decisions called for summary dismissal of the offending employees. Labor unions were anathema."[62] This was as true in the nineteenth century as it was in the twentieth, particularly in the Phelps Dodge mining towns in Arizona. Ajo, Bisbee, Clifton, Douglas, and Morenci were tough towns. Perhaps the most notorious was Bisbee, which is located just a few miles from the infamous town of Tombstone. Bandits and, for a while, Apache raiders made Bisbee a precarious place to live. But even when the company, backed by the power of the state and federal governments, had brought law and order to the mining frontier, life was difficult. Mining itself, of course, was quite dangerous, and Phelps Dodge was slow to alleviate the bad working conditions. Its mines at Bisbee and Morenci were particularly awful. In 1925 alone, four hundred workers were either seriously injured or killed at Morenci.[63]

Phelps Dodge's Arizona miners quickly figured that the only way they could change their lives was by joining a union. The company met the union organizers head on. When the Western Federation of Miners began to operate in Arizona, Phelps Dodge helped to form "citizen's alliances" to ward them off. The strong-arm tactic worked. The union lost strikes at Morenci (1903), Bisbee (1907), and Clifton (1915). Not only did the WFM lose the strikes, but the more conservative American Federation of Labor stepped in by 1915 to negotiate contracts with the company on behalf of the miners. The arrangements did not last long, and by 1917 both the Industrial Workers of the World and the International Union of Mine, Mill, and Smelter Workers (formerly the WFM) were back vying for workers' support. As miner strikes spread during the spring of 1917, Phelps Dodge took drastic action. With the blessing of the U.S. Army, which cut telegraph wires and stood by in silence, company officials had the county sheriff arm a posse of local men (the reincarnated citizen's alliance), who then rounded up at gunpoint more than two thousand suspected unionists. They were herded into a local baseball stadium and then put on cattle cars. A train drove them west to New Mexico, where they were taken into custody by the Army. The Bisbee and Douglas Deportations began a black chapter in the history of American civil liberties. Despite a scathing investigative report by Felix Frankfurter, of the wartime National Mediation Commission, all legal proceedings against Phelps Dodge failed. There was no redress for the deportees, and Phelps Dodge had smashed all its union opponents.[64]

All this changed with the election of Franklin D. Roosevelt and the creation of the New Deal. Not surprisingly, Phelps Dodge's managers vehemently opposed the National Labor Relations Act. Even after the National Labor Relations Board imposed sanctions on the company, it still continued to fire organizers and unionists. The NLRB had no choice other than to seek redress in federal court. By 1941, Phelps Dodge's legal challenge had reached the U.S. Supreme Court. In an opinion written and delivered by none other than Justice Frankfurter, the Court upheld the Wagner Act and thus forced the company to finally accept unions and deal with them fairly.[65] Not only did this decision represent a watershed moment for Phelps Dodge and its miners, but, in the words of the legal historian Marshall Oldman, it was "to become one of the seminal decisions on the act and labor relations."[66]

For our purposes here, the ruling meant that Phelps Dodge now had to engage a union and sign a collective bargaining agreement. Although the International Union of Mine, Mill, and Smelter Workers had been the union involved in the original 1935 lawsuit, the company initially dealt with other unions, particularly those affiliated with the American Federation of Labor, which had won local NLRB elections. For all intents and purposes, the AFL unions were the only ones to deal with.

The Federation and its associated Arizona State Federation of Labor had chased the CIO out of the state in the late 1930s. First, in 1937, the Arizona State Federation of Labor had expelled all unions that had affiliated with the CIO.[67] Then, to add insult to injury, the AFL out-organized the remnants of the CIO in the state's copper-mining fields. As the key Federation organizer, A. H. Peterson, wrote William Green in the summer of 1937:

> I assisted the Machinists, Boilermakers, Carpenters and Electricians of Jerome in presenting the first union shop agreement for these crafts to the Phelps Dodge Cooper Co, [*sic*]. The CIO organizer who was in the state has not met with any degree of success and I believe that the mines are ripe for the installation of Federal Labor Charters. . . . I am writing to let you know that it seems very ripe at present.[68]

In early 1941, the CIO, under the guise of an organization called the United Arizona Labor Legislative Committee, tried to make a comeback. Although the CIO did not make immediate headway, it did re-establish a beachhead in the state.[69]

Despite the resurgence of the CIO—or perhaps partly because of it—between March 28 (two weeks after its lawyers argued before the Supreme Court) and November 11, 1941, Phelps Dodge signed several agreements with the AFL's Metal Trades Department. Specifically, it negotiated with the metal trades councils of Ajo, Bisbee, Clifton, Douglas, and Morenci. These councils each had jurisdiction over dozens of local unions, including the boilermakers, carpenters, electrical workers, engineers, miners, office and technical workers, plumbers, and teamsters. This relationship with Phelps Dodge was unique to the AFL. Its craft-union structure made it possible for local unions to fashion their own agreements with companies. Phelps Dodge officials wanted to avoid this, for one reason. Working with a single metal trades council was simpler than hammering out agreements with dozens of unions at each mine. In March 1941, the Metal Trades Council of the United Verde Branch of Phelps Dodge (near Globe, Arizona) reached the first mine-wide agreement. The National Labor Relations Board later scrutinized this deal at Globe and found it acceptable as long as the member unions agreed to the contract.[70]

As union contracts went, the ones with the metal trades councils were relatively simple, outlining policies regarding pay, seniority, griev-

TABLE 5.1
Copper Production in the United States, 1935–1945 (1939 = 100)

Year	*Production of Recoverable Copper*
1935	51.7
1936	84.3
1937	116.1
1938	76.5
1939	*100*
1940	120.8
1941	131.8
1942	149.1
1943	149.8
1944	133.1
1945	105.9

SOURCE: US Department of Labor, Bureau of Labor Statistics, "Productivity and Unit Labor Cost in Selected Mining Industries, 1935–1945," 7, AFL Papers, Series 4, Box 84.

ance procedures, discharge, suspension, and vacation. Additionally, and importantly, the AFL secured closed-shop arrangements with Phelps Dodge.[71] The problem was that by November 1942, when the contract came up for renewal, the metal trades councils and Phelps Dodge no longer saw eye to eye. Generally speaking, the coming of the Second World War had altered the relationship between employer and workers. Phelps Dodge had benefited greatly from wartime contracts and had finally emerged from terrible economic doldrums of the Great Depression. In the early 1930s, production, employment, and productivity in the copper production industry were at twenty-year lows.[72] As tables 5.1 and 5.2 indicate, the wartime demand for copper led to a tripling of copper production in the United States between 1935 and 1942.[73] As a result, Phelps Dodge finally began to turn a profit again after several years of operating at a loss. This economic upturn was, of course, aided by the federal government. Federal contracts allowed the company to expand dramatically its operation at Morenci. Additionally, its involvement in Operation Pluto, which laid metal fuel pipes beneath the English Channel in advance of the Allied invasion of northern Europe, also increased the company's profits.[74] And Phelps Dodge's AFL unions wanted part of the profits. The workers also wanted higher wages and some relief. The company worked its employees hard. For example, at Ajo, Phelps Dodge managers maintained three shifts a day, seven days a week. Jobs were plentiful at the mine, and the population of the small

TABLE 5.2
Phelps Dodge Copper Production, 1935–1945

Year	Production of Recoverable Copper
1935	176,876
1936	252,708
1937	314,449
1938	258,045
1939	299,337
1940	319,063
1941	363,581
1942	446,938
1943	478,319
1944	458,154
1945	360,581

SOURCE: Robert Glass Cleland, *A History of Phelps Dodge, 1834–1950* (New York: Knopf, 1952) 303.

town ballooned from four hundred in 1935 to six thousand in 1943. And yet, with the breakneck pace came more accidents and exceedingly high turnover. In the next contract, the union wanted more control over the working conditions. The pace had to be slowed, and wages had to be increased.[75]

By late summer 1942, negotiations between various AFL metal trade councils and Phelps Dodge had broken down. By December 1942, the talks were hopelessly deadlocked. AFL negotiators felt that Phelps Dodge officials were trying to break the union. "Old yellow-dogs on those [company] committees," one metal trades council member wrote, "[were] stalling on major grievances, ignoring the union."[76] While the AFL and the company wrangled, the door was left open for the return of the International Union of Mine, Mill, and Smelter Workers, which by then had became a mainstay of the CIO. In fact, the CIO, as well as the Mine and Mill Workers, had made a significant recovery in the early 1940s. After the great upheavals of the First World War, the dark days of the open-shop 1920s, and the pyrrhic Supreme Court victory of 1941, the union had made some inroads against many employers, including Phelps Dodge. With a new and radical leadership, the Mine and Mill Workers had become the bargaining unit at the Phelps Dodge mine in Douglas, Arizona. Emboldened by this advance, Mine and Mill leaders set their sights on other Phelps Dodge mines.[77]

In November 1942, the Mine and Mill Workers petitioned the NLRB for elections at the mines in Bisbee and Morenci. The Morenci Metal

Trades Council immediately objected on the grounds that the NLRB had decided, in its Globe decision, that the Arizona mines would be represented by craft and not by industrial unions.[78] In January, the NLRB held a hearing to hear both sides, but this time the board ruled:

> In our opinion, the recent history of labor organization and collective bargaining has been on the basis of an industrial unit. As stated above, the AFL Unions, that is the MTC [i.e., the Metal Trades Council] and the intervening unions affiliated with it, have bargained with the Company on the basis of an industrial unit.[79]

Shortly thereafter, elections were held. In defiant protest, the AFL unions set up picket lines at the election booths, and metal trade council officials told its members not to vote. Predictably, the AFL's metal trade councils lost. On May 1, 1943 (a date that must have made the Communist leadership of the Mine and Mill Workers smile), the NLRB certified the International Union of Mine, Mill, and Smelter Workers (CIO) as the bargaining agent for the workers at the old Bisbee mine and the new, gigantic surface mine at Morenci.[80] The CIO and the Mine and Mill Workers were especially proud of their "historic" victory at Bisbee. To them, it was the righting of an old wrong.[81]

Officials at Phelps Dodge were, of course, less sanguine about the Mine and Mill resurgence. Hadn't they all but eliminated the union during the last war? But dealing with working-class radicals was only part of the problem, from Phelps Dodge's point of view. According to the company's labor relations director, C. R. Kuzell, the decision of the NLRB and the subsequent union election had "unsettle[d] labor relations [in Arizona] and interfere[d] with the prosecution of the war." The CIO had successfully raided the AFL's Arizona mining unions. Those loyal to the Federation were seeking ways to reverse their misfortune. In a letter to the National War Labor Board, President Roosevelt's wartime labor dispute troubleshooter Kuzell called for an investigation "for redetermination [*sic*] of bargaining units in order to bring about harmony." Kuzell seemed to express sympathy for the AFL metal trade councils, which were "unable to reconcile the [National Labor Relations] Board's decision with past actions."[82]

A few days after Kuzell's letter to the NWLB, G. A. Pennapacker, the head of the Morenci Metal Trades Council, formally filed a request with the NWLB to review the entire matter, including the January 1943

NLRB ruling. The War Labor Board took up the thorny issue and handed down its ruling on September 5, 1943. Seeking to avoid interagency rivalry, NWLB member Wayne L. Morse publicly reported the unanimous decision. "The National War Labor Board," he announced, "will not use its power to nullify decisions of the National Labor Relations Board, since to do so would nullify an Act of Congress."[83] The NWLB concluded further that "utter chaos would result if the War Labor Board should ever undertake to set aside, review or modify the decisions" of the NLRB.[84]

Although the AFL's member on the War Labor Board, Robert J. Watt, concurred with the decision, he felt compelled to issue his own special statement after the ruling. In it, he wrote:

> Because I agree with the unanimous decision that the National War Labor Board lacks jurisdiction to review the finding of the National labor Relations Board, I have joined in the unanimous decision of the National War Labor Board in this case. In so doing, I must express my belief that the finding of the National Labor Relations Board is utterly unwarranted on precedent or merit, wrong in principle and destructive in consequence. . . . I have found no explanation as to why the National Labor Relations Board should have ignored its own standards, and the obvious preference of skilled craftsmen for craft representation in this case. If the National Labor Relations Board took this course for the purpose of experimenting with the destruction of craft unions they are perpetrating an ideological excursion, which is inexcusable during a national emergency in a nation at war.[85]

It is doubtful that Watt's words had much of an impact. And yet, in June 1944, the National Labor Relations Board decided to reconsider its pro-CIO ruling at Phelps Dodge. As the Mine and Mill Workers' contract with Phelps Dodge expired, the Morenci Metal Trade Council petitioned the NLRB for investigation and certification as the bargaining unit at the mine. Turnabout was fair play. The Mine and Mill Workers' leaders immediately challenged the AFL's request. In a nearly inexplicable reversal, the NLRB admitted that it had been in error and that the Metal Trades Council was the legitimate and proper representational unit. A new election was ordered. In May 1945, the Morenci Metal Trades Council defeated the Mine and Mill Workers and regained its place at the bargaining table.[86]

Conclusion

The labor conflict at Phelps Dodge by no means was the nastiest fight ever between the American Federation of Labor and the Congress of Industrial Organizations. However, it does illustrate that the "peace without unity" deal pushed by Roosevelt, Murray, and Green was, in practical terms, a mere political expediency and often a farce at the local level. With so much at stake, neither labor organization was very interested in the phony peace. Rather, the war provided opportunities for the unions to add members, expand control of industries, and fill their coffers. And as long as the war industries were not too adversely affected, it seems, little was done to damper the spirited conflict between the AFL and the CIO. In the case of Phelps Dodge, the federal government, through the National Labor Relations Board, actually made things worse, going back and forth three times on the issue of the proper representative bargaining unit. All the while, however, Phelps Dodge got its metal. Near the war's height in 1943, its workers extracted 239 million tons of copper, 10 million coming from the huge surface mine at Morenci. Had the rivalry at Phelps Dodge or even elsewhere stopped production for an extended period of time, one assumes, that Dr. Win-the-War might have offered some stronger medicine, which would have compelled the AFL and the CIO to sacrifice their civil war, at least for the duration. But, by the end of the war, the arsenal of democracy had withstood its internal problems. Of course, even after World War II, the fight between the AFL and CIO continued for ten more years.

6

Death in the Factories

Worker Safety and the AFL

American factories are America's first line of defense, and throughout the vast industrial machine soldiers with tools were dying by the thousands, being maimed and disabled by more thousands, in a "blitzkrieg" led by General Carelessness.

—*Popular Mechanics,* March 1942[1]

When Management takes the overzealous view that production must be achieved at all costs—accidents are in the making.

—*Fortune,* July 1942[2]

As on the battlefront, life on America's home front all too often required the ultimate sacrifice for the war effort. "John Jones was killed yesterday when his shirt was caught in the machine he was operating, pulling him to his death. Mr. Jones was one of the founders of Local 236 Amalgamated Machine Workers of America. He is survived by his wife, Esther Jones." This obituary, on the cover of the U.S. Department of Labor's 1944 pamphlet *Is This the Payoff,* was used to call attention to a virtually unpublicized crisis in American factories during the war: the dramatic loss of life on the shop floor.[3] Quite literally, during the first few years of the Second World War, it was safer for Americans to be on the battlefront than it was for them to work on the home front of the arsenal of democracy (see tables 6.1 and 6.2).[4] Almost simultaneously with the terrific upswing in defense-related employment in 1940, accident rates rose precipitously across all industries (see table 6.3).

The injured worker on the shop floor was not a new experience. Since the early nineteenth century, the United States had suffered unusually high worker death and injury rates, particularly on the railroads, in the steel industry, in the lumber industry, and in coal mines. But, during the war, the crumpled, twisted man lying on the grease-stained floor became more than an object of pity, fear, and grief. He was a wartime liability. Aside from the compensation paid to the family and the costs to clean and repair the machinery, 6,000 man-days were lost if he died (4,500 man-days if he just lost a leg or an arm).[5] In practical terms, this kind of wartime sacrifice casualties meant fewer guns, planes, tanks, and ships to fight the Axis powers. High accident rates threatened the Allies' ability to win the war.

This chapter examines what amounts to the hidden history of factory safety during World War II. Historians who have investigated industrial accidents have not focused on the war years. Instead, job safety studies have tended to fall into three categories. First, there are examinations of particular industrial disasters. Examples of this are Claudia Clark's excellent book on dial painters poisoned by radium and Martin Cherniack's book on the Hawk's Nest incident, in which more than seven hundred workers succumbed to silicosis after drilling a tunnel near Gauley Bridge, West Virginia. Second, there are examinations of dangerous trades and industrial diseases, such as Richard A. Greenwald's study of mercury poisoning among hatters and Robert E. Botsch's investigation into the cotton industry and "brown lung" disease.[6] The vast majority of the scholarly work in this category concerns mining.[7] Third, there are some general accounts like Christopher C. Sellers's *Hazards on the Job,*

TABLE 6.1

Factory Injuries and Deaths, 1941–1946: U.S. Census Bureau Figures

	1941	*1942*	*1943*	*1944*	*1945*	*1946*
Deaths and Permanent Total Disabilities	19,200	19,900	20,100	17,600	17,800	18,300
Permanent Partial Disabilities	100,600	100,800	108,000	94,400	88,100	92,400
Temporary Total Disabilities	2,060,400	2,147,000	2,285,900	2,118,400	1,913,900	1,945,300
Total	2,180,200	2,267,700	2,414,000	2,230,400	2,019,800	2,056,000

SOURCE: "Estimated Number of Disabling Industrial Injuries, 1941–1943" in *Statistical Abstracts of the United States, 1944–1945* (Washington, DC: GPO, 1945), 217; and "Estimated Number of Disabling Industrial Injuries, 1943–1947" in *Statistical Abstracts of the United States, 1948* (Washington, DC: GPO, 1948), 223.

TABLE 6.2
Factory Deaths, 1928–1945: National Safety Council Figures

Year	*Deaths*
1928	19,000
1933	14,500
1936	18,500
1938	16,000
1939	15,500
1940	17,000
1941	18,000
1942	18,500
1943	17,500
1944	16,000
1945	16,000

SOURCE: National Safety Council, *Accident Facts, 1946* (Chicago: NSC, 1947), 9.

TABLE 6.3
Industrial Injury Frequency Rates, 1926–1945

Year	*Work-Injury Frequency Rate**
1926	24.2
1927	22.6
1928	22.5
1929	24.0
1930	23.1
1931	18.9
1932	19.6
1933	19.3
1934	20.2
1935	17.9
1936	16.6
1937	17.8
1938	15.1
1939	14.9
1940	15.3
1941	18.1
1942	19.9
1943	20.0
1944	18.4
1945	18.6

* Rate is average number of disabling injuries per million man-hours worked.

SOURCE: U.S. Census Bureau, *Historical Statistics of the United States, Colonial Times to 1970* (Washington, DC: GPO, 1975), 182.

Mark Aldrich's *Safety First,* both published in 1997, and John Fabian Witt's *The Accidental Republic* (2004). The main question that drives most of these histories is whether it was labor, management, or government (or some combination) that was the force behind improvements in industrial safety. In other words, just how important was organized labor in the creation of a safer shop floor? This chapter directly answers this question while exploring a neglected aspect of industrial-safety history. Virtually nothing has been written about this aspect of the Second World War, let alone the American Federation of Labor's role in reducing injuries and deaths in the factories.[8]

This chapter helps to fill that gap by discussing wartime safety generally and by offering the American Federation of Labor's view of the subject, and specifically the experiences of one of its locals, at the International Harvester Corporation's plant in Milwaukee, Wisconsin. Taken as a whole, this story of factory safety during World War II shows not only how dangerous the shop floor was but also the glacial pace of reform. Moreover, unlike other wartime labor issues, such as the open-shop movement, factory safety appears not to have been at the top of the AFL's agenda. Despite pressure from the federal government, the Federation continued to see job safety as management's responsibility. In fact, the AFL gladly remained on the sidelines, acting as a cheerleader for government and business campaigns to reduce workplace injuries and deaths. This is another example of a tradition that the wartime AFL refused to abandon.

Workplace Injury and Safety Before World War II

Concerns over work injuries were by no means new in the 1940s. Occupational accidents are as old as work itself. As paleontologists have known for decades, Stone Age hunters risked life and limb attacking large mammals. Neolithic bones in the archaeological records show fractures most likely caused by injuries sustained during hunts. Historically, industrial disease has been a topic of discussion at least since the time of Hippocrates and Pliny. But serious investigations into workplace hazards began in the fifteenth century when the German physician Ulrich Ellenbog wrote *Von den gifftigen besen tempffen und reuchen* (On the poisonous wicked fumes and smokes [1473]), a treatise on the dangers of working with metals, particularly the fumes from heated lead, mercury, and gold. Following in Ellenbog's footsteps were Paracelsus and the Italian physician Bernardino Ramazzini, whose 1700 book, *A Treatise of the Diseases of Tradesmen, Shewing the Various Influence of Particular Trades upon the State of Health* (first English translation, 1705) is sometimes considered the first modern investigation into occupational hazards. Interest in job injuries in the United States developed during the Age of Andrew Jackson. In 1837, the New York Medical Society sponsored the publication *On the Influence of Trades, Professions and Occupations,* which discussed work-related illness in the United States.[9]

It took almost another fifteen years for governments to take action to improve the occupational health of America. The goal of this state intervention was to compel employers to act responsibly and to create safe work environments. From the nineteenth century, the prevailing and operative idea was that managers were accountable for factory safety. With the backing of workers and unions, several state governments led the movement to improve industrial safety. First came factory inspection. Massachusetts became the pioneer when, in 1852, it passed a law to improve the safety of steam machines. Requirements for the inspection of steam boilers followed in 1870 and were modified in 1877. Inspectors were granted the right to enter factories to gauge safety and to enforce regulations. Similar inspection laws were passed in New Jersey (1884), Wisconsin (1884), Ohio (1884), New York (1886), Connecticut (1887), Minnesota, (1887), Maine (1887), Pennsylvania (1889), Missouri (1891), and Tennessee (1891). By 1930, all states had elaborate factory-inspection laws.[10]

A second area of state regulation was labor protection. The first state to act in this area was Utah, whose legislature, in 1896, passed a law to establish an eight-hour day in mining to foster safety. Almost immediately, a mine operator was arrested, charged, and convicted of working his crews longer than ten hours a day. The operator was fined $57 and jailed for fifty-seven days. In jail, the employer began appeal proceedings, which eventually made their way to the U.S. Supreme Court. In 1898, the Court gave its decision in *Holden v. Hardy,* siding with the State of Utah and affirming the constitutionality of laws protecting workers' health. The law was "a valid exercise of the police power of the state," the majority wrote. "These employments," they concluded, "when too long pursued [are] detrimental to the health of the employees; and so long as there are reasonable grounds for believing that this is so, [the Utah law] cannot be reviewed by the federal courts."[11]

By the turn of the twentieth century, the patchwork system of state inspection and protection laws had failed to create safer work environments. Inspectors rarely fined careless, irresponsible, and noncompliant employers, and, in any case, the penalties were usually too small to effect change. During the early 1900s, workers themselves took bolder actions to fight for safer jobs. Unionists called wildcat strikes when jobs became too hazardous. But strong union organization was required, and unions rarely had the power to sustain such activity. Unions also backed lawsuits in the names of injured workers against employers. At first, the workers were at a clear financial and legal disadvantage. For decades, the courts across the nation used the common-law theory of "due care" that guided the old master-and-apprentice case law: as long as the employer showed "due care" for the employee, in injury cases, the employer was not liable. Thus, for decades, workers usually lost of their suits against employers. But, during the early 1900s, so many injury cases were being brought before judges that employers' common-law defense began to crack. Growing fears among businessmen that they would be found liable for unsafe work environments, as well as the failure of factory owners and operators to create a safe work environment, led to the third governmental action: the creation of workmen's compensation.[12]

During the Progressive Era, spurred by reformers such as John R. Commons, Alice Hamilton, and Florence Kelley, states passed laws that provided payments at the employer's expense to the families of workers injured or killed. Payments were made through a state fund or an insurance company under the direction of a governmental agency. Insurance premium rates encouraged employers to adopt safer practices. These laws had some weaknesses, however. The initial workmen's compensation statutes enacted between 1910 and 1917 omitted most farm and domestic workers, as well as workers at small companies that employed fewer than six employees. Additionally, these first laws did not cover occupational diseases such as silicosis, a lung disease caused by inhaling quartz dust. Still, workmen's compensation had the strong support of unions. In fact, the AFL and its affiliates were particularly active in proposing, supporting, and reforming state workmen's compensation laws. The Wisconsin State Federation of Labor (WSFL) was one of the most energetic and helped Wisconsin adopt the most progressive laws in the nation. In particular, the state accepted the WSFL's idea to tie companies' insurance rates to their safety records. This was the carrot-and-stick method, which reformers thought would bring down the number of industrial accidents. By 1932, at the dawn of the Roosevelt era, most states had adopted the "Wisconsin system." Only four states did not have workmen's compensation laws: Arkansas, Florida, Mississippi, and South Carolina.[13]

Despite the legislative and bureaucratic efforts in the Progressive Era to reduce workplace injuries and deaths, significant decline was achieved only during the New Deal. During the First World War, the number of injuries and deaths was staggeringly high; there were an estimated thirty thousand deaths in 1917 and a similar number in 1918.[14] Through the 1920s, accident frequency rates (based on the average number of disabling injuries per million man-hours worked) remained largely unchanged. As in an earlier period, inspectors even in Wisconsin did shoddy work, and employers continued to factor in accidents (rather than safety) as a cost of business.[15] Additionally, the most noteworthy organization fighting for workers' safety, the Workers' Health Bureau of America (WHB), failed to achieve its goal of empowering workers to create safe factories and thus to reduce industrial accidents and deaths. Created in 1921 by a group of radical women workers, the WHB worked closely with local and state affiliates of the American Federation of Labor. But, at a critical junction, when the WHB needed the political and financial backing of the AFL's Executive Council, the Federation turned its back on the Bureau, which disbanded in 1928. Although the WHB counted public awareness of factory safety, the expansion of workers' compensation, and the organization of scientists and health professionals behind a worker-led safety movement as its accomplishments, it did not dramatically affect accident frequency rates (see table 6.3).[16]

Even without the WHB, during the 1930s, the rate declined significantly. There are three reasons for this. First was the dedicated and effective safety campaigns of the National Safety Council, organized in 1912 as a cooperative service organization established to advance industrial safety.[17] Second, the Great Depression encouraged employers to retain their best employees and to lay off their inefficient workers, who, as the sociologist Earl E. Muntz wrote, were "a group in which industrial casualties are prone to be high."[18] Third, President Franklin D. Roosevelt's administration, especially the Department of Labor under Frances Perkins, made reducing industrial accidents a priority.[19] As a result of these factors, by the mid-1930s, factory injuries and deaths were down. Take, for example, the construction industry in the mid-1930s. In 1936, the U.S. Bureau of Labor Statistics estimated that 2,700 construction workers were killed on the job; 15,400 more were permanently injured, and 265,000 were temporarily disabled. These numbers were truly astonishing. To put it another way, in 1936, one out every four construction workers suffered a disabling accident or worse. By 1938, however, the Labor Department's safety awareness programs —as well as the Roosevelt recession—brought those numbers down. That year, there were only 2,000 deaths on construction sites (a 25 percent decrease), 10,700 permanent injuries (a 30 percent decrease), and 191,000 temporary injuries (a 30 percent decrease).[20] The message was clear: safety campaigns worked if undertaken seriously and vigorously. In 1939, there were fifteen thousand occupational deaths, a low that had not been seen for decades.[21] In 1937, the United States Public Health Service's National Institute of Health conducted an accident assessment in eight cities. It found that most injuries and deaths did not occur in the factories. Thirty percent happened in the home, 40 percent occurred in public places, particularly highways, and 23 percent took place on the shop floor.[22]

Factory Safety and World War II

The gains made in factory safety during the New Deal were quickly lost during the defense emergency of 1940. In that year alone, the accident rate jumped 20 percent over that for 1939. Simply put, there were six injuries in 1940 for every five in 1939. Moreover, there were 1,500 more factory deaths.[23] In the year of Franklin D. Roosevelt's penultimate presidential election, more than 1,410,000 workers sustained injuries while on the job in their factories, and 17,000 were killed. About 170 million man-days were lost. This was fifty times the number of hours lost to strikes and lockouts.[24] The exact reasons for the increase in accidents and deaths were hotly contested then as they are now. There were two basic positions: the high accident rate was either management's fault or the workers'. Strangely enough, but well within the lines of tradition thinking on the issue, the generally pro-industry *Fortune* magazine proclaimed that management was ultimately responsible.

In the magazine's view, the mixture of war and industrial accidents had created a vicious cycle:

> War calls for stepped-up production. Stepped-up production involved increased hazards. The hazards, if not controlled, result in accidents and lost manpower just when the loss may be disastrous.[25]

By the hundreds, managers took up President Roosevelt's call to transform and increase their production. They hastily built annexes, quickly installed new machinery and power systems, hired thousands of untrained and under-trained workers, and thrust them into newly established second and third shifts. *Fortune* concluded: "when Management takes the overzealous view that production must be achieved at all costs —accidents are in the making."[26] Because of their rushed and rash actions, the magazine posited, employers were to blame.

Most managers refused to acknowledge any responsibility in factory injuries and deaths. Their "moth-eaten alibi" (as *Fortune* called it) was that the workers who got injured were careless. Accident statistics provide little clue as to whether they were right that the "personal factor," as they called it, was the key issue.[27] National factory accident statistics were based largely on state estimates, which were not terribly accurate. Not only were statistics not rigorously collected, but also often they did not include incidents of industrial disease, such as silicosis.[28] The most definitive statistics came from the National Safety Council, whose 1941 study of one thousand accidents that led to either permanent disabilities or deaths showed that 68 percent of the accidents were caused by both personal and mechanical faults. Seventeen percent of the cases had no personal cause, and 15 percent had no mechanical cause.[29] Nevertheless, some employers, politicians, and journalists no doubt agreed with a March 1942 *Popular Mechanics* article that proclaimed that thousands had been maimed and killed "in a 'blitzkrieg' led by General Carelessness." Misquoting the National Safety Council's statistics, the magazine opined that the responsibility for the increase in accidents lay with " 'rusty' old hands recalled from retirement" and "green" workers who did not understand their jobs. The director of the U.S. Vocational Training for Defense Workers, L. S. Hawkins, supported this view and stated, in 1942, that "the great majority of accidents result from the failure of some individual rather than from causes which cannot be foreseen." Still, Hawkins, like most journalists and employers, believed that advances were just around the corner.[30] Unfortunately, they were not.

The years 1941 and 1942 were bloody years on the factory shop floor. From 1941 to 1942, the number of accidents rose from 2,180,200 to 2,267,700, and the number of deaths increased from 19,200 to 19,900 (see tables 6.1 and 6.2).[31] The loss of manpower had devastating effects on the industrial effort. One hundred more Liberty ships could have been built, a navy official estimated, if shipyard accidents had been 15 percent fewer. Furthermore, the total cost of lost wages, medical expenses, insurance, property damage, and various indirect costs for all accidents in 1942 was more than $900 million.[32]

By the middle of 1942, some patterns in the accidents that were recorded were evident, suggesting that the work environment, and not the worker, was the primary cause behind the high accident rates. First, injuries most often occurred on the second and particularly third (or graveyard) shifts. Fatigue was a major factor.[33] A few employers recognized this and offered their late-night workers nutritious hot meals as a means to make them more alert. But most managers did not do this. Furthermore, employers had a hard time finding hawk-eyed foremen willing to work late hours and thus help maintain a safe work environment. Second, as had been the case for decades before the war, smaller war plants had higher accident rates than larger, more established plants.[34] In 1941 alone, accident frequency was 36 percent higher in small factories than in larger ones. Several examples make this trend clear. Omaha's gigantic Glenn L. Martin bomber factory did not have a single fatal industrial accident in more than 108 million man-hours of work. In fact, one of the few serious accidents that did occur there was a fluke: on September 22, 1943, a B-25 Mitchell bomber on a test flight crashed into the assembly building's roof, killing three members of the plane's crew. Fortunately, most of the workers were eating lunch outside and escaped serious injury.[35] Another airplane manufacturer, North American Aviation, which made the famous P-51 Mustang fighter, boasted a lower accident frequency rate during the war years at its Inglewood, California, plant than it had before the war. This safety improvement took place despite the influx of "green" workers, the steep rise in the number of man-hours worked, and the installation of new machinery. North American managers credited the plant's success to its rigorous safety program. In late 1941, company officials discovered that

60 percent of all worker injuries were inflicted by sharp metal, particularly on jobs connected to power shears, punch presses, and hand-and-power brakes. Safety engineers installed finger guards on all power shears, replaced foot pedals on punch presses with hand levers, and substituted large foot treadles on brakes with small movable pedals, thus removing a shop-floor obstacle. Combined with North American's goggle and face-shield campaigns, the changes reduced the company's accident rate by half by mid-1942.[36]

This highly publicized and relatively uncommon achievement not only provided a ray of hope that improvements were possible but also pointed to the vastness of the safety problem. There were thousands of factories just like North American, most of which had little or nothing in the way of safety programs. What was more shocking was how little Americans seemed to notice the safety crisis. As one War Production Board (WPB) official explained, "if a full division of American soldiers were wiped out by the enemy on some battlefield, it would cause screaming page one headlines," but "individual accidents get small headlines occasionally."[37] Nonetheless, each year, the United States was losing at least an entire battalion to injury and death on the shop floor, and very little was being done to rectify the situation. Finally, in 1942, the federal government began to focus seriously on the issue. Initially, the Roosevelt administration was hampered by the sheer plethora of government agencies responsible for overseeing factory safety. Simply put, no one person or government entity was in charge. By the Second World War, there were dozens of government safety organizations at the state and federal level. An examination of just the federal overseers reveals a confusing bureaucratic network involving the U.S. Public Health Service, the Office of Defense Health and Welfare Services, the Bureau of the Mines, and the safety committees inside the War Department, the Maritime Commission, and the U.S. Navy. In addition, each wartime agency concerned with production or mobilizing manpower had its own safety apparatus. Each federal safety group acted independently, and each had its own special mission.[38]

For example, after hearing of the safety successes of North American and other corporations, in 1943, the War Production Board's Safety and Technical Equipment Division began a publicity campaign to encourage employers to buy more safety equipment. As its name suggests, the Division had as its job to provide technical information on safety equipment. By the end of the year, managers of war facilities had spent almost $41 million on safety equipment. In its study of the purchase and use of safety equipment, published in 1944, WPB safety division officials found what they must have suspected to be the case. In many industries—with the exception of shipbuilding—the higher the safety equipment expenditure per employee, the lower the frequency of accidents. The converse was also true. The WPB's report also outlined several problems on the safety front. One was that employers had a hard time purchasing equipment because of omnipresent wartime shortages. They simply could not get enough steel-tipped boots or protective goggles. As one employer wrote the WPB:

> Our inability to secure necessary protective equipment for the use of our employees is a matter of grave concern to our Safety Division. The principles of safety are built up in an organization only through a long and unceasing program of education and insistence on safe working practices. A prime requisite in furthering safe working conditions is to supply workers with adequate equipment to enable them to comply with all rules. In regard to goggles and respirators we are now in the illogical position of insisting on their use without being able to furnish them to our employees.[39]

These isolated efforts, like the WPB's safety equipment campaign, were unsuccessful in stemming the rising tide of industrial accidents. In 1943, the numbers rose yet again. By December, there had been 2,414,000 accidents, 20,100 of which resulted in death. In 1943, there had been enough accidents to shut down the entire nation's industrial home front for seven days and seven nights. Moreover, by the middle of the war, there were more casualties in the factories than on the battle front. In the first sixteen and a half months of war, 12,123 servicemen in the U.S. armed forces had been killed, 15,049 had been wounded, and 51,063 were missing-in-action or captured. In the same period, nearly 20,000 died because of industrial accidents, and more than two million were injured.[40]

The AFL and Factory Safety

Given these grim statistics, it is a fair historical question to ask what, if anything did, labor, management, and government did to stem the rising tide of industrial accidents. Further, what did the AFL do? The short answer is that the federal government sponsored several wartime safety campaigns that management led with the moderate support of organized labor. To understand why management had the upper hand in conducting the wartime factory safety program, one has to understand that it was an unquestioned assumption in the 1940s that it was management's responsibility to establish a safe environment for workers. Every industrial safety textbook, as well as every statement from the federal government, management, and labor organizations, recognized, as the eminent safety expert H. W. Heinrich put it, "the moral obligation of an employer [that] requires [that he maintain] a reasonably safe working environment."[41] The foreman, management's direct daily link with its workforce, had the job of training workers in safety, policing the shop floor, maintaining equipment, and reporting unsafe machinery and safety violations.[42]

Despite the industrial safety programs that were undertaken before the United States entered the war (e.g., those at Glenn Martin and North American Aviation), generally speaking, while acknowledging their responsibility for plant safety, most American employers initially did not take the problem too seriously. Rather, the spark for change came from the federal government. In typical New Deal fashion, to meet the crisis of shop-floor safety, President Franklin D. Roosevelt fostered two new bureaucratic initiatives. First, FDR created a new governmental entity to solve the safety crisis. On October 17, 1941, FDR sent a letter to his secretary of labor, Frances Perkins, calling for action:

> The urgency of our production needs under the defense program cannot help but deepen concern over the disclosure that work accidents in 1940 caused an aggregate time loss of close to one and one half billion man hours.
>
> Aside from the heavy social burden this inflicted upon workers and their families, and the money loss occasioned to management, this staggering wastage of effective manpower seriously slows up plant output today when quick delivery of equipment and supplies is so vitally essential to our security.[43]

Roosevelt ordered that Perkins create under her leadership what became known as the National Committee for the Conservation of Manpower in Defense Industries. The Committee was composed of labor, management, and government officials. The AFL's representative was John P. Frey, head of the Metal Trades Department, which oversaw work in some of the most dangerous industries, including shipbuilding. The Committee had two basic activities. First, it led a public relations campaign to emphasize the need for safer factories. Secretary Perkins, who had been a strong advocate for safety even before the war, stumped for the cause. For instance, in November 1942, she attended the National Safety Council's annual meeting, in Chicago, and appealed to the delegates to do all they could to "stop this mounting toll of industrial deaths and disabilities."[44] In all their public announcements, Perkins and the Committee were quite blunt. In the pamphlet *Safety Speeds Production,* the committee members stated that "accidents are unintentional sabotage . . . [a] loss and delay of materials for Uncle Sam; for the boys at the front; a gain for Hitler, Hirohito, and Mussolini."[45] In addition to making speeches in person and on the radio, members of the National Committee also published several dozen publications on particular industries and on safety in general.[46] All the pamphlets generally followed the suggestions of what the federal government labeled its "minimum safety program." The Walsh-Healy Public Contracts Act of 1936 required all government contractors (such as defense contractors) to collect injury-frequency data quarterly and to provide working conditions that were not "unsanitary or hazardous or dangerous to the health and safety of employees engaged in the performance of said contract."[47] During the war, the minimum safety program was expanded to include other measures such as the creation of safety organizations within the contracting companies consisting of a safety director, a safety inspector, and clerks and staff. Moreover, the federal government called for the creation of central safety committees of workers and plant officials to plan and carry out safety training. But, again, the National Committee clearly expressed the prevailing view that "the primary responsibility for safety rests squarely on the shoulders of top management."[48] Managers were the ones who were expected to ensure that work practices were safe, that workers had access to protective equipment and clothing, as well as to first aid and medical facilities, and that accident records were properly kept.

Roosevelt's second initiative came later in the war. As home-front factory injuries and deaths continued to mount, in early 1943, the Roosevelt administration proposed a temporary interdepartmental committee on health and safety to better coordinate efforts. By the summer of

1943, the group was formalized and became the Industrial Health and Safety Section of the Plant and Community Facilities Services Division of the Office of Labor Production in the War Production Board. The Service consisted of representatives from civilian agencies, the War Department, private organizations (such as the U.S. Chamber of Commerce and the National Safety Council), the CIO, and the AFL. The Service's chief, John M. Fewkes, quickly rediscovered the problem: neither management nor labor was willing to change its thinking on safety, despite the war. At the December 20, 1943, Service meeting, both the CIO representative, John Gibson, and the AFL's member, Martin Durkin, argued strongly "that there was considerable work to do to bring a large portion of management around to the realization of their responsibility for installing safe working conditions."[49] In the end, the Service formally called for a national publicity campaign to convince employers to take safety seriously and for unions to aid employers in creating safe working conditions, greater conformity in safety requirements in wartime federal contracts, a new federal procedure to carry out remedial action against unsafe employers, and the fostering of labor-management safety committees for each war factory. Only the Service's campaigns to encourage safety and labor-management cooperative ever got off the ground.

Getting American employers on board this safety bandwagon was not as difficult as getting the support of organized labor, including the American Federation of Labor. When the National Committee for the Conservation of Manpower released a film on safety training for foremen, the first five hundred copies sold out immediately. The committee then ordered another thousand copies to fill the "unexpected demand" of employers.[50] The WPB's Industrial Health and Safety Section had similar success with its movies for managers. Labor's attention was harder to get. At various times, the National Committee and other government agencies (e.g., the Industrial Health and Safety Section) sent out pamphlets with catchy titles such as *Is This the Payoff?* and *Industrial Health and Safety: Some Suggestions to Organized Labor.* While the former publication was just a trifold payroll stuffer, the latter document was ostensibly written by Joseph D. Keenan, who was the main AFL's representative on the WPB and the Board's labor point man in its safety campaign. In the pamphlet, Keenan implored labor to take safety more seriously. He understood that safety was a muted issue during wartime. As he wrote:

> If there were a film record of the accidents which took the lives of the thousands of production line victims since Pearl Harbor, it would give a portrayal of human suffering equal to the horror of front line films.[51]

Keenan argued that "labor must bestir itself." Although no one could argue with that position, the rest of the WPB pamphlet reflected the Board's confused and somewhat contradictory position on wartime safety. The WPB, like the Department of Labor and other interested groups, including organized labor, continued to maintain that, while "there [was] a real job to be done," in the words of Keenan, "organized labor should help." It remained the responsibility of "top management" to demonstrate "an active and continued interest in the safety program and its application at all times."[52] Keenan then laid out the plan for an effective safety program, which included the widespread use of safety equipment, systematic plant safety inspection, safety education, accident investigation, and, significantly, a labor-management safety committee. Perhaps typical of the AFL approach to labor relations, Keenan emphasized employer and employee cooperation over, for example, new contract provisions detailing the responsibilities of safety programs. Instead, he proposed that the Joint Safety and Health Committees create the conditions so that workers and managers could "work together to end . . . industrial accidents and diseases . . . [and help bring] the war to a speedy victorious conclusion."[53]

The WPB's publicity campaign had little effect in slowing the home-front accident rates. The problem was twofold. On the one hand, the government had failed to force managers to live up to their safety responsibilities. On the other hand, organized labor had yet to sacrifice its prewar views on safety and shoulder some of the burden. In the early summer of 1944, the WPB's codirector Charles E. Wilson reported accident statistics from Pearl Harbor to D-Day. Forty-two thousand workers had been killed, 160,000 had been permanently disabled, and 4.2 million had been temporarily injured. Wilson then sent a plaintive letter to William Green calling for his help in yet another publicity campaign. The centerpiece again would be the establishment of more Joint Plant Health and Safety Committees. "It is our hope that this typically American approach," Wilson wrote, "will bring about an immediate and very marked reduction in injuries and illness among our workers in all war industries."[54] Green responded quickly to the Board's formal request. A day after receiving Wilson's letter, Green penned his own to the leaders of all national and international unions, all state federations, and all city central bodies. In it, he stated that labor "must take immediate and effective action to reduce industrial accidents and occupational diseases." And he urged the formation of new Joint Plant Health and Safety Committees. But he also wrote that "it is primarily the responsibility of management to initiate and carry on an effective and adequate health and safety program."[55]

The WPB's safety wartime campaigns thus reflected well the general recognition that management was essentially in charge of safety and the skeptical stance of labor. It was not that workers and their unions opposed safety. Of course, they supported it, generally speaking.[56] Since the early 1900s, the AFL had taken a strong public stance on industrial health and safety. At its 1906 convention, the Federation had pushed for better working conditions to prevent such diseases as tuberculosis. Still, the AFL had opposed the Worker's Health Bureau in the 1920s and was not as supportive of workers as the Western Federation of Miners, which organized its own hospitals and hired its own doctors. The Congress of Industrial Organizations was also more progressive and supported its unions, such as the United Automobile Workers, which created its own medical department, with union doctors, during the war. But in the eyes of the AFL and, to some extent, even the CIO, it was management's responsibility to initiate and maintain workplace safety programs.[57]

The skepticism that many AFL unionists felt toward management-led safety campaigns had something to do with their previous experiences with industrial safety programs. Safety experts were seen as (and often were actually) efficiency experts in disguise, telling workers not necessarily how to work safer but how to work harder. Employer-sponsored safety committees sometimes had labor spies or were composed of the plant's "best men," who were sympathetic to the employer. This was particularly true in the mining fields of Pennsylvania, where employees who worked with employers on safety issues were known as "suckers."[58] Even the plant physician was not trusted. Pre-employment examinations were sometimes used to keep certain (often prounion) workers from getting jobs, and subsequent examinations were occasionally used as grounds for reassignment or discharge. A few progressive states, such as Wisconsin, forbade such practices, but they were all too common.[59] Finally, the AFL had clearly internalized the notion that managers were primarily responsible for safety. The onus for maintaining plant safety was on them, not on AFL workers or leaders. One can see this mindset at work in the example of the International Harvester Corporation and its tractor plant, the Milwaukee Works, in Milwaukee, Wisconsin.

A Case Study of the AFL and Wartime Job Safety

By the time of the Second World War, International Harvester was a corporate behemoth, with historical roots extending more than one hundred years into the past. In 1831, Cyrus Hall McCormick built his first horse-powered reaper. He received a patent three years later. In 1847, he built his first factory, near Chicago. In 1902, McCormick's sons and four other industrialists attempted to corner the farm implement market by forming International Harvester Corporation (IHC). IHC, which produced 85 percent of the nation's farm equipment, was an industry leader, often on the cutting edge of industrial developments. This was especially true for labor relations. By the 1940s, McCormick and his sons had waged a multigenerational war against unions. Organized labor first made inroads in McCormick's plants during the Civil War, when workers struck for higher wages and an eight-hour day. Following the economic collapse of 1872, Cyrus McCormick II began a concerted effort to destroy the unions within his shops. At first, McCormick utilized a three-pronged attack. Like many employers, he used violence, intimidation, and other strong-arm methods to discourage unionizations. When these failed, he replaced workers with machines. These methods were only partially successful, and, by the turn of the twentieth century, McCormick had opted for another method. In advance of many of his peers, McCormick established IHC as a leader in welfare capitalism. In 1901, McCormick hired Gertrude Becks, of the conservative National Civic Federation, to head up "betterment work" at the corporation. On her recommendations, McCormick dramatically increased worker benefits, which included, among other things, accident compensation and sick leave. Additionally, IHC was a pioneer when it came to worker safety.[60]

All IHC plants had a medical department staffed with doctors and nurses. Hurt workers were expected to go to the department first, before going for medical treatment outside the plant. In serious cases, workers were sent directly to the hospital. IHC paid for the bills out of its relief fund, which was endowed largely by the company itself. In 1905, Harvester's new welfare manager, C. W. Price, made an intensive investigation of industrial disease and accidents and devised a benefit-plan proposal, which was widely adopted in the company's plants. The program was voluntary; participants paid 2 percent of their wages into the fund in return for benefits that included fifty-two weeks' leave at half-pay for sickness; fifty-two weeks' leave at half-pay for accidents on the job or at home; one year's wages for death; two years' wages for accidental death; and one year's wages for loss of a hand. Furthermore, workers did not have to sign a waiver giving up their right to sue for damages. Price justified this unique aspect of the program on the ground that including the waiver would only breed resentment among the workers, jeopardizing their participation in the program and actually encouraging them to sue when accidents did happen.[61]

Harvester also had an elaborate safety organization. The corporation itself had a safety department, with a supervisor, general inspector, and assistant. Among their tasks was education. They created safety handbooks for workers and foremen. Twice a week, Harvester's safety supervisor issued safety bulletins to workers, raising awareness and encouraging everyone to work carefully. Every plant had a safety inspector, a safety committee (composed of managers and foremen), and a workers safety council, with representatives elected by employees in every department, including the foundries, which were almost entirely staffed by African Americans. In turn, the council selected a safety deputy to be the link between workers and managers. The council also worked closely with foremen and each week held joint safety meetings. The results were positive. Like many other companies in the 1930s, Harvester enjoyed low accident-frequency rates.[62]

Again, in addition to any altruistic motives, McCormick's goal in creating strong safety and medical components to IHC was to discourage the formation and expansion of unions. This goal went unrealized. Rather, workers resented the tradeoff for all welfare benefits, which was a signed pledge not to strike. Workers also resisted what one historian has called McCormick's "guerrilla war" against unions. Company officials forbade any meetings—including ones involving safety—that involved workers from more than one plant. They even eliminated interplant athletics, fearing that ballgames fostered worker solidarity. The combination of an excellent benefit system, company hostility toward unions, and a weak economy in the 1930s did sap—but did not destroy—Harvester's unions. They still existed, but in a weakened state. During the Second World War, Harvester maintained its commitment to

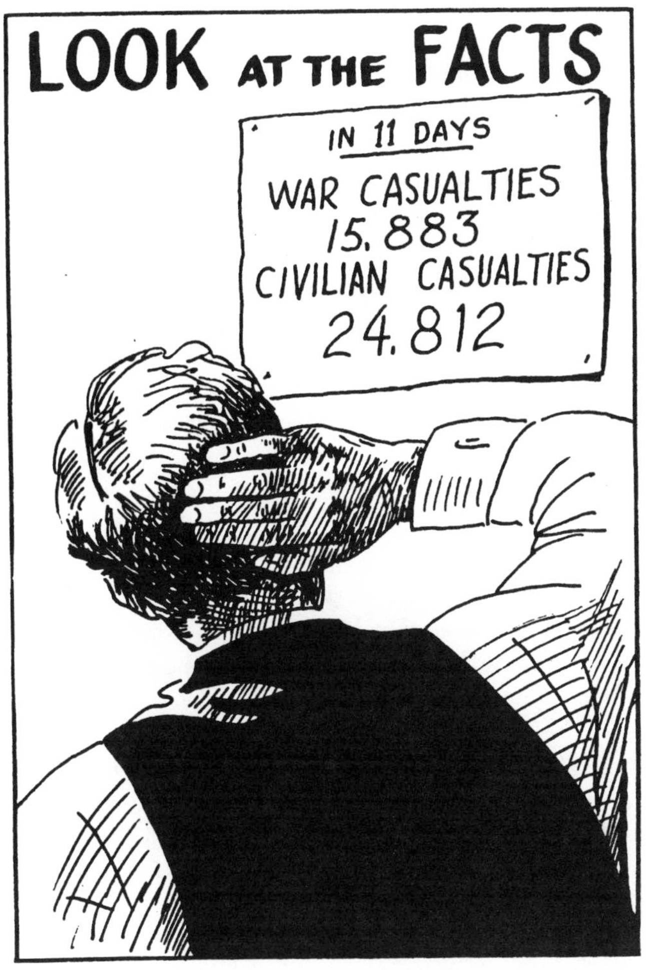

Safety Bulletin No. 40, IHC Tractor Works, 9 October 1944. Original caption read: "American Forces, fighting their way into Fortress Europe suffered 15,883 causalities during the first 11 days of the invasion. Of these, 3,283 were killed and 12,600 wounded. They were on a necessary mission of liberation. Compare their sacrifices with the useless slaughter and injury from carelessness at home. Even with last year's wartime restrictions on motoring, the traffic causalities *each 11 days* averaged 24,812—702 killed and 24,110 injured. Last year's record also indicates that there were more than two times that many industrial accidents in an 11-day period throughout the country." From *Safety: 51 Safety Messages* (Chicago: International Harvester Corporation, 1945), p. 44, International Harvester Collection, courtesy of the Wisconsin Historical Society, image ID 34379.

corporate welfare without much objection from the unions.[63] In the case of industrial safety, the unions at IHC seemed to take it for granted that the company would lead the campaign against accidents, which were on the rise in the 1940s. Although accident statistics for those years at Harvester no longer exist, the problem was severe. At the 1942 meeting of International Harvester plant safety inspectors, the corporation's chief safety supervisor, John Young, reported:

> The safety record thus far this year has been most disheartening. At the close of last year, all of us in this field of accident-prevention had set our sights to "cut accidents in two during 1942" and we sincerely hoped to reduce the severity as well as the frequency rate by at least 50 per cent. As we know, such has not been the case; on the contrary, our experience in severity for this year has steadily increased, until now we can only conclude that when the year's figures are compiled it will probably be the highest in many years.[64]

Despite this increase, workers were content to let the company handle the problem. International Harvester's Milwaukee Works provides one example of this. The 3,500 employees at the plant made farm tractors and other types of implements. They belonged to the AFL Federal Labor Union No. 22631. By 1941, there was only one other IHC plant that had an AFL union—Farmall, in Rock Island, Illinois. The rest had gone over to the Congress of Industrial Organizations in the 1930s.[65] As in all Harvester plants, the company led an efficient and wide-ranging safety campaign. Milwaukee Works' safety superintendent was R. E. Bloye, and its safety inspector was C.W. Coutts. Like all safety superintendents, Bloye sent out weekly bulletins. Written in a punchy style, they no doubt caught workers' attention. Coutts was also quite active in the plant and appears to have been a humanitarian. In commenting on why the Milwaukee Works upheld strict safety and inspection rules, he explained that it was not "solely because [of] existing [state] law or safety orders, but because these are prized assets in the life of a human being."[66]

Union employees at Milwaukee Works supported the plant safety program and were quite content to let management lead the campaign for a safe shop floor. Even when given the opportunity to assert more influence, the union did not. In the spring of 1942, Federal Union 22631 officials began to negotiate a new contract with Harvester. Com-

Milwaukee Harvester Works, ca. 1940, International Harvester Collection, image 33310, courtesy of the Wisconsin Historical Society.

pany officials did not like the wage proposals, and there was conflict between management and labor. Eventually, the National War Labor Board stepped in, and, in May, the union signed a contract, which provided for a retroactive 4.5 percent raise.[67] In the contract, no specific reference was made to safety. However, the union approved of two provisions that clearly gave management control of that aspect of the shop floor. First, it agreed that a main function of management was to keep "abreast of scientific and technical advances." In other words, the machines and their improvements, such as safety guards, were in managers' control. Second, the granting of leaves of absence in case of accidents and other situations was completely management's prerogative. Time off to recover from an accident was not a worker's right. Rather, workers had to make a request, which management then might or might not approve.[68]

In no wartime document that survives is it apparent that the AFL Federal Union 22631 opposed IHC's control over safety and accidents on the shop floor. Rather, it seems that that it conceded managers' control in this area, and Harvester was more than happy to maintain its power. In fact, IHC officials were quite pleased with their ability to expand their authority. In a 1945 speech titled "Management's Prerogatives," George Hodge, Harvester's lead labor-relations manager, acknowledged that the company's 114 unions refused to tackle "knotty" problems; he suggested that they preferred, in effect, to say,"well, that's your problem—you're running the business."[69] Hodge was exaggerating, no doubt to impress his peers. Nonetheless, it seems clear that Federal Union 22631 did indeed leave accident prevention up to the company. Union officials were not alone in acting this way and were in fact in line with the American Federation of Labor. It is important to recognize, however, that if managers assumed the power to set and enforce safety rules, they had also to take responsibility for the disastrous injury rates during the war. It was in large part—as *Fortune* magazine pointed out, in 1942—management's attitudes and inactions that created the dire shop-floor situation. The AFL's unwillingness to challenge management's prerogative in this area, however, did not improve the working conditions for its members. Rather, in some ways, the Federation's position on wartime safety ensured that many of its members would continue to sacrifice more than they should have on the home front of the Second World War.

7

Planning America's Future
The AFL and Postwar Planning

> We know our objectives. We want lasting peace. We want equality between nations. We want freedom and opportunity for all nations. We want social and economic security for all peoples. These are the things labor in America is working and fighting for. These are the objectives which will spell the real victory and the permanent destruction of the forces of hate and oppression against which we are now engaged in a desperate war.
>
> —William Green, 1942[1]

> When I indicate the prospect of the coming depression toward which we are headed unless we act, I sound the warning, not in the way of a threat. I sound the warning for the prospect of mass unemployment as a real one—not imaginary. I sound it not because it is inevitable, but because it is not too late to change our future course.
>
> —Boris Shishkin, AFL economist, 1944[2]

Although those close to him knew that he was seriously ill, President Franklin D. Roosevelt's death on April 12, 1945, came as a great shock to a nation still at war. Perhaps no one was more astonished than Vice President Harry S. Truman. At approximately 5:00 P.M., Truman was summoned to the White House for what he thought was an impromptu meeting with FDR. There he was greeted by Stephen Early, Roosevelt's long-time secretary and adviser; Eleanor Roosevelt; her daughter Anna; and Anna's husband, John Boettiger. Mrs. Roosevelt approached Truman, put her hand on his shoulder, and gave him the sad news. Stunned silent for a few moments, Truman recovered to ask the former firstlady, "Is there anything I can do for you?" She replied,

"Is there anything *we* can do for you? For you are the one in trouble now." Indeed, Truman had to finish all the Herculean tasks remaining on FDR's desk, namely winning the war and forging a lasting postwar peace. In many ways, the first issue was really a matter of time, while the second was a tangled mess made even more complicated by various competing political factions, including big business and organized labor. Eventually, President Truman cast his support with labor, specifically the American Federation of Labor. Together, they sought to forge a postwar America free from economic depression and supportive of the needs and desires of workers. That vision, however, was only partly realized. As they did with so much of Truman's domestic policy initiatives, congressional conservatives thwarted many of his plans for reconversion in the United States. And, since their fates were linked, by defeating Truman, conservatives also dealt a crushing blow to the AFL's liberal postwar goals.[3]

The Lingering Fear of Unemployment

While Americans grieved and began to adjust to life without Roosevelt, they wondered who, exactly, Harry S. Truman was. As both a Democratic senator from Missouri and vice president, he had earned a reputation as a hardworking, unassuming Roosevelt loyalist. He did not have the political gravity of his vice presidential predecessor, Henry Wallace, nor in the least his presidential one. Nonetheless, Americans quickly rallied behind the new president. In August 1945, he enjoyed an 87 percent approval rating. Twelve months later, however, his job performance ratings had plummeted to 33 percent.[4] Truman won the war in stunning fashion, but he never secured widespread support for his vision of the postwar economy and society. As Truman's approval ratings fell, he became the object of ridicule. Americans made fun of his personal and presidential styles. Many mocked his close attachment to his mother. "Every day is Mother's Day in the White House" was the snide quip. A joke that concerned Truman's handling of the postwar economy came from Texas. The raconteur speculated on how Franklin Roosevelt might have dealt with the postwar crises and ended by wondering "what Truman would do if he were alive."[5] The truth was, however, that, while he lived, Franklin Roosevelt was neither entirely clear nor effective in setting out his administration's goals for the postwar period. Although one might have expected as much from the president who bragged that he never let his right hand know what his left was doing, FDR's seeming and apparent indecisiveness did not calm Americans' fears about the postwar period.

The most salient fear of most American workers was simple, yet all-consuming. They worried greatly about the return of the Great Depression. Even at the height of wartime production, in the summer of 1944, when the total labor force totaled more than sixty-six million and the unemployed numbered a meager 600,000, memories of hard times were not too distant. Only four years earlier, workers had been struggling through the "Roosevelt recession," which had begun in 1937. FDR and his New Deal seemed tired, unable to move the country far beyond a modest recovery. In July 1940, unemployment hovered near 16 percent.[6] The Second World War, of course, spurred rapid economic growth. But the question on the minds of many was: would that growth be sustained? Or, as the *American Federationist,* the AFL's house organ, put it: "Will that first day of peace herald the dawn of a new era of prosperity, of equity and of stable growth?" Or "will it merely reflect the afterglow of dying fires in the blast furnaces, smelters and kilns which will have done their job of feverish 'all out' production of defense material and equipment and which are no longer needed?"[7] Clearly, like many Americans, the heads of the AFL feared the latter.

Two members of the AFL's national leadership, Boris B. Shishkin and Matthew Woll, led the charge to prevent the return of economic depression. As an economist, Shishkin was the first to draw the Federation's attention to the challenges of the postwar period. He was born in 1906 in Odessa, Russia. Unlike so many immigrants who joined the labor movement in the United States, neither Shishkin nor any of his immediate family had been active trade unionists in the Old World. Shishkin's father was an officer in the czar's army. In 1919, the Shishkins fled to Turkey to escape the Bolsheviks. At his mother's urging, the family relocated again in 1923. This time they came to New York City. In 1927, he entered Columbia University and graduated three years later with a A.B. in economics. Two years later, he moved to Washington, D.C., to accept a fellowship at the Brookings Institution. In 1933, he left his post to join the AFL as a researcher. He worked with Florence Thorne, the Federation's director of research, who was also the confidant and

Boris Shishkin (1911–1973), courtesy of the George Meany Memorial Archives, image 1859.

personal secretary of both Samuel Gompers and William Green. Thus began a career in the labor movement that spanned four decades. In addition to serving as the Federation's top economist, he served on various government agencies, committees, and boards, including the War Production Board, the Office of Price Administration, and the President's Committee on Fair Employment Practice.[8]

Although Shishkin eventually became one of the AFL-CIO's elder statesmen, his initial encounter with organized labor was somewhat awkward. It came after he arrived in New York City, in 1923. Shortly after finding an apartment, Shishkin's parents sent their teenager out to find a job. With few language or job skills, Shishkin had a very hard

Matthew Woll (1880–1956), courtesy of the George Meany Memorial Archives, Photograph Collection, P-24/115, Chase Studios-301.986.1050.

time finding work. The economic collapse that had followed World War I only made his job hunt worse. Desperate for work, he sought some assistance. Out job-searching one day, Shishkin stopped a man on the street and asked for help. The man gave him the location of the local employment agency and told him to say, "I want a job." Before Shishkin could walk off, the man thought again and corrected himself. He told Shishkin to just go to the manager and say, "IWW." Not knowing what he was saying, Boris did as he was told. The employment officer got very red in the face and told him to "get the hell out here!" Eventually Boris found employment, later joining the local teamsters and driving truck for the American News Company.[9]

Even once in the AFL, Shishkin still seemed to struggle a bit. He was no organizer, and yet his immediate superior, Florence Thorne, often sent him on speaking engagements. After some bad outings, his office-mate, Spencer Miller, head of worker education, offered some advice, suggesting that it was easier to talk before a big group with one's eyes shut. As Shishkin told a Columbia University oral history interviewer, what happened next became part of Federation lore:

> So I started doing that a couple times, and then in the midst of one of those orations, a very beautiful thought passed through my head, and I was interested to see what the audience's reaction to it would be immediately, so I opened my eyes and look, and there was nobody in the hall. There was a fellow sitting next to me, and I said, "Where is everybody?" This fellow said, "everyone left." I said, "What are you doing here?" He said, "I'm the next speaker."[10]

Eventually Shishkin would become a superb and tremendously witty public speaker, giving more than 425 network radio broadcast speeches by the late 1950s.[11] In addition to his skill as a spokesman for labor and the AFL, Shishkin's importance to the Federation and the labor movement generally centered on his ability to distill economic facts and figures and put them into simple prose that the average worker could understand. He was a kind of John K. Galbraith for the labor movement. In the early 1940s, Shishkin related in the clearest terms the potential crisis lying in wait after the war.

Well before the United States officially entered the Second World War, Shishkin, as well as other AFL leaders, including Federation president William Green, expressed their concerns about what would happen to the American economy after the "emergency" in Europe, which had sparked an upswing in domestic factory production. Americans were once again beating plowshares into swords. But, as the editors of the *American Federationist* wrote, in early 1941, the United States needed to be ready for "the economic shock of peace."[12] Shishkin put it this way in a 1944 article titled "The Next Depression?":

> What matters is to make sure that our ship is kept on a stable and forward course and we don't chart the course once again in such a way as to find that our only escape from the path of another economic hurricane is into the path of another war.[13]

He then made the case by the numbers. Shishkin predicted that at least eleven million workers would be laid off after V-E Day and that another nine million would join the ranks of the unemployed following the fall of Japan. Thus, shortly after V-J Day, America would be in the clutches of a "deadly depression" far greater than that of the 1930s, with at least twenty million out of work. This worst-case scenario would be realized as the federal government terminated defense contracts and as employers laid off workers, cut hours, eliminated overtime, and downgraded jobs. Normally, a statement like this (or any statement) in the pages of the *American Federationist* would have a limited effect. Only those who regularly received the magazine would have seen Shishkin's dire forecast. But, in this instance, the AFL disseminated Shishkin's views as a formal press release, which was picked up by several major newspapers and news magazines, including the *New York Times,* the *Washington Post,* and *The Nation.* Additionally, *Stars and Stripes* published a summary of "The Next Depression?" in an article titled "AFL Economist Warns of Postwar Depression."[14]

Of course, soldiers were not immune to the fear that Shishkin so poignantly named. In fact, in many of their minds, the concern centered not only on the recent depression but also on what had happened to veterans after the First World War. No returning veteran wanted to be that haggard man selling apples in the street, the icon of the postwar period that followed the Armistice in 1918. The abrupt end of that war had caught American officials off guard. Wilson and his administration had started to plan for the postwar period only in late summer 1918. And those plans were still at the most abstract level. Written primarily by War Labor Policies Board officials, the position memoranda sent to Wilson sought ways to avoid lengthy periods of "idleness and dependency" and to solve the conundrum of how to provide jobs for returning American Expeditionary Force veterans while not denying opportunities to laid-off munitions workers.[15] The planners within the Wilson administration hoped to maintain the high levels of employment and income achieved in 1918. The problem was, however, that no one ever turned these goals into a plan of action. As a result, when the war ended, factory managers laid off wartime workers by the hundreds of thousands. They were joined by a similarly large numbers of unemployed veterans. Initially, the officials in the Wilson administration urged patience and expressed optimism. But, by the winter of 1919, there was no ignoring the economic collapse. Even the directors of the

Federal Reserve, which had been bullish on the prospects for the post-war economy, now sounded a pessimistic note in their monthly bulletin:

> Practically throughout the country the month of January has been characterized by the uncertainty incident to a period of transition in business. In some cases more readjustment than had been expected has proved to be necessary. Favorable developments which some had thought would present themselves immediately after the Armistice with Germany have been delayed. There has therefore been "hesitation" in business.[16]

The Federal Reserve Board still maintained that there had been "no essential loss of confidence in the future of the general situation."[17] This provided little solace for the out-of-work veterans and factory workers. Through the summer of 1919, unemployment was high, as was labor unrest. As demobilization and reconversion were completed over the next two years, things only got worse. In 1921, there were five million laborers out of work and 3,600 strikes, the highest peacetime total since 1903.[18]

Planning for Prosperity

While significant and perhaps influential, Shishkin's 1944 article was not really news. In fact, his call to action served only as a reminder, especially to New Dealers, that the work of fixing the American economy was unfinished. As the Second World War began, FDR himself had seemed to turn away from this central mission of the New Deal. As he said publicly, Dr. New Deal had become Dr. Win-the-War. Still, Roosevelt knew that sooner or later he would have to deal with the economic problems that he seemingly had never solved. In other words, the lurking fear must have even haunted Roosevelt. Yet, in rethinking the problems of the Great Depression, FDR also had to fight the euphoric notion, already present by early 1944, that the war would be over soon and that the "good old days" would return. As his closest advisers, such as his budget director, Harold D. Smith, reminded the commander-in-chief, there had been no good economic days during the first six years of his administration. There had been only crisis.[19]

The economic crisis that had most shocked Roosevelt and the New

Dealers came in 1937. Shortly after his reelection, FDR began to consider how he could put the economy on a firmer footing. His secretary of the Treasury, Henry J. Morgenthau, strongly urged him to balance the federal budget, which had been running deficits since 1933. A balanced budget, it was reasoned, would instill both business and consumer confidence. Just the opposite happened. Without the financial crutch that the New Dealers had fashioned, the economy began to falter and collapse. Industrial production quickly declined, and unemployment rapidly rose. Initially, President Roosevelt seemed unmoved, and he told his cabinet to remain calm and stay the course. But, by October 1937, when the stock market had taken a major tumble, the White House began to get what Morgenthau called the "jitters."[20] Only the economic spark provided by the defense effort in 1939 and 1940 pulled the United States out of what was termed the Roosevelt recession. Nonetheless, for New Dealers, questions remained: after the war, would the sick economy return? Would Dr. Win-the-War have to become once again Dr. New Deal?

Although the United States was engaged in a fateful war, this question nonetheless dominated the wartime political and economic thoughts of liberals and their allies. In the late 1930s and early 1940s, there had been something of a battle among New Dealers to find the path out of the recession. Those in the Roosevelt administration tended to agree with the British economist John Maynard Keynes, who believed that the American economic recovery depended on two things: increased federal spending and increased consumption. Consensus broke down on the best method to achieve those goals. One group within the Roosevelt administration, whose membership included Attorney General Thurman Arnold, sought to revive the economy by attacking monopolies and labor unions. Smashing economic concentration, it was thought, would encourage competition. Increasing the number of businesses vying for consumer sales would lower prices and thus raise consumer purchasing power and therefore consumer spending.

This second cadre within the administration—whose members were older than those in the other group—firmly believed that social and economic planning would lead to prosperity. When Roosevelt launched the New Deal in 1933, the planners were in control. Their desire was to create a harmonious economy through cooperation among business, organized labor, and government. Initially, they were somewhat successful, working under the aegis of the National Recovery Administration

(NRA). The mechanism that was to bring about economic stability, predictability, and prosperity was the NRA codes. These codes—of which there were 541 by 1935—were intended to be the result of careful reasoning, planning, and analysis by the various economic stakeholders. And, to some degree, the codes were in fact the product of such tripartite collaborations. The AFL's Boris Shishkin himself participated in many code-writing sessions in 1933 and 1934.[21]

In 1935, however, the U.S. Supreme Court invalidated the NRA codes. This allowed other political forces to gain power during the later years of the New Deal. Nonetheless, planning advocates remained in the administration. Many quickly found a home in Harold Ickes's Public Works Administration (PWA). The PWA's National Resource Board did much of the initial planning for federal construction projects. In 1939, the New Deal's planning group was renamed the National Resource Planning Board (NRPB). The NRPB, whose membership, staff, and advisers represented literally a who's who of the American liberal intelligentsia, was led by the President's seventy-year-old uncle, Frederic A. Delano. The Board members participated in the policy debates on how to end the Roosevelt recession and later fashioned a blueprint for the postwar United States. Their conclusions on this matter were best summarized in two lengthy and groundbreaking reports, titled *Security, Work, and Relief Policies* (1942) and *Post-War Plan and Program* (1943), as well as two smaller pamphlets, titled *After Defense—What?* (1941) and *After the War—Full Employment* (1943).[22] In general, the NRPB called for the creation of a comprehensive and thoughtful system of social programs and economic planning in order to establish a more permanent prosperity in America. Although the NRPB's reports (which we discuss in more detail later) were exceedingly controversial, they nonetheless illustrate the high regard that some liberals had for planning and represent the high-water mark in the national planning movement. Their work resonated with many observers inside and outside the federal government.[23]

Like the NRPB, the AFL was deeply committed to social and economic planning after the war. In fact, its national leaders believed that only through planning could the looming postwar economic crisis be avoided. On August 9, 1941, the AFL Executive Council issued a public statement reiterating its fear that "the United States faces a dangerous and perhaps fatal depression." To council members, the solution was clear. "Long-range plans for the future," they said, "must be prepared without delay or the economic security and political freedom of our country will be menaced." Finally, the AFL's leaders called on President Roosevelt to create a labor-business-government agency to lay the groundwork for a plan to shift the United States "from war production to peace production."[24]

Roosevelt made no formal or recorded response to the AFL's request, although in November 1940 he had directed the NRPB to focus its energies on postwar planning.[25] As a result, the Federation moved to jump-start the planning process. At the October 1941 AFL Convention, the Federation's membership authorized William Green to appoint a post-emergency planning committee. Fourteen months later, in late December 1942, Green set up his committee. Called the Post-War Planning Committee, it was headed by AFL vice president Matthew Woll. Committee members included David Dubinsky, of the International Ladies Garment Workers Union; John Childs, of the American Federation of Teachers; Harvey Brown, president of the International Association of Machinists; George M. Harrison, president of the Brotherhood of Railway Clerks; Richard Gray, secretary of the International Union of Bricklayers, Masons and Plasterers; and Rubin Soderstrom, president of the Illinois State Federation of Labor. Importantly, Green also named to the committee one African American, Milton Webster, of the Brotherhood of Sleeping Car Porters, and one woman, Agnes Nestor, of the AFL's research bureau. The group had a four-point mission. First, it was to investigate and report on a "plan for labor representation in the peace conferences which will follow victory." Second, the committee was to develop "specific proposals which the labor representatives should seek to have incorporated in the peace treaty." Third, it was to develop a "broad program of post-war reconstruction to prevent a disastrous depression." Fourth, it was to devise ways to expand "social, economic and political security for America and the people of all lands."[26]

The charge and composition of the AFL's Post-War Planning Committee were rather straightforward, except perhaps for one point: the appointment of Woll. One probably should not interpret this as a snub directed at Shishkin, who already held critical posts with the Office of Price Administration, the War Production Board, and the Fair Employment Practice Committee. Giving him one more job like that would only have spread the AFL's economist even thinner. Furthermore, just because Shishkin did not directly sit on the committee did not mean he could not help. In fact, he fed the committee members statistical data for their speeches, articles, and pamphlets.[27] Similarly, regardless of his lack of an official position, Shishkin provided the committee with a connection to the community of American planners by his membership in the National Planning Association (NPA), the most influential planning organization, which had formed in 1934 as a cooperative venture of progressive-minded business, labor, and academic leaders.[28] Shishkin, along with the AFL's other representative on the NPA, gave the committee not only access to a wealth of knowledge about planning but also contacts to some of the foremost political and economic thinkers of the time.[29] Finally, by placing the AFL's number two man at the head of the committee (and not the Federation's economist), Green was signifying to the union's membership, to the public, and to the Roosevelt administration just how important and serious the AFL considered the problem.

Born in 1880, in Luxembourg, Woll was a photoengraver by trade. In 1906, he became the president of the International Photoengraving Union of North America, a post he held for nearly twenty-five years. A staunch conservative Republican for most of his life, Woll was well connected in Washington, D.C.; he served on various government boards, including the War Labor Board during the First World War, and advised presidents from Wilson to Truman. He was Samuel Gompers's protégé and had been groomed to succeed the cigar maker when he died. But, as fate would have it, William Green, not Woll, was tapped. Despite the disappointment, Woll continued to serve the AFL as its first vice president. His energetic style, his florid dress (always wing collars and frock coats), and his gifted oratory made him the perfect leader for the AFL's most critical wartime project. It was Woll's responsibility to devise and rally support for the Federation's plan to recast and reshape the American economy, guaranteeing not only prosperity for all but also working-class security.[30] AFL president Green put it this way:

> We must start planning now for the emergencies that will face us when the war is over. We can't afford to wait until victory is won. Without adequate preparation and a specific program to meet that day of victory, we may find—as in the last war—that the battle was in vain.
>
> We know our objectives. We want lasting peace. We want equality between nations. We want freedom and opportunity for all nations. We want social and economic security for all peoples.
>
> These are the things labor in America is working and fighting for. These are the objectives which will spell the real victory and the perma-

nent destruction of the forces of hate and oppression against which we are now engaged in a desperate war.

I firmly hope that through the finds of this committee the American Federation of Labor will be able to show that labor is measuring up to its responsibilities and is capable of exerting real leadership for a better world.[31]

The Federation's Plan for Reconversion

The AFL's Post-War Planning Committee worked along two connected but different tracks: economic reconversion and postwar social policy. The Woll team first developed detailed recommendation regarding the federal government's immediate economic response to victory. Released to the public in late February 1944, the committee's report on reconversion (which was distributed as a pamphlet titled "Reconstruction Administration") focused on the mechanics of changing the economy back to a peacetime footing. The committee's suggestions were practical. First, the U.S. Congress was to pass legislation creating a Reconstruction Administration (RA) consisting of representatives of labor, farmers, and employers, appointed by the president and confirmed by the Senate. Second, working with wartime agencies such as the War Production Board, the RA was to coordinate defense contract cancellation, all manpower issues from demobilization to job placement, disposal of government stockpiles and property, the continuation or elimination of price and wage controls, and the expansion of federal social services to aid returning veterans or unfortunate workers caught in the chaos of reconversion.[32]

Each of the RA's jobs reflected not only the AFL's newly found belief in social and economic planning but also a clear sense of history. What the AFL Post-War Planning Committee hoped to avoid was a repeat of the situation that had followed World War I, when there was no planned termination of contracts, when the federal government quickly dumped surplus equipment and factories onto the markets, and when no thought was given to the situation that would face returning veterans. The lack of federal coordination and consideration caused chaos and depressed consumer, business, and labor markets. The rapid removal of federal contracts was bad enough, but when it was followed by the flooding of markets with cheap parts, plants, and equipment, the economy sputtered even more. Moreover, since there was no forethought given to the release of veterans into cities, unemployed workers pooled in large cities, unable to find work but unable to leave. At the same time, the immediate elimination of price controls created skyrocketing inflation in the early 1920s. Woll and his colleagues sincerely hoped that by creating a kind of Reconversion czar, they could help the country understand the lessons of the post–World War I era and avoid its hardships.[33]

The AFL's Executive Council approved the Post-War Planning Committee's report during its January 1944 meeting. In giving its stamp of approval, the Council issued a statement saying that the "clear-cut and orderly plan" was essential to avoiding any postwar economic downturn. Moreover, the Council reiterated its political position on reconversion. Civilians, and not military officials, should supervise the transition of the wartime economy to peacetime. Additionally, it was essential that labor have representation on the proposed RA.

On February 23, 1944, Green sent the report to President Roosevelt. In the cover letter, he tried to impress upon the FDR a sense of urgency, suggesting that thirty million people might be unemployed following the war, ten million more than Shishkin had predicted. In any case, Green urged Roosevelt to accept the Federation's suggestions, particularly regarding the inclusion of labor in the administration of the reconversion period. This was a direct criticism of the report issued by the president's own postwar planning group, headed by Bernard M. Baruch, the financier and World War I's chief industrial production administrator, and his long-time collaborator, John M. Hancock. Baruch's and Hancock's *Report on War and Post-War Adjustment Policies* had been published just a week prior to the release of the AFL's plan and had quickly met a firestorm of criticism. Green's comments were mild in comparison to those of others. He kindly urged that FDR "consider these recommendations in connection with the recommendations of Mr. Baruch which is splendid in many respects but does not provide a representative economic commission to be the over-all policy making body, providing the framework and controls to guide the agencies of conversion."[35]

Everything about the Baruch-Hancock report—even the creation of his committee—had been controversial and part of the bureaucratic mess in Washington.[36] At no time during the defense emergency or during the war itself was Roosevelt or Congress completely satisfied with the administration of the mobilization. Unsurprisingly, FDR's response was to tinker with the bureaucratic structure. In 1939, he had created (or more accurately re-created) the War Resources Board, which gave way to the National Defense Advisory Commission (1940), then to the Office of Production Management (1941), then to the War Production Board (1942). Under the leadership of Donald Nelson, the WPB did an enormous and terrific job of coordinating the production of munitions. And yet, problems remained. In 1943, in part to forestall congressional action, Roosevelt created the Office of War Mobilization (OWM) to handle everything from manpower to factory production issues. The OWM's director was James F. Byrnes. Known as "Mr. Assistant President" (a phrase that Roosevelt hated), Jimmy Byrnes oversaw the final phases of war production and resource utilization.[37] But, almost as that work reached completion, critics, including many members of Congress, began to voice their worry that the OWM was not doing enough to plan for the postwar period.[38] In fact, there had been several congressional hearings on the issue of federal contract termination, and congressmen such as Senator Harry S. Truman (D-Missouri), Senator Walter George (D-Georgia), and Representative William Colmer (D-Mississippi) took the lead on the issue and initiated legislation to expand the purview of the OWM to include the postwar reconstruction. FDR opposed this idea, as it seemed to swing political power away from him. To forestall action, he instructed Director Byrnes to commission a postwar planning document. Byrnes in turn appointed the Wall Street mogul Bernard Baruch to the task of planning reconversion.[39]

Although FDR was not completely happy about the selection of Baruch, who had been Roosevelt's political adversary since the early 1930s, the president did accept the Baruch-Hancock report, even before its formal release. During his 1944 budget message, on January 10, 1944, Roosevelt publicly gave his imprimatur to the report.[40] Baruch and Hancock justified their work with the maxim that "just as we prepare for war in time of peace, so we should prepare for peace in time of war."[41] Their discussion of the peacetime economy centered on two main issues: the termination of war contracts and the disposal of surplus property. They also discussed at length the issue of planning the end of war production slowly so that the demobilization would not hamper the final military defeat of the Axis powers. At first glance, the Baruch-Hancock report seemed appealing to those concerned about postwar planning. In fact, the AFL's report had covered much the same ground. But the two reports did differ in one critical aspect. Only the

Federation report clearly dealt with what was termed the "human side" of reconversion. Only twice in the 108-page Baruch-Hancock report did the authors suggest what kind of program would be needed for veterans and unemployed factory workers. First, they recommended that the government create a "work director" to "unify the forces of the Executive Branch and to work with Congress on the whole human side of demobilization." Then, on page 77, they wrote:

> The war has brought abnormal conditions of employment which have given rise to human problems which become reflected in every situation requiring administrative or legislative decision. These problems cannot be separated from others. They will be greater or smaller directly according to the way in which such programs as contract termination, surplus disposal, the mustering out from the Armed Forces, public works, social security, education and benefits for veterans, and international agreements are handled. There is no way of isolating problems of human interest from others. But there is no necessity for losing sight of the personal element in any of the fields of adjustment—and there will be no excuse for ignoring it.[42]

The statement was sympathetic enough to assuage some liberals such as Eleanor Roosevelt. As she wrote Harry Hopkins (who criticized the report), "I read the Baruch report and it does not seem to me it ignores all the human side of demobilization."[43] But neither did the document spell out in any detail how public works, training programs, or social security would fit into the federal government's postwar plan. This criticism was at the root of William Green's request to President Roosevelt to include labor in the government's postwar policymaking commissions. Other critics of the Baruch-Hancock plan were less polite and even more to the point. In an influential essay that appeared in *The Nation* in March 1944, the liberal journalist Irving F. Stone called the Baruch-Hancock plan and its quick (in fact preemptive) approval by the Roosevelt administration "a kind of right-wing economic coup" staged by foes of liberalism and progressive planning. Even more telling, Stone wrote, was the idea coming from the White House that Brigadier General F. T. Hines would be appointed to the "work director" post. As Stone wrote, Hines was "a mediocre reactionary, a hangover from the Coolidge-Hoover era, and notorious in Washington for his opposition to work relief." "His appointment," Stone concluded, "makes the job a kind of cruel joke."[44]

As the ramifications of the plan sank in, others began to agree with Stone. Uncertain about Roosevelt's commitment to postwar planning, Senator George and Representative Colmer returned to their draft legislation to create a federal agency to handle reconversion. Their bill passed in October 1944, and FDR had no other choice but to sign it, thus transforming the Office of War Mobilization into the Office of War Mobilization and Reconversion.[45] The OWMR's mission was changed to include all issues related to the wartime economy. Perhaps no other federal agency has had as much power before or since.[46] There was yet another, and perhaps even more important, reaction to the Baruch-Hancock report. Groups such as the AFL that were interested in the "human side" of reconversion began to think of ways to fashion a postwar America where the needs of veterans and workers were met. In other words, they began to compose an American counterpart to the "Beveridge Plan," Great Britain's detailed postwar blueprint, which emphasized not only economic reconstruction but also social economic security.

The Federation's "Beveridge Plan"

The journalist I. F. Stone derisively labeled the Baruch-Hancock report "a Beveridge Plan for millionaires."[47] He was referring to Sir William Beveridge's report, sent to the British government in late 1942, which laid out a range of economic and social policy recommendations to improve the health and wealth of the average British citizen. Stone accused Baruch and Hancock of devising a postwar program to help those who had profited the most during the war, that is, the dollar-a-year men who owned the factories and who had accepted the war contracts to build the arsenal of democracy. The workers who had done the actual labor, though, seemed an afterthought to Baruch and Hancock, but not to the AFL. Drawing inspiration from President Franklin Roosevelt's notion of an "economic bill of rights," which including the right to decent housing, to adequate medical care, to protection from "the economic fears of old age, sickness, accident, and unemployment," and to education, the Federation sought to create its own working-class "Beveridge" plan.[48]

On February 1, 1944, in advance of the public release of the AFL's and OWM's postwar planning documents, the Federation's Executive Council announced that it was calling a national conference "to seek united policies on actions on vital post-war problems."[49] The event, formally titled the American Federation of Labor's National Post-War Forum, was held in New York City on April 12–13, 1944 and attended by more than five hundred union members, government officials, and business leaders. It was a buttoned-down, rather proper affair, complete with formal dinners. The menu for April 12 included grapefruit a l'orange, chicken gumbo with rice, filet of Boston sole bonne femme with mushrooms, roast turkey stuffed à l'americaine with cranberry and giblet sauce, sweet potato glace, new green peas, pave fraiselia, petit fours, and demitasse. Not regular worker fare, but perhaps it was conducive to the meeting of the minds of labor, business, and government.[50]

The conference had four main sessions and two plenary dinner meetings. Three of the topics focused on domestic issues, while the fourth concerned the postwar world order. The meeting began with international issues. Chaired by Matthew Woll, the session, which featured Professor James T. Shotwell, of Columbia University, Professor J. B. Condliffe, of Yale University and E. J. Phelan, director of the International Labor Organization, focused on national security in a hostile world and global economic security. April 12's afternoon session had perhaps the most important speaker of the forum, Alvin H. Hansen. This session was chaired by Percy Bengough, president of the Canadian Trades and Labor Congress, and featured Donald Davenport, of the Curtiss-Wright Corporation, Paul Hoffman, of the businessmen's planning organization, the Committee for Economic Development, and Hansen, the preeminent Keynesian economist, of Harvard University. The topic session was "Full Employment in Post-War America." Hansen's address, titled "Full Employment After the War," painted the possibility of a very rosy, prosperous America following the cessation of fighting. He contended that the rapid and dramatic increases in productivity and income experienced during the war years could continue into the peace. The war, he stated, would

> likely be followed by a general all around restocking boom. The elements of such a boom are: (a) an accumulation of inventory stocks by retailers, wholesalers, and manufacturers; (b) a large demand for consumers durables (automobiles, household equipment, etc.); (c) manufac-

> turers' and other business demand for machinery and equipment; (d) a huge net export surplus of foodstuffs and other materials for relief and rehabilitation.

The postwar economic expansion would also require significant government investment and major public spending initiatives. Hansen suggested that there existed "a great new frontier for investment," urban redevelopment. This new frontier, he reasoned, would be reached only through concerted governmental action. "[I]t will not happen automatically." Rather, urban redevelopment and the full-employment economy that it would help bring about would be attained in a "rational and planned way."[51]

Although both sessions were incredibly important for helping mold the AFL's policy and political positions about the postwar world, the press focused on April 12's dinner meeting, which, following a series of toasts by President Green, featured the now-infamous diplomat Assistant Secretary of State Breckinridge Long.[52] Long first thanked the AFL for stimulating the American "conscience . . . in behalf of human welfare." He then spoke about the need for cooperation among the Allies in building a peaceful, democratic postwar world, and he offered some veiled criticism of the Soviet Union and Joseph Stalin, who had seemingly disregarded the Atlantic Charter's admonition about territorial aggrandizement.[53]

The second day of the forum was entirely devoted to domestic issues. The first session, chaired by Agnes Nestor, collectively called for an expansion of social services. The eminent health insurance crusader Alice Hamilton spoke about the need to change the insurance systems that govern industrial accidents to grant "full coverage . . . for every injury that can be traced to the workers' occupation."[54] Alvin Hansen's equally famous Harvard colleague Sumner Slichter presented an address titled "The Contributions of Unemployment Compensation to Economic Stability," which called for raising unemployment benefits and increasing the number of weeks for which they were available to at least thirty.

Up to this point—lunch on the second day of the Post-War Forum—there does not seem to have been any controversy. At least for those attending the forum, full employment, more health insurance, and greater unemployment compensation were welcome additions to the American social system. But the apparent consensus cracked a bit after lunch.

During the afternoon session, titled "Free Labor and Free Enterprise in the Post-War Period," chaired by George Meany, the president of the U.S. Chamber of Commerce, Eric Johnston, spoke to the convention via radio. Whereas the earlier speeches seemed to have a progressive bent, Johnston's certainly did not. Rather, to many, his words were reactionary. He stated clearly that he favored unrestrained capitalism as the only means to achieve higher standards of living in the United States and the world. Any programs that sought to improve the lot of the poor were antithetical to this goal. Johnston, moreover, said:

> I do not yield to any Socialist in deploring the conditions of the so-called submerged tenth or underprivileged third. I share their sorrow, often their shame, for the sharecroppers, the migrant workers, the slum dwellers, the ill-housed and the undernourished. If I could honestly agree with them that there is a short-cut to perpetual plenty, freedom and glory, I would join them. But I cannot agree. There are no short-cuts. Our task of improving the lot of those at the bottom is a long, hard one.

Finally, Johnston said that it was the responsibility of management to evade the "haunting specter of mass unemployment." He gave government no specific role and said of labor that it would only help managers in "achiev[ing] this end."[55] Not one to pull punches, Meany later launched into a critique of Johnston's position that lasted several minutes. Stating that American capitalists must "bear the brunt of the blame" for the Great Depression, he questioned whether they could be trusted to secure a prosperous postwar period. Meany stated that the members of the AFL believed in capitalism and free enterprise but added that the economic system must be based also on "honest dealing and fair value." To that end, he concluded that in addition to labor organizations, industry "will need the cooperation of federal, state and local governments in the post-war transition period."[56]

The AFL's conference generated some positive press, particularly in the *New York Times,* which covered the forum in some detail and even published a glowing editorial that praised the work of the Woll committee.[57] A few weeks after the forum, the Federation's Post-War Planning Committee released a pamphlet that contained the entire AFL postwar program. The AFL maintained that the immediate responsibility of organized labor was to help win the war. But it acknowledged that the nation was living "in a revolutionary age [when] America [was] in the process of making far-reaching adjustments in both her domestic institutions and her foreign relations." "We believe that these changes in economy, government, and foreign affairs," the Planning Committee wrote, "can and must be made by and for the people."[58] In that spirit, the document laid out in a systematic manner its guiding principles. The first concerned the international scene. The AFL condemned war and pledged full support for the Atlantic Charter and Roosevelt's Four Freedoms, while stating that "lasing peace must rest on social justice and include all peoples."[59] The AFL also threw its weight behind the leadership of the United Nations, as well as the International Labor Organization, as a means to "provide lasting security."[60] On the domestic front, the Federation was dedicated to creating a "higher level of production and employment." In addition to full employment, the document called for new training and educational opportunities, the extension of federal unemployment benefits for two years, new public works, including urban renewal, and the broadening of various kinds of health insurance. Moreover, the report denounced "any and all forms of discrimination whether in the sphere of politics, of education or of work." And it called "equality of opportunity" an "authentic goal of American democracy."[61] Finally, the AFL called on labor, management, and the federal government to join in a partnership to address the problems of the postwar world.

Neither the AFL's postwar forum nor the conclusions that the unionists drew were exceptional. There were other such conferences, three in particular in 1944, sponsored by the National Association of Manufacturers (NAM).[62] Although the positions that came out of the NAM-sponsored events were typically conservative, the AFL's suggestions were not radical. In fact, they meshed nicely with what was fast becoming the liberal political agenda for the postwar period. This agenda had three main points: (1) the establishment of full employment, (2) the expansion of social security, and (3) the creation of a nationwide housing redevelopment program.

By far, full employment was the most discussed issue. It was on the lips of nearly all liberals and had become, in the words of I.,F. Stone, "that new, glamorous, and socially explosive slogan."[63] The ideas behind the concept are related to those of the British economist John M. Keynes, whose strongest proponent in America was Alvin Hansen. Born in 1887 to Danish immigrants living in South Dakota, Hansen became socially active academic but never lost his midwestern touch, that unquantifable quality of being able to relate to the common folk. Eventually making his way to Harvard University, Hansen worked off-campus for various New Deal agencies, including the Temporary National Economic Committee and the National Resource Planning Board, and for nongovernmental think tanks such as the National Planning Association, where he encountered the AFL's Boris Shishkin and R. J. Watts. Initially, Hansen was not keen on Keynes, and in 1936 he penned a critical review of Keynes's magnum opus, *General Theory of Employment, Interest, and Money* (1936). By 1939, however, a conversion had taken place, and now Hansen was the spokesman for those who advocated systematic economic planning and countercycle spending. During the Second World War, he loudly urged liberals and conservatives alike to take up the full-employment position.

On a macro level, the ideas behind full employment were rather simple. Advocates sought to avoid economic collapse after the war. These liberals and economists all shared that nagging fear of the return of massive unemployment. Economists figured that initially the postwar period would be a boom time because of all the pent-up consumer spending. For five years, Americans had not been able to purchase the cars, trucks, radios, refrigerators, and washing machines that they wanted. But, after that boom, they reasoned, there would be a dreadful economic bust. To prevent that ill, economic and resource planning, government-sponsored large- and small-work projects, the expansion of social security insurance to include at least more unemployment compensation and health care, and government investment in the economy were all necessary.[64] How much money? In a late 1944 article titled "Planning Full Employment," which appeared in *The Nation,* Hansen suggested that $20 billion might be enough to buoy the economic structure and prevent the return of the Great Depression.[65]

The American Federation of Labor's leadership signed on wholesale to the notion of full employment. Beginning in 1944, the *American Federationist* began running several full-length articles on the topic. Hansen, of course, summarized his ideas. Additionally, John H. G. Pierson, the Labor Department's Keynesian, wrote a couple of long essays, too.[66] By printing these articles, the AFL joined a public debate about full employment. Only the most conservative people, including the Chamber's Eric Johnston, and business organizations did not support the idea. Members of the U.S. Congress, members of the Federal Reserve Board, academics, Republican, Democrats, and even Socialists, and importantly, the general public (rich and poor alike) endorsed full employment. A *Fortune* magazine poll in 1944 indicated that nearly 75 percent of those asked supported some sort of federally engineered full-employment program. The main reservation, often expressed by conservatives, was that the public investment would explode the federal budget. Liberal retorted that a full-employment program and a balanced budget were not mutually exclusive goals. In fact, as the National Planning Association (of which both Alvin Hansen and Boris Shishkin were members) pointed out, the higher levels of income in a full-employment economy would increase the amount of taxes collected even without a tax increase. It seemed like a win-win, and the AFL found it easy to throw its weight behind it.[67]

The next agenda item was substantially more controversial—the expansion of the social security program. Although innovative and progressive by American standards, the Social Security Act of 1935 was nonetheless limited in scope, funding, and coverage. In 1945, the main architect of the law, Senator Robert F. Wagner (D-New York) proposed sweeping changes. If enacted, Wagner's new bill, whose Senate cosponsor was James E. Murray (D-Montana) and whose House sponsor was John D. Dingell (D-Michigan), would have funded the construction of new hospitals and medical facilities, broadened community health programs such as child and maternal health and welfare services, established government-funded health insurance, and created national employment service and national unemployment insurance systems. The American Federation of Labor, particularly William Green, gave these new provisions strong support. President Green had been intimately involved in the design and passage of the first Social Security Act as a member of the Advisory Council on Economic Security (ACES). ACES and, importantly, the National Planning Association, both of which had AFL representatives, also helped draft the underlying principles of the Wagner-Murray-Dingell bill.[68]

To amass the support of the members of the AFL as well as that of the general public, the AFL Executive Council, in 1944, hired Nelson H. Cruikshank as its full-time director of social insurance activities. He was the perfect choice for the job. He had been not only a business agent for a local AFL union but also a New Dealer who worked at various federal agencies in the 1930s. Thus, while holding liberal views, he also understood and could talk to the Federation's arch-conservatives, such as Matthew Woll, John Frey, and Florence Thorne. With the assistance and support of Federation leaders like Woll, Green, and Shishkin, Cruikshank worked with liberal congressional lobbyist groups like the Social Security Charter Committee and appealed directly to the AFL membership. In a series of articles published in the *American Federationist,* Cruikshank tried to build support for the Wagner-Murray-Dingell bill.[69] Unfortunately for Cruikshank, the AFL, and other liberal groups, such as the NPA, their amendments to the Social Security Act met a wall of criticism and political opposition from conservatives of all stripes and from organizations like the American Medical Association (AMA), which homed in on national health insurance as anathema to the American way. To the AMA, it was "socialized medicine" that would lower standards and regiment doctors and patients.[70]

The final part of the AFL's postwar platform was as universally accepted as the Wagner-Murray-Dingell bill was controversial. The Federation's leadership wanted the federal government to sponsor massive public works to rebuild America's cities and fabricate homes for the next generation. This suggestion came from the AFL's Housing Committee, which during the war was chaired initially by Boris Shishkin and later by Harry C. Bates. The AFL's Housing Committee made three arguments in favor of such a building plan. First, the condition of American housing was poor and getting worse. A Twentieth Century Fund report found that in 1940, nearly a quarter of all urban dwellings lacked bathrooms and more than 10 percent needed major repairs. Things were worse in rural areas of the United States, where nearly one out of every three houses needed major repairs.[71] The second argument related to wartime population changes. In addition to the new construction made necessary by internal migration of workers from one part of the country to another, housing requirements were going to increase with the population. By AFL estimates, country would need to build 1.5 million housing units for ten years after the war.[72] Finally, the AFL's Housing Committee contended that urban and rural redevelopment was a positive good.

> Blighted districts have developed which must be rehabilitated before they deteriorate still further. Slums, both an economic burden and a social liability, will continue to spread if not checked. Development on

> the boarders of our cities must be controlled or we will have further sprawling and uneconomic decentralization.[73]

Moreover, this building program would provide, in words of Harry Bates, the "things we all want, like 'full employment.' "[74]

The Fight for an American "Beveridge" Plan

Unlike the AFL's first postwar planning document, there was no imperative to send President Roosevelt the Woll Committee's second report. In a sense, FDR already had it, and both the AFL and CIO approved of it.[75] In November 1940, Roosevelt had asked his National Resource Planning Board to investigate the issue of postemergency (and, after December 7, 1941, postwar) economic and social planning. During the conversion and war years, the NRPB published more than two hundred reports. Put another way, the Board published 1,200 pages on the issue of housing, 1,500 pages on public works, 2,300 pages on the postwar economy, and 13,000 pages on general planning.[76] Despite all this work, the NRPB is known for one report: *Security, Work, and Relief Policies*. Sent to the president just three days before Japan's attack on Pearl Harbor, the report was kept under wraps by FDR for more than a year for fear of raising the ire of conservative congressmen. When it was finally released, in March 1943, *Security, Work, and Relief Policies* was heralded (and damned) as an American version of the Beveridge Report, which had been sent to the British Parliament in November 1942. Although both reports had marked differences because of the idiosyncratic nature of politics, society, and economics in each country, they did share a common outlook. Simply put, William Beveridge and his British staff and Frederic Delano and his American Board sought to—in the words of Beveridge—find "the way to freedom from want."[77] Central to the NRPB's plan was the idea of full employment. Although the NRPB (and, in particular, its economist, Alvin Hansen) had been arguing for full-employment policies since 1940, *Security, Work, and Relief Policies* was perhaps the Board's boldest statement:

> We can have work for all, and we can have much higher levels of income, particularly for the lowest income groups. Full employment makes possible these higher income levels, and without full employment

> such levels are impossible. The National Resource Planning Board has repeatedly stated its conclusion, based on careful study of American resources, that full employment and high national income are indispensable parts of the American goals for which we strive.[78]

Security, Work, and Relief Policies also called for a series of reforms to the current system of social security, such as an expansion of old-age and survivors insurance, an increase in unemployment compensation and public assistance, the creation of federal work programs, the establishment of various educational opportunities for young people, and the creation of a range of public services to improve child-welfare services, promote the health of mothers and their children, and institute such novel programs such as "free school lunches . . . for all school children."[79]

If *Security, Work, and Relief Policies* seemed to move the country in a radical direction, the NRPB's other major wartime report, *Post-War Plan and Program,* might be considered revolutionary. Transmitted to President Roosevelt roughly a year after its first report, *Post-War Plan and Program* had two parts that summarized the Board's recommendations for the immediate postwar reconversion and for the restructuring of the American economy after the war. It was the second set of suggestions that seemed to break new ground. The NRPB crystallized its position in one large resolution:

> The National Resource Planning Board believes that it should be the declared policy of the United States Government to promote and maintain a high level of national production and consumption by all appropriate measures necessary for this purpose. The Board further believes that it should be the declared policy of the United States Government:
>
> To underwrite full employment for the employables;
> To guarantee a job for every man released from the armed forces and the war industries at the close of the war, with fair pay and working conditions;
> To guarantee and, when necessary, underwrite:
> Equal access to security,
> Equal access to education for all,
> Equal access to health and nutrition for all, and
> Wholesale housing conditions for all.[80]

The NRPB was suggesting the same things as the AFL. It wanted full employment, public works, urban and rural housing development, an expanded social security system, and a new national health care system.

Liberals inside and outside the federal government heralded the NRPB reports, particularly *Security, Work, and Relief Policies*. Several congressmen, such as Representative William Colmer (D-Mississippi), Senator Robert Wagner (D-New York), and Senator Walter F. George (D-Georgia), had taken special interest in issues like housing, health care, and postwar public works.[81] The American Federation of Labor, the National Farmers Union, and the Congress of Industrial Organizations (CIO) all rallied behind it. Like the AFL, the CIO had its own postwar planning committee, whose adherence to full employment and whose recommendations mirrored the AFL's and the NRPB's.[82] In fact, the CIO may have had a more decentralized postwar planning mechanism that involved more member unions and locals and encouraged them to develop ideas for long-term prosperity. The stellar example is Walter Reuther's plan for full employment. In 1945, Reuther, who was then a vice president in the UAW-CIO, devised a plan to raise wages and maintain (not increase) consumer prices, while achieving full employment. In a widely distributed pamphlet titled "How to Raise Wages Without Increasing Prices," Reuther used quotations from Alvin Hansen to support his position that if workers' wages were increased, workers would in turn buy more consumer goods, such as automobiles. For employers and managers, higher sales would maintain or increase profits and thus avoid any urge to raise prices to offset the higher wages.[83] Although, given the serious and continuing tension between the AFL and CIO, union leaders might not have admitted that they agreed with one another, in fact they did.

While Roosevelt and his supporters seemed to have reached a consensus behind the NRPB's reports and ideas, conservatives similarly united to oppose the postwar plan. Their counterargument had two main parts. First, many feared that Keynesian countercycle spending would create such large budget deficits that the economy would be gravely—and perhaps fatally—harmed, instead of improved. As one University of California at Los Angeles economist, Benjamin M. Anderson, Jr., a critic of both Keynes and Hansen, put it, in 1940:

> Our great American economy, functioning with full efficiency, can carry a heavy load. But a chronically unbalanced government budget is a

> poor foundation for social security for anybody; and a crippled economic mechanism is a poor foundation for a more abundant life.[84]

This argument appealed greatly to conservative Republicans and Democrats in Congress. Senator Robert A. Taft (R-Ohio), who became Congress's leading critic of postwar planning, voiced his opposition as early as 1943, asserting that the NRPB's program was "a combination of hooey and false promises" and that it would lead to financial ruin "long before the war was over."[85] Taft's congressional colleague Representative Stephen Pace (D-Georgia), concluded similarly that the Roosevelt postwar plan "looks like a $50-million-a-year proposition." "I don't see," Pace continued, "where we get that kind of money."[86]

The second argument against the postwar plan supported by the AFL and the NRPB was based on an overriding fear that planning itself would lead to totalitarianism. The *New York Times* editorialized that the NRPB's proposals were akin to "Bismarck's state insurance systems which laid the foundation for the German welfare state that ended in naziism." The U.S. Chamber of Commerce agreed. In 1945, the Chamber's director of economic research, Emerson P. Schmidt, speaking for the organization, published a pamphlet condemning the concept of full employment as antithetical to "individual freedom in this country." Only "a dictatorship—fascist, socialist or communist—controlling prices, wages and workers, can secure and maintain full employment so long as its power endures."[87] Certainly not all conservatives shared the depth of this fear of creeping totalitarianism. UCLA professor Benjamin Anderson called it governmental "back seat driving" that would lead to various economic fender-benders.[88] Others, however, shared Friedrich A. von Hayek's view, expressed in his best-seller, *The Road to Serfdom* (1944), that governmental planning led to totalitarianism.[89]

The first action congressional conservatives took to stop Roosevelt's postwar plan—and those of the AFL and the CIO—was to eliminate the National Resource Planning Board. They did so the same way that they killed other New Deal agencies they opposed, such as the Fair Employment Practice Committee. Congress denied the NRPB money to continue its operations. Senator Taft led this charge, denouncing the Board, criticizing its publication *Security, Work, and Relief Policies* and its pamphlet *After the War—Full Employment*, and claiming that "Congress has never passed a planning law, has never created a planning agency, and has never given the board authority to do the kind of things it is doing."[90] Taft's supporters in both houses agreed, and in 1944 the NRPB ceased to exist.

From Plans to Action

Congress might have killed the messenger, but the message was nonetheless out. And it was not the National Resource Planning Board alone that had created the liberal postwar goals. The NRPB's ideas reflected a broad consensus among New Dealers and their allies, such as the AFL, about the shape of postwar America.[91] This battle of ideas that some in Congress had tried to stop came to a head in the summer of 1944. The D-Day invasion marked a significant turning point on both the battlefront and the home front. As Allied forces began to push toward Berlin, employers and government officials began to consider the future of the American workforce. By late fall 1944, as an end to the war in Europe was within sight, defense contractors began to lay off workers. Although serious attempts were made to keep workforce reductions quiet, workers soon read the writing on the wall, and they began to quit their war jobs by the thousands. As the *Wall Street Journal* announced, in October 1944:

> America's migrant war workers are going home by the tens of thousands. They are moving back to the farms, the small communities and the towns from which they were drawn by high wages in the arms plants. They want employment with a peace-time future.[92]

This was not an isolated phenomenon. In late 1944, in Los Angeles, about nine thousand workers were leaving the city each month. At the same time, in Philadelphia, turnover was about 6 percent, despite rigid manpower restrictions placed upon employers by federal officials who were concerned that munitions makers would be hamstrung by movement of workers out of the city. The situation became more fluid after V-E Day and V-J Day. Within two weeks of the victory over Japan, almost three million defense workers were laid off at major factories, such as Ford's Willow Run and Kaiser's Portland shipyards. Organizations like the American Federation of Labor saw the rise of unemployment as the coming of the next depression. In September 1945, the AFL announced that the three million out of work were just the tip of the iceberg and that Americans should brace themselves for three times that number of unemployed by the spring of 1946.[93]

But the American economy was not sunk after the war. Close observers might have been heartened by the news that by late 1944 nondefense jobs were available. Indeed, unemployment increased but never reached epidemic levels, because the Office of War Mobilization and Reconversion slowly and quietly had allowed the resumption of domestic consumer production by late 1944. Well before the surrender of Germany, the OWMR allowed a select number of factories to begin to produce household items such as garbage cans, floor lamps, electrical heating pads, vacuum cleaners, electric flat irons, and fishing rods and tackle.[94] Similarly, in late 1944, the OWMR relaxed rules on the construction of private dwellings and business structures. In other words, by the war's peak, the Office of War Mobilization and Reconversion had indeed begun the process of reconversion. Roosevelt's "assistant president," Jimmy Byrnes, still headed the OWMR. In his report to FDR on reconversion, published in September 1944, the reconversion chief outlined his plan for the nation's transformation to a peacetime economy. Basically, he planned to follow the Baruch-Hancock report, which emphasized thoughtful defense cutbacks, as well as a streamlined contract termination process. Interestingly enough, Byrnes also included in his report several sections on what the AFL had termed the "human side" of reconversion. Byrnes called on the president to expand unemployment compensation and to institute a new public works program to be supervised by the newly established Federal Works Agency.[95]

Under Director Byrnes, reconversion was well under way when FDR died unexpectedly, on April 12, 1945. President Harry Truman was not unaware of the problems of the economy or reconversion. In fact, as a Missouri senator, he had chaired a committee, which bore his name, that investigated these issues. As president, Truman continued to rely upon the OWMR director, who, after March 1945, was Fred M. Vinson, who was in turn replaced by John W. Snyder and then by John R. Steelman. And the OWMR continued to rely upon its advisory board, which was made up of various economic stakeholders. In particular, the AFL's William Green served on the board. On April 17, 1945, he submitted a five-point plan, most likely drafted by Boris Shishkin, to further refine the role of the federal government in the immediate economic transition. The plan called for government to oversee these functions:

1. To safeguard war production for continued military needs.
2. To expedite reconversion wherever that is possible and clearly desirable, but always with the objective of full employment.
3. To safeguard the *initial* flow of necessities of life, such as low-cost shelter, clothing and food, against encroachment of claims of less essential production and against price inflation through direct price increases, uptrading or downgrading.
4. To facilitate prompt flow of civilian production and employment into the areas threatened with distress in which impending cutbacks and terminations will bring idleness to plants and men.
5. To assure prior aid and consideration to such segments of production and distribution as are determined to be essential for the restoration of balanced, full production and full employment throughout the entire economy.[96]

On the evening of August 9, 1945, President Truman addressed the American people and outlined the steps that the federal government was going to take to ensure a smooth reconversion. He basically provided a summary of the AFL's five points.[97] Boris Shishkin was so surprised that the next morning he telegrammed William Green, stating:

> Reconversion program announced by President Truman last night contains exactly the five point program submitted by you at advisory board meeting of OWMR on April 17. Press statement from you to that effect today would do much to enhance AFL prestige and assure consultation on procedures.[98]

Truman's final plan for reconversion was embodied in a report by OWMR director John W. Snyder, delivered the week after the president announced his (and the AFL's) five points. In *From War to Peace: A Challenge,* Snyder did not break new ground. Rather, like the two other OWMR directors, he continued to draw inspiration from the Baruch-Hancock report. But, unlike Byrnes, Snyder did not suggest any new federal assistance for displaced workers or for the unemployed.[99]

Truman and Snyder were neither heartless nor conservative. Rather, as with the AFL's Post-War Planning Committee, headed by Woll, the Truman administration saw the immediate issues surrounded the mechanics of reconversion and the issues related to the structure of the

American economy and the future of social security as separate. The day after the release of the Snyder report, President Truman called for a government-labor-business conference to ensure "the peaceful settlement of disputes that might adversely affect the transition to a peacetime economy." Additionally, the conference was to handle economic "maladjustments and inequities."[100] The job of organizing the event was handed to the OWMR's last director, John R. Steelman. The fact that Steelman assembled the parties at all was rather remarkable. The AFL had alienated the U.S. Chamber of Commerce after George Meany's rebuke of Eric Johnston. The Chamber, in turn, had distanced itself from the movement to reshape the postwar economy by publishing its critique of Hansen and the idea of full employment. The conflict between the AFL and the final key member of the Truman conference, the CIO, needs no repeating. During the war, the squabbles between the AFL and the CIO were not only at the local level but also at the national and international levels. By late 1944, passions seemed to have reached a boiling point as the AFL publicly refused to work with the CIO on postwar planning at a conference sponsored by the National Association of Manufacturers and refused to invite the CIO to the International Labor Organization's 1944 meeting.[101] By 1945, however, President Roosevelt's calls for unity had worked a little, and both the AFL and the CIO, as well as Eric Johnston, of the Chamber, had agreed in principle to cooperate and to try to avoid contentious postwar labor relations. Building upon this momentary spirit of unity, Steelman convened his meeting on November 5, 1945. President Truman attended and sought to convince the representatives of the AFL, the CIO, and major industries "to handle their affairs in the traditional, American, democratic way."[102] To the president's disappointment, the month-long meeting ended in complete failure. As the Truman historian Donald R. McCoy has written, "the proceedings of the conference resembled less a Quaker meeting or a legislative session than the shoot out at the OK Corral."[103]

Undaunted, liberals kept pressuring Congress to act on their proposals for full employment, national health insurance, and urban and rural redevelopment. They had the strong backing of President Truman. On September 6, 1945, Truman had presented Congress with his twenty-one-point program for the restructuring of the American economy in the postwar period. Perhaps no president before or since has provided such a farsighted and far-reaching vision. Among his suggestions were the extension of unemployment compensation benefits for fifty-two weeks, the creation of federal work and building programs to foster full employment, and the establishment of a urban and rural development program. Two months later, President Truman outlined to Congress his ideas on comprehensive national health insurance.[104] Although they did not work in concert, the AFL and the CIO backed these proposals, but eventually all parts of the liberal postwar agenda were either defeated or significantly watered down. For example, in February 1946, Congress passed and Truman signed the Employment Act (the controversial word "full" as well as mention of the concept of full employment had been deleted). The legislation declared that it was the responsibility of the federal government to promote maximum employment, production, and consumer purchasing power. However, aside from the creation of the President's Council of Economic Advisors, there were no new financial initiatives or new public works included in the law.[105] Similarly, in May 1949, Congress passed and Truman signed a housing bill, written by Robert Taft, an Ohio Republican, that did provide new money for home construction and urban redevelopment. But the projects were quite limited and fell far short of what was actually needed.[106] Finally, on the issue of national health insurance, nothing at all was accomplished. Senator Taft and his conservative allies in Congress successfully blocked Truman's proposal. In fact, they barely gave it the time of day. In early 1946, at the hearing before the Senate Committee on Education and Labor that discussed the Wagner-Murray-Dingell health-care bill, Senator Taft interrupted the opening statement of Senator Murray to denounce the bill as "the most socialistic measure that this Congress has ever had before it." Taft then walked out of the hearing.[107]

Historians have well documented the efforts of conservatives to frustrate Truman and what he eventually called his Fair Deal.[108] It is worth noting, however, that Truman's program, which had been developed by the AFL and others, in fact found its way into American life. In 1944, the Servicemen's Readjustment Act became law. The so-called G.I. Bill provided veterans with unemployment benefits, educational opportunities, home and business loans, and expanded medical services. In the end, those who had served on the battlefronts received more than those who had served on the home front. What the AFL and others were asking for was labor's bill of rights. Roosevelt had thought about it, liberals had supported it, but it never materialized for workers. In so many ways, the years of the Second World War were organized labor's moment to transform the United States. But, in the end, a divided labor movement, combined with the end of the liberal reform movement and the rise of conservatism nationally, resulted in stunning and stinging political defeats for the AFL as well as for leading liberals like President Truman. These defeats were total, and the vision of a full-employment economy that provided a broad safety net for citizens while supporting the development and refurbishing of America's infrastructure remained the unrealized goals of twentieth-century America.

Epilogue
Labor's Moment

In late February 2005, twenty-one-year-old Joshua Noble lost his latest and perhaps final battle with his employer, Wal-Mart Stores, to unionize his workplace. Noble worked at the Wal-Mart tire and oil change shop in Loveland, Colorado, just north of Denver. When he began his struggle to bring a union into Wal-Mart's Tire & Lube Express, his coworkers were mostly behind him. They, too, felt that they had been neglected, cheated, and oppressed by America's largest employer. Two issues dominated the workers' thoughts. First, Wal-Mart paid starvation wages and offered no affordable health insurance. Alicia Sylvia, a single mother of ten-year-old twins, initially backed Noble's efforts. As she told reporters, "compared to other stores, we don't even make what cashiers make." At the time, Wal-Mart paid its automotive shop workers about $9 per hour; Colorado's unionized grocery workers earned roughly $15.50 per hour. Second, the employees were angry about the working conditions. "We have to stand out in the cold and heat," Sylvia commented. "If you're working 10-hour days in the rain and getting your pants wet and freezing all day, it's not fun."[1]

Noble's quest to unionize this Wal-Mart shop was nearly unprecedented. To date, the handful of attempts to organize unions in the company's North American stores have failed miserably. In 2000, meat cutters at Wal-Mart's Jacksonville, Texas, store voted to form a union. But immediately afterward, the company announced that it planned to subcontract its meat-cutting operation and sell prepackaged beef, chicken, fish, and pork. All the butchers were summarily laid off. A troubled unionization drive in Quebec, Canada, followed. There, an entire store moved to establish a union. Company executives responded by closing the store, citing financial difficulties. Joshua Noble knew of these episodes but kept on battling. "We thought the only way they'd listen to us is to have a union." "There's strength in numbers," Noble told a reporter.[2] He had a majority of his shop coworkers behind him, as well as organizers from the United Food and Commercial Workers, who encouraged him to carry on despite the odds. But Wal-Mart officials were ready. First, they hired a "consulting firm" to talk to the workers about the problems with unions and to show them anti-union videos. Then, under the guise of improving efficiency, Wal-Mart managers began to remove pro-union employees and replace them with outspoken anti-union workers. Just weeks earlier, a Pennsylvania judge had admonished Wal-Mart executives for similar illegal transfers in New Castle, where workers had tried to organize that town's Wal-Mart Tire & Lube Express. The ploy worked as well in Loveland as it had in New Castle. When the National Labor Relations Board (NLRB) held the election for Noble's shop, the employees voted seventeen to none against the union. Noble himself did not get a chance to vote. He had had an epileptic seizure earlier that morning that prevented him from voting. Wal-Mart's open-shop attitude and anti-union actions clearly affected the outcome of the election. Cody Fields originally backed Noble, because he felt "we need a change." But Fields had been susceptible to the barrage of slick videos shown day after day. "It's just a bunch of brainwashing," he admitted, "but it kind of worked." Wal-Mart's actions also emboldened anti-union employees like Dan Wright. "My grandfather said that during World War II, unions were helpful—they had their place. But I don't feel I need one."[3]

This story illustrates a major difference between the working world of Dan Wright and that of his grandfather. At one time, especially during the Second World War, not only were unions prevalent, but workers perceived them to be "helpful." Times have changed. Organized labor has reached another nadir. It is once again on its "deathbed," as the 1930s labor economist Lewis L. Lorwin might say. A combination of factors has come together to drive labor into the dirt. The modern open-shop campaign, which began during the Second World War and which achieved early success with the 1947 Taft-Hartley Act, has succeeded nicely in creating many unionfree work environments. Wal-Mart executives can still proudly claim that none of its 1.2 million American workers belong to a union. Other wartime issues, such as equality and equity for black and women workers, have also played into organized labor's troubles. And there are a host of other problems, large and small. In fact, there is an entire scholarly literature about the fall of the house of labor. Theories abound, some well reasoned and others quite off base.[4] Most tend to focus on divisive forces both outside and within the unions, such as the anti-union movement and racial, gender, and ethnic tensions. Additionally, writers have criticized many labor leaders for a lack of vision and American consumers for supporting the economic systems that drive down wages and benefits in order to drive down costs. Recently, President Bill Clinton's secretary of labor, Robert B. Reich, acerbically wrote, "it's not as if Wal-Mart's founder, Sam Walton, and his successors created the world's largest retailer by putting a gun to our heads and forcing us to shop there."[5] True enough. Shoppers do not look for the union label as they once did.

It is important to note, however, that these issues are not new. The generation of unionists, particularly in the American Federation of Labor, that fought the Second World War had been dealing with them since the 1930s. And, as this book recounts, the members of the Federation, as well as those of the Congress of Industrial Organizations, continued to struggle with them as the nation went to war. Thus, the AFL battled the open shop while fighting against the fascists. It also waged a home-front fight over racial, gender, and shop-floor politics. A notable difference with the past, however, is the current lack of forethought on the part of organized labor and its allies. During the Second World War, the AFL sought boldly to recast American politics and society by offering a new vision for the future. Based on FDR's Four Freedoms and Second Bill of Rights, this AFL blueprint for a better America included expansions of the New Deal state to aid workers in every phase of their lives. At root, the plan was to utilize the power and machinery of the federal government to advance the social and economic position of the average American unionist. The anti-union movement, along with the centrifugal tensions within organized labor, no doubt stymied the AFL's Beveridge Plan. But the decline of liberal politics may have had even more to do with labor's demise.[6] Following FDR's death, in 1945, conservatives made a pronounced return to American politics. They did not, however, eliminate the New Deal, as so many liberals feared. Rather, they limited its growth and later took over its machinery. The process continues today. For example, President George W. Bush has appointed very conservative bureaucrats to run the National Labor Relations Board. The results have been disastrous. The NLRB has made it difficult to organize, hold elections, and bargain for contracts. All sorts of workers have been turned down, from New York University graduate students to IBM's high-tech workers.[7] The NLRB has also sided with employers in many cases where unfair labor practices have been alleged. The situation is so uncompromisingly bad that recently AFL-CIO president John Sweeney has pledged to lead a new organizational drive "despite the law" and despite the NLRB.[8]

Thus, the old battles over working-class politics and over union membership that were so vividly fought out during the Second World War will continue. In fact, they have been a kind of historical constant over the past eighty years. Winning these battles may not solve all workers' problems in today's America. Rather, changing the current doldrums and reversing organized labor's fortunes will require a fresh ideological outlook. In particular, unions will have to devise new arguments to attract new members. As the failed Colorado Wal-Mart drive indicates, union organizers have a long way to go to win over the hearts of coworkers. If history is a guide, organized labor might benefit from recapturing parts of the AFL wartime ideology and its plans for a stronger, more economically stable, and more socially secure America. It might then also return to Franklin D. Roosevelt's ideas. As FDR stated in 1942:

> The better world for which you fight—and for which some of you give your lives—will not come merely because we shall have won the war. It will not come merely because we wish very hard that it would come. It will be made possible only by bold vision, intelligent planning, and hard work. It cannot be brought about overnight; but only by years of effort and perseverance and unfaltering faith.[9]

For a moment, as this book has shown, that vision and that world seemed well within grasp. Unfortunately for American workers, their political reach was not long enough. It will be up to the new, revitalized labor movement that is to come to finally complete the work set out by those grandfathers and grandmothers, many of whom belonged to the AFL and whose sacrifices and hard work helped defeat the Axis powers and win the Second World War.

Notes

NOTES TO THE PREFACE

1. Franklin D. Roosevelt, "A Statement on Labor Day, September 5, 1942," in Samuel I. Rosenman, comp., *The Public Papers and Addresses of Franklin D. Roosevelt, Volume Eleven: Humanity on the Defensive, 1942* (New York: Russell & Russell, 1950), 354–355.

2. Andrew E. Kersten, *Race, Jobs, and the War: The FEPC in the Midwest, 1941–1946* (Urbana: University of Illinois Press, 2000); Martin Glaberman, *Wartime Strikes: The Struggle Against the No-Strike Pledge* (Detroit: Bewick, 1980); Nelson Lichtenstein, *Labor's War at Home: The CIO in World War II* (New York: Cambridge University Press, 1982); August Meier and Elliott Rudwick, *Black Detroit and the Rise of the UAW* (New York: Oxford University Press, 1979); Joe W. Trotter, Jr., *Black Milwaukee: The Making of an Industrial Proletariat, 1915–1945* (Urbana: University of Illinois Press, 1985); Ruth Milkman, *Gender at Work: The Dynamics of Job Segregation by Sex During World War II* (Urbana: University of Illinois Press, 1987); and Robert H. Zieger, *The CIO, 1935–1955* (Chapel Hill: University of North Carolina Press, 1995). This list is merely a sampling of a much larger bibliography. On the new labor history, see David Brody, "The Old Labor History and the New: In Search of an American Working Class," *Labor History* 20 (1979): 111–126; Brody, "Reconciling the Old Labor History with the New," *Pacific Northwest Quarterly* 62 (1993): 1–18; Melvyn Dubofsky, "Give Us That Old Time Labor History: Philip S. Foner and the American Worker," *Labor History* 26 (1985): 118–137; Howard Kimeldorf, "Bringing Unions Back In (Or Why We Need a New Old Labor History)," *Labor History* 32 (1991): 91–103; and especially the updated introduction to Nelson Lichtenstein's *Labor's War at Home* (Philadelphia: Temple University Press, 2003), vii–xxviii. See Roger Daniels's review of Irving Bernstein's *The Turbulent Years: A History of the American Worker, 1933–1941* (Boston: Houghton Mifflin, 1970) in *Pacific Northwest Quarterly* (April 1971): 87. Some exceptions to this trend are Christopher Tomlins, *The State and the Unions: Labor Relations, Law, and the Orgnaized Labor Movement in America, 1880–1960* (New York: Cambridge University Press, 1985); and James B. Alteson, *Labor and the Wartime State: Labor Relations During World War II* (Urbana: University of Illinois Press, 1998).

3. See for example, Gwendolyn Mink, *Old Labor and New Immigrants in American Political Development: Union, Party, and State, 1875–1920* (Ithaca: Cornell University Press, 1986); Michael Kazin, *Barons of Labor: The San Francisco Building Trades and Union Power in the Progressive Era* (Urbana: University of Illinois Press, 1987); David Montgomery, *The Fall of the House of Labor: The Workplace, the State, and American Labor Activism, 1865–1925* (Cambridge: Cambridge University Press, 1987); Dana Frank, *Purchasing Power: Consumer Organizing, Gender, and the Seattle Labor Movement, 1919–1929* (Cambridge: Cambridge University Press, 1994); Joseph A. McCartin, *Labor's Great War: The Struggle for Industrial Democracy and the Origins of Modern American Labor Relations, 1912–1921* (Chapel Hill: University of North Carolina Press, 1970); Julie Greene, *Pure and Simple Politics: The American Federation of Labor and Political Activism, 1881–1917* (Cambridge:

Cambridge University Press, 1998); and Ileen A. DeVault, *United Apart: Gender and the Rise of Craft Unionism* (Ithaca: Cornell University Press, 2004).

4. Christopher L. Tomlins, "AFL Unions in the 1930s: Their Performance in Historical Perspective," *Journal of American History* 65 (March 1979): 1021–1042; and Dorothy Sue Cobble, "Lost Ways of Organizing: Reviving the AFL's Direct Affiliate Strategy," *Industrial Relations* 36 (July 1997): 278–301.

5. Philip S. Foner, *History of the Labor Movement: From Colonial Times to the Founding of the American Federation of Labor,* Vol. 1 (New York: International Publishers, 1947), 10–12; Leon Fink, *Progressive Intellectuals and the Dilemmas of Democratic Commitment* (Cambridge, MA: Harvard University Press, 1997), 52–79; and Dubofsky, "Give Us That Old Time Labor History," 119–120.

6. Philip Taft, *The A. F. of L. from the Death of Gompers to the Merger* (New York: Harper & Brothers, 1959), 230; and Greene, *Pure and Simple Politics,* 1.

7. See Kimeldorf, "Bringing Unions Back In (Or Why We Need a New Old Labor History)," and Brody, "Reconciling the Old Labor History and the New." To read an example of my last point, see Nelson Lichtenstein, *The Most Dangerous Man in Detroit: Walter Reuther and the Fate of American Labor* (New York: Basic Books, 1995).

8. Brody, "The Old Labor History and the New," 126.

NOTES TO CHAPTER 1

1. "American Labor Goes to War," *American Federationist* 50 (January 1942): 5.

2. Franklin D. Roosevelt, Fireside Chat, 28 April 1942, in Russell D. Buhite and David W. Levy, eds., *FDR's Fireside Chats* (Norman: University of Oklahoma Press, 1992), 225.

3. See Tom Brokaw, *The Greatest Generation* (New York: Random House, 1998).

4. Philip Pearl, "An A.F. of L. Mother," *American Federationist* 51 (April 1944): 22. During the war, a blue star in the window meant that that family had a son in the military. Blue stars became gold stars when the serviceman died.

5. Philip Taft, *The A.F. of L. from the Death of Gompers to the Merger* (New York: Harper and Brothers, 1959), 204.

6. William Green, *No European Entanglements* (Washington, DC: American Federation of Labor, 1939), 3–4.

7. See Harvey C. Mansfield, *A Short History of OPA* (Washington, DC: GPO, 1947), 14.

8. Green, *No European Entanglements,* 7.

9. Taft, *The A. F. of L. from the Death of Gompers,* 207.

10. Ibid., 208.

11. AFL Executive Council Meeting Minutes, 8 May 1940, as quoted in ibid., 209.

12. "Labor and Defense," *American Federationist* 47 (July 1940): 3.

13. Letter, Frank P. Fenton, Robert J. Watt, and Harvey W. Brown to Franklin D. Roosevelt, 15 June 1940, Frances Perkins Papers, box 1, Franklin D. Roosevelt Presidential Library (FDRL).

14. "Labor and Defense," 3–4.

15. "Defense Profits Are Enormous," *American Federationist* 48 (July 1941): 18–19 (emphasis in original); and "Labor's Increasing Role in the War Effort," *Labor's Monthly Survey* 3 (December 1942): 1.

16. On this battle with the Knights of Labor see Philip Taft, *The A. F. of L. in the Time of Gompers* (New York: Harper, 1957), 26–29; Samuel Gompers, *Seventy Years of Life and Labor: An Autobiography* (New York: E. P. Dutton, 1957), 144–152; and Florence Calvert Thorne, *Samuel Gompers, American Statesman* (New York: Philosophical Library, 1957), 10.

17. Taft, *The A. F. of L. in the Time of Gompers,* 1–18.

18. Ibid., 35.

19. Ibid., 38; and Gompers, *Seventy Years of Life and Labor,* 119–120.

20. Gompers, *Seventy Years,* 6.

21. Thorne, *Samuel Gompers,* 13. Thorne claimed to have written Gompers's autobiography. See Florence C. Thorne, interview by Donald F. Shaughnessy, tape recording transcript, 28 November 1958, Oral History Research Office, Columbia University, New York, p. 95. Thorne wrote nearly all the editorials in the *American Federationist* that were signed by either Samuel Gompers or William Green.

22. Thorne, *Samuel Gompers,* 56, and see 56–62.

23. Gompers's testimony before the House Lobby Investigation Committee,

1913, as quoted in Thorne, *Samuel Gompers,* 58.

24. Gompers quoted in Thorne, *Samuel Gompers,* 106.

25. Taft, *The A.F. of L. in the Time of Gompers,* 150.

26. Vernon A. Jensen, *Heritage of Conflict: Labor Relations in the Nonferrous Metals Industry up to 1930* (Ithaca: Cornell University Press, 1950), 160.

27. Lewis L. Lorwin with the assistance of Jean Atherton Flexner, *The American Federation of Labor: History, Policies, and Prospects* (Washington, DC: Brookings Institution, 1933), 185.

28. Gompers quoted in Priscilla Murolo and A. B. Chitty, *From the Folks Who Brought You the Weekend: A Short Illustrated History of Labor in the United States* (New York: New Press, 2001), 160.

29. Lorwin, *The American Federation of Labor,* 91. For examples of the AFL's involvement in local politics see Michael Kazin, *Barons of Labor: The San Francisco Building Trades and Union Power in the Progressive Era* (Urbana: University of Illinois Press, 1989).

30. Taft, *The A. F. of L. in the Time of Gompers,* 303.

31. Ibid., 302.

32. Gompers quoted in Thorne, *Samuel Gompers,* 89.

33. Ibid., 18.

34. Craig Phelan, *William Green: Biography of a Labor Leader* (Albany: State University of New York Press, 1989), 4.

35. Phelan, *William Green,* 22.

36. Lorwin, *The American Federation of Labor,* 241–264; and Phelan, *William Green,* viii–x; 29–47.

37. Lorwin, *The American Federation of Labor,* 454.

38. Phelan, *William Green,* 102, 120, and 164.

39. Florence C. Thorne, interview by Donald F. Shaughnessy, tape recording transcript, 31 October 1956, Oral History Research Office, Columbia University, New York, p. 41.

40. William Green, *Labor and Democracy: A Plan of Action to Safeguard the American Way* (Princeton: Princeton University Press, 1939), 10.

41. Christopher L. Tomlins, "AFL Unions in the 1930s: Their Performance in Historical Perspective," *Journal of American History* 65 (March 1979): 1024.

42. Ibid., 1035.

43. See "Green Condemns Militarized Labor Camps for Jobless," *American Federation of Labor Weekly News Service* 23 (25 March 1933): 1.

44. See also letter, Daniel J. Tobin to President Franklin D. Roosevelt, 11 December 1933, President's Official File, OF 142, container 1, FDRL.

45. See National Defense Advisory Commission, *Handbook of the Advisory Commission to the Council of National Defense* (Washington, DC: GPO, 1940), 1–2.

46. "Defense Is MAJOR Topic at Building Trades Session," *American Federationist* 47 (December 1940): 22; and John P. Coyne, "Building Trades and Defense," *American Federationist* 47 (November 1940): 12.

47. Unidentified clipping, Drew Pearson and Robert S. Allen, "Washington Merry-Go-Round: Arnold and Hillman in Heated Dispute," 14 October 1941, 11, AFL Papers, series 4, box 30.

48. Richard J. Purcell, *Labor Policies of the National Defense Advisory Commission and the Office of Production Management, May 1940 to April 1942* (Washington, DC: Civilian Production Administration, 1946), 242.

49. Eventually the War Production Board, the OPM's successor, eliminated all nonessential building with its Order L-41 and Order L-121. See "OPM Restriction on Use of Materials in Construction," AFL Papers, series 4, box 27; "The Extreme Importance of the Issue of This Meeting to the Construction Industry," AFL Papers, series 4, box 27; and "Construction Before and After Pearl Harbor," AFL Papers, series 4, box 27; and "The Milwaukee Plan for Priority Allocation for Non-Defense Building," AFL Papers, series 4, box 30. See Civilian Production Administration, *Industrial Mobilization for War: History of the War Production Board and Predecessor Agencies, 1940–1945: Vol. I, Program and Administration* (Washington, DC: GPO, 1947, New York: Greenwood Press, 1969 reprint), 396–399.

50. File memo, "Defense Labor Advisory Committee on the Construction Industry," AFL Papers, series 4, box 27.

51. "Building Trades Sign Epochal Pact,"

American Federationist 48 (August 1941): 19; OWI press release, 23 August 1942, AFL Papers, series 4, box 30; and Joel Seidman, *American Labor from Defense to Reconstruction* (Chicago: University of Chicago, 1953), 29–30.

52. *Officers' Report to the Thirty-fifth Annual Convention of the Building and Construction Trade Department, American Federation of Labor, Seattle, Washington, October 1941,* p. 15, AFL Papers, series 4, box 26; and testimony of Samuel L. Gompers before the Industrial Commission on the Relations and Conditions of Capital and Labor, U.S. Congress, House of Representatives, *Report of the Industrial Commission on the Relations and Conditions of Capital and Labor,* 56th Congress, 2nd Session, House Document 495, Part 7, 605. See also "The Building Industry in Defense and After, an Address by Richard J. Gray, Acting President of the AFL Building and Construction Trades Department, 7 November 1941," AFL Papers, series 4, box 30.

53. See Western Homes Foundation (Seattle, Washington) press release, 21 June 1939, AFL Papers, series 4, box 25; and John T. Flynn, "Why Rent Is High," *Collier's* (17 June 1939): 52.

54. Letter, Martin Christiansen to William Green, 21 March 1943, AFL Papers, series 4, box 27; letter Christiansen to Green, 9 December 1942, AFL Papers, series 4, box 27; FEPC file memo, George M. Johnson to Boris Shishkin, 15 January 1943, AFL Papers, series 4, box 27; letter, Green to Christiansen, 18 January 1943; letter, Green to William L. Hutcheson, 18 January 1943, and letter, Christiansen to Green, 28 January 1943. For more information on the AFL and corruption see David Witwer, *Corruption and Reform in the Teamsters Union* (Urbana: University of Illinois Press, 2003).

55. Press Release, Western Homes Federation (Seattle, Washington), 21 June 1939, AFL Papers, series 4, box 25.

56. Coyne, "Building Trades and Defense," 12.

57. Ibid., 32; and Kermit B. Mohn, "Union Wages and Hours in the Building Trades, June 1, 1941," *Monthly Labor Review* 50 (November 1941): 5.

58. Press Release, Western Homes Federation (Seattle, Washington), 21 June 1939, AFL Papers, series 4, box 25.

59. "The Case for Construction," *Nation's Business* (April 1941): 35–63.

60. OPM press release, 14 October 1941, AFL Papers, series 4, box 27.

61. "Proposed Policies and Programs for Traditional & Post-War Construction [1944?]," AFL Papers, series 4, box 25; and U.S. Department of Labor, Bureau of Labor Statistics, "Construction Expenditures in Continental United States, 1915–1944" [typescript], AFL Papers, series 4, box 30; See also, D. Stevens Wilson, "Wartime Construction and Plant Expansion," *Survey of Current Business* (October 1944): 1–6.

62. "Building Trades Sign Epochal Pact," 19; and unidentified clipping, Drew Pearson and Robert S. Allen, "Washington Merry-Go-Round: Arnold and Hillman in Heated Dispute," 14 October 1941, 11, AFL Papers, series 4, box 30.

63. "Statement to Truman Committee by R. J. Gray, Acting President of the Building and Construction Trades Department of the American Federation of Labor" [typescript], 5, AFL Papers, series 4, box 29; and Seidman, *American Labor from Defense to Reconstruction,* 30.

64. See Senate Special Committee Investigating the National Defense Program, *Investigation of the National Defense Program: Part 14, Interim Report on Lumber and Forest Products,* 77th Cong., 1st sess., 1941.

65. "President Gets Poster Painting," *American Federationist* 48 (June 1941): 5.

66. AFL, *Responsibility of Central Labor Unions* (Washington, DC: AFL, 1942). 1; AFL, *Defense Contracts* (Washington, DC: AFL, 1941); AFL, *A.F. of L. Program Priority Unemployment* (Washington, DC: AFL, 1941); AFL, *Priorities* (Washington, DC: AFL, 1941): and AFL, *Price Control* (Washington, DC: AFL, 1941).

67. Letter, William Green to President Franklin D. Roosevelt, 7 December 1941, OF 142, container 2, FDR Papers; and AFL press release, 15 December 1941, FDR Papers, OF 142, box 2, FDRL. One can find various no-strike pledges of several AFL international unions in "No Strikes During the War," *The Bricklayer, Mason and Plasterer* (December 1941): 199, 204.

68. Letter, John Frey to President Franklin D. Roosevelt, 4 January 1941, OF 142, container 2, FDR Papers, FDRL; and AFL Metal Trades Department, press

release, 20 June 1940, Frances Perkins Papers, box 1, FDRL.

69. On the CIO's wartime equality of sacrifice plans, see Nelson Lichtenstein, *Labor's War at Home: The CIO in World War II* (Cambridge: Cambridge University Press, 1982), 82–109.

70. Lichtenstein, *Labor's War at Home,* 102.

71. William Green, *We Work for the Future* (Washington, DC: AFL, 1941), 18.

72. Stella Stewart, "Government Price Control in the First World War," *Monthly Labor Review* 51 (February 1941): 271–285.

73. "Danger Signals for Labor," *Labor's Monthly Survey* 2 (July 1941): 1; "New Controls Test Democracy," *Labor's Monthly Survey* 3 (August–September 1942): 1; and Saul Nelson and Aryness Joy, "Prices and the War," *Monthly Labor Review* 50 (July 1941): 49–65.

74. National Defense Mediation Board, *Report of the Work of the National Defense Mediation Board, March 19, 1941–January 12, 1942* (Washington, DC: GPO, 1942), 1. For more information on wartime strikes see Martin Glaberman, *Wartime Strikes: The Struggle Against the No-Strike Pledge in the UAW During World War II* (Detroit, 1980); George Lipsitz, *Rainbow at Midnight: Labor and Culture in the 1940s* (Urbana: University of Illinois Press, 1994); and Andrew E. Kersten, *Race, Jobs, and the War: The FEPC in the Midwest, 1941–46* (Urbana: University of Illinois Press, 2000).

75. John R. Steelman, "Conciliation in the Defense Picture," *American Federationist* 48 (October 1941): 21; and Purcell, *Labor Policies of the National Defense Advisory Commission and the Office of Production Management,* 168.

76. William Green, "Amendments to the National Labor Relations Act," *American Federationist* 46 (February 1939): 129–130; and see letter, Eddie R. Stahl to Joseph Padway, 4 April 1944, AFL Papers, series 4, box 6. See also Congress of Industrial Organizations, *Conspiracy Against Labor: Full Proof of the Plot by William Green of the AFL and Agents of the Most Anti-Labor Corporations in America to Destroy the Wagner Act* (Washington, DC: CIO, 1940).

77. Seidman, *American Labor from Defense to Reconstruction,* 179–180; and Fred Witney, *Wartime Experiences of the NLRB* (Urbana: University of Illinois Press, 1949), 30–48. See also NDMB, *Report on the Work of the National Defense Mediation Board,* 34–35; and James A. Gross, *The Reshaping of the National Labor Relations Board: National Labor Policy in Transition, 1937–1947* (Albany: SUNY Press, 1981). On the Frey rider itself see *Congressional Record,* 78th Cong., 1st sess. (1943): 800, A346–A347, A655–A656, and A2260. Frey and the AFL initiated their rider in direct response to a dispute with the CIO at the Kaiser Shipyards. See Joseph A. Padway, "The Kaiser Shipyards Case," *American Federationist* 51 (February 1943): 18–20.

78. See for example Nelson Lichtenstein, *Labor's War at Home: The CIO in World War II* (Cambridge: Cambridge University Press, 1982); and James B. Alteson, *Labor and the Wartime State: Labor Relations and Law During World War II* (Urbana: University of Illinois Press, 1998).

79. Purcell, *Labor Policies,* 168–173, and Edith W. First, *Industry and Labor Advisory Committees in the National Defense Advisory Commission and the Office of Production Management, May 1940 to January 1942* (Washington, DC: GPO, 1946), 169–218; and NDMB, *Report on the Work on the National Defense Mediation Board,* 53–54.

80. "Weyerhaeuser Timber Company, Case #5, 1006-MB," National War Labor Board Headquarter Dispute Case Files, 1941–1943, RG 202, box 4, National Archives and Records Administration, Silver Spring, MD; Seidman, *American Labor from Defense to Reconstruction,* 91–108; Bryce M. Stewart and Walter J. Couper, *Maintenance of Union Membership: A Study of Official Cases and Company Experiences* (New York: Industrial Relations Counselors, 1943); "M. of M.—A Wartime Fixture," *Business Week* (20 November 1943): 92–103; Marcus Manoff, "The National War Labor Board and the Maintenance-of-Membership Clause," *Harvard Law Review* 57 (December 1944): 183–219; *Labor Disputes and the War Labor Board* (New York: International Statistical Bureau, 1944); and A. F. Hinrichs, *Maintenance-of-Membership Awards of National War Labor Board, Bulletin No. 753 of the United States Bureau of Labor Statistics* (Washington, DC: U.S. Bureau of Labor Statistics, 1943).

81. "Danger Signals for Labor," 1.

82. Philip Pearl, "Facing the Facts," *American Federation of Labor Weekly News Service* (28 October 1941), 1, as quoted in Seidman, *American Labor from Defense to Reconstruction,* 64.

83. Seidman, *American Labor from Defense to Reconstruction,* 64.

84. On the NWLB see John Chamberlain, "Will Davis of the War Labor Board," *Fortune* (March 1942): 70–71, 166–176; Wayne L. Morse, "The National War Labor Board, Its Power and Duties," *Oregon Law Review* 22 (December 1942): 1–45; NWLB, *WLB, What It Is . . . How It Operates* (Washington, DC: NWLB, 1943); William H. Davis, "Collective Bargaining and the War," *American Federationist* 51 (January 1943): 12–13, 28; Robert J. Watt, "Labor-Management Cooperation," *American Federationist* 52 (February 1944): 21–24; and NWLB, *The Termination Report of the National War Labor Board, Vol. I: Industrial Disputes and Wage Stabilization in Wartime, January 12, 1942–December 31, 1945* (Washington, DC: GPO, 1948), xii–xviii.

85. Franklin D. Roosevelt, Fireside Chat, 28 April 1942, in Buhite and Levy, eds., *FDR's Fireside Chats,* 225, 229.

86. U.S. Bureau of the Budget, *United States at War: The Development and Administration of the War Program by the Federal Government* (Washington, DC: GPO, 1946), 254–257; and Frank Freidel, *Franklin D. Roosevelt: A Rendezvous with Destiny* (Boston: Little, Brown and Company, 1990), 432–434.

87. Harvey C. Mansfield. *A Short History of OPA* (Washington, DC: GPO, 1947), 145.

88. "A. F. of L. President Predicts Workers Will Accept Wage Sacrifices in Labor Day Address from Omaha," *Boilermakers Journal* 54 (October 1942): 310.

89. Letter, William Green to Franklin D. Roosevelt, 31 July 1942, FDR Papers, OF 142, box 2, FDRL.

90. Letter, Franklin D. Roosevelt to William Green, 6 August 1942, FDR Papers, OF 142, box 2; Boris Shishkin, "Wages and Inflation," *American Federationist* 48 (August 1942): 4; "Price Control Program for Women's Auxiliaries of Labor," AFL Papers, series 5C, box 20; and letter, Green [?] to Women's Auxiliaries, nd, AFL Papers, series 5C, box 25.

91. Mansfield, *A Short History of OPA,* 9.

92. "A Crisis: Will It Be Met by Democratic or Fascist Controls?" *Labor's Monthly Survey* 4 (April 1943): 1; "Labor's New Wartime Responsibilities," *Labor's Monthly Survey* 4 (May 1943): 1; "Food Prices in January 1943," *Monthly Labor Review* 56 (March 1943): 600–609; "Food Prices in May and June 1943," *Monthly Labor Review* 57 (August 1943): 362–373; "Cost of Living in Large Cities, April 1944," *Monthly Labor Review* 58 (June 1944): 1279–1291; "Cost of Living and Retail Prices," *Monthly Labor Review* 59 (December 1944): 1258–1282; and "Index of Consumers' Prices in Large Cities, February 1946," *Monthly Labor Review* 62 (April 1946): 647–661.

93. "Stabilization: Have All Groups Made Equal Sacrifices?" *Labor's Monthly Survey* 4 (November 1943): 1–2; and "Labor's Sacrifice Has Not Stopped Inflation," *Labor's Monthly Survey* 4 (March 1943): 1–2.

94. Don Q. Crowther, "Work Stoppages Caused by Labor-Management Disputes in 1945," *Monthly Labor Review* 62 (May 1946): 721.

95. Letter, William Green to Franklin D. Roosevelt, 20 July 1942, FDR Papers, OF 142, container 2.

96. Boris Shishkin, "Wages and Inflation," *American Federationist* 48 (August 1942): 3–4.

97. Speech, Franklin D. Roosevelt, "If the Vicious Spiral of Inflation Ever Get Under Way, the Whole Economic System Will Stagger—Fireside Chat on the Cost of Living and the Progress of the War, 7 September 1942," in Samuel I. Rosenman, comp., *The Public Papers and Addresses of Franklin D. Roosevelt, Vol. 11: Humanity on the Defensive, 1942* (New York: Russell & Russell, 1950), 368–369.

98. On the fight against the wartime labor draft, see "Forced Labor?" *American Federationist* 48 (February 1941): 8–11; George Meany, "Slave Labor Is No Solution," *American Federationist* 48 (June 1941): 9–10, 23; "Federation Presses Fight on Slavery Bills," *American Federationist* 48 (July 1941): 11; "Spring Offensive Against Labor," *American Federationist* 49 (April 1942): 3–6, 28–30; Joseph A. Padway, "Involuntary Servitude," *American Federationist* 50 (July 1943): 3–5; "Dishonest and

Dangerous," *Nation* (5 February 1944): 148; William Green, "Slavery Is What We Are Fighting *Against," American Federationist* 51 (March 1944): 10–13; "Shall Labor Be Drafted?" *Labor's Monthly Survey* 5 (April 1944): 1–2; and William Green, "Labor Conscription?" *American Federationist* 51 (May 1944): 23.

99. Mansfield, *A Short History of OPA,* 55–56; Seidman, *American Labor from Defense to Reconversion,* 238–245; "President's Committee Finds Living Costs Rise Understated," *Washington Post,* 23 June 1944; George Meany, "Labor Must Have a *Real* Cost-of-Living Index," *American Federationist* (July 1944): 4–7; and "Report of President's Committee on Cost of Living," *Monthly Labor Review* 60 (January 1945): 168–187.

100. Few seemed to protest the demise of this taxation idea. See "Has the President's Program of Equal Sacrifice Been Carried Out?" *Labor's Monthly Survey* 3 (June 1942): 1–6; "Equality of Sacrifice," *New York Times,* 27 March 1943, 12; and "Equality of Sacrifice," *New York Times,* 18 April 1943, E12.

NOTES TO CHAPTER 2

1. "Closed Shop," *Journal of Electrical Workers and Operators* 40 (December 1941): 645.

2. Andrew E. Kersten, "Taft-Hartley Act," in *The Encyclopedia of American Labor,* ed. Robert Weir and James Hardin (Westport, CT: Greenwood Press, 2004), 485–487.

3. American Federation of Labor, *Report on Proceedings of the Sixty-sixth Convention of the American Federation of Labor* (Washington, DC: AFL, 1947), 98; "Labor Pays Final Tribute to Joseph A. Padway," *American Federationist* 55 (November 1947): 16–17; and *New York Times,* 9 October 1947, 1, 26. See Joseph A. Padway, "Shackling Labor by Legislation," *American Federationist* 47 (August 1940): 10–11, 22. On Lewis's legal troubles in 1947, see Melvyn Dubofsky and Warren Van Tine, *John L. Lewis: A Biography* (Urbana: University of Illinois Press, 1986), 336.

4. "Labor Pays Final Tribute to Joseph A. Padway," 16–17.

5. Gilbert Gall has investigated the right-to-work movement thoroughly. For his analysis of the war years see Gilbert J. Gall, *The Politics of Right to Work: The Labor Federations as Special Interests, 1943–1979* (Westport, CT: Greenwood Press, 1988).

6. "Labor Pays Final Tribute to Joseph A. Padway," 16. See also Padway's obituary in *New York Times,* 9 October 1947; "Joseph Arthur Padway," *Biographical Dictionary of American Labor,* ed. Gary M. Fink (Westport, CT: Greenwood, 1974), 281–282; American Civil Liberties Union, *Labor's Civil Rights: The Position of the American Civil Liberties Union on the Basic Issues* (New York: ACLU, 1941); and Thomas W. Gavett, *Development of the Labor Movement in Milwaukee* (Madison: University of Wisconsin Press, 1965).

7. See Melvyn Dubofsky, ed., *American Labor Since the New Deal* (Chicago: Quadrangle Books, 1971), 54–57; and Walter H. Uphoff, "The Riot at Kohler, 1934," in *Workers and Unions in Wisconsin: A Labor Anthology,* ed. Darrel Holter (Madison: University of Wisconsin Press, 1999): 143–146.

8. The AFL Executive Council had employed other lawyers, such as Charles Ogburn, when legal issues arose. Padway worked on a full-time, not part-time, basis.

9. "Labor Personality of the Month: John Frey," *American Federation of Labor*48 (April 1944): 17.

10. Philip Taft, *The A. F. of L. from the Death of Gompers to the Merger* (New York: Harper & Brothers, 1959, 15–61; Christopher L. Tomlins, "AFL Unions in the 1930s: Their Performance in Historical Perspective," *Journal of American History* 65(4) (March 1979): 1021–1042; Robert H. Zieger, *American Workers, American Unions,* 2nd ed. (Baltimore: Johns Hopkins University Press, 1994), 21–57; and "Wagner Charta," *Time* 33 (April 10, 1939): 16.

11. AFL, *Report on Proceedings,* 377; Taft, *The A.F. of L. from the Death of Gompers to the Merger,* 303; James R. Green, *The World of the Worker: Labor in Twentieth-Century America* (Urbana: University of Illinois Press, 1980), 141–154; James A. Gross, *The Making of the National Labor Relations Board: A Study in Economics, Politics, and the Law* (Albany: State University of New York Press, 1974); and James A. Gross, *The Reshaping of the National Labor Relations Board: National Labor Policy in Transition, 1937–1947* (Albany: State University of New York Press, 1981). Padway's

career and political outlook were not unique. The CIO's Lee Pressman had similar pro–New Deal views but focused on other issues during the 1940s. See Gilbert J. Gall, *Pursuing Justice: Lee Pressman, the New Deal, and the CIO* (Albany: SUNY Press, 1999); Gall, "Rights Which Have Meaning: Reconceiving Labor Liberty in the 1940s," *Labor History* 39 (1998): 273–289; and Nelson Lichtenstein, *Labor's War at Home: The CIO in World War II* (Cambridge: University of Cambridge Press, 1982). For the AFL's partisan activities see Michael Kazin, *Barons of Labor: The San Francisco Building Trades and Union Power in the Progressive Era, 1896–1922* (Urbana: University of Illinois Press, 1987); and Julie Greene, *Pure and Simple Politics: The American Federation of Labor and Political Activism, 1881–1917* (New York: Cambridge University Press, 1998).

12. Fred Witney, *Wartime Experiences of the National Labor Relations Board, 1941–1945* (Urbana: University of Illinois Press, 1949), 34.

13. "Plain Men in Houston," *Time* 32 (17 October 1938): 15; "Wagner Charta," 15–16; and "Judge Padway Is Seattle Visitor," *Washington Times* (15 September 1939), microfilmed papers of Joseph A. Padway, reel 2 (hereinafter Padway Micro), Wisconsin Historical Society. Interestingly enough, Padway was also the Teamsters' chief counsel.

14. Witney, *Wartime Experiences of the NLRB*, 30–61. Eventually the AFL realized its mistake. The Frey Amendment in essence made illegal and unfair labor practices potentially legal. By 1948, all vestiges of the amendment were removed.

15. See Taft, *The A.F. of L. from the Death of Gompers to the Merger*, 268–269; and Louis P. Goldbert, "Thurman Arnold: Backfiring Liberal," *American Federationist* 47 (March 1940): 262–270.

16. 310 *U.S. Reports* 88 (quotation); Sidney Fine, "Frank Murphy, the Thornhill Decision, and Picketing as Free Speech," *Labor History* 6 (Spring 1965): 99–120; "United States Supreme Court Voids Anti-Picketing Laws," *American Federationist* 47 (June 1940): 603–608; Joseph A. Padway, "Supreme Court Decisions on Labor," *American Federationist* 49 (September 1942): 18; and Paul L. Murphy, *The Constitution in Crisis Times, 1918–1969* (New York: Harper and Row, 1972), 203–205.

17. Padway, "Supreme Court Decisions on Labor," 18.

18. 310 U.S. 88 (1940). See also Fine, "Frank Murphy, the Thornhill Decision, and Picketing as Free Speech"; and Archibald Cox, "The Influence of Mr. Justice Murphy on Labor Law," *Michigan Law Review* 48 (April 1950): 767–810.

19. There is an enormous historiography surrounding the Wagner Act. For an interesting exchange see Michael Goldfield, "Worker Insurgency, Radical Organization, and New Deal Labor Legislation," *American Political Science Review* 83 (December 1989): 1257–1282; and Theda Skocpol, Kenneth Finegold, and Michael Goldfield, "Explaining New Deal Labor Policy," *American Political Science Review* 84 (December 1990): 1297–1315.

20. Zieger, *American Workers, American Unions*, 29 (quotation); and Christopher L. Tomlins, "AFL Unions in the 1930s: Their Performance in Historical Perspective," *Journal of American History* (March 1979): 1021–1042.

21. *Wisconsin Session Laws, 1939* (Madison: Wisconsin Farmer Company, 1939), 77–94; Hammond, "The Closed Shop Issue in Wartime Labor Disputes," 45; James B. Alteson, *Labor and the Wartime State: Labor Relations and Law During World War II* (Urbana: University of Illinois Press, 1998), 5, 10; Mason C. Doan, "State Labor Relations Acts," *Quarterly Journal of Economics* 56 (August 1942): 507–559, esp. 525–526; "Wagner Charta," 15; John V. Spielmans, "The Dilemma of the Closed Shop," *Journal of Political Economy* 51 (April 1943): 124–125; *Wisconsin News*, 29 January 1937; *Milwaukee Journal*, 29 January 1937; and "M. of M. Prevails," *Business Week* (4 November 1944): 104–105.

22. "Wagner Charta," 15; and Padway, "Shackling Labor by Legislation," 10–11, 22.

23. Joseph A. Padway, "Supreme Court Decisions on Labor," *American Federationist* 49 (August 1942): 14; and William Green, "Oregon Anti-Union Law," *American Federationist* 46 (March 1939): 241–242.

24. Padway, "Supreme Court Decisions on Labor," *American Federationist* 49

(August 1942): 14; and 315 U.S. 437 (1942).

25. For more information on 1940s state antilabor union laws see letter, Joseph A. Padway to William Green, 11 March 1943, American Federation of Labor Papers, series 3, box 2, State Historical Society of Wisconsin (hereinafter AFL Papers); letter Joseph A. Padway to William Green, 6 September 1943, AFL Papers, series 3, box 5; letter, James F. Barrett to William Green, 22 August 1942, AFL Papers, series 3, box 4; letter, Thomas E. Wilkinson to William Green, February 26, 1943, AFL Papers, box 2, series 3; Padway, "Shackling Labor by Legislation," 10–11, 22; Joseph A. Padway and B. A. Green, "We Move Away from Legal Bondage," *American Federationist* 48 (January 1941): 14–15, 32; Joseph A. Padway, "Judicial Gymnastics in Wisconsin," *American Federationist* 48 (February 1941): 14–15, 32; Joseph A. Padway, "Bills to Fetter Trade Unionism," *American Federationist* 49 (July 1942): 22–23; Padway, "Supreme Court Decisions on Labor," *American Federationist* 49 (August 1942): 14–15, 29; Joseph A. Padway, "Supreme Court Decisions on Labor," *American Federationist* 49 (September 1942): 18–19; Richard L. Neuberger, "Oregon Strikes Back," *Collier's* (28 January 1939): 12–13, 59–61; Joseph A. Padway, "Colorado Victory," *American Federationist* 50 (October 1943): 8–9; and "Padway Advises Fight on Oregon Labor Law," *Milwaukee Evening Post* (September 1939), Padway Micro, reel 2.

26. Spielmans, "The Dilemma of the Closed Shop," 114.

27. A considerable number of government employees also belonged to unions. See "Extent of Collective Bargaining and Union Status, January 1944," *Monthly Labor Review* 57 (April 1944), 697.

28. "Types of Union Recognition in Effect in January 1943," *Monthly Labor Review* 56 (February 1943), 284–291; "Extent of Collective Bargaining and Union Status, January 1944," 697–705; National Defense Mediation Board, *Report on the Work of the National Defense Mediation Board, March 19, 1941–January 12, 1942* (Washington, DC: GPO, 1942); International Statistical Bureau, *Labor Disputes and the War Labor Board* (New York: International Statistical Bureau, 1944); Howell John Harris, *The Right to Manage: Industrial Relations Policies of American Businesses in the 1940s* (Madison: University of Wisconsin Press, 1982), 41–89; Joel Seidman, *American Labor from Defense to Reconversion* (Chicago: University of Chicago Press, 1953); "Closed Shop Provision Aids Labor Relations," *Boilermakers Journal* (November 1941): 345; and Alteson, *Labor and the Wartime State,* 58.

29. Charles W. Baird, "Right to Work Before and After 14(b)," *Journal of Labor Research* 19 (Summer 1998): 471–493.

30. Thomas Taylor Hammond, "The Closed Shop Issue in the Wartime Labor Disputes," M.A. thesis (University of North Carolina, 1942), 30–32; Allen M. Wakstein, "The Origins of the Open-Shop Movement, 1919–1920," *Journal of American History* 51 (December 1964): 460–475; and Sidney Fine, *'Without Blare of Trumpets': Walter Drew, the National Erectors' Association, and the Open Shop Movement, 1903–1957* (Ann Arbor: University of Michigan Press, 1995).

31. Florence Calvert Thorne, *Samuel Gompers, American Statesman* (New York: Philosophical Library, 1957), 34; and Seidman, *American Labor from Defense to Reconversion,* 93.

32. Fine, *'Without Blare of Trumpet,'* 270; Jerold S. Auerbach, "The La Follette Committee: Labor and Civil Liberties in the New Deal," *Journal of American History* 51 (December 1964): 445, 452–454; Jerold S. Auerbach, *Labor and Liberty: The La Follette Committee and the New Deal* (Indianapolis: Bobbs-Merrill, 1966): 97–218; Los Angeles Industrial Council (CIO), *Unions Mean Higher Wages: The Story of the La Follette Committee in Los Angeles* (Los Angeles: Los Angeles Industrial Council, 1940), 6; J. W. Buzzell, "An Open Shop Citadel Falls," *American Federationist* 47 (April 1941): 6–7, 30–31; and Joseph A. Padway, "Enemies of Labor Slapped Down," *American Federationist* 52 (November 1945): 9–11. Interestingly enough, the AFL's support for the La Follette Committee waned significantly as the committee seemed to develop a pro-CIO stance. See Auerbach, "The La Follette Committee," 443.

33. Uphoff, "The Riot at Kohler, 1934," 143–146; and Walter H. Uphoff, *Kohler on Strike: Thirty Years of Conflict* (Boston: Beacon Press, 1966), 28–29, 85.

34. On Drew see Fine, *'Without Blare of Trumpets'*; and Walter Drew, *The Open or Closed Shop?* (New York: National Association of Manufacturers of the United States of America, nd), copy in AFL Papers, series 11, box 5, file B.

35. Robert H. Zieger, *American Workers, American Unions,* 2nd ed. (Baltimore: Johns Hopkins University Press, 1994), 85–87.

36. Spielmans, "The Dilemma of the Closed Shop," 127–128, esp. n. 31. In a footnote, Spielmans mentioned that "no attempt has been made to study [open shop] bills . . . introduced into state legislatures."

37. For another example of anticlosed shop employers' groups see Lois Quam and Peter J. Rachleff, "Keeping Minneapolis an Open-Shop Town: The Citizens' Alliance in the 1930s," *Minnesota History* (Fall 1986): 105–117; and William Millikan, *A Union Against Unions: The Minneapolis Citizen Alliance and Its Fight Against Organized Labor, 1903–1947* (Minneapolis: Minnesota Historical Society Press, 2001).

38. William Frew Long, *The Closed Shop Threat to National Defense* (Cleveland: Associated Industries of Cleveland), 4, 13, 18. See also John Chamberlain, *Democracy and the Closed Shop* (New York: National Association of Manufacturers); Julia E. Johnson, ed., *The Closed Shop* (New York: H. W. Wilson, 1942); and Robert M. La Follette, "Oppression of Labor," *American Federationist* 51 (August 1944): 28.

39. David Witwer, "Westbook Pegler and the Anti-Union Movement," unpublished paper, in author's possession.

40. Ray Parr, *America Is Also Fighting for Freedom to Work: The Actual Experience of an Oklahoman and* Times *Reporter in Starting Work on an Oklahoma War Work Project* (Oklahoma City: Daily Oklahoman, 1942), 1. See also S. W. Moore, "Effect of Closed Shop Agreements Upon a Labor Union's Right to Determine Who May Be Members," *Oklahoma Business Association Journal* 16 (28 July 1945): 1110–1113.

41. Parr, *America Is Also Fighting for Freedom to Work,* 3.

42. Ibid., 2, 5.

43. Ibid., 1.

44. Interestingly enough, the "right-to-work" movement in Oklahoma started slowly and offered its first antiunion referendum in 1964; it was defeated. However, in September 2001, a similar referendum was passed by the state's electorate. See "Oklahoma Voters Approve Work Measure," *New York Times,* 26 September 2001, A15.

45. John Roy Carlson, *Under Cover: My Four Years in the Nazi Underworld of America—The Amazing Revelation of How Axis Agents and Our Enemies Within Are Now Plotting to Destroy the United States* (New York: E. P. Dutton, 1943).

46. Parr, *America Is Also Fighting for Freedom to Work,* 1; "Men and Money Behind the Scenes," *The Southern Patriot* 2 (December 1944), 2; and Carlson, *Under Cover,* particularly 166–176, 169 (quotation).

47. Joseph Padway, "Report on Present Status of Litigation Involving State Anti-Labor Laws and Other Matters" [typescript], January 1944, AFL Papers, series 3, box 1; Joseph A. Padway, "Three-State Test," *American Federationist* 51 (October 1944): 11–13; and "Monopoly Control of Christian Americans Shown by Conference," *Boilermakers Journal* 57 (April 1945): 95. See also Gilbert J. Gall, *The Politics of Right to Work: The Labor Federations as Special Interests, 1943–1979* (New York: Greenwood Press, 1988): 13–49.

48. See Gall, *The Politics of Right to Work;* Gall, "Rights Which Have Meaning,"; and letter, Joseph A. Padway to W.C. Roberts, 11 May 1939, AFL Papers, series 11, file B, box 5.

49. "Opposition Grows," *Business Week* (15 July 1944): 98; "Security at Stake," *Business Week* (21 October 1944): 98–99; "Outlawing Closed Shops," *Business Week* (20 November 1944): 69; and "Closed Shop Provision Aids Labor Relations," *Boilermakers Journal* (November 1941): 345 (quotation). A year later, the same antiunion forces proposed another amendment with Proposition 12, which would have limited strikes, picketing, and boycotts. This proposition also failed. See Edward D. Vandeleur, "Labor Fights California Slave Bill," *American Federationist* 49 (October 1942): 21–22. The Franklin D. Roosevelt Library has some rare materials relating to Proposition 12. See FDR Papers, Office File 407, box 4, folder August–December 1944. See also Philip Taft, *Labor Politics American Style: The California State Federation of Labor* (Cambridge, MA: Harvard University Press, 1968), 232–279.

50. "Christian American Record So Far: Thirteen Anti-Labor Laws," *The Southern Patriot* 2 (December 1944): 2.

51. Arkansas State Constitution, [Online] Available at http://w3.trib.com/FACT/1st.arkconst.html, 24 July 2000. The constitution still contains the right-to-work amendment. See James E. Youngdahl, "Thirteen Years of the 'Right to Work' in Arkansas," *Arkansas Law Review and Bar Association Journal* 14 (Fall 1960): 289–301.

52. Letter Wesley High to Mr. Schmidt, 3 December 1944, AFL Papers, series 3, box 1.

53. Florida State Constitution, [Online], www.leg.state.fl.us/citizen/documents/constitution/1998/index, 24 July 2000. The Florida state constitution also still contains this amendment.

54. Gilbert Gall, "Southern Industrial Workers and Anti-Union Sentiments: Arkansas and Florida in 1944," 231 in Zieger, ed. *Organized Labor in the Twentieth Century South.*

55. Joseph A. Padway, "The Closed Shop Is Upheld," *American Federationist* 50 (December 1943): 12–13; Joseph A. Padway, "Florida Supreme Court Upholds Constitutionality of Closed Shop Agreements," *Boilermakers Journal* 55 (December 1943): 301; and "Validity of Closed-Shop Contract," *Monthly Labor Review* 58 (February 1944): 266.

56. Attorney General Watson had acted similarly when, in early 1943, Florida passed another law sponsored by the Christian American Association, which forced labor unions to register with the state and to acquire a license for operation. When Watson tried to use the law to prevent the United Association of Journeymen Plumbers and Steamfitters, Local 234, from functioning, a suit was initiated, and the plumbers and steamfitters won in the Florida Supreme Court, which voided the law. See Joseph A. Padway, "Supreme Court Kills Florida Anti-Labor Law," *American Federationist* 52 (July 1945): 10–11.

57. Letter, Joseph A. Padway to William Green, 7 April 1945, AFL Papers, series 3, box 1; American Federation of Labor, *Report on Proceedings of the Sixty-third Convention of the American Federation of Labor* (Washington, DC: AFL, 1944), 353; and 327 US 582. See also Padway, "Judicial Gymnastics in Wisconsin," 14–15, 31 and Padway, "Supreme Court Decisions on Labor," *American Federationist* 49 (August 1942): 14–15, 29.

58. Letter, Padway to Green, 7 July 1943, AFL Papers, series 3, box 1; and 327 U.S. 582 (1946).

59. Indeed, Padway had beaten Watson in front of the U.S. Supreme Court once before. In 1945, Padway had challenged and won a decision that threw out a different Florida antiunion law. See Padway, "Supreme Court Kills Florida Anti-Labor Law"; and "Hill v. State of Florida, Ex Rel. Watson," 325 U.S. 538 (1945).

60. The historians Paul L. Murphy and Sidney Fine have argued that the Thornhill case marked the "high-water mark in the Constitutional rights of labor." Following that decision the Supreme Court, according to Murphy, the "pendulum [swung] back." See Paul L. Murphy, *The Constitution in Crisis Times, 1918–1969* (New York: Harper and Row, 1972), 203–204; and Fine, "Frank Murphy, the Thornhill Decision, and Picketing as Free Speech," 108–109.

61. 327 U.S. 582 (1946) and *New York Times,* 26 March 1946.

62. 327 *U.S. Reports* 582 (1946).

63. "Alabama Renegade," *Business Week* (15 July 1944): 99; "Employer Loses Appeal," *Business Week* (19 August 1944): 108; "Union Fights Ban," *Business Week* (21 October 1944): 99; "M. of M. Prevails," *Business Week* (4 November 1944): 104–105; "How Issues Faired," *Business Week* (18 November 1944): 18–19; "Regional War Labor Board Dents the Florida Anti-Closed Shop Law," *Boilermakers Journal* 57 (April 1945): 86; and National War Labor Board, *The Termination Report of the National War Labor Board: Industrial Disputes and Wage Stabilization in Wartime,* Vol. I (Washington, DC: GPO, 1947), 98 (quotation). See also Fred Witney, *Wartime Experiences of the National Labor Relations Board, 1941–1945* (Urbana: University of Illinois Press, 1949), 13, 116, 118–119.

64. Zieger, *American Workers, American Unions,* 108–114; Green, *The World of the Worker,* 198–200; Gall, *The Politics of Right to Work,* 13–14; Robert A. Taft, *The New Labor Law—What It Really Means* (Milwaukee: Milwaukee *Sentinel,* 1947); Congress of Industrial Organizations,

Analysis of the Taft-Hartley Act (Washington, DC: CIO Legal Department, 1947); and U.S. Congress, *Labor-Management Relations Act, 1947: Message from the President of the United States Returning Without His Approval the Bill (H.R. 3020) Entitled the "Labor Management Relations Act, 1947,"* 80th Congress, 1st Session, 1947, H. Doc. 334.

65. AFL, *Report on Proceedings,* 105.

66. AFL, *Report on Proceedings,* 105–106, 107 (quotation).

67. Murray is quoted in Zieger, *American Workers, American Unions,* 114.

68. AFL, *Report on Proceedings,* 114.

NOTES TO CHAPTER 3

1. Transcript, President's Committee on Fair Employment Practice, In the Matter of Kaiser Company, Inc., Vancouver, Washington, Kaiser Company, Inc., Portland, Oregon, and Oregon Shipbuilding Corporation, 15 November 1943, Microfilmed Records of the President's Committee on Fair Employment Practice (hereafter FEPC micro), reel 13.

2. Memorandum, Clarence Mitchell to George M. Johnson, 27 October 1943, reel 14; and Josh Sides, "Battle on the Home Front: African American Shipyard Workers in World War II Los Angeles," *California History* 75 (Fall 1996): 255.

3. Sides, "Battle on the Home Front," 255.

4. Affidavit of Thomas Doram, 18 November 1943, FEPC micro, reel 14.

5. Memorandum, Clarence Mitchell to George M. Johnson, 27 October 1943, FEPC micro, reel 14.

6. Affidavit of Thomas Doram, 18 November 1943, FEPC micro, reel 14.

7. Memorandum, Clarence Mitchell to George M. Johnson, 27 October 1943, FEPC micro, reel 14.

8. See James S. Rush, Jr., "The Fair Employment Practice Committee and the Shipyard Hearings, 1943–1944," *Prologue* (Winter 1997): 278–289; Merl E. Reed, *Seedtime for the Modern Civil Rights Movement: The President's Committee on Fair Employment Practice, 1941–1946* (Baton Rouge: Louisiana State University Press, 1991), 267–317; Herbert Hill, *Black Labor and the American Legal System: Race, Work, and the Law* (Madison: University of Wisconsin Press, 1985), 185–208; and William H. Harris, "Federal Intervention in Union Discrimination: FEPC and West Coast Shipyards During World War II," *Labor History* 22 (Summer 1981): 325–347.

9. U.S. Commerce Department, Bureau of the Census, *Historical Statistics of the United States: Colonial Times to 1970,* part 2 (Washington, DC: GPO, 1975), 753–754.

10. U.S. Labor Department, *Estimated Labor Requirements for the Shipbuilding Industry Under the National Defense Program, November 22, 1941* (Washington, DC: GPO[?], 1941), 7.

11. Howard L. Vickery, "Ships Galore," *American Federationist* 50 (May 1943): 19.

12. John P. Frey, "Ships for Freedom," *American Federationist* 49 (April 1942): 8–11, 26; Frederic C. Lane, *Ships for Victory: A History of Shipbuilding Under the U.S. Maritime Commission in World War II* (Baltimore: Johns Hopkins Press, 1951), 1–100; Office of Production Management, press release, 29 August 1941, Papers of the American Federation of Labor, series 4, box 116, State of Wisconsin Historical Society (hereinafter AFL Papers, series 4, box 116); War Production Board, press release, 27 January 1942, AFL Papers. For an example of how the Metal Trades Department's conference and program became a model for subsequent negotiations see "Building and Construction Trade Agreement on Defense Work," *The Boilermakers Journal* 53 (September 1941): 268–269.

13. Vickery, "Ships Galore," 19–20; Lane, *Ships for Victory,* 72–100; U.S. Census Bureau, *Historical Statistics,* 753; and "Land Praises Union Shipyard Men," *American Federationist* 50 (September 1942): 19. See also press release, Office of War Information, August 23, 1942, AFL Papers, series 4, box 116.

14. U.S. Labor Department, *Estimated Labor Requirements for the Shipbuilding Industry Under the National Defense Program,* 7; and Vickery, "Ships Galore," 19, 20.

15. Jack M. Skirboll, "Mt. Hood Lodge No. 72, Portland, Ore.," *Boilermakers Journal* 55 (August 1943): 221.

16. John Morton Blum, *V Was for Victory: Politics and American Culture During World War II* (New York: Harcourt, Brace, Jovanovich, 1976), 113.

17. *Master Agreement Covering New Ship Construction Between the Pacific Coast Shipbuilders and the Metal Trades Dept. A.F. of L., the Pacific Coast District Metal Trades Council, the Local Metal Trades Councils, and Affiliated International Unions, April 23, 1941, Seattle, Washington*, 4, 6, 10, and 16, AFL Papers, series 4, box 116.

18. Skirboll, "Mt. Hood Lodge No. 72, Portland, Ore.," 221.

19. Robert L. Andresen, *Providence Shipyard: Walsh-Kaiser Company, Inc., Shipbuilding Division, Providence, R.I., 1943–1945* (Providence: Bank Lithograph Co., 1945), 1–9; Lane, *Ships for Victory*, 536; and U.S. Congress, House Committee on the Merchant Marine and Fisheries, *Walsh-Kaiser Co, Inc.: Investigation of the National Defense Program as It Relates to the Committee on the Merchant Marine and Fisheries*, 78th Cong., 2nd sess., 4–5 and 26–27 April 1944 (Washington, DC: GPO, 1944), 307, 333.

20. Andresen, *Providence Shipyard*, 16.

21. U.S. Congress, House, Committee on the Merchant Marine and Fisheries, *Investigation of the National Defense Program as It Relates to the Committee on the Merchant Marine and Fisheries*, 307–308; and Lane, *Ships for Victory*, 411–455.

22. Andresen, *Providence Shipyard*, 6, 34.

23. Vickery, "Ships Galore," 21.

24. "Stabilization in War Industry by Metal Trades Department," *Boilermakers Journal* 56 (August 1944): 187; and "West Coast Visit," *Boilermakers Journal* 56 (April 1944): 85.

25. Clyde W. Summers, "Admission of Labor Unions," *Quarterly Journal of Economics* 61 (November 1946): 68–69. In a much wider study of American unions (not limited to internationals), Herbert Northrup found racial exclusion to be more widespread. See Herbert R. Northrup, "Organized Labor and Negro Workers," *Journal of Political Economy* 51 (June 1943): 206–221 and the article's errata, *Journal of Political Economy* 51 (December 1943): 550.

26. See Sterling D. Spero and Abram L. Harris, *The Black Worker: The Negro and the Labor Movement* (New York: Columbia University Press, 1931); Eric Arnesen, *Waterfront Workers of New Orleans: Race, Class, and Politics, 1863–1923* (Urbana: University of Illinois Press, 1991); and Bruce Nelson, *Divided We Stand: American Workers and the Struggle for Black Equality* (Princeton: Princeton University Press, 2001).

27. Summers, "Admission of Policies of Labor Unions," 69; and Robert C. Weaver, "Recent Events in Negro Union Relationships," *Journal of Political Economy* 52 (September 1944): 234. On the railway unions see Eric Arnesen, *Brotherhoods of Color: Black Railroad Workers and the Struggle for Equality* (Cambridge, MA: Harvard University Press, 2001). The practice of creating separate locals continued into the 1960s for many unions, including the Boilermakers. See Herbert Hill, *Black Labor and the American Legal System: Race, Work, and the Law* (Madison: University of Wisconsin Press, 1985), 185–208. For information on the IBB and Chinese workers, see Xiaojian Zhoa, "Chinese American Women Defense Workers in World War II," *California History* 73 (1996): 138–153.

28. Herman D. Bloch, "Labor and the Negro, 1866–1910," *Journal of Negro History* 50 (July 1965): 173–175.

29. Summers, "Admission of Policies of Labor Unions,"69–71; and Northrup, "Organized Labor and Negro Workers," 211.

30. Northrup, "Organized Labor and Negro Workers," 207–208. For excepts on racial exclusion in the AFL see Paul Hartman, "Negro Longshoremen Make Gains," *American Federationist* 47 (June 1940): 585–586; and D. G. Garland, "Negro Workers and the AFL," *American Federationist* 52 (March 1945): 13–14, 31.

31. Northrup, "Organized Labor and Negro Workers," 211. For a wartime example see William Green's roundtable response to "Which Union Is Fairer to the Negro: AFL or CIO?," *Negro Digest* (July 1945): 41–43. Green claimed that "the American Federation of Labor . . . pioneered in the fight against discrimination."

32. Northrup, "Organized Labor and Negro Workers," 212.

33. Ibid. (quotation). See also "The Urban League and the AFL: A Statement on Racial Discrimination," *Opportunity* 13 (August 1935): 247; Herman D. Bloch, "Craft Unions and the Negro in Historical

Perspective," *Journal of Negro History* 43 (January 1958): 10–33; Robert C. Weaver, "Negro Labor Since 1929," *Journal of Negro History* 35 (January 1950): 20–38; and F. Ray Marshall, *The Negro and Organized Labor* (New York: Wiley, 1965).

34. Northrup, "Organized Labor and Negro Workers," 209.

35. It is not clear why the column ended in 1943. Since its cancellation roughly coincides with the FEPC's Boilermaker hearings, one might speculate that the IBB's leadership sought to appear kinder and less racist.

36. See for example the "Uncle Twink Sez" columns, *Boilermakers Journal* 53 (May 1941): 142 and (July 1941): 224.

37. *Proceedings of the Sixteenth Convention of the International Brotherhood of Boilermakers, Iron Ship Builders, and Helpers of America, 1937* (Kansas City: IBB, 1937), 361. See also 143, 332–333, 360–363.

38. *Proceedings of the Sixteenth Convention of the International Brotherhood of Boilermakers, Iron Ship Builders, and Helpers of America, 1937* (Kansas City: IBB, 1937), 363 (quotation); Malcolm Ross, *All Manner of Men* (New York: Reynal and Hitchcock, 1948): 144–145; Herbert R. Northrup, "Negroes in a War Industry: The Case of Shipbuilding," *Journal of Business* 16 (July 1943): 162; Thurgood Marshall, "Negro Status in the Boilermakers Union," *Crisis* 35 (March 1944): 77–78; and see also "Boilermakers Resolution, April 23, 1946," NAACP Micro, part 13, series C, reel 1.

39. Herbert R. Northrup, "An Analysis of the Discrimination Against Negroes in the Boilermakers Union," FEPC Micro, Reel 14.

40. See Arnesen, *Brotherhoods of Color.*

41. Northrup, "Negroes in a War Industry," 163–164.

42. Edwin C. Berry, "Profiles: Portland," *Journal of Educational Sociology* 19 (November 1945): 158–159; and John Gunther, *Inside U.S.A.* (New York: Harper and Brothers, 1947), 88.

43. Berry, "Profiles," 160–163.

44. Ibid., 161; Testimony of Leland Tanner, United States of America, President's Committee on Fair Employment Practice, In the Matter of Oregon Shipbuilding Corporation and Vancouver and Swan Island Shipyards, Portland, Oregon, 15 November 1943, 36–38, FEPC Micro, Reel 13; and Gunther, *Inside U.S.A.*, 96.

45. Ross, *All Manner of Men,* 149.

46. Transcript, President's Committee on Fair Employment Practice, In the Matter of Kaiser Company, Inc., Vancouver, Washington, Kaiser Company Inc., Portland, Oregon, and Oregon Shipbuilding Corporation, 19 October 1944, 15–39, 271–274, FEPC Micro, Reel 13 (hereinafter Kaiser FEPC hearing, 19 October 1944).

47. Kaiser FEPC hearing, 19 October 1944, 271–274, FEPC Micro, reel 13; and "Train with 465 Recruits for Kaiser Yards on Way," *Oregonian,* 10 October 1942.

48. "AFL to Investigate Anti-Negro Union Activities," *PM,* 2 October 1942, and "Negroes Ask Better Jobs," *Oregonian,* 9 October 1942.

49. "Negro Victory Committee Decries Local's 'Dictator,'" *PM,* 2 October 1942.

50. "AFL to Investigate Anti-Negro Union Activities," *PM,* 2 October 1942.

51. "Union at Kaiser's Shipyard Insists on Negro Ban," *PM,* 5 October 1942.

52. "Train with 465 Recruits for Kaiser Yards on Way," *Oregonian,* 10 October 1942.

53. "Union at Kaiser's Shipyard Insists on Negro Ban," *PM,* 5 October 1942. The exact number of African Americans on the train is not known. By October 1942, Kaiser had recruited more than 2,400 New Yorkers, roughly 140 (6 percent) of whom were black. See "Train with 465 Recruits for Kaiser Yards on Way," *Oregonian,* 10 October 1942.

54. "Negroes Ask Better Jobs," *Oregonian,* 9 October 1942; Lane, *Ships for Victory,* 254; and see testimony of Sidney Wolf, United States of America, President's Committee on Fair Employment Practice, In the Matter of Kaiser Company, Inc., Vancouver, Washington, Kaiser Company Inc., Portland, Oregon, and Oregon Shipbuilding Corporation, 15 November 1943, 193–197, FEPC Micro, reel 13.

55. "Mr. Ray Relents," *Oregonian,* 9 October 1942.

56. "NAACP Drops Portland Aide," *PM,* 24 October 1943.

57. Letter, Lawrence Cramer to William Green, 11 September 1941, FEPC Micro, Reel 15; and letter, Green to Cramer, 15 September 1941, FEPC Micro, Reel 15.

58. "Committee Wires Protest to Roosevelt," *PM,* 2 October 1942.

59. Letter, Francis K. Haas to James H.

Wolfe, 14 August 1943, FEPC Micro, Reel 15.

60. In October 1944, the FEPC convened another hearing regarding Portland shipbuilding and racial discrimination. Kaiser had requested a rehearing, because its officials wanted to stress that they had done all they could to alleviate the situation. Were it not for the Boilermakers and the closed-shop agreement, they charged, the yard would have been integrated. They testified about their extensive meeting with AFL officials, leaders of the Boilermakers, city politicians, and African American community spokesmen. Although the FEPC eventually agreed in essence to drop the case against Kaiser (while keeping the pressure on the IBB), it was clear that Kaiser in fact discriminated, too. At the hearing, an FEPC official asked Kaiser's industrial relations director, J. O. Murray, why the company did not employ more black women. Murray answered that "white women . . . seem to expect to follow instructions. They seem to learn quicker than the colored women. They seem more anxious to work than the colored women also." Despite such racist beliefs, Kaiser did in fact employ a lot of black workers, nearly eleven thousand in the Portland area by late 1944, which constituted about 13 percent of Kaiser's workforce in Oregon. See testimony of J. O. Murray, in United States of America, President's Committee on Fair Employment Practice, In the Matter of Kaiser Company, Inc., Vancouver, Washington, Kaiser Company, Inc., Portland Oregon, and Oregon Shipbuilding Corporation, 19 October 1944, 15–39, FEPC Micro, Reel 13; and "Distribution of Force by Shift, Hourly Employees Only as of October 1, 1944," FEPC Micro, Reel 13.

61. FEPC Portland hearing, 15 November 1943, 1–6, 193–197, FEPC Micro, reel 13.

62. Lane, *Ships for Victory,* 296–297.

63. FEPC Portland hearing, 15 November 1943, 30–49, FEPC Micro, reel 13.

64. Charles J. MacGowan, "A.F. of L. Report of Committee on Resolutions: Racial Discrimination," *Boilermakers Journal* 55 (November 1943): 283, 295.

65. Before the President's Committee on Fair Employment Practice, November 15–16, 1943, Summary, Findings, and Directives, Boilermakers Subordinate Lodge 72, 9 December 1943, FEPC Micro, Reel 14.

66. Ibid.

67. Charles Wollenberg, "James v. Marinship: Trouble on the New Black Frontier," *California History* 60 (1981): 262–279; and Skirboll, "Mt. Hood Lodge 72, Portland, Ore.," 221.

68. Ross, *All Manner of Men,* 142, 147.

69. Letter, Franklin D. Roosevelt to Joseph A. Franklin, 1 February 1944, President's Personal File 8653, Franklin D. Roosevelt Presidential Library (FDRL).

70. "Resolution Defining Policy with Regard to Colored Members," *Boilermakers Journal* 56 (March 1944): 73, 76, 79; Congress, House, Roger C. Slaughter, extension of remarks, Fair Employment Practice Committee, 79th Cong., 1st sess., *Congressional Record* (21 June 1945), vol. 91, pt. 12, A2983–2984; and *Gerald R. Hill et al. v. International Brotherhood of Boilermakers, Iron Shipbuilders, and Helpers of America, and Local 308 of the International Brotherhood of Boilermakers, Iron Shipbuilders, and Helpers of America,* Memorandum Brief for Complainants, Microfilmed Papers of the National Association for the Advancement of Colored People, part 13, series C, reel 1, 1171–1189.

71. Statement of basis for committee's decisions of March 17, 1945, in regard to Boilermakers' proposal of February 10, 1945, FEPC Micro, Reel 15; and Presentation of the International Brotherhood of Boilermakers, Iron Ship Builders, and Helpers of America on H.R. 2232, 79th Cong., 1st sess., *Congressional Record* (21 June 1945), vol. 91, pt. 12, A2981–2983.

72. Federal Writers' Project (WPA), *Rhode Island: A Guide to the Smallest State* (Boston: Houghton Mifflin, 1937), 99, 260 (quotation); and Neal R. Peirce, *The New England States: People, Politics, and Power in the Six New England States* (New York: Norton, 1972), 171–174.

73. Gunther, *Inside U.S.A.,* 498; Peirce, *The New England States,* 144–145, 151–152; Federal Writers' Project, *Rhode Island,* 58–59; Erwin L. Levine, *Theodore Francis Green: The Rhode Island Years, 1906–1936* (Providence: Brown University Press, 1963), 108–195; and Mason C. Doan, "State Labor Relations Acts," *Quarterly Journal of Economics* 56 (August 1942): 532.

74. "A Review of the Month: Recreation," *A Monthly Summary of Events and*

Trends in Race Relations (Fisk University), 1, no. 4 (November 1943): 7–8.

75. Robert A. Hill, ed. and comp., *The FBI's RACON: Racial Conditions in the United States During World War II* (Boston: Northeastern University Press, 1995), 236–237, 677; Richard F. Irving, *Toward Equal Opportunity: The Story of the Providence Urban League in the 1940s* (Providence: Urban League of Rhode Island, 1974), 5–15; and "Negroes at Yard Rest Their Case," *Providence Journal,* 30 May 1944.

76. Many contemporaries noted Local 308's uniqueness. See "Unions and Race," *A Monthly Summary of Events and Trends in Race Relations* (Fisk University), 1, no. 3 (October 1943): 4; Marshall, "Negro Status in the Boilermakers Union," 77–78; Weaver, "Recent Events in Negro Union Relationships," 245; Colston E. Warne et al., *Yearbook of American Labor: Vol. I: War Labor Policies* (New York: Philosophical Library, 1945), 375; and Summers, "Admission Policies of Labor Unions," 70.

77. Irving, *Toward Equal Opportunity,* 20–22.

78. "Timeline," n.d., NAACP Micro, part 13, series C, reel 2, 17 (quote); "Unions and Race," *A Summary of Events and Trends in Race Relations* (Fisk University), 1, no. 3 (October 1943): 4; "Negroes Press Injunction Plea," *Providence Journal,* 16 May 1944; and Irving, *Toward Equal Opportunity,* 21–22, 28.

79. Irving, *Toward Equal Opportunity,* 28; and "Timeline," n.d., NAACP Micro, part 13, series C, reel 2, 17.

80. Irving, *Toward Equal Opportunity,* 28.

81. "Timeline," n.d.; "Negroes at Yard Rest Their Case," *Providence Journal,* 30 May 1944; and *Gerald R. Hill et al. v. International Brotherhood of Boilermakers, Iron Shipbuilders, and Helpers of America, and Local 308 of the International Brotherhood of Boilermakers, Iron Shipbuilders, and Helpers of America,* Memorandum Brief for Complainants, Microfilmed Papers of the National Association for the Advancement of Colored People, part 13, series C, reel 1, 1171–1189;

82. Telegram, John F. Lopez to Roy Wilkins, December 14, 1943, NAACP Micro, part 13, series C, reel 2, 864; file memo, n.a., December 17, 1943, NAACP Micro, part 13, series C, reel 2, 865; letter, James N. Williams to Roy Wilkins, December 18, 1943, NAACP Micro, part 13, series C, reel 2, 867; and memo, Thurgood Marshall to Walter White and Roy Wilkins, December 22, 1943, NAACP Micro, part 13, series C, reel 2, 872. For information on the James case, see the sources mentioned in footnote 7 and Wollenberg, "James vs. Marinship."

83. Memo, Milton Konvitz to Thurgood Marshall, 20 April 1944, NAACP Micro, part 13, series C, reel 1, 922; memo, Konvitz to Marshall, n.d., NAACP Micro, part 13, series C, reel 2, 160; and State of Rhode Island, Providence, Superior Court, *Gerald R. Hill et al. vs. International Brotherhood of Boilermakers, Iron Shipbuilders and Helpers of America and Local No. 308 of the International Brotherhood of Boilermakers, Iron Shipbuilders and Helpers of America, et al.,* Answer of the Respondent, NAACP Micro, part 13, series C, reel 1, 1118–1123; "New Union Poll Sought in Court," *Providence Evening Bulletin,* 17 December 1943; and Marshall, "Negro Status in the Boilermakers Union," 77.

84. Resolution of John J. Norton, December 29, 1943, NAACP Micro, part 13, series C, reel 2, 18; and "Buckley Denies Ordering Marks," *Providence Evening Bulletin,* 6 January 1944.

85. "Court Told Negro Votes Accepted," *Providence Evening Bulletin,* 4 January 1944; "Buckley Denies Ordering Marks," *Providence Evening Bulletin,* 6 January 1944; "Negro Union Vote Action Nears End," *Providence Journal,* 7 January 1944; "Negro Union Vote Action Nears End," *Providence Journal,* 7 January 1944.

86. Marshall, "Negro Status in the Boilermakers Union," 78; letter, Thurgood Marshall to Ira B. Lewis, January 18, 1944, NAACP Micro, part 13, series C, reel 1, 888; and Irving, *Toward Equal Opportunity,* 31–32.

87. "Negroes Press Injunction Plea," *Providence Journal,* 16 May 1944; "Negroes at Yard Rest Their Case," *Providence Journal,* 30 May 1944; Wollenberg, "James vs. Marinship," 274–276; Anderson, *Providence Shipyard,* 63; Congress, House, Committee on the Merchant Marine and Fisheries, *Walsh-Kaiser Co, Inc,* 315; and Irving, *Toward Equal Opportunity,* 32–33.

88. Hill, *Black Labor and the American Legal System,* 205–208.

NOTES TO CHAPTER 4

1. Frances Perkins, "Women's Work in Wartime," *Monthly Labor Review* 56 (April 1943): 661.

2. Mary Robinson, *Woman Workers in Two Wars* (Washington, DC: GPO, 1944), 13.

3. Alice Kessler-Harris, "Where Are the Organized Women Workers?" *Feminist Studies* 3 (Fall 1975): 92–110.

4. A very small sample of this literature includes Sharon Hartman Storm, "Challenging 'Woman's Place': Feminism, the Left, and Industrial Unionism in the 1930s," *Feminist Studies* 9 (Summer 1983): 359–386; Philip S. Foner, *Women and the American Labor Movement: From the First Trade Unions to the Present* (New York: Free Press, 1979); Susan M. Hartmann, *The Home Front and Beyond: American Women in the 1940s* (Boston: Twayne, 1982); Ruth Milkman, *Gender at Work: The Dynamics of Job Segregation by Sex During World War II* (Urbana: University of Illinois Press, 1987); Michael J. Lewandowski, "Democracy in the Workplace: Working Women in Midwestern Unions, 1943–1945," *Prologue* 25 (Summer 1993): 157–169; Melina Chateauvert, *Marching Together: Women of the Brotherhood of Sleeping Car Porters* (Urbana: University of Illinois Press, 1998); Alice Kessler-Harris, *In Pursuit of Equity: Women, Men, and the Quest for Economic Citizenship in 20th-Century America* (New York: Oxford University Press, 2001); and Dorothy Sue Cobble, *The Other Women's Movement: Workplace Justice and Social Rights in Modern America* (Princeton: Princeton University Press, 2004).

5. Robinson, *Women Workers in Two Wars,* 1; and Gladys Dickason, "Women in Labor Unions," *Annals of the American Academy of Political and Social Science* 251 (May 1947): 71.

6. "Economic Position of Married Business and Professional Women," *Monthly Labor Review* 51 (December 1940): 1371; Lewandowski, "Democracy in the Workplace," 158; and Hartmann, *The Home Front and Beyond: American Women in the 1940s,* 17. One of the best explanations of the 1932 Economy Act can be found in Kessler-Harris, *In Pursuit of Equity,* 59–62. Section 213 was repealed in 1937. An example of how ingrained these notions of women and work were can be seen in Ann Shofield's excellent article "Rebel Girls and Union Maids: The Woman Question in the Journals of the AFL and IWW, 1905–1920," *Feminist Studies* 9 (Summer 1983): 335–358. Although the IWW and the AFL were in many ways polar opposites, both, according to Shofield, demonstrated similar "sexist and paternalistic behavior." See p. 355.

7. Frieda S. Miller, "The Female Worker," *American Federationist* 52 (November 1945): 20; and Miller, "Economic Position of Married Business and Professional Women," *Monthly Labor Review* 51 (December 1940): 1371–1374.

8. As quoted in Hartmann, *The Home Front and Beyond,* 54.

9. Federal Security Agency, "Survey of Employment Prospects for Women in War Industries, January to June 1942," AFL Papers, series 8A, box 44; Hartmann, *The Home Front and Beyond,* 21; and Cobble, *The Other Women's Movement,* 11.

10. "Women in Defense Industry," *American Federationist* 48 (July 1941): 6.

11. Mary Anderson, "A Silver Milestone for Women Workers," *American Federationist* 50 (July 1943): 20.

12. U.S. Women's Bureau, *The New Position of Women in American Industry: Bulletin No. 12* (Washington, DC: GPO, 1920), 18–19.

13. John F. Hart's statement from *Butcher Workman* (May 1917), as quoted in Foner, *Women and the American Labor Movement,* 246.

14. Foner, *Women and the American Labor Movement,* 247.

15. American Federation of Labor, *Report on the Proceedings of the Thirty-eighth Annual Convention* (Washington, DC: American Federation of Labor, 1918), 38.

16. See Samuel Gompers, "Don't Sacrifice Womanhood," *American Federationist* 24 (August 1917): 640–641; and Gompers, "Women Workers in War Time," *American Federationist* 24 (September 1917): 747–749.

17. Foner, *Women and the American Labor Movement,* 256–264; and Benjamin M. Squires, "Women Street Railway Employees," *Monthly Labor Review* 6 (May 1918): 1049–1050.

18. Women's importance to organized

labor's history was made clear in Frieda S. Miller, "The Female Worker," *American Federationist* 52 (November 1945). For more information see Foner, *Women and the American Labor Movement,* 1–266. See also Mary Blewett, *Men, Women, and Work: Class, Gender, and Protest in the New England Shoe Industry, 1780–1910* (Urbana: University of Illinois Press, 1988).

19. Florence Thorne [?], "American Federation of Labor Policies and Declarations on Women Workers" [typescript], AFL Papers, series 8A, box 44.

20. Ida M. Van Etten, *The Condition of Women Workers Under the Present Industrial System: An Address by Ida M. Van Etten at the National Convention of the American Federation of Labor, Detroit, Michigan, December 8, 1890* (Washington, DC: American Federation of Labor, 1891), 3.

21. On the AFL, volunteerism, and masculinity, see Alice Kessler-Harris, *In Pursuit of Equity,* 8, 23–25. See also Florence Calvert Thorne, *Samuel Gompers: American Statesman* (New York: Philosophical Society, 1952), 41–42.

22. Van Etten, *The Conditions of Women Workers Under the Present Industrial System,* 3.

23. Ibid., 15.

24. Ibid., 16.

25. For a summary of the convention resolutions concerning women from 1882 through 1921, see David Mandel Halfant, "Attitudes of the American Federation of Labor Toward Unskilled and Women Workers," M.A. thesis (University of Chicago, 1922). See also Thorne [?], "American Federation of Labor Policies and Declarations on Women Workers."

26. Halfant, "Attitudes of the American Federation of Labor Toward Unskilled and Women Workers," 83–84.

27. 208 U.S. 412 (1908).

28. For more on this issue see Kessler-Harris, *In Pursuit of Equity,* 29–33.

29. Ibid., 69.

30. *Constitution of the National Women's Trade Union League of America Adopted in Faneuil Hall, Boston, November 17–19, 1903,* as quoted in Foner, *Women and the Labor Movement,* 130.

31. Foner, *Women and the American Labor Movement,* 279–280.

32. See for example letter, Selma M. Borschardt to William Green, 8 November 1932, AFL Papers, series 11B, box 2.

33. "Equal Rights Amendment," *American Federationist* 45 (March 1938) 245.

34. Cobble, *The Other Women's Movement,* 3–4. In Cobble's analysis, this "missing" wave of feminism is closely aligned with the New Deal and with the World War II years. For my purposes I take the concept a few decades back in time.

35. Agnes Nestor, *Women's Labor Leader: An Autobiography of Agnes Nestor* (Rockford, IL: Bellevue Books, 1954), 35–36.

36. Ibid., 41.

37. Ibid., 65.

38. Ibid., 131.

39. Ibid., 236 (quotation)–238.

40. The National Defense Advisory Commission's Women in Industry Committee was different from the U.S. Department of Labor's Women in Industry Committee, which was headed by Mary Anderson and which after the war became the U.S. Women's Bureau.

41. Nestor, *Women's Labor Leader,* 174.

42. Ibid., 174.

43. Beulah was a subject in Katherine Archibald's study of wartime shipyards. Typical of such projects, last names were withheld to protect true identities.

44. For more information on the Dust Bowl migrants see Seymour J. Janow and William Gilmartin, "Labor and Agricultural Migration to California, 1935–40," *Monthly Labor Review* 53 (July 1941): 18–34; and James N. Gregory, *American Exodus: Dust Bowl Migration and Okie Culture in California* (New York: Oxford University Press, 1989).

45. Robinson, *Woman Workers in Two Wars,* 13; and Eleanor V. Kennedy, "Employment of Women in Shipyards, 1942," *Monthly Labor Review* 56 (February 1943): 277–282.

46. Katherine Archibald, *Wartime Shipyard: A Study in Social Disunity* (Berkeley: University of California Press, 1947), 25; Foner, *Women and the American Labor Movement,* 362–364; and Hartmann, *The Home Front and Beyond,* 57–65.

47. U.S. Women's Bureau, "Women in Unions in a Mid-west War Industry Area [typescript], p. 5, Records of the Women's Bureau, RG-86, box 1, 56-A-50, National

Archives and Records Administration (Silver Spring, MD).

48. "Women in Defense Industry," *American Federationist* 48 (July 1941): 7.

49. William Green, "War Jobs for Women," *American Federationist* 49 (May 1942): 20.

50. Archibald, *Wartime Shipyard,* 25.

51. Lewandowski, "Democracy in the Workplace," 164.

52. Foner, *Women and the American Labor Movement,* 364.

53. The only union that continued to refuse women as members was the International Brotherhood of Bookbinder, which had a separate women's organization, the Bindery Women's Local Unions. See Dickason, "Women in Labor Movements," 72.

54. Foner, *Women and the American Labor Movement,* 364.

55. Archibald, *Wartime Shipyard,* 3.

56. Ibid., 16.

57. Ibid., 17.

58. U.S. Women's Bureau, "Women in Unions in a Mid-west War Industry Area [typescript], 6. 59. Archibald, *Wartime Shipyard.* 24.

60. Seymour J. Janow and William Gilmartin, "Labor and Agricultural Migration to California, 1935–1940," *Monthly Labor Review* 53 (July 1941): 21.

61. Emile Benoit-Smullyan and Bettina G. Conant, "State Variations in War Migration and Post-War Demobilization," *Monthly Labor Review* (September 1944): 485.

62. Archibald, *Wartime Shipyard,* 47.

63. Ibid., 46.

64. Ibid., 51.

65. Ibid., 63.

66. "Equal Pay for Equal Work" [typescript], AFL Papers, series 8A, box 44.

67. Ibid.; and National War Labor Board, *The Termination Report of the National War Labor Board,* Vol. 1 (Washington, DC: GPO, 1947), 292.

68. NWLB, *The Termination Report of the National War Labor Board,* Vol. 1, 290.

69. Ruth Milkman, *Gender at Work: The Dynamics of Job Segregation by Sex During World War II* (Urbana: University of Illinois Press, 1987), 42–48, 74–79.

70. U.S. Women's Bureau, "Women in Unions in a Mid-west War Industry Area," 12–14.

71. NWLB, *The Termination Report of the National War Labor Board,* Vol. 1, 296

72. U.S. Department of Labor, Women's Bureau, "Women's Wages in Wartime" [typescript], AFL Papers, series 8A, box 32.

73. AFL Women in Industry Committee, "Women in Industry" [typescript], AFL Papers, series 8A, box 32.

74. "Standards for Employment of Women in Defense Program," *Monthly Labor Review* 51 (September 1940): 564–567.

75. Foner, *Women and the American Labor Movement,* 356.

76. American Federation of Women's Auxiliaries of Labor, *History of the American Federation of Women's Auxiliaries of Labor* (Washington, DC: AFWAL, nd [1940?]), 3.

77. Ibid., 6.

78. Ibid., 11 (emphasis added).

79. The AFWAL came nowhere near realizing that goal. In 1955, it had only fifty thousand members. See Cobble, *The Other Women's Movement,* 149.

80. Melinda Chateauvert, *Marching Together: Women of the Brotherhood of Sleeping Car Porters* (Urbana: University of Illinois Press, 1998), 92, 180–184.

81. See for example Tri-City Women's Trade Union League, meeting minutes, 6 February 1942, Tri-City American Federation of Women's Auxiliaries of Labor Papers, box 1, State Historical Society of Iowa.

82. Tri-City Women's Trade Union League, meeting minutes, 16 January 1942, Tri-City AFWAL Papers, box 1.

83. Tri-City Women's Trade Union League, meeting minutes, 6 February 1942; and AFL Union Label Trades Department, *What Is the AFWAL?: It Is the American Federation of Women's Auxiliaries of Labor* (Washington, DC: AFL, nd). There were two other organizer pamphlets: *How to Organize a Women's Auxiliary and Affiliate with the American Federation of Women's Auxiliaries of Labor* and *How to Conduct Meetings of Women's Auxiliaries.*

84. Tri-City Women's Trade Union League, meeting minutes, 20 March 1942, Tri-City AFWAL Papers, box 1. The WTUL ceased to exist in 1950. The AFWAL survived the merger, becoming, in 1957, the American Federation of Labor and Congress of Industrial Organizations Auxiliaries. Mrs. Herman Lowe remained AFWAL president

until 1951, when Anna P. Kelsey took over the Federation. In the 1960s, the Federation lost members and power within the AFL-CIO. It does continue to exist, but its name and activities are subsumed under the AFL-CIO's Organization and Field Services Department.

85. Letter, I. M. Ornburn to Arnold Zander, 27 November 1941, AFWAL Papers, box 13.

86. AFWAL, *The History of the American Federation of Women's Auxiliaries of Labor,* 5.

87. "Women's Auxiliaries Hold Convention," *American Federationist* 50 (July 1942): 7.

88. AFWAL press release, 19 June 1942, American Federation of Women's Auxiliaries of Labor Records, RG52-001, box 11, George Meany Library (Silver Spring, MD). See also AFWAL, *Proceedings of the Second Convention of the American Federation of Women's Auxiliaries of Labor, St. Louis, Missouri, June 19 and 20, 1942* (Washington, DC: AWFAL, 1942).

89. AFWAL, *Proceedings of the Second Convention of the American Federation of Women's Auxiliaries of Labor,* 66–69.

90. AFWAL Bulletin 2, no. 8 (October 1944), American Federation of Women's Auxiliaries of Labor, box 11.

91. Meeting Minutes, May 1943, Women's Auxiliary to the Tri-City Federation of Trade Unions Papers, box 1.

92. Hartmann, *The Home Front and Beyond,* 134–135. See also "New York State's Equal Pay Law" [typescript], AFL Papers, series 3, box 4.

93. AFL file memo, 6 April 1944, AFL Papers, series 8A, box 32. See also "Effect of 'Cutbacks' on Women's Employment," *Monthly Labor Review* 59 (September 1944): 585–588.

94. As quoted in Hartmann, *The Home Front and Beyond,* 63.

95. As quoted in Mary Elizabeth Pidgeon, *A Preview as to Women Workers in Transition from War to Peace* (Washington, DC: GPO, 1944), 9.

96. As quoted in ibid., 10.

97. Ibid., 6.

98. Nestor, *Women's Labor Leader,* 174.

99. See AFL Postwar Planning Committee, *Women Workers* (Washington, DC: AFL, 1944); and Agnes Nestor, "Working Women After Victory," *American Federationist* 52 (February 1945): 17, 32.

100. Ibid., 3.

101. Ibid., 4.

102. Ibid., 5–6.

103. Ibid., 7.

104. N.a. [Philip Murray?], "Organized Labor Faces the Problems of Post-War Employment of Women" [typescript], n.d. [1944?], AFL Papers, series 5C, box 24.

105. Congress of Industrial Organizations, *Report of President Philip Murray to the Seventh Constitutional Convention of the Congress of Industrial Organizations, Chicago, Illinois, November 20, 1944* (Washington, DC: CIO, 1945), 44.

106. U.S. Women's Bureau press release, 5 December 1944, AFL Papers, series 8A, box 32; and Bess Furman, "Post-War Job Plan Drawn for Women," *New York Times,* 7 December 1944, p. 28.

107. Congress, Senate, Committee on Banking and Currency, *Full Employment Act of 1945,* 79th Cong., 1st sess., 30 July–1 September 1945, 19–20, as quoted in Kessler-Harris, *In Pursuit of Equity,* 19–21; and Pidgeon, *A Preview as to Women Workers in Transition From War to Peace,* 18–19.

108. Office of War Information press release, 17 May 1943, AFL Papers, series 5C, box 26.

109. Letter, William Green to All Women's Auxiliaries, nd [1944], AFL Papers, series 5C, box 25.

110. U.S. Women's Bureau, "Women in Unions in a Mid-west War Industry Area" [typescript], 6, 7.

111. See Cobble, *The Other Women's Movement,* 149–223.

NOTES TO CHAPTER 5

1. Herbert Harris, *Labor's Civil War* (New York: Greenwood Press, 1940; repr. ed., 1969), 4.

2. American Federation of Labor, *Report of Proceedings of the Fifty-fifth Annual Convention of the American Federation of Labor, 1935* (Washington, DC: AFL, 1935), 727.

3. James R. Green, *The World of the Worker: Labor in Twentieth-Century America* (Urbana: University of Illinois Press, 1980), 32–66; Philip Taft, *The A.F. of L. from the Death of Gompers to the Merger*

(New York: Harper & Brothers, 1959), 1–14; and Robert H. Zieger, *American Workers, American Unions* (Baltimore: Johns Hopkins University Press, 1986), 3–25.

4. American Federation of Labor, *Industrial Unionism in Its Relation to Trade Unionism, Being a Report of the Executive Council of the American Federation of Labor to the Rochester, N.Y., Convention, 1912, in Which the Subject Iis Fairly Presented* (Washington, DC: AFL, 1912), 2–7, Franklin D. Roosevelt Presidential Library Vertical Files, "American Federation of Labor" folder, Franklin D. Roosevelt Presidential Library (FDRL).

5. Taft, *The A.F. of L. from the Death of Gompers,* 96–101; and Harris, *Labor's Civil War,* 38.

6. Zieger, *American Workers, American Unions,* 29.

7. My treatment of the "great schism," as it became known, is drawn from Taft's *The A.F. of L. from the Death of Gompers,* 140–180; and Robert H. Zieger, *The CIO, 1935–1955* (Chapel Hill: University of North Carolina Press, 1995), 1–111.

8. See John Frey, *Craft Unions of Ancient and Modern Times* (Washington, DC, s.n., 1945).

9. *Report of the Proceedings of the Metal Trades Department of the American Federation of Labor,* 1935, 99, as quoted in Taft, *The A. F. of L. from the Death of Gompers,* 146.

10. American Federation of Labor, *A.F.L. vs. C.I.O.: The Record* (Washington, DC: AFL 1939), 5–6, Franklin D. Roosevelt Presidential Library Vertical Files, "American Federation of Labor" folder.

11. Ibid.

12. Form letter, John Brophy to union leaders, 27 November 1935, American Federation of Labor Papers (AFL Papers), series 11C, box 24, Wisconsin Historical Society; and Minutes of Meeting of Committee for Industrial Organization, Washington, DC, 9 November, 1935, as quoted in Taft, *The A.F. of L. from the Death of Gompers,* 145 (quotation).

13. Letter, John L. Lewis to William Green, 7 December 1935, as quoted in Taft, *The A. F. of L. from the Death of Gompers,* 148.

14. Letter, Green to Lewis, 9 December 1935, AFL Papers, series 11C, box 24. See also *President Green Declares That American Federation of Labor's Relentless Opposition to Minority Rule in Labor Movement Is Real Issue in CIO Controversy* (Washington, DC: AFL, 1937), Franklin D. Roosevelt Library Vertical Files, "American Federation of Labor" file.

15. Craig Phelan, *William Green: Biography of a Labor Leader* (Albany: SUNY Press, 1989), 24–28.

16. See letter, Charles P. Howard to William Green, 2 December 1935, in American Federation of Labor, *A.F.L. vs. C.I.O.: The Record* (Washington, DC, 1939), 11–12, Franklin D. Roosevelt Presidential Library Vertical Files, "American Federation of Labor" File.

17. Phelan discusses how Green intertwined his religious and union belief in *William Green.*

18. Letter, Charles Ogburn to William Green, 30 September 1936, AFL Papers, series 11C, box 24.

19. Taft, *The A.F. of L. from the Death of Gompers,* 156.

20. Vernon A. Jensen, *Heritage of Conflict: Labor Relations in the Nonferrous Metals Industry up to 1930* (Ithaca: Cornell University Press, 1950), 160.

21. Ibid., 169.

22. *Industrial Unionism in Its Relation to Trade Unionism, Being a Report of the Executive Council of the American Federation of Labor to the Rochester, N.Y., Convention, 1912, In Which the Subject Is Fairly Presented.*

23. Taft, *The A.F. of L. from the Death of Gompers,* 163.

24. Ibid., 162–180.

25. The unions were the United Mine Workers, the Amalgamated Clothing Workers, the Oil Field, Gas Well, and Refinery Workers, the International Union of Mine, Mill, and Smelter Workers, the International Ladies' Garment Workers, the United Textile Workers, the Federation of Flat Glass Workers, the Amalgamated Association of Iron, Steel, and Tin Workers, the International United Automobile Workers Union, and the United Rubber Workers Union.

26. Taft, *The A.F. of L. from the Death of Gompers,* 172–173.

27. Harris, *Labor's Civil War,* 35–36.

28. Ibid., 210–214.

29. Ibid., 214–222; and Joseph A. Padway, "Shackling Labor by Legislation,"

American Federationist 47 (August 1940): 10–11, 22.

30. Harris, *Labor's Civil War,* 281–288.

31. Ibid., 283.

32. John W. Baily, "Unions in Kenosha," in Darryl Holter, *Workers and Unions in Wisconsin: A Labor History Anthology* (Madison: State Historical Society of Wisconsin, 1999), 47–51, quotation from 51. See also John A. Neuenschwander, *Kenosha County in the Twentieth Century* (Kenosha: Kenosha County Historical Society, 1976) and Robert W. Ozanne, *The Labor Movement in Wisconsin: A History* (Madison: State Historical Society of Wisconsin, 1984), 51–52, 56, 64–65.

33. James R. Prickett, "Communist Conspiracy or Wage Dispute?: The 1941 Strike at North American Aviation," *Pacific Historical Review* 50 (November 1981): 215–233.

34. Melvyn Dubofsky and Warren Van Tine, *John L. Lewis: A Biography,* abridged (Urbana: University of Illinois Press, 1986), 228.

35. See cross-reference file memo, Secretary of Labor, 29 October 1937, FDR Papers, OF 142, container 1, FDRL.

36. American Federation of Labor, *A.F.L. vs. C.I.O.: The Record* (Washington, DC, 1939), 16–17, Franklin D. Roosevelt Presidential Library Vertical Files, "American Federation of Labor" folder, FDRL.

37. Taft, *The A.F. of L. from the Death of Gompers,* 196–199; Dubofsky and Van Tine, *John L. Lewis,* 222–226; AFL, *A.F.L. vs. C.I.O.,* 5258.

38. Speech, William Green, ca. 1938, AFL Papers, series 11C, box 24.

39. American Federation of Labor, *Woll Charges CIO Leaders Wrecked Labor Peace Conference* (Washington, DC: AFL, [1937?]), 8, Franklin D. Roosevelt Presidential Library Vertical Files, "American Federation of Labor" folder, FDRL; Louis Stark, "Labor Peace Drive Finally Collapses," *New York Times,* 22 December 1937, p. 18; and "Woll Charges CIO Wrecked Peace," *New York Times,* 27 December 1937, p. 4.

40. Taft, *The A.F. of L. from the Death of Gompers,* 198; and Dubofsky and Van Tine, *John L. Lewis,* 268–347.

41. Letter, FDR to William Green, 23 February 1939, FDR Papers, OF 407, box 2, FDRL.

42. Letter, Green to FDR, 24 February 1939, FDR Papers, OF 407, box 2, FDRL.

43. Telegram, Sausage Makers Union Number 615 (Minneapolis, MN) to William Green, 15 March 1939, AFL Papers, series 11C, box 29.

44. Resolution, International Association of Machinists, Lodge No. 364 (Stockton, CA), 20 March 1939, AFL Papers, series 11C, box 29.

45. White House press release, 7 March 1939, FDR Papers, OF 142, container 1, FDRL.

46. White House press release, 3 March 1939, FDR Papers, OF 407, box 2, FDRL.

47. AFL Executive Council Minutes (Miami), 29 January to 9 February, 1940, 141–142, AFL Papers, series C, box 24; file memo of telephone call, John L. Lewis to William Green, 5 April 1939, AFL Papers, series C, box 24; and file memo of telephone call, Frances Perkins to Matthew Woll, 10 April 1939, AFL Papers, series C, box 24 (quotation).

48. Letter, Matthew Woll to President Franklin D. Roosevelt, 16 June 1939, FDR Papers, OF 142, container 1, FDRL. The statement was attached to the letter. See also Louis Stark, "To Renew Effort for Labor Peace," *New York Times,* 16 June 1939, p. 1.

49. Letter, President Franklin D. Roosevelt to William Green, 30 September 1939, AFL Papers, series 11C, box 24.

50. Telegram, William Green to President Franklin D. Roosevelt, 3 October 1939, AFL Papers, series 11C, box 24; and letter, William Green to President Franklin D. Roosevelt, 3 October 1939, AFL Papers, series 11C, box 24.

51. Letter, President Franklin D. Roosevelt to John L. Lewis, 6 October 1939, FDR Papers, President's Personal File, box 5623–5660, folder 5640.

52. Letter, Lewis to Roosevelt, 15 October 1939, FDR Papers, PPF, Box 5623–5660, File 5640.

53. In his messages to the AFL and CIO conventions from 1940 through 1944, FDR made no mention of the rivalry between the organizations and did not call for peace. See Letter, President Franklin D. Roosevelt to William Green, 13 November 1940, FDR Papers, President's Personal File, box 3172–3189, file 3189; letter, President Franklin D. Roosevelt to William Green, 2 October

1941, FDR Papers, President's Personal File, box 3172–3189, file 3189; letter, President Franklin D. Roosevelt to William Green, 3 October 1942, FDR Papers, President's Personal File, box 3172–3189, file 3189; letter, President Franklin D. Roosevelt to William Green, 29 September 1943, FDR Papers, President's Personal File, box 3172–3189, file 3189; letter, President Franklin D. Roosevelt to William Green, 13 October 1944, FDR Papers, President's Personal File, box 3172–3189, file 3189; letter, President Franklin D. Roosevelt to Philip Murray, 15 November 1941, FDR Papers, President's Personal File, box 5623–5660, file 5640a; letter, President Franklin D. Roosevelt to Philip Murray, 25 March 1942, FDR Papers, President's Personal File, box 5623–5660, file 5640b; letter, President Franklin D. Roosevelt to Philip Murray, 23 October 1942, FDR Papers, President's Personal File, box 5623–5660, file 5640b; letter, President Franklin D. Roosevelt to Philip Murray, 21 October 1943, FDR Papers, President's Personal File, box 5623–5660, file 5640b; and President Franklin D. Roosevelt to Philip Murray, 8 June 1944, FDR Papers, President's Personal File, box 5623–5660, file 5640b.

54. Zieger, *The CIO,* 108 (quotation), 110.

55. "Personal Feud Shown at Parley," *New York Times,* 18 January 1942, p. 33; and cross-reference file memo, Gardner Jackson, 20 January 1942, FDR Papers, OF 142, container 2.

56. Letter, Gardner Jackson to President Franklin D. Roosevelt, 20 January 1942, FDR Papers, OF 4747; and A. H. Raskin, "President Supports Murray in Row on Lewis," *New York Times,* 22 January 1942, p. 1.

57. Letter, Gardner Jackson to President Franklin D. Roosevelt, 20 January 1942, FDR Papers, OF 4747 (quote); and see cross-reference file memo, Gardner Jackson, 20 January 1942, FDR Papers, OF 142, Container 2; "Murray Puts Aside Labor Peace Talks," *New York Times,* 20 January 1942, p. 1; Raskin, "President Supports Murray in Row on Lewis Peace Deal"; and Dubofsky and Van Tine, *John L. Lewis,* 294–296.

58. W. H. Lawrence, "President Offers Labor Peace Plan Countering Lewis," *New York Times,* 23 January 1942 (quotation), p. 1; A. H. Raskin, "President Offers Labor Peace Plan," *New York Times,* 23 January 1942, p. 36; A. H. Raskin, "CIO Heads Back Roosevelt Truce," *New York Times,* 24 January 1942, p. 1; and cross-reference file memo, Philip Murray and William Green, 22 January 1942, FDR Papers, OF 407, Box 3, File 2.

59. Press Release, 17 March 1942, FDR Papers, OF 4747; and " 'War Labor Cabinet' for U.S.," *American Federationist* 49 (February 1942): 3.

60. Cross-reference file memo, 9 May 1943, FDR Papers, OF 4747.

61. See Robert Glass Cleland, *A History of Phelps Dodge, 1834–1950* (New York: Knopf, 1952); and Carlos A. Schwantes, *Vision and Enterprise: Exploring the History of Phelps Dodge Corporation* (Tucson: University of Arizona Press and Phelps Dodge Corporation, 2000).

62. Cleland, *A History of Phelps Dodge,* 72–73.

63. U.S. Bureau of Mines, *Safety at the Morenci Branch of the Phelps Dodge Corporation* (Washington, DC: Bureau of Mines, 1930), 16; Mark Aldrich, *Safety First: Technology, Labor, and Business in the Building of American Work Safety, 1870–1939* (Baltimore: Johns Hopkins University Press, 1997), 248–250.

64. Marshal A. Oldman, "Phelps Dodge and Organized Labor in Bisbee and Douglas," *Western Legal History* 5 (Winter/Spring 1992): 83–95; Melvyn Dubofsky, *We Shall Be All: A History of the Industrial Workers of the World* (New York: Quadrangle, 1969), 385–391; Jensen, *Heritage of Conflict,* 381–410; and Cleland, *A History of Phelps Dodge,* 165–188.

65. Phelps Dodge Corp. v. National Labor Relations Board, 313 U.S.177 (1941) and Schwantes, *Vision and Enterprise,* 202–204.

66. Oldman, "Phelps Dodge and Organized Labor in Bisbee and Douglas," 92.

67. Arizona State Federation of Labor, Resolution, 27 June 1937, AFL Papers, series 11C, box 34

68. Letter, A. H. Peterson to William Green, 29 June 1937, AFL Papers, series 11C, box 34.

69. Letter, William Green to C.P. Flynn, 22 January 1941, AFL Papers, series 11C, box 34; and letter, John J. Durkin to

William Green, 4 February 1941, AFL Papers, series 11C, box 34.

70. See *In the Matter of Phelps Dodge Corporation, United Verde Branch,* 15 NLRB 732; and *In the Matter of Phelps Dodge Corporation and Mill and Smelter Workers Union, No. 22893 (AFL),* 60 NLRB 249.

71. Contract agreement for Morenci Metal Trades Council, No. 22893, AFL Papers, series 7, box 66, folder 22893; and *In the Matter of Phelps Dodge Corporation and Mill and Smelter Workers Union, No. 22893 (AFL),* 60 NLRB 249.

72. "Labor Productivity and Employment in Copper Mining," *Monthly Labor Review* 53 (July 1940): 51.

73. In 1942, less than 1 percent of the copper produced in the United States was utilized for civilian purposes. See "Recent Productivity Changes in Copper Mining," *Monthly Labor Review* (August 1943): 258–264.

74. See letter, William Green to Luella R. Witte, 23 May 1934, AFL Papers, Series 4, Box 82; and Schwantes, *Vision and Enterprise,* 207–215.

75. Schwantes, *Vision and Enterprise,* 211.

76. Letter, Jess Nicols to Allan D. McNeil, 4 December 1942, Records of the National War Labor Board, RG 202, Entry 277, Box 6, Phelps-Dodge folder (2), National Archives and Records Administration, Denver, Colorado.

77. Jensen, *Heritage of Conflict,* 465; Vernon Jenson, *Nonferrous Metal Industry Unionism, 1932–1954: A Story of Leadership Controversy* (Ithaca: Cornell University, 1954), 51–65; "Phelps Dodge Corp.," *War Labor Reports* 2 (24 June 1942), 58–59; and Morris Wright, *"Takes More Than Guns": A Brief History of the International Union of Mine, Mill, and Smelter Workers, CIO* (Denver: IUMMSW, 1944), 30–35.

78. "Phelps Dodge Corp.," *War Labor Reports* 2 (June 24, 1942), 58.

79. *In the Matter of Phelps Dodge Corporation and International Union of Mine, Mill, and Smelter Workers, CIO,* 48 N.L.R.B 58, 493.

80. "Synopsis," na, nd, Records of the National War Labor Board, RG 202, Entry 277, Box 5, Phelps-Dodge folder, National Archives and Records Administration, Denver, Colorado.

81. Nonferrous Metal Commission, National War Labor Board, *Decision in the Matter of Phelps Dodge,* Case No. 22-635, Records of the National War Labor Board, RG 202, Entry 278, Box 26, National Archives and Records Administration, Denver, Colorado; and Wright, *"Takes More Than Guns,"* 46.

82. Letter, C. R. Kuzell to Walter T. Margetts, 7 August 1943, Records of the National War Labor Board, RG 202, entry 277, box 5, Phelps-Dodge folder, National Archives and Records Administration, Denver, Colorado. See also Letter, C. R. Kuzell to Nathan Siensinger, 6 August 1943, Records of the National War Labor Board, RG 202, entry 277, box 5, Phelps-Dodge folder, National Archives and Records Administration, Denver, Colorado; and National War Labor Board, "Jurisdictional Disputes," in *The Termination Report of the National War Labor Board,* vol. 1 (Washington, DC: GPO, 1947): 71–79.

83. NWLB press release, 5 September 1943, Records of the National War Labor Board, RG 202, entry 277, box 23, Phelps-Dodge folder, National Archives and Records Administration, Denver, Colorado.

84. NWLB, *In the Matter of Phelps-Dodge Corporation and Clifton-Morenci Metal Trades Council (AFL), 2 September 1943,* Records of the National War Labor Board, RG 202, Entry 277, Box 23, Phelps-Dodge folder, National Archives and Records Administration, Denver, Colorado. See Fred Witney, *Wartime Experiences of the National Labor Relations Board, 1941–1945* (Urbana: University of Illinois Press, 1949), 125.

85. National War Labor Board, *In the Matter of Phelps Dodge Corporation and Clifton-Morenci Metal Trades Council (AFL): Special Concurring Opinion of Robert J. Watt, Labor Member, National War Labor Board, 2 September 1943,* Records of the National War Labor Board, RG 202, Entry 277, Box 23, Phelps-Dodge folder, National Archives and Records Administration, Denver, Colorado.

86. *In the Matter of Phelps Dodge Corporation and Mill and Smelter Workers Union, No. 22893, et al., 60 NLRB* 249, 1431–1458; *In the Matter of Phelps Dodge Corporation and Bricklayers, Masons, and Plasterers International Union of America,*

Local No. 3 of Arizona (AFL) et al., 62 *NLRB* 174, 1287–1293; and letter, C. R. Kuzell to Charles F. Mulford, 5 May 1945, Records of the National War Labor Board, RG 202, entry 277, box 47, Phelps-Dodge folder, National Archives and Records Administration, Denver, Colorado. The CIO remained in control of the Bisbee mine.

NOTES TO CHAPTER 6

1. "The Battle for Safety," *Popular Mechanics* 77 (March 1942): 67.
2. "Death on the Working Front," *Fortune* (supplement) 26 (July 1942): 2.
3. U.S. Department of Labor, *Is This the Payoff* (Washington, DC: GPO[?], 1944), 1.
4. See Ned H. Dearborn, "Labor and Safety," *American Federationist* 52 (March 1945): 16–17.
5. "Death on the Working Front," 1.
6. One of the most dangerous industries during World War II was shipbuilding. See Frank S. McElroy and Arthur L. Svenson, "Shipyard Injuries and Their Causes, 1941," *Monthly Labor Review* 31 (October 1942): 680–696; Frank S. McElroy and Arthur L. Svenson, "Basic Accident Factors in Shipyards," *Monthly Labor Review* 33 (July 1944): 13–23; and Frederic C. Lane, *Ships for Victory: A History of Shipbuilding Under the U.S. Maritime Commission in World War II* (Baltimore: Johns Hopkins Press, 1951), 446–451.
7. See Alan Derickson, "Participative Regulation of Hazardous Working Conditions: Safety Committees of the United Mine Workers of America, 1941–1969," *Labor Studies Journal* 18 (Summer 1993): 25–38; Lillian Trettin, "The Case of the Crippled Blockholder: Miners, Managers, and Talk about Early Twentieth-Century Industrial Accidents," *Oral History Review* 18 (Spring 1990): 1–27; Alan Derickson, *Workers' Health, Workers' Democracy: The Western Miners' Struggle, 1891–1925* (Ithaca: Cornell University Press, 1988); Harold W. Aurand, "Mine Safety and Social Control in the Anthracite Industry," *Pennsylvania History* 52 (1985): 227–241; Price V. Fishback, "Workplace Safety During the Progressive Era: Fatal Accidents in Bituminous Coal Mining, 1912–1923," *Explorations in Economic History* 23 (1986): 269–298; and William Graebner, *Coal-Mining Safety in the Progressive Period: The Political Economy of Reform* (Lexington: University Press of Kentucky, 1976).
8. To get a flavor of the historiography see John Fabian Witt, *The Accidental Republic: Crippled Workingmen, Destitute Widows, and the Remaking of American Law* (Cambridge, MA: Harvard University Press, 2004); Mark Aldrich, *Safety First: Technology, Labor, and Business in the Building of American Work Safety, 1870–1939* (Baltimore: Johns Hopkins University Press, 1997); Robert E. Botsch, *Organizing the Breathless: Cotton Dust, Southern Politics, and the Brown Lung Association* (Lexington: University Press of Kentucky, 1993); Martin Cherniack, *The Hawk's Nest Incident: America's Worst Industrial Disaster* (New Haven: Yale University Press, 1986); Claudia Clark, *Radium Girls: Women and Industrial Health Reform, 1910–1935* (Chapel Hill: University of North Carolina Press, 1997); Richard Greenwald, "Work, Health, and Community: Danbury, Connecticut's Struggle with an Industrial Disease," *Labor Heritage* 2 (1990): 4–21; Carl Gersuny, *Work Hazards and Industrial Conflict* (Hanover, NH: University Press of New England, 1981); David Rosner and Gerald Markowitz, eds., *Dying for Work: Workers' Safety and Health in Twentieth-Century America* (Bloomington: Indiana University Press, 1987); and Christopher C. Sellers, *Hazards on the Job: From Industrial Disease to Environmental Health Science* (Chapel Hill: University of North Carolina Press, 1997). See also these review essays: Allan M. Brandt, "Exploring the Dangerous Trades," *Reviews in American History* 17 (March 1989): 101–107; and Gerald Markowitz, "Hazardous History: Researching the Dangerous Trades," *Reviews in American History* 26 (1998): 408–414.
9. Henry E. Sigerist, "Historical Background of Industrial and Occupational Diseases," *Bulletin of the New York Academy of Medicine* 12 (1936): 597–609.
10. Earl E. Muntz, "Industrial Accidents and Safety Work," *Journal of Educational Sociology* 5 (March 1932): 401.
11. *Holden v. Hardy*, 169 U.S. 366 (1898); and see Sellers, *Hazards on the Job*, 47–48.
12. Robert Asher, "Organized Labor and the Origins of the Occupational Safety and Health Act," *Labor's Heritage* 3 (January 1991): 57–60. See also E. H. Downey,

"Workmen's Compensation in the United States: A Review," *Journal of Political Economy* 21 (December 1913): 913–930; E. H. Downey, "Essentials of Workmen's Compensation Statistics," *Journal of Political Economy* 22 (December 1914): 955–968; Willard C. Fisher, "American Experience with Workmen's Compensation," *American Economic Review* 10 (March 1920): 18–47; Lawrence M. Friedman and Jack Ladinsky, "Social Change and the Law of Industrial Accidents," *Columbia Law Review* 67 (1967): 50–82; Julian Go III, "Inventing Industrial Accidents and Their Insurance: Discourse and Workers' Compensation in the United States, 1880s–1910s," *Social Science History* 20 (Fall 1996): 401–430; Ryken Grattet, "Sociological Perspectives on Legal Change: The Role of the Legal Field in the Transformation of the Common Law of Industrial Accidents," *Social Science History* 21 (Fall 1997): 359–397; and R. Rudy Higgens-Evenson, "From Industrial Police to Workmen's Compensation: Public Policy and Industrial Accidents in New York, 1880–1910," *Labor History* 39 (1998): 365–380.

13. Asher, "Organized Labor and the Origins of the Occupational Safety and Health Act," 62–63; Muntz, "Industrial Accidents and Safety Work," 401–404; Roger D. Horne, "Practical Idealism at the Zenith of Progressivism: John R. Commons as an Industrial Reformer," *Mid-America: An Historical Review* 76 (Winter 1994): 53–70; Sandra D. Harmon, "Florence Kelley in Illinois," *Journal of the Illinois State Historical Society* 74 (1981): 163–178; Kathryn Kish Sklar, *Florence Kelley and the Nation's Work* (New Haven: Yale University Press, 1995); Alice Hamilton, *Exploring the Dangerous Trades: The Autobiography of Alice Hamilton* (Boston: Little, Brown, 1943); and Barbara Sicherman, *Alice Hamilton: A Life in Letters* (Cambridge, MA: Harvard University Press, 1984). In 1948, Mississippi became the last state to pass a workers' compensation law. See Gersuny, *Work Hazards and Industrial Conflict,* 54.

14. "More Deadly Than War," *Popular Mechanics* 79 (March 1944): 67. Factory accident statistics are virtually unavailable for the years of the First World War. It was not until 1928 that the U.S. Bureau of Labor Statistics and the National Safety Council began reported reliable statistics on factory injuries and deaths. See "War Worker Deaths Below '17–'18," *Accident Facts, 1943 Edition* (Chicago: National Safety Council, 1944), 10.

15. Donald W. Rogers, "From Common Law to Factory Laws: The Transformation of Workplace Safety Law in Wisconsin Before Progressivism," *American Journal of Legal History* 39 (2) (1995): 177–210.

16. David Rosner and Gerald Markowitz, "Safety and Health as a Class Issue: The Workers' Health Bureau of America During the 1920s," 53–64, in Rosner and Markowitz, eds., *Dying for Work: Workers' Safety and Health in Twentieth-Century America* (Bloomington: Indiana University Press, 1987).

17. Eventually the National Safety Council expanded its mission to include safety in the home and traffic safety. Since accident statistics have been kept, the number of factory injuries and deaths has always been smaller than the number of accidents in the home and on the roads. See Earl E. Muntz, "Accidents and Safety Education," *Journal of Educational Sociology* 5 (December 1931): 215–224; and National Safety Council, *National Safety Council's Golden Anniversary* (Washington: NSC, 1963).

18. Muntz, "Industrial Accidents and Safety Work," 399.

19. For the dropping accident rates in the 1930s see also C. L. Sankey, "Safety from an Industrial Viewpoint," *Journal of Educational Sociology* 11 (September 1937): 48–54; and Dan W. Dodson, "E. George Payne, Pioneer in Safety Education," *Journal of Educational Sociology* 20 (October 1946): 65–67. For an excellent summary of the factory safety policies of the Labor Department under the New Deal see David Rosner and Gerald Markowitz, "Research or Advocacy: Federal Occupational Safety and Health Policies During the New Deal," 83–102, in Rosner and Markowitz, eds. *Dying for Work.*

20. Max D. Kossoris and Swen Kjaer, *Causes and Prevention of Accidents in the Construction Industry, 1936* (Washington, DC: GPO, 1938), 1–12; and Max D. Kossoris and Swen Kjaer, *Causes and Prevention of Accidents in the Construction Industry, 1938* (Washington, DC: GPO, 1939), 1–16.

21. *Accident Facts, 1946* (Chicago: National Safety Council, 1947), 9. See also Sankey, "Safety from an Industrial Viewpoint," 48.

22. U.S. Public Health Service, National Institute of Health, Division of Public Health Methods, *The National Health Survey, 1935–1936: Accidents as a Cause of Disability, Bulletin No. 3* (Washington, DC: GPO, 1938), 1–8.

23. Letter, A. F. Hinrichs to William Green, July 3, 1941, AFL Papers, series 8A, box 5; and "The Battle for Safety," 67.

24. John B. Andrews, "Not 'Business-As-Usual'," *American Labor Legislation Review* 31 (June 1941): 51.

25. "Death on the Working Front," 2.

26. Ibid.

27. War Production Board, *Distribution of Safety Equipment by Major Consuming Industries—1943* (Washington, DC: GPO, 1944), 1; and "Death on the Working Front," 2.

28. Alice Hamilton, "Let's Look at Labor: Death in the Factories," *The Nation* 157 (July 17, 1943): 67.

29. "Death on the Working Front," 6–7.

30. "The Battle for Safety," 67–68, 174; Howard P. Wall, "Workers' Accidents Bad," *The American City* (April 1942): 89; "Purely Co-Accidental," *Time* (19 January 1942): 68.

31. "Estimated Number of Disabling Industrial Injuries, 1941–1943," in *Statistical Abstracts of the United States, 1944–1945* (Washington, DC: GPO, 1945), 217; and "Accidents Slow Up Defense," *American Labor Legislation Review* 31 (September 1941): 98. See also "Speed vs. Safety," *Business Week* (23 August 1941): 44; "Safety on the Job: Occupational Deaths Are Up but Not in Proportion to New Hazards," *Business Week* (7 November 1942): 27–28; and "Industrial Accidents: Factory Mishaps Jump in Wartime," *Life* (6 April 1942): 47.

32. Hamilton, "Let's Look at Labor: Death in the Factories," 66; and "More Deadly Than War," 148.

33. "Fatigue and Productivity," *Industrial Relations Digest*, no. 12 (September 1942): 3–8; and Robert H. Flinn, "Fatigue and War Production," *The Medical Clinics of North America* (July 1942): 1121–1143.

34. On the trouble with smaller factories compared to larger ones, see Muntz, "Industrial Accidents and Safety Work," 408.

35. George A. Larson, "Nebraska's World War II Bomber Plant: The Glenn L. Martin-Nebraska Company," *Nebraska History* 74 (1993): 36.

36. "Death on the Working Front," 2, 9.

37. Address of Joseph D. Keenan on Industrial Safety at the National Safety Council, 7 October 1943, Records of the War Production Board, RG 179, box 1028.

38. See file memo on the purposes and functions of the Industrial Health and Safety Secrive of the Labor Production Division, 15 January 1943, WPB Records, RG 179, box 643.

39. War Production Board, *Distribution of Safety Equipment by Major Consuming Industries—1943*, 5.

40. "Estimated Number of Disabling Industrial Injuries, 1941–1943," in *Statistical Abstracts of the United States, 1944–1945* (Washington, DC: GPO, 1945), 217; and "More Deadly Than War," 66–67, 69.

41. H. W. Heinrich, *Industrial Accident Prevention: A Scientific Approach* (New York: McGraw-Hill, 1941), 42–43. See also Roland P. Blake, ed., *Industrial Safety* (Englewood Cliffs, NJ: Prentice Hall, 1943).

42. American Mutual Liability Insurance Company, *Foremanship and Accident Prevention in Industry* (Boston: American Mutual, 1943); and C. M. MacMillan, *Foremanship and Safety* (New York: Wiley, 1943). The standard historical treatment of management during the war is Howell John Harris, *The Right to Manage: Industrial Relations Policies of American Business in the 1940s* (Madison: University of Wisconsin Press, 1982). Harris does not, however, deal with safety.

43. U.S. Department of Labor, *Labor Safety Service: A Report by the Labor Members of the National Committee for the Conservation of Manpower in the War Industries* (Washington, DC: Department of Labor, 1942), 3.

44. "Safety on the Job," 27–28; and Rosner and Markowitz, "Research or Advocacy," 83–102.

45. U.S. Department of Labor, *Safety Speeds Production: A Message for Supervisors* (Washington: GPO, 1943), 2.

46. See for example *Safe Handling of Nitric Acid* (1942); *A Guide to the Prevention of Weight-Lifting Injuries* (1943); *What Would You Pay for 8,000 Years' Experience* (1943); and *Safety Speeds Production: A Message for Supervisors* (1943).

47. 49 Stat. 2036; 41 U.S. Code 35-45.

See also U.S. War Department, *Minimum Safety Program* (Washington, DC: GPO, 1943).

48. U.S. Department of Labor, *Men, Minutes, and Victory: Three-Year Progress Report of the National Committee for the Conservation of Manpower in War Industries* (Washington: GPO, 1944), 1.

49. Meeting minutes of the National Advisory Committee to the Industrial Health and Safety Section, War Production Board, 20 December 1943, WPB Records, RG 179, box 643.

50. U.S. Department of Labor, *Field Letter* (August 23, 1943), in Wisconsin Industrial Commission Records, series 1006, box 22, Wisconsin State Historical Society.

51. War Production Board, *Some Suggestions to Organized Labor* (Washington, DC: GPO, 1944), 2.

52. Ibid., 4.

53. Ibid., 9.

54. Letter, C. E. Wilson to William Green, 22 July 1944, AFL Papers, series 8A, box 42.

55. Letter, William Green to Officers of National and International Unions, State Federations of Labor, and City Central Bodies, 26 July 1944, AFL Papers, series 8A, box 42.

56. "AFL Wars on Accidents," *American Federationist* 50 (November 1943): 23.

57. Gerald Markowitz, "Hazardous History: Researching the Dangerous Trades," *Reviews in American History* 26 (1998): 408–414; Rosner and Markowitz, "Safety and Health as a Class Issue: The Workers' Health Bureau of America During the 1920s," 53–64; and Hamilton, "Death in the Factories," 68.

58. Aurand, "Mine Safety and Social Control in the Anthracite Industry," 237.

59. Industrial Commission of Wisconsin, *Physical Examinations of Industrial Workers* (Madison: ICW, 1939), 6.

60. Robert W. Ozanne, *A Century of Labor-Management Relations at McCormick and International Harvester* (Madison: University of Wisconsin Press, 1967), xv–28.

61. Ibid., 29–95.

62. *Safety at McCormick Works, 1934* (Chicago: International Harvester, 1934); *Safety at McCormick Works, 1935* (Chicago: International Harvester, 1935); *Safety at McCormick Works, 1934 and 1935* (Chicago: International Harvester, 1935); *Safety Rules and Regulations* (Chicago: International Harvester, 1938); and *A Foreman's Safety Handbook* (Chicago: International Harvester, 1943). All these pamphlets are found in the unprocessed International Harvester Archives, box 458, file 00416, Wisconsin State Historical Society.

63. Ozanne, *A Century of Labor-Management Relations at McCormick and International Harvester,* 44–70.

64. "Report of the Safety Inspectors' Meeting, November 19–20, 1942, Chicago, Illinois," 1, International Harvester Corporation Collection, unprocessed papers, box 473, file 00903, Wisconsin State Historical Society.

65. Ozanne, *A Century of Labor-Management Relations at McCormick and International Harvester,* 206–207.

66. "Report of the Safety Inspectors' Meeting, November 28–29, 1944, Chicago, Illinois," 4, International Harvester Corporation Collection, unprocessed papers, box 473, file 00903, Wisconsin State Historical Society.

67. "File memo, nd. from David Sigman, 5 May 1942, American Federation of Labor Papers, series 7, box 64, folder 22631, Wisconsin State Historical Society.

68. "Agreement between Harvester Company and Federal Union 22631, May 11, 1942," AFL Papers, series 7, box 64, folder 22631.

69. George Hodge, *Management's Prerogatives: Address by George Hodge, Manager of Labor Relations, International Harvester Company, April 19, 1945* (Chicago: International Harvester Company, 1945), 1, International Harvester Corporation Collection, unprocessed papers, box 855, file 12578, Wisconsin State Historical Society.

NOTES TO CHAPTER 7

1. AFL press release, 27 December 1942, American Federation of Labor Papers (AFL Papers), series 5C, Files of the Economist, General File, box 23, folder "Post War Planning, AFL Committee."

2. Boris Shishkin, "The Crisis Ahead," *The Nation* (21 October 1944): 495.

3. David McCullough, *Truman* (New York: Simon & Schuster, 1992), 342. See also Jim Bishop, *FDR's Last Year, April 1944–April 1945* (New York: Morrow,

1974); Robert H. Ferrell, *The Dying President: Franklin D. Roosevelt, 1944–1945* (Columbia: University of Missouri Press, 1998); Robert E. Miller, "April 12, 1945: The Other Day That Lives in Infamy," 117–132, in Andrew E. Kersten and Kriste Lindenmeyer, eds., *Politics and Progress: American Society and State Since 1865* (Westport, CT: Praeger, 2001); and Hugh E. Evans, *The Hidden Campaign: FDR's Health and the 1944 Election* (Armonk, NY: M. E. Sharpe, 2002).

4. "The Roper Center: Presidential Job Performance," n.d., available at http://roperweb.ropercenter.uconn.edu/cgi-bin/hsrun.exe/Roperweb/PresJobRatings40/StateId/C1DI7my8t-US61r7cib_YhzY1g-WE-4OId/HAHTpage/HS_presapproval_home_fH (2 March 2004).

5. McCullough, *Truman,* 520.

6. Confidential report, U.S. Labor Department, Bureau of Labor Statistics, "Estimated Distribution of the United States Labor Force, 1930–1944, and Hypothetical Distribution Two Years After Victory," AFL Papers, series 5C, box 23, folder "Post War Planning, Aircraft."

7. "After the Emergency . . . What Then?" *American Federationist* 49 (March 1941): 9–11.

8. See Boris Basil Shishkin, interview by John A. Tooney, 5 July to 10 August 1956, tape-recording transcript, Columbia Oral History Interview. Shishkin's prewar and postwar years are covered nicely in Robert D. Reynolds, Jr., "A Career at Labor Headquarters: The Papers of Boris Shishkin," *Labor's Heritage* 1 (October 1989): 58–75. On Shishkin's service with the Fair Employment Practice Committee see Andrew E. Kersten, *Race, Jobs, and the War: The FEPC in the Midwest, 1941–1946* (Urbana: University of Illinois Press, 2000).

9. Boris Basil Shishkin, interview by John A. Tooney, 2 August 1956, tape #14, 2–3, tape-recording transcript, Columbia Oral History Interview.

10. Boris Basil Shishkin, interview by Donald Shaughnessy, 2 October 1956, tape #1, 14–15, tape-recording transcript, Columbia Oral History Interview.

11. Reynolds, "A Career at Labor Headquarters," 65.

12. "After the Emergency . . . Then What?," 10.

13. Boris Shishkin, "The Next Depression?" *American Federationist* 52 (October 1944): 3.

14. Shishkin, "The Next Depression?" 3–6, 21–22; AFL press release, 6 October 1944, AFL Papers, series 5C, box 24, folder "Post War Planning, Employment June 1944 to Present"; "AFL Expert Fears 20,000,000 Jobless," *New York Times,* 9 October 1944, p. 25; "AFL Warns of Idleness," *Washington Post,* 9 October 1944; and "AFL Economist Warns of Postwar Depression," *Stars and Stripes,* 11 October 1944. See also Boris Shishkin, "The Crisis Ahead," *The Nation* (21 October 1944): 495.

15. Stella Stewart, "Demobilization of Manpower, 1918–1919: Bulletin No. 784," *Bulletin of the Bureau of Labor Statistics* (1944): 8.

16. "Business Conditions in January, 1919," *Federal Reserve Bulletin* 5 (1 February 1919): 109. See also Stewart, "Demobilization of Manpower, 1918–1919," 29.

17. Stewart, "Demobilization of Manpower, 1918–1919," 29.

18. U.S. Census Bureau, *Historical Statistics of the United States, Colonial Times to 1970,* Part 1 (Washington, DC: GPO, 1975), 126, 179.

19. Harold D. Smith, *The Management of Your Government* (New York: Whittlesy House, 1945), ix.

20. Dairy entry, 19 October 1937, Morgenthau Diaries 92: 230, as quoted in Alan Brinkley, *End of Reform: New Deal Liberalism in Recession and War* (New York: Vintage, 1996), 29. See also John Morton Blum, *Roosevelt and Morgenthau: A Revision and Condensation of* From the Morgenthau Diaries (Boston: Houghton Mifflin, 1970), 172–209, esp. 175.

21. On the NRA see Robert F. Himmelberg, *The Origins of the National Recovery Administration* (New York: Fordham University Press, 1976); Ellis W. Hawley, *The New Deal and the Problem of Monopoly* (Princeton: Princeton University Press, 1966); and Brinkley, *The End of Reform,* 36–47.

22. National Resource Planning Board, *After Defense—What?: Full Employment, Security, and Up-Building America* (Washington, DC: GPO, 1941); National Resource Planning Board, *Security, Work, and Relief Policies* (Washington, DC: GPO, 1942); National Resource Planning Board, *After the War—Full Employment* (Washington, DC:

GPO, 1943); and National Resource Planning Board, *Post-War Plan and Program* (Washington, DC: GPO, 1943). Alvin Hansen was the sole author for the pamphlet *After the War—Full Employment.* Like *After the War* (1943), *After Defense* (1941) focuses on "full employment."

23. On the New Deal and planning see Marion Clawson, *New Deal Planning: The National Resources Planning Board* (Baltimore: Johns Hopkins University Press, 1981); Philip W. Warken, *A History of the National Resources Planning Board, 1933–1943* (New York: Garland, 1979); David E. Wilson, *The National Planning Idea in United States Public Policy* (Boulder: Westview Press, 1980); and George Soule, *Planning USA* (New York: Viking Press, 1967).

24. "A.F.L. Stresses Post-War Plan," *New York Times,* 10 August 1941, p. 34.

25. Clawson, *New Deal Planning,* 181.

26. AFL press release, 27 December 1942, AFL Papers, series 5C, box 23, folder "Post War Planning, AFL Committee."

27. See for example Matthew Woll, "Are We Preparing for Unemployment?" *American Federationist* 52 (August 1944): 4–5, 31.

28. See letter, E. J. Coil to Boris Shishkin, 17 November 1942, AFL Papers, series 5C, box 25, folder "Postwar Planning National Planning Association."

29. The NPA's chairman was William L. Batt, a New Dealer and former member of Governor Franklin D. Roosevelt's Temporary Emergency Relief Administration. The vice chairman was Robert J. Watt, former executive secretary of the Massachusetts Federation of Labor and one of the AFL's representatives on the National War Labor Board. Among the other members of the NPA were the renowned Harvard economist Alvin Hansen, the old-time progressive Luther Gulick, the planning advocate and *New Republic* editor George Soule, E. J. Coil, of the National Economic and Social Planning Association, and Charles E. Wilson, the former head of General Electric.

30. See "Matthew Woll Dies at Age of 76," *New York Times,* 2 June 1956, p. 19.

31. AFL press release, 27 December 1942, AFL Papers, series 5C, Files of the Economist, General File, box 23, folder "Post War Planning, AFL Committee."

32. AFL Post-War Planning Committee, *Reconstruction Administration: Report of the A.F. of L. Committee on Post-War Planning* (Washington, DC: AFL, 1943).

33. Ibid.

34. "Executive Council Meets," *American Federationist* 51 (February 1944): 3 (quotation), 7, 32; and William Green, "Reconversion," *American Federationist* 51 (January 1944): 25.

35. Letter, William Green to Franklin D. Roosevelt, 23 February 1944, FDR Papers, OF 142, box 2, folder "AFL, 1943–1945," FDRL.

36. For the bureaucratic difficulties in the federal government during the Second World War see George Q. Flynn, *The Mess in Washington: Manpower Mobilization in World War II* (Westport, CT: Greenwood Press, 1979). For more on the debates surrounding wartime contract termination see "War Contract Termination, Part I," *Law and Contemporary Problems* 10 (Winter 1944): 427–558, and "War Contract Termination, Part II," *Law and Contemporary Problems* 10 (Spring 1945): 561–692.

37. Herman Miles Somers, *Presidential Agency: The Office of War Mobilization and Reconversion, OWMR* (Cambridge, MA: Harvard University Press, 1950), 6–46, 54. On Byrnes see David Robertson, *Sly and Able: A Political Biography of James F. Byrnes* (New York: Norton, 1994); and John William Partin, "Assistant President for the Home Front: James F. Byrnes and World War II," Ph.D. diss., University of Florida, 1977. A useful if untapped source on the American wartime production accomplishments is the War Production Board's final report to President Harry S. Truman: WPB, *Wartime Production Achievements and the Reconversion Outlook* (Washington, DC: GPO, 1945).

38. The OWM was not the only agency responsible for postwar planning. All major agencies, like the Office of Price Administration and the War Production Board, had postwar plans. The WPB's was the most complete, and it did influence the OWM's thinking on the issue. See Civilian Production Administration, *Development of the Reconversion Policies of the War Production Board* (Washington, DC: CPA, 1946). The WBP's postwar planning document was known as the Kanzler Report.

39. On the chronology of mobilization agencies see Civilian Production Administration, *Chronology of the War Production*

Board and Predecessor Agencies, August 1939 to November 1945 (Washington, DC: GPO, 1946). On Congress see Congress, Senate, Subcommittee to the Committee on Military Affairs, *Contract Termination and Related Post-War Legislation: Report of the War Contracts, Pursuant to S. Res. 198, A Resolution to Investigate War Contracts, the Termination of War Contracts, and Related Problems,* 78th Cong., 2nd sess., 1944, Committee Print; and Congress, Senate, Special Committee on Post-War Economic Policy and Planning, *Report,* parts 1–5, 78th Cong., 1st and 2nd sess., 1944; and Congress, House, Special Committee on Post-War Economic Policy and Planning, *Hearings Before the Special Committee on Post-War Economic Policy and Planning,* 78th Cong., 2nd sess., 1944–1946.

40. "Annual Budget Message, January 10, 1944," Samuel I. Rosenman, comp., *Presidential Papers of Franklin D. Roosevelt, 1944* (New York: Russell & Russell, 1969), Item 3, 7–31.

41. Bernard M. Baruch and John M. Hancock, *Report on War and Post-War Adjustment Policies* (Washington, DC: Office of War Mobilization, 1944), 1. See also Benard M. Baruch, *Baruch: The Public Years* (New York: Holt, Rinehart & Winston, 1960): 321–334; and Jordan A. Schwarz, *The Speculator: Bernard M. Baruch in Washington, 1917–1965* (Chapel Hill: University of North Carolina Press, 1981), 457–466.

42. Baruch and Hancock, *Report on War and Post-War Adjustment Policies,* 5–6, 77.

43. Letter, Eleanor Roosevelt to Harry Hopkins, 12 August 1944, as quoted in Brinkley, *The End of Reform,* 244.

44. I. F. Stone, "Millionaires' Beveridge Plan," *The Nation* (25 March 1944): 355. For more commentary on the Baruch-Hancock plan see "The Baruch Plan," *New Republic* 110 (28 February 1944): 263–264; "Baruch Report (Cont'd)," *New Republic* 110 (6 March 1944): 304; Erwin Esser Nemmers, "Economic Aspects of Termination of War Contracts," *Quarterly Journal of Economics* 59 (May 1945): 386–404; and John D. Sumner, "The Disposition of Surplus War Property," *American Economic Review* 34 (September 1944): 457–471.

45. *War Mobilization and Reconversion Act, Statutes at Large,* 58, Ch. 480, PL 458, 785–792, (1944).

46. On the OWMR see Somers, *Presidential Agency.*

47. Stone, "Millionaires' Beveridge Plan," 355. Beveridge's report was published in the United States in 1942: William Beveridge, *Social Insurance and Allied Services: Report by Sir William Beveridge* (New York: Macmillan, 1942). The AFL's position on the Beveridge plan is not entirely clear. The Federation did, however, publish a positive review of it. See "Britain Plans Postwar Work for All," *American Federationist* 52 (June 1944): 31.

48. "Unless There Is Security Here at Home, There Cannot Be Lasting Peace in the World: Message to the Congress on the State of the Union, 11 January 1944," *The Public Papers and Addresses of Franklin D. Roosevelt, Compiled with Special Material and Explanatory Notes by Samuel I. Rosenman, Vol. 13: Victory and the Threshold of Peace, 1944–1945* (New York: Russell & Russell, 1969), 41.

49. "Federation Bans Local Strikes for Any Cause; Charts National Conclave on Post-War Policy," *American Federation of Labor Weekly New Service* (1 February 1944): 1.

50. Menu for American Federation of Labor National Post-War Forum, 12 April 1944, AFL Papers, series 5C, box 23, folder "Postwar Planning, AFL Postwar Forum, April 12–13, 1944, NYC."

51. Alvin H. Hansen, "Full Employment After the War," Address delivered at the AFL National Post-War Forum, New York City, New York, 12 April 1944, AFL Papers, series 5C, box 23, folder "Postwar Planning, AFL Postwar Forum, April 12–13, 1944, NYC." The Forum's program lists the original title of his talk, which was "Fiscal Policy and Full Employment." See also Alexander C. Findlay, "Post-War Capacity and Characteristics of the Construction Industry," *Monthly Labor Review* 58 (May 1944): 925.

52. For examinations of Long's role in the American response to the Holocaust see David S. Wymann, *America and the Holocaust: A Thirteen-Volume Set Documenting the Editor's Book: The Abandonment of the Jews, Vol. 6* (Amherst: University of Massachusetts Press, 1989), 238–255.

53. Breckridge Long's address was published in the *New York Times.* For analysis of the speech see "Long Assures AFL on

U.S. Peace Aims," *New York Times,* 13 April 1944, p. 1.

54. Alice Hamilton, "The Health of the Nation," Address delivered at the AFL National Post-War Forum, New York City, New York, 12 April 1944, AFL Papers, series 5C, box 23, folder "Postwar Planning, AFL Postwar Forum, April 12–13, 1944, NYC"; and see Sumner Slichter, "The Contribution of Unemployment Compensation to Economic Stability," Address delivered at the AFL National Post-War Forum, New York City, New York, 12 April 1944, AFL Papers, series 5C, box 23, folder "Postwar Planning, AFL Postwar Forum, April 12–13, 1944, NYC."

55. Eric Johnston, "There Are No Short-Cuts," *American Federationist* 52 (May 1944): 8.

56. George Meany, "Free Labor and Free Enterprise in the Post-War World," Address delivered at the AFL National Post-War Forum, New York City, New York, 12 April 1944, AFL Papers, series 5C, box 23, folder "Postwar Planning, AFL Postwar Forum, April 12–13, 1944, NYC." Interestingly, after the conference, the *American Federationist* published Johnston's remarks, but not Meany's retort.

57. See "Labor as Statesman," *New York Times,* 13 April 1944, p. 18.

58. AFL Post-War Planning Committee, *Post-War Program of the American Federation of Labor* (Washington, DC: AFL, 1944), 20.

59. Ibid., 3.

60. Ibid., 5.

61. Ibid., 15, 19–20. One can imagine that Milton Webster, who was also a member of Roosevelt's Fair Employment Practice Committee, wrote this statement.

62. For more information on the NAM postwar conferences see "Conference Seeks U.S. Post-War Unity," *New York Times,* 18 February 1944, p. 4; "22 Groups to Meet on Post-War Plans," *New York Times,* 19 May 1944, p. 12; and "AFL Shuns Meeting, Widens CIO Rift," *New York Times,* 8 September 1944, p. 32.

63. I. F. Stone, "What F.D.R. Forgot," *The Nation* 59 (8 January 1944): 35.

64. On full employment see Alvin H. Hansen, *Economic Policy and Full Employment* (New York: McGraw-Hill, 1947); John H. G. Pierson, *Full Employment & Free Enterprise* (Washington, DC: Public Affairs Press, 1947); and Brinkley, *The End of Reform,* 227–264.

65. Alvin H. Hansen, "Planning Full Employment," *The Nation* 59 (21 October 1944): 492–493.

66. See John H. G. Pierson, "Employment After the War," *American Federationist* 51 (October 1943): 10–13; John H. G. Pierson, "The Underwriting of Aggregate Consumer Spending as a Pillar of Full-Employment Policy," *American Economic Review* 34 (March 1944): 21–55; Alvin H. Hansen, "Full Employment After the War," *American Federationist* 52 (July 1944): 10–12; and John H. G. Pierson, "A Full Employment Program," *American Federationist* 53 (August 1945): 28–31.

67. "The Fortune Survey," *Fortune* 29 (February 1944): 94, 104, 112, 114; Congress, Senate, War Contracts Subcommittee of the Committee on Military Affairs, *Legislation for Reconversion and Full Employment,* 78th Cong., 2nd sess., 18 December 1944; E. A. Goldenweiser and Everett E. Hagen, "Jobs After the War," *Federal Reserve Bulletin* 30 (May 1944): 421–431; Sumner H. Slichter, "Jobs After the War," *Atlantic Monthly* (October 1944): 87–91; William Withers, "The Meaning of Full Employment," *The New Leader,* 14 April 1944; and National Planning Association, *National Budgets for Full Employment* (Washington, DC: NPA, 1945).

68. Robert F. Wagner, *Social Security for the American People* (Washington, DC: GPO, 1945). See also Alan Derickson, "Health Security for All?: Social Unionism and Universal Health Insurance, 1935–1958," *Journal of American History* 80 (March 1994): 1333–1356; and Colin Gordon, *Dead on Arrival: The Politics of Health Care in Twentieth-Century America* (Princeton: Princeton University Press, 2003).

69. See Derickson, "Health Security for All?" 1341; Nelson H. Cruikshank, "Wagner-Murray-Dingell Bill," *American Federationist* 52 (July 1945): 14–17; Nelson H. Cruikshank, "The New Wagner-Murray-Dingell Bill," *American Federationist* 52 (August 1945): 15–17, 32; and Alan Derickson, *Health Security for All: Dreams of Universal Health Care in America* (Baltimore: Johns Hopkins University Press, 2005), 72–100. See also Miles Atkinson, "Medical Care for All," *American Federationist* 52 (June 1945): 25–27. For more information

on Cruikshank see Nelson H. Cruikshank, *The Cruikshank Chronicle: Anecdotes, Stories, and Memoirs of a New Deal Liberal,* ed. Alice M. Hoffman and Howard S. Hoffman (Hamden, CT: Archon Books, 1989); and C. Wright Mills, *The New Men of Power: America's Labor Leaders* (New York: Harcourt, Brace, 1948): 285–287.

70. Wagner, *Social Security for the American People,* 6.

71. "Postwar Housing Needs," *American Federationist* 51 (April 1944): 32; and Miles Colean, *American Housing: Problems and Prospects: The Factual Findings* (New York: Twentieth Century Fund, 1944).

72. Harry C. Bates, "Homes for the Future," *American Federationist* 51 (June 1944): 11.

73. Harry C. Bates, "Housing for the Nation," *American Federationist* 52 (February 1945): 16.

74. Bates, "Homes for the Future," 9.

75. "Ask Quick Action on Post-War Plan," *New York Times,* 14 March 1943, p. 13.

76. Marion Clawson, *New Deal Planning: The National Resources Planning Board* (Baltimore: Johns Hopkins University Press, 1981), 100–101, 332–345.

77. Beveridge, *Social Insurance and Allied Services* 7. See also Beulah Amidon, "The NRPB and the Beveridge Reports," *Survey Midmonthly* (May 1943): 141–142; and Brinkley, *End of Reform,* 250–258.

78. National Resource Planning Board, *Security, Work, and Relief Policies* (Washington, DC: GPO, 1942), 2. See also Alvin H. Hansen, *Price Flexibility and Full Employment of Resources* (Washington, DC: National Resources Planning Board, 1940).

79. Ibid., 545–549. Quotation from 549.

80. National Resources Planning Board, *National Resources Development Report for 1943, Part I. Post-War Plan and Program* (Washington, DC: GPO, 1943), 3. An abbreviated version of this report was released as a pamphlet titled *Post-War Plan and Program.*

81. Both the House and the Senate had special committees on the postwar economic structure. See Congress, Senate, Special Committee on Post-War Economic Policy and Planning, *Post-War Economic Policy and Planning,* 78th Cong., 2nd sess., 1944; Congress, Senate, Special Committee on Post-War Economic Policy and Planning, Subcommittee on Housing and Urban Development, *Hearings, parts 1–15,* 78th Cong., 2nd sess. to 79th Cong., 1st sess., 1944–1945. Both William Green and Matthew Woll appeared before the House Special Committee on Post-War Economic Policy and Planning. Their statements were published in the hearings reports and separately by the AFL. See William Green, *A. F. of L. and Reconversion* (Washington, DC: AFL, 1944); and Matthew Woll, *Machinery for Reconversion* (Washington, DC: AFL, 1944).

82. The CIO's Reconversion Committee consisted of Ted F. Silvey, CIO executive board member; Harold J. Ruttenberg, of the United Steelworkers; Lincoln Fairley, from the United Automobile Workers; Gladys Dickason, of the Clothing Workers; Neil Brant, of the United Electrical Workers; Leo Goodman, from the Retail, Wholesale, and Department Store Workers; Tom Owens, representing the United Rubber Workers; Michael Ross, of the Shipbuilding Workers; and John Edelman, of the Textile Workers. See CIO, *Report of President Philip Murray to the Seventh Constitutional Convention of the Congress of Industrial Organizations* (Chicago: CIO, 1945), 20; CIO, *Re-Employment* (Washington, DC: CIO, 1944); CIO Research and Education Department, "As Victory Comes," *Economic Outlook* 5 (June 1944): 1; CIO Press Release, 7 July 1943, AFL Papers, series 5C, Files of the Economist, General Files, box 23, folder "Post-War Planning, CIO"; CIO Press Release, 10 March 1944, AFL Papers, Series 5C, Files of the Economist, General Files, box 23, folder "Post-War Planning, CIO"; and Clinton S. Golden, "CIO Leader Offers Post-War Plan," *The New Leader,* 8 January 1944, 4.

83. Walter P. Reuther, *How to Raise Wages Without Increasing Prices* (Detroit: United Automobile Workers, 1945), especially 13.

84. Benjamin M. Anderson, Jr., "Governmental Economic Planning," *American Economic Review* 30 (March 1940): 262.

85. *Congressional Record,* 78th Cong., 1st sess., 4294. See also Brinkley, *The End of Reform,* 254; and Richard N. Chapman, *Contours of Public Policy, 1939–1945* (New York: Garland, 1981), 257.

86. Louis Stark quotes Stephen Pace in "Congress at Odds on Security Plan," *New York Times,* 12 March 1943, p. 1. See also

Philip W. Warken, *A History of the National Resources Planning Board, 1933–1943* (New York: Garland, 1979), 227.

87. Emerson P. Schmidt, *Can Government Guarantee Full Employment?: Post-War Readjustments Bulletin, No. 13* (Washington, DC: Chamber of Commerce of the United States of America, 1945), 2–3.

88. Anderson, "Governmental Economic Planning," 247.

89. See Friedrich von Hayek, *Road to Serfdom* (Chicago: University of Chicago Press, 1944). See also Ludwig Von Mises and Rufus S. Tucker, *Economic Planning* (New York: Dynamic America, 1945); and Ludwig Von Mises, *Planned Chaos* (Irvington-on-Hudson, NY: Foundation for Economic Education, 1947).

90. As quoted in Clawson, *New Deal Planning,* 232.

91. "Ask Quick Action on Post-War Plan," *New York Times,* 14 March 1943, p. 13.

92. "Restive Workers: They Quit Arms Jobs by Thousands to Get Permanent Peace Work," *Wall Street Journal,* 10 October 1944.

93. "Reconvert to What?" *American Federationist* 52 (September 1944): 21; "Your Job After Victory: Mobilization for Peace Is Behind Schedule," *American Federationist* 53 (May 1945): 5–7, 30; "Reconversion," *American Federationist* 53 (May 1945): 16; and "The Problem Is Jobs," *American Federationist* 53 (September 1945): 4.

94. Civilian Production Administration, *Resumption of Production of Domestic Electric Flat Irons* (Washington, DC: GPO, 1946); and "Start Made Here in Reconversion," *New York Times,* 23 September 1944, p. 15. On unemployment statistics and predictions see U.S. Department of Labor, Bureau of Labor Statistics, "Estimated Distribution of the United States Labor Force, 1930–1944, and Hypothetical Distribution Two Years After Victory."

95. James F. Byrnes, *Reconversion: A Report to the President from the Director of War Mobilization* (Washington, DC: GPO, 1944). Byrnes's report was widely distributed and appeared verbatim in several newspapers. See "Text of the Byrnes Report to President on Progress of Plans for Return to Peacetime Economy," *New York Times,* 10 September 1944, p. 41.

96. File copy, "Some AFL Recommendations on Reconversion," 17 April 1945, AFL Papers, series 5C, box 25, folder "Post-War Reconversion—1944 to present,"

97. See "Letter to the Chairman, War Production Board, on Measures to Speed Reconversion, August 9, 1945," *Public Papers of the Presidents of the United States, Harry S. Truman, April 12 to December 31, 1945* (Washington, DC: GPO, 1961), 200–202.

98. Telegram, Boris Shishkin to William Green, 10 August 1945, AFL Papers, series 5C, box 25, folder "Post-War Reconversion—1944 to present."

99. See John W. Snyder, *From War to Peace: A Challenge* (Washington, DC: Office of War Mobilization and Reconversion, 1945).

100. "Statement by the President Proposing Measures to Insure Industrial Peace in the Reconversion Period, August 16, 1945," *Public Papers of the Presidents of the United States, Harry S. Truman, 1945,* 220–222.

101. "AFL Shuns Meeting, Widens CIO Rift," *New York Times,* 8 September 1944, p. 32; and "Hillman Proposes New Labor Parley," *New York Times,* 19 May 1944, p. 12.

102. As quoted in Donald R. McCoy, *The Presidency of Harry S. Truman* (Lawrence: University Press of Kansas, 1984), 51.

103. Ibid., 51.

104. "Special Message to the Congress Presenting a 21-Point Program for the Reconversion Period," *Public Papers of the Presidents of the United States, Harry S. Truman, 1945,* 263–309; and "Special Message to the Congress Recommending a Comprehensive Health Program, November 19, 1945," *Public Papers of the Presidents of the United States, Harry S. Truman, 1945,* 475–491.

105. Brinkley, *The End of Reform,* 262–264.

106. James T. Patterson, *Mr. Republican: A Biography of Robert A. Taft* (Boston: Houghton Mifflin, 1972), 432–434; and Richard O. Davies, *Housing Reform During the Truman Administration* (Columbia, MO: University of Missouri Press, 1966).

107. As quoted in Derickson, "Health Security for All?" 1342.

108. See Susan M. Hartmann, *Truman and the 80th Congress* (Columbia: Univer-

sity of Missouri Press, 1971); and Francis H. Thompson, *The Frustration of Politics: Truman, Congress, and the Loyalty Issue, 1945–1953* (Rutherford, NJ: Fairleigh Dickinson University Press, 1979).

NOTES TO THE EPILOGUE

1. Steven Greenhouse, "At a Small Shop in Colorado, Wal-Mart Beats a Union Once More," *New York Times,* 26 February 2005, p. 8.
2. Ibid.
3. Ibid.
4. Charles J. Morris, *The Blue Eagle at Work: Reclaiming Democratic Rights in the Workplace* (Ithaca: ILR Press, 2005); Rick Fantasia and Kim Voss, *Hard Work: Remaking the American Labor Movement* (Ithaca: ILR Press, 2004); Ruth Milkman and Kim Voss, eds., *Rebuilding Labor: Organizing and Organizers in the New Union Movement* (Ithaca: ILR Press, 2004); Nelson Lichtenstein, *State of the Union: A Century of American Labor* (Princeton: Princeton University Press, 2002); Vernon M. Briggs, *Immigration and American Unionism* (Ithaca: ILR Press, 2001); Stanley Aronowitz, *From the Ashes of the Old: American Labor and America's Future* (New York: Basic Books, 1998); Michael Yates, *Why Unions Matter* (New York: Monthly Review Press, 1998); Peter J. Rachleff, *Hard-Pressed in the Heartland: The Hormel Strike and the Future of the Labor Movement* (Boston: South End Press, 1992); and Michael Goldfield, *The Decline of Organized Labor in the United States* (Chicago: University of Chicago Press, 1987).
5. Robert B. Reich, "Don't Blame Wal-Mart," *New York Times,* 28 February 2005, p. 19.
6. See for example Kevin Boyle, *The UAW and the Heyday of American Liberalism, 1945–1968* (Ithaca: Cornell University Press, 1995); and Nelson Lichtenstein, *The Most Dangerous Man in Detroit: Walter Reuther and the Fate of American Labor* (New York: Basic Books, 1995).
7. See Steven Greenhouse, "Labor's Board Detractors See a Bias Against Workers," *New York Times,* 2 January 2005, p. 12.
8. Dorothee Benz, "Sisyphus and the State: On the Front Lines of Union Organizing," *Dissent* (Fall 2005): 80.
9. Franklin D. Roosevelt, "The Better World . . . Will Be Made Possible Only by Bold Vision, Intelligent Planning, and Hard Work"—The President Addresses the International Student Assembly, 3 September 1942," in Samuel I. Rosenman, comp., *The Public Papers and Addresses of Franklin D. Roosevelt: Vol. 11, Humanity on the Defensive, 1942* (New York: Russell & Russell, 1950), 352.

A Note on Sources

When I began researching the American Federation of Labor during World War II, I expected wrongly that there would not be many primary and secondary sources. The historical sources and literature about the AFL in this era is broad, extensive, and growing.

The Wisconsin Historical Society in Madison, Wisconsin, has the records of the American Federation of Labor before 1955. For everything after 1955 and for the personal papers of AFL leaders, one needs to travel to the George Meany Memorial Archives. That said, the AFL Papers at the Wisconsin Historical Society do contain a lot of information on certain people, such as Boris Shishkin and Matthew Woll. Also, the Joseph A. Padway Papers are not in either location. They are at the University of Wisconsin-Milwaukee Archives. One should also be aware that the Columbia Oral History Project has the remembrances of dozens of labor activists and bureaucrats. Other largely heretofore untapped sources include organized labor's periodical literature from the 1940s. In addition to the wonderfully illustrated *American Federationist,* one should consult the AFL's *Monthly Labor Review* and its *Weekly News Service,* trade-specific journals such as *The Boilermakers' Journal* and the *Journal of Electrical Workers and Operators.* Finally, the proceedings of the AFL's annual conventions and those of its member unions are particularly useful.

For studying any aspect of labor history, government records and publications offer a treasure trove. For World War II–specific topics, the Franklin D. Roosevelt Library is essential. Additionally, one should consult the papers of the National War Labor Board and its predecessor, the National Defense Mediation Board. It is important to note that the records of President Roosevelt's Advisory Commission of the Council on National Defense are located at his presidential library in Hyde Park, New York. Using the federal government's *Monthly Catalog* remains the best way to find its published materials. Of special use are the periodicals *Monthly Labor Review* and *War Labor Reports*. One should also look for the dozens of key reports by the National Defense Advisory Committee, the National Defense Mediation Board, the National Resources Planning Board, and the National War Labor Board. In the late 1940s, the Civilian Production Administration began publishing histories of wartime agencies. They are extraordinarily useful as are the agencies' own histories such as Harvey C. Mansfield's *A Short History of OPA* (Washington, DC: GPO, 1947). One should also read the landmark reports issued by officials of the federal government including Bernard H. Baruch and John M. Hancock as well as James F. Byrnes. Finally, the U.S. Congress generated a lot of documents. In addition to the *Congressional Record,* one should explore the Serial Set and committee reports.

For the general history of the AFL, one still has to rely on Philip Taft's decades-old two-volume history *The AFL in the Time of Gompers* (New York: Harper, 1957) and *The A.F. of L. from the Death of Gompers to the Merger* (New York: Harper, 1959). Both tomes are still important, but dated and incomplete. To begin to piece together the story of the AFL during World War II, consult James B. Altesons, *Labor and the Wartime State: Labor Relations and Law During World War II* (Urbana: University of Illinois Press, 1998); Melvyn Dubofsky, *The State and Labor in Modern America* (Chapel Hill: University of North Carolina Press, 1994); Nelson Lichtenstein, *Labor's War at Home: The CIO in World War II* (Cambridge: Cambridge University Press, 1982); and Fred Witney, *Wartime Experiences of the National Labor Relations Board, 1941–1945* (Urbana: University of Illinois Press, 1949). Additionally, one must read Christopher L. Tomlins, "AFL Unions in the 1930s: Their Performance in Historical Perspective," *Journal of American History* 65 (March 1979): 1021–1042.

In this book, my approach has been topical. The books listed here will help the interested reader foray into the wider literature about the specific issues and organized labor's approach to them. The open-shop movement during World War II has not been covered completely yet. One should start with Jerold S. Auerbach, *Labor and Liberty: The La Follette Committee and the New Deal* (Indianapolis: Bobbs-Merrill, 1966); Charles W. Baird, "Right to Work Before and After 14(b)," *Journal of Labor Research* 3 (Summer 1998): 471–493; Sidney Fine, *Without Blare of Trumpets: Walter Drew, the National Erectors' Association, and the Open Shop Movement, 1903–1957* (Ann Arbor: University of Michigan Press, 1995); Gilbert J. Gall, *The Politics of Right to Work: The Labor Federations as Special Interests, 1943–1978* (New York: Greenwood Press, 1998); Howell John Harris, *The Right to Manage: Industrial Relations Policies of American Business in the 1940s* (Madison: University of Wisconsin Press, 1982); and William Millikan, *A Union Against Unions: The Minneapolis Citizens Alliance and Its Fight Against Organized Labor, 1903–1947* (Minneapolis: Minnesota Historical Society Press, 2000).

The issue of race and the AFL has a much wider historiographical tradition. Among the most useful works are Eric Arnesen, *Brotherhoods of Color: Black Railroad Workers and the Struggle for Equality* (Cambridge, MA: Harvard University Press, 2001); Clete Daniel, *Chicago Workers and the Politics of Fairness: The FEPC in the Southwest, 1941–1945* (Austin: University of Texas Press, 1991); William B. Gould, *Black Workers in White Unions: Job Discrimination in the United States* (Ithaca: Cornell University Press, 1977); Rick Halpern, *Down on the Killing Floor: Black and White Workers in Chicago's Packinghouses, 1904–1954* (Urbana: University of Illinois Press, 1997); Herbert Hill, *Black Labor and the American Legal System* (Madison: University of Wisconsin Press, 1977); and Andrew E. Kersten, *Race, Jobs, and the War: The FEPC in the Midwest, 1941–46* (Urbana: University of Illinois Press, 2000). For the most complete history of shipbuilding during the war see Frederic C. Lane, *Ships for Victory: A History of Shipbuilding Under the U.S. Marine Commission in World War II* (Baltimore: Johns Hopkins University Press, 1951).

Over the past five decades, historians have focused a lot of attention on the history of women in the labor movement. Particularly important recent works are Melinda Chateauvert, *Marching Together: Women of the Brotherhood of Sleeping Car Porters* (Urbana: University of Illinois Press, 1998); Dorothy Sue Cobble, *The Other Women's Movement: Workplace Justice and Social Rights in Modern America* (Princeton: Princeton University Press, 2004); Ileen A. DeVault, *United Apart: Gender and the Rise of Craft Unionism* (Ithaca: Cornell University Press, 2004); Philip S. Foner, *Women and the American Labor Movement: From the First Trade Unions to the Present* (New York: Free Press, 1979); Nancy Gabin, *Feminism in the Labor Movement: Women and the United Auto Workers, 1933–1975* (Ithaca: Cornell University Press, 1990); Alice Kessler-Harris, *In Pursuit of Equity: Women, Men, and the Quest for Economic Citizenship in 20th-Century America* (New York:

Oxford University Press, 2001); and Ruth Milkman, *Gender at Work: The Dynamics of Job Segregation by Sex During World War II* (Urbana: University of Illinois Press, 1987).

Despite the dramatic fight between the AFL and CIO, there remains much work to be done on organized labor's rivalry during World War II. Still one of the most readable books is Irving Bernstein, *The Turbulent Years: A History of the American Workers, 1933–1941* (New York: Houghton Mifflin, 1968). Other books to consult are Steven Fraser, *Labor Will Rule: Sidney Hillman and the Rise of the American Labor Movement* (New York: The Free Press, 1991); and Walter Galenson, *The CIO Challenge to the AFL: A History of the American Labor Movement, 1935–1941* (Cambridge, MA: Harvard University Press, 1960). Especially useful for my chapter on union rivalry was Vernon A. Jenson, *Heritage of Conflict: Labor Relations in the Nonferrous Metals Industry up to 1930* (Ithaca: Cornell University Press, 1950).

Historians are devoting more and more attention to workplace safety and disability issues. My chapter on wartime safety relied heavily upon Mark Aldrich, *Safety First: Technology, Labor, and Business in the Building of American Work Safety, 1870–1939* (Baltimore: Johns Hopkins University Press, 1997); Robert E. Botsch, *Organizing the Breathless: Cotton Dust, Southern Politics, and the Brown Lung Association* (Lexington: University Press of Kentucky, 1993); Martin Cherniak, *The Hawk's Nest Incident: America's Worst Industrial Disaster* (New Haven: Yale University Press, 1986); Claudia Clark, *Radium Girls: Women and Industrial Health Reform, 1910–1935* (Chapel Hill: University of North Carolina Press, 1997); and William Graebner, *Coal-Mining Safety in the Progressive Period: The Political Economy of Reform* (Lexington: University Press of Kentucky, 1976).

Finally, to begin any study of post–World War II planning, one has to consult William Beveridge, *Social Insurance and Allied Services: Report by Sir William Beveridge* (New York: Macmillan, 1942); the attempted American versions including: Bernard M. Baruch and John M. Hancock, *Report on War and Post-War Adjustment Policies* (Washington, DC: Office of War Mobilization, 1944); and James F. Byrnes, *Reconversion: A Report to the President from the Director of War Mobilization* (Washington, DC: GPO, 1944). For historical treatments, see Alan Brinkley, *End of Reform: New Liberalism in Recession and War* (New York: Vintage, 1996); Marion Clawson, *New Deal Planning: The National Resources Planning Board* (Baltimore: Johns Hopkins University Press, 1981); Nelson H. Cruikshank, *The Cruikshank Chronicle: Anecdotes, Stories, and Memoirs of A New Deal Liberal* (Hamden, CT: Archon Books, 1989); and Colin Gordon, *Dead on Arrival: The Politics of Health Care in Twentieth-Century America* (Princeton: Princeton University Press, 2003).

Index

Absenteeism, 76
Accidents. *See* Safety
Addams, Jane, 114, 116
African Americans, 12, 14–15, 63, 68–99, 101, 110, 118, 120, 121–122, 127, 240n53
Airline Dispatchers Union, 77
Amalgamated Association of Iron and Steel Workers, 10
Amalgamated Clothing Workers of America, 8
Amalgamated Meat Cutters and Butcher Workmen, 106–107
American Amalgamated Association of Street and Railway Employees, 108
American Federation of Labor (AFL): Building and Construction Trades, 20, 21–26; "equality of sacrifice," xi, 1–40; exclusivity, 11, 14–15, 101; gender discrimination, xi, 71, 90, 100–138; isolationism, 4–6, 156; origins, 9–18; Metal Trades Department, 3, 16, 28, 44, 72, 74, 76, 141, 160; National Defense Committee, 27–28; no-strike pledge, 22–23, 28, 51, 72; postwar planning, 132, 189–222, 225; Post–War Planning Committee, 132, 191–192, 202, 203, 225; "pure and simple" unionism, xi, 3, 11, 12–14, 15, 40, 45; racial discrimination, xi, 63, 68–99; relations with Communists, 13; relations with Industrial Workers of the World, 13, 14, 16, 141, 145–146; relations with Socialists, 13, 14; relations with Western Federation of Miners, 145–146; rivalry with CIO, xi, 8–9, 21, 29, 139–165, 248n53; safety, xi, 166–188; Scranton Declaration, 16; unemployment, 24–25, 191–196; volunteerism, 3, 11–12, 14, 38, 40, 44, 67; women's auxiliaries, 104
American Federation of Women's Auxiliaries of Labor (AFWAL), 36, 126–130, 137
American Medical Association (AMA), 212
Anderson, Benjamin M., Jr., 215–216
Anderson, Mary, 112, 126, 135, 136
Archibald, Katherine, 120–122
Arizona Federation of Labor, 160
Arnold, Thurman, 26, 48, 197
Asbestos Workers Union, 78

Baruch, Bernard, 157, 202–204, 205, 218, 219
Bates, Harry C., 20, 153, 212–213
Beichman, Arnold, 85
Bengough, Percy, 206
Berks, Gertrude, 183
Beveridge Report, 205, 213
Bittner, Van A., 20
Blacksmiths Union, 77
Brandeis, Louis D., 111
Brewer, David J., 111
Brophy, John, 143
Brotherhood of Locomotive Engineers, 77
Brotherhood of Locomotive Firemen and Enginemen, 77
Brotherhood of Railway Carmen, 77
Brotherhood of Railway Trainmen, 77
Brotherhood of Sleeping Car Porters, 78; Ladies Auxiliary of the Brotherhood of Sleeping Car Porters, 127
Brown, Harvey W., 7, 20, 199
Brown, Thomas H., 143
Burke, Edward R., 47
Bush, George W., 225
Byrnes, James F., 38, 157, 203, 218, 219

California Federation of Labor, 43, 61
Carlson, John Roy, 59
Carpenters Union, 120
Case, Clifford P., 66
Chicago Federation of Labor, 115
Childs, John, 199
Chinese workers, 14–15, 239n27
Christian Americans, 59–64, 66, 237n56
Cigarmakers' International Union (CIU), 9–10
Civilian Conservation Corps, 19–20
Clayton Act (1914), 15, 16
Clinebell, Sallie, 125, 133
Closed shop, 42, 43, 48, 49, 50–51, 54, 72, 74, 76, 161

Collins, Charles, 84
Colmer, William, 203, 215
Combined Labor War Victory Board, 38, 157
Commons, John R., 100, 171
Condliffe, J. B., 206
Congress of Industrial Organizations (CIO), viii–ix, 3, 7, 8, 17, 25–26, 28–29, 31, 33, 38, 43, 46, 47–48, 50, 61, 67, 80, 83, 84, 100, 101, 104, 123, 132, 134–135, 136, 137, 139–165, 182, 215, 220–221, 225, 259n82
Construction industry, 21–26, 229n49
Coyne, John P., 20, 22, 24
Cruikshank, Nelson H., 211–212

Dalrymple, S. H., 20
Davenport, Donald, 206
Debs, Eugene, 13
Delano, Frederic A., 198, 213
DeLeon, Daniel, 13
Dewey, Thomas, 61
Dingell, John D., 211
Doram, Thomas, 68–70
Douglas, William O., 64
Drew, Walter, 56
Dubinsky, David, 134, 142–143, 199
Duncan, James, 16
Durkin, Martin, 180
Durr, Goldthwaite, 106
Dykstra, Clarence, 32

Early, Stephen, 189
Economy Act (1932), 102
Emspack, Julius, 157
Equal Rights Amendment (ERA), 114, 117

Fair Employment Practice Committee (FEPC), 24, 69–70, 83–84, 86–92, 95, 192, 199, 241n60, 258n61
Federal Security Agency, 103
Federal Works Agency, 218
Federation of Organized Trade and Labor Unions (FOTLU), 10–11, 14, 109, 140
Fenton, Frank P., 7
Fitzpatrick, John, 115
Flint and Glass Workers Union, 78
Flint, Michigan, 55
Flynn, John, 23
Frankensteen, Richard, 28
Frankfurter, Felix, 159
Franklin, Joseph A., 88, 89, 94
Fremming, Harvey C., 143
Frey, John, 16, 31, 44–45, 47–48, 73, 79, 85, 116, 141, 142–143, 151, 179, 212; "Frey" amendment, 31, 47–48
Full employment, 210–211, 214–215
Full Employment Bill (1946), 136

George, Walter, 203, 215
Gerald R. Hill v. International Brotherhood of Boilermakers et al., 96–98
G.I. Bill (Servicemen's Readjustment Act of 1944), 221
Glenn L. Martin Company, 175, 178
Gold star mothers, 1–2, 228n4
Golden, Clinton, 20
Goldmark, Josephine, 111
Gompers, Samuel, 9–12, 13, 14, 15, 16, 17, 18, 23, 41, 55, 107–108, 110, 112, 116, 119, 122, 145–146, 191, 192, 199, 200, 228n21
Government printing office, 106
Granite Workers Union, 16, 78
Gray, Richard, 199
Green, Theodore Francis, 92
Green, William, 4–8, 16–18, 19, 20, 23, 27, 35–38, 43, 47, 67, 79, 85, 87, 119, 132, 137, 142, 144–146, 150–157, 165, 181–182, 191, 192, 194, 199, 200–201, 202, 207, 211, 212, 218–219

Hamilton, Alice, 171, 207
Hancock, John M., 202–204, 205, 218, 219
Hansen, Alvin H., 206–207, 209–210, 213, 215
Harrison, George, 199
Hart, John F., 106–107
Hartley, Fred A., 66
Hawkins, L. S., 174–175
Haymarket Square Massacre, 10, 140
Haywood, Allen S., 20
Haywood, William, 145–147
Heinrich, H. W., 178
Hillman, Sidney, 8, 18, 19, 20, 21–22, 25–26, 32, 116, 143, 156
Hillquit, Morris, 13
Hines, F. T., 204
Hoffman, Clare, 47
Hoffman, Paul, 206
Holden v. Hardy (1898), 170
Hopkins, Harry, 157, 204
Howard, Charles P., 142–143
Hutcheson, William L., 24, 51, 139–140, 143, 146–147

Ickes, Harold, 198
Illinois State Federation of Labor, 199
Industrial Union of Mine, Mill, and Smelting Workers, 143 159–164
Industrial Workers of the World (IWW), x, 13, 14, 16, 141, 145–146, 159, 193
Inflation, 29–30, 34–38
International Association of Machinists (IAM), 7, 20, 29, 77–78, 120, 124, 141, 149, 152
International Brotherhood of Boilermakers, Iron

Ship Builders, and Helpers of America (IBB), 48, 63, 68–99, 118, 120, 240n35
International Brotherhood of Electrical Workers (IBEW), 20, 77, 120
International Brotherhood of Teamsters, 47, 120, 146, 147
International Glove Workers Union, 116
International Harvester Corporation, 169, 183–188
International Hod Carriers, Building and Common Laborers Union of America, 58
International Labor Organization, 209–220
International Ladies Garment Workers Union (ILGWU), 1–2, 142
International Molders and Foundry Workers Union, 120
International Photo-Engravers Union, 16, 200
International Typographical Union, 10
International Union of Bricklayers and Allied Craftworkers, 20
International Union of Marine and Shipbuilding Workers, 48, 80

Jackson, Gardner, 153–154
Johnson, Charles S., 84
Johnston, Eric, 132, 208, 210, 220

Kaiser Company, 48, 73–76, 83–84, 88, 92, 217, 240n53, 241n60
Kaiser, Edgar F., 83–85, 87
Kaiser, Henry J., 83
Keenan, Joseph D., 20, 76, 180–181
Kelley, Florence, 111, 114, 171
Kennedy, Thomas, 33, 34
Kenney, Mary E., 110
Kenosha, Wisconsin, 140, 147–149
Keynes, John Maynard, 197, 209–210, 215
Knights of Labor (KOL), 9–11, 13, 14, 100, 109, 140
Knudsen, William S., 8
Koehler Company, 44, 56
Ku Klux Klan, 81, 88

La Follette, Robert M., 44, 46
La Follette, Robert M., Jr., 41; La Follette Committee, 55, 57
Land, Emory S., 73
Laurrell, Karl, 9
Leahy, William D., 157
Leffingwell, Samuel, 10
Lenin, Vladimir, 11
Lewis, Denny, 26
Lewis, John L., 16, 25–26, 33–34, 39, 42, 139–140, 142–143, 144–146, 150–157
Lochner v. New York (1905), 111
Lohr, George, 27
Long, Breckinridge, 207, 257n52
Long, William Frew, 57–58
Los Angeles, California, 24, 55–56, 68, 217
Lynch, George Q., 20

MacGowen, Charles J., 20, 89, 90–91
Maintenance of membership, 34
March on Washington Movement (MOWM), 86–87
Marshall, Thurgood, 95–98
Masterton, George, 20
McBride, John, 13
McDowell, 116
McMahon, Thomas F., 143
Meany, George, 21, 27, 33, 38, 39, 156, 157, 208, 220
Miller, Frieda, 135, 136
Miller, Spencer, 194
Milwaukee, Wisconsin, 169, 183–188
Minneapolis Sausage Makers Union, 152
Moore Dry Dock Company, 118–122
Morgenthau, Henry, 197
Morse, Wayne S., 164
Muller v. Oregon (1908), 111
Murdock, Abe, 136
Murphy, Frank, 49, 65
Murray, James E., 136, 211
Murray, Philip, 28, 33, 34, 67, 150, 153, 156, 157, 165
Muse, Vance, 59

National Association for the Advancement of Colored People (NAACP), 69, 83, 86, 87, 93, 95–98
National Association of Manufacturers (NAM), 47, 59, 209, 220
National Civic Federation, 14, 183
National Committee for the Conservation of Manpower in Defense Industries, 178–179, 180
National Defense Act (1917), 30
National Defense Advisory Commission (NDAC, First World War), 16, 117
National Defense Advisory Commission (NDAC, Second World War), 8, 18, 19, 20–26, 28, 30, 32, 203
National Defense Mediation Board (NDMB), 30, 31–34, 51, 54
National health insurance, 211–212, 214–215
National Labor Relations Board (NLRB), 20, 29, 30–31, 46–48, 59–64, 66, 159, 163–165, 224–226; Globe decision, 160
National Mediation Commission (First World War), 159
National Planning Association (NPA), 200, 210, 211, 256n29

National Recovery Administration (NRA), 197–198
National Resource Planning Board (NRPB), 198, 213–215, 216, 217
National Safety Council (NSC), 172, 174, 179, 252n17
National War Labor Board (First World War), 108
National War Labor Board (Second World War), ix, 30, 31–34, 37, 38, 39, 54, 65–66, 123–124, 163–165
Negro Victory Committee of New York, 84
Nelson, Donald, 203
Nestor, Agnes, 114–117, 125, 127, 132, 134, 137, 199, 207
NLRB v. Jones & Laughlin Steel Company (1937), 50, 54
North American Aviation Company, 149, 175–176, 178

O'Daniel, Wilbert, 59
O'Sullivan, Mary Kenney, 112, 116
Office of Defense Health and Welfare Services, 176
Office of Economic Stabilization (OES), 38
Office of Price Administration (OPA), 35–36, 38, 39, 129, 192, 199, 256n38
Office of Production Management (OPM), 21–26, 33, 104, 229n49
Office of War Mobilization (OWM), 203, 206, 256n38
Office of War Mobilization and Reconversion (OWMR), 205, 218
Ogburn, Charlton, 145–147
Ohl, Henry, 146
Oklahoma migrants, 121
Open shop movement, 16, 41–67; Arkansas open shop state constitutional amendment, 61–62, 66; California open shop referendum, 61; Florida open shop state constitutional amendment, 62–65
Order of Railway Conductors, 77
Ornburn, Ira M., 126, 128, 129

Pace, Stephen, 216
Padway, Joseph A., 42–49, 50, 56, 60–67, 116
Parr, Ray, 58–59
Pattern Makers Union, 20
Patterson, Robert P, 131
Paul, Alice, 114
Pegler, Westbrook, 24, 58
Perkins, Frances, 20, 150–153, 172, 178–179
Peterson, A.H., 160
Petrini, Americo, 71, 93–95
Phelan, E. J., 206
Phelps-Dodge Company, 158–164
Pierson, John H.G., 210
Plessy v. Ferguson (1896), 91
Portland, Oregon, 48, 70, 73–74, 81–89, 217
Postwar planning, 189–222, 259n81, 259n82
Powderly, Terence V., 10–11
President's Committee on Cost of Living, 39
Pressman, Lee, 61
Providence, Rhode Island, 70, 74, 92–98
Public Works Administration, 198

Racketeering, 23
Railroad Firemen's Union, 77
Railroad Telegraphers Union, 77
Railway and Steamship Clerks Union, 77
Railway Mail Association, 77
Randolph, A. Philip, x, 78, 79, 86, 87, 89
Ray, Tom, 71, 83–90
Reich, Robert, 225
Reuther, Walter, 28, 215
Reynolds Metal Company, 124
Rheem Shipbuilding Company, 74–75
Rickert, Tom, 16
Rieve, Emil, 20
Roberts v. City of Boston (1849), 91
Roosevelt, Eleanor, 136, 189, 204
Roosevelt, Franklin D., vii, viii, xi, 2, 3, 4, 6–7, 8, 18, 19, 20, 26, 27, 29, 32, 34–38, 39, 44, 50, 51, 71–72, 83, 90, 118, 126, 129, 141, 142, 149–157, 165, 172, 173, 174, 178–180, 189–191, 196–197, 199, 202–204, 205, 215, 218, 220, 225, 226, 248n53
Rosenberg, Anna, 84, 85, 136, 156–157
Ross, Malcolm, 90–91
Rubber Workers' Union, 139, 143

Safety, 76, 162, 166–188
Schlichter, Sumner, 207
Schmidt, Emerson P., 216
Schneiderman, Rose, 114, 125, 133, 134
Sheet Metal Workers Union, 77
Shelley, John L., 43
Sherman, Val, 59
Shipbuilding, 71–76, 79, 92–93
Shipyard Negro Organization for Victory (SNOV), 87
Shishkin, Boris, 18, 116, 191–196, 199, 202, 210, 218–219
Shotwell, James T., 206
Smith, Gerald L. K., 59
Smith, Harold D., 196
Smith, Howard K., 31, 57
Snyder, John W., 218, 219
Socialists, 10, 13, 14
St. Louis, Missouri, 131, 133
Starr, Ellen Gates, 116
Steel Workers Organizing Committee, 20
Steelman, John R., 30, 218, 220

Stone, Harlan Fiske, 65
Stone, Irving F., 204–205
Strasser, Adolph, 9
Strikes, 29–31, 34, 37, 38–40, 41, 44, 54, 56, 76, 84, 117, 146–147, 148, 149, 158–159, 171, 196
Sullivan, J. H., 122
Sweeney, John, 226
Switchmen's Union of North America, 77

Taft, Robert A., 66, 216, 217, 221
Taft-Hartley Act (Labor-Management Relations Act of 1947), 42–44, 66–67, 224
Tampa, Florida, 63, 81
Tanner, Leland, 88–89
Textile Workers Union, 20
Thomas, Elbert D., 47
Thomas, R. J., 20, 28, 39, 157
Thorne, Florence, 11, 18, 112, 119, 125, 137, 191–192, 194, 212, 228n21
Thornhill v. State of Alabama (1940), 48–49, 64, 237n60
Tobin, Daniel J. 20, 38, 47, 146, 157
Tracey, D. W., 20
Trade Unity League, 13
Truman, Harry S., 26, 42, 66, 189–191, 200, 203, 218–222

Ulrey, S. Valentine, 59
United Association of Plumbers and Steamfitters, 20, 63, 78, 118, 120
United Automobile Workers (UAW), 20, 29, 124, 149, 182, 215
United Brotherhood of Carpenters and Joiners (UBCJ), 24, 33, 146
United Brotherhood of Maintenance of Way Employees, 77
United Construction Workers Union, 26
United Electrical Workers (UE), 124
United Garment Workers, 16
United Mine Workers (UMW), 14, 17, 34, 39, 42, 153
United Nations, 209
United Rubber Workers, 20
United States Chamber of Commerce, 132, 216, 220
United States Conciliation Service (USCS), 30, 51
United States Congress, 34, 35, 38, 39, 47–48, 136–137, 201, 205, 216–217, 220–222, 259n81
United States Department of Labor, 108, 172–173, 181
United States Employment Service (USES), 58, 84, 86, 93, 104
United States Maritime Commission, 71–73, 74, 79, 93, 98
United States Public Health Service National Institute of Health, 173, 176
United States Supreme Court, 49, 50, 51, 64–65, 67, 111, 159, 162, 170, 198
United States Women's Bureau, 101, 103, 125, 132, 134–135, 136, 137
Urban League, 93–94
Urban renewal, 212–213, 214–215
Utility Workers Organizing Committee, 20

Van Etten, Ida M., 109–110
Vickery, Howard L., 76
Vinson, Carl, 57
Vinson, Frederick M., 38, 218
Von Hayek, Friedich A., 216

Wagner Act (National Labor Relations Act of 1935), 31, 42, 46, 47, 49, 50, 54, 56, 59, 64, 65, 67, 159
Wagner, Robert F., 211, 215
Wal-Mart, 223–224, 226
Walsh-Kaiser Company, 75–76, 93–99
War Labor Disputes Act (Smith-Connally Act), 39, 48, 57, 129
War Manpower Commission (WMC), 84, 104, 130, 133, 136
War Production Board (WPB), 76, 126, 176–177, 180, 181, 192, 201, 203, 229n49, 256n38; Safety and Technical Equipment Division, 176–177
War Resources Board (WPB), 6, 8, 203
Watson, J. Tom, 62–65, 237n56
Watt, Robert J., 7, 164, 210
Webster, Milton, 199, 258n61
Western Federation of Miners (WFM), 145–146, 158, 182
Weyerhaeuser Timber Company, 33
Wheeler, Burton K., 157
Wilkie, Wendell, 156
Wilson, Charles E., 181
Wilson, Woodrow, 16, 30, 106, 118, 195, 200
Winrod, Gerald, 59
Wisconsin State Federation of Labor (WSFL), 44, 146, 171–172
Woll, Mathew, 15, 79, 132, 134, 143, 150–151, 153, 199, 200, 206, 191, 212, 219
Women, 12, 100–138
Women's Trade Union League (WTUL), 112, 116, 123, 126, 127, 130, 135
Work Progress Administration (WPA), 82; Works Projects Administration, 22, 92
Workers' Health Bureau (WHB), 172, 182
World War, First, viii, 7, 15, 29–30, 57, 71, 83, 105–106, 117, 123, 132, 133, 135, 159, 162, 172, 193, 195–196, 200, 201–202

Zaritsky, Max, 143

About the Author

Andrew E. Kersten is Associate Professor of American History in the Social Change and Development Department of the University of Wisconsin–Green Bay. He is the author of *Race, Jobs, and the War.* He is currently working on a history of the AFL and the AFL-CIO from 1881 to the present.